FREE MARKETS
& FOOD RIOTS

Studies in Urban and Social Change

Published by Blackwell in association with the *International Journal of Urban and Regional Research*. Series editors: Chris Pickvance, Margit Mayer and John Walton

Published

Divided Cities
Susan S. Fainstein, Ian Gordon, and Michael Harloe (eds.)

The City Builders
Susan S. Fainstein

Fragmented Societies
Enzo Mingione

Free Markets and Food Riots
John Walton and David Seddon

Forthcoming

Post-Fordism
Ash Amin (ed.)

The Resources of Poverty
Mercedes González de la Rocha

Social Rented Housing in Europe and America
Michael Harloe

Cities after Socialism
Michael Harloe, Ivan Szelenyi and Gregory Andrusz

Urban Social Movements and the State
Margit Mayer

FREE MARKETS
& FOOD RIOTS
THE POLITICS OF GLOBAL ADJUSTMENT

John Walton & David Seddon

BLACKWELL
Oxford UK & Cambridge USA

First published 1994

Blackwell Publishers
238 Main Street,
Cambridge, Massachusetts 02142
USA

108 Cowley Road
Oxford OX4 1JF
UK

Library of Congress Cataloguing-in-Publication Data

Walton, John, 1937–
    Free markets and food riots: the politics of global adjustment /
John Walton and David Seddon, with contributions by Victoria Daines ... [et al.].
        p.   cm. – (Studies in urban and social change)
    Includes bibliographical references and index.
    ISBN 0–631–18245–4. – ISBN 0–631–18247–0 (pbk.)
    1. Structural adjustment (Economic policy) – Developing countries.
    2. Developing countries – Economic conditions.   3. Free trade – Developing countries.
    4. Social conflict – Developing countries.   5. Capitalism – Developing countries.
    6. Post-communism – Europe, Eastern.   7. Economic history – 1971–1990.
    8. Economic history – 1990–   I. Seddon, David.   II. Daines, Victoria.   III. Title.
    IV. Series.
    HC59.7.W263   1994
    339.5′09172′4–dc20   93–30890
                                                                      CIP

British Library Cataloguing in Publication Data

A CIP catalogue record for this book is available from the British Library.

Typeset in 10½ on 12 pt Baskerville
by Apex Products, Singapore
Printed in Great Britain by Hartnolls Ltd., Bodmin, Cornwall

This book is printed on acid-free paper

Contents

Tables

Acknowledgements

Although John Walton and David Seddon are the principal authors and editors of this volume, its contents and conception rely on additional contributors. Victoria Daines coauthored with David Seddon chapter 3 on women's responses to austerity. Ronald Herring wrote chapter 8 on Sri Lanka's exceptionalism. Trevor Parfitt and Stephen Riley contributed chapter 5 on Africa. Jonathan Shefner coauthored with John Walton chapter 4 on Latin America. Mridula Udayagiri wrote chapter 7 on India. John Walton is grateful to the Woodrow Wilson International Center for Scholars, Washington, DC for a fellowship that supported work on this project.

Part I

Introduction

1

Global Adjustment

In this book we examine the relationship between widespread popular unrest in the cities of the developing world (including the "new" developing world of Central and Eastern Europe) and the process of economic and social transformation – associated with a renewed emphasis on liberalization and the promotion of "free markets" – that has taken place on a global scale over the last two decades.

We argue that, despite its roots in the distinctive historical development of the state within which it takes place, popular protest must also be seen as a more general social and political response to the systematic undermining of previous economic and social structures and of an earlier moral order, in the name of "adjustment," to ensure renewed capitalist development on a world scale. The period of "global adjustment" extends, roughly, from the late 1960s to the present. This period, we would argue, has been characterized by crisis and reconstruction on a world scale.

1 GLOBAL CRISIS

Few disagree that the period under consideration is one of significant change and transformation; but interpretations of the precise significance, and of the economic and political causes and effects, of the changes taking place differ considerably.

Most orthodox economists (including those in the World Bank, at least until very recently) have seen the changes of this period simply as aspects of a process of "transition." as the emergence of new developing (industrializing) countries (NICs) challenges the old international economic order and the global economy "adjusts" to these new circumstances (e.g. Beenstock 1989). The period of "transition," however, has been redefined periodically as things have failed to turn out as predicted. In 1979, the World Bank recognized that "the 1970s were a period of turmoil and transition for the world economy," but predicted that the 1980s would see renewed growth, with the developing countries averaging GDP growth of 5.6 percent between 1980 and 1990 (*World Development Report* 1979, cited in World Bank 1988: 13–14). In 1985, after the severe recession of 1979–83, and the development of "the debt crisis" in the early 1980s, the World Bank was prepared to argue that "we are now in a period of transition – an essential and intermediate phase before returning to sustained growth and normal relationships between debtors and creditors" (World Bank 1985). For this school of thought, the development of capitalism on a world scale is characterized by a general tendency towards economic development and social improvement, despite occasional "setbacks" and "shocks." This analysis is remarkably similar in crucial respects to that of the school of neo-classical Marxists (exemplified by Warren 1980; see also Harris 1986: 187–203) who also have seen, in the 1970s and 1980s, a world in transition, characterized by temporary inequalities and difficulties but tending generally towards economic and social development as capitalism progressively integrates every state and society within a single global system. These schools of thought have little to say regarding the wave of social unrest and popular protest that has characterized the last two decades of restructuring and adjustment, seeing them (when they are considered at all) either (in the orthodox neo-classical perspective) as reflections of "rigidities" and "constraints" to be overcome, or (in the neo-classical Marxist conception) as misguided "populist" reactions to a painful but generally progressive process of transformation and capitalist development.

For economists more influenced by the theories of Keynes, the evident changes of the period under consideration are in part at least associated with a deepening crisis in international economic and political relations associated with a lack of effective international management of an increasingly interdependent global economy and giving rise to conflict between and within states, growing inequality (both international and national) and mass poverty (cf. Pearson 1969; Brandt et al. 1980; Brandt and Manley 1985, UNICEF 1987). For this school of thought, deep-seated conflicts of interest between states threaten the process of development but can nevertheless be reconciled, given the political will and a greater degree of coordinated intervention on the part of international institutions and the governments of the more powerful states in particular. This school of thought has seen social unrest and popular protest as an indication of, and reaction to, the pain (real costs) experienced by the most vulnerable sections of the population in the current world crisis.

For others, writing from a more radical perspective (and often referred to as "neo-Marxists") the crisis is a classical crisis of over-accumulation and is thus intrinsic to the international capitalist economy and its associated political regime. This gives rise to heightened conflict both at the international and at the national level as different interests struggle to resolve the crisis to their own benefit. Mediation in this struggle (class struggle within states, and international competition and conflict at the global level) is likely to be ineffective and based on wishful thinking. In this perspective, popular protest against the austerity measures that have accompanied "structural adjustment" throughout the developing world is an integral part of the struggle around the very process of capital accumulation and in defense of the interests of those suffering most from the process of restructuring and adjustment. Popular struggle is thus linked to class struggle.

While we share much of the analysis of this last body of thinking, we also see the recent growth of popular struggles and protest as a distinctive political development of the last two decades, involving an exceptionally wide range of social forces, both responding to, and itself shaping, the process of global adjustment that has accompanied a global crisis.

The roots of the current crisis lie back in the 1960s, when the industrial capitalist economies began to experience a profits squeeze reflecting a crisis of overaccumulation (Armstrong, Glyn, and Harrison 1984). Measures adopted by western governments to help resolve the crisis included austerity measures directed primarily at reducing real wages, particularly in the public sector. According to this analysis, it was the induced recession and austerity measures of the mid-1960s, designed to restructure and rationalize working processes, which established the conditions for the subsequent crisis (Armstrong, Glyn, and Harrison 1984: 276). The austerity measures introduced as part of the process of restructuring provoked unprecedented popular protest and a wave of strikes swept across Europe between 1968 and 1970, resulting in a rapid increase in money wages. Broadly similar developments took place in north America around the same time (cf. Armstrong, Glyn, and Harrison 1984: 271–90). The clampdown which followed was associated with a "mini-recession" in 1970–1 and succeeded by a "mini-boom" in 1972–3, which proved to be the final phase of the long postwar boom.

The mini-boom effectively marked the end of an era. The US dollar devaluation of 1971, the "oil crisis" of winter 1973–4 and an international "crash" in the summer of 1974 brought the golden years to an abrupt and painful halt. The remainder of the decade fell into two phases: a fragile recovery, followed by a renewed and more serious recession in the wake of the second major oil-price rise of 1979 what some referred to as "the second slump" (Mandel 1980). The two deep recessions (of the mid-1970s and of the early 1980s) experienced by the advanced capitalist countries were followed by a period of uneven recovery (1983–9), but it would appear clear now that another recession, starting around 1989, has begun to affect them once again. Despite periods of recovery, it is possible to see the entire period from the late 1960s to the present as one marked essentially by recession and crisis.

Frank, for example, has written of "a deep and widespread economic, social and political crisis in the world, which seems to be centred on a new crisis of overaccumulation of capital in the capitalist West, and on the consequent transformation of its relations with the socialist East and the underdeveloped South" (Frank 1981: ix). Others concur with this view of the last two decades as a period of significant transformation on a world scale, and emphasize that the crisis is associated with a long recession. Thus Fröbel remarks that "in the two decades following the Second World War, the capitalist world-economy experienced the greatest boom in its history. This boom came to an end toward the close of the 1960s. Since then the world-economy has been in a phase of decelerated growth, intensified structural change, and heightened political instability" (Fröbel 1982: 507). Even the World Bank, with its very different perspective, recognized towards the end of the 1980s that "in some developing countries the severity of this prolonged economic slump already surpasses that of the Great Depression in the industrial countries, and in many countries poverty is on the rise" (World Bank 1988b: 3).

But while some emphasize the similarities between this "contemporary crisis" and previous capitalist crises (in the 1930s and 1870s, for example), others draw attention to the novel features of this latest crisis:

> the post-war period, at least up to 1973, saw the greatest boom in economic history. Since then there has been slower growth, marked

by two recessions which, some have argued, make this later period rather more like the condition of capitalism prior to 1939. However, in this more recent period, there are signs that a new stage in the development of the political economy has emerged, with conditions which differ considerably from those which prevailed in the 1930s. (*Gill and Law 1988: 127*)

The distinctive character of the last two decades is associated with the increasing integration of capitalism on a world scale, its "internationalization."

This has ensured that a crisis of capitalism is, increasingly, and unavoidably, a crisis on a world scale, even if that crisis is experienced unevenly and differently at different moments and in different places. For Gill and Law,

the global political economy has reached an unprecedented stage of development. The present is not like the past. Today, the security, trade, money, direct investment, communications, and cultural dimensions of global interdependence, are such that there is now an integrated global political economy, whereas in the past, there was a less complex international political economy (and before 1500 a series of regional political economies). (*Gill and Law 1988: 378*)

One of the major consequences of this deepening integration is a greater "synchronicity" or "simultaneity" of events in different parts of the world and in different countries. Evidence suggests that, from the late 1960s onwards, the advanced capitalist countries of the West in particular have become both more closely integrated and mutually interdependent. Consequently, they demonstrate, in recession and in recovery, an increasingly high degree of synchronicity in economic rhythms relative to earlier periods; only Japan stands somewhat apart. By the early 1980s the same was becoming more generally the case for the developing world as a whole, although the unevenness of capitalist development in the Third World and the continuing survival of state socialism in the Second World until the late 1980s ensured that global synchronicity was still not achieved at the beginning of the 1990s. Increasingly, however, the successive booms and recessions of the advanced capitalist West have been "passed on" to the rest of the world in a variety of ways and as a consequence a major process of restructuring on a world scale has taken place.

2   THE END OF THE SECOND WORLD

For some 40 years, analysts tended to accept the distinction between the advanced capitalist countries of the West (First World), the developing countries of the South (Third World) and the "state socialist" countries of the East (Second World) as systematic. With the dramatic transformation of the political economy of Eastern Europe during the 1980s, culminating in the "revolutions" of 1989–90, such a distinction has become more evidently problematic.

In this book, the countries of the Second World are treated not as part of a separate economic and political system, but as countries with their own distinctive heritage experiencing a process of rapid change, in which their progressive integration into the capitalist world and associated domestic economic and political transformation has generated many contradictions and conflicts that resemble those identified with crisis and "economic reform" in the developing Third World.

During the late 1960s and 1970s trade between the state socialist countries and the capitalist world increased significantly. Average annual growth rates of export trade with the West and the South which were 10.9 percent and 11.4 percent respectively in the period 1965 to 1970, increased to an average of 23.5 percent and 21.0 percent in the period 1970 to 1975. But rates of growth in imports accelerated even more dramatically, with imports from the West rising from an annual average of 12.2 percent in 1965–70 to 31.2 percent in the period 1970 to 1975 and imports from the South increasing from 7.5 percent to 26.0 percent. Even if inflation is taken into consideration these figures represent a startling increase in overall trade outside the Council of Mutual Economic Assistance (CMEA) and a significant growth in the balance-of-trade deficit.

The increasing balance-of-trade deficit was associated with a rising balance-of-payments deficit. It is estimated that by 1972 the accumulated combined balance-of-payments deficit of the Soviet Union and Eastern Europe with the West (excluding Japan) reached $7.6 billion; by 1975 the deficit of Eastern Europe alone was calculated at $9 billion – largely through trade with the United States, Japan, France and West Germany (Frank 1980: 188).

As the balance-of-payments deficit grew, so too did foreign borrowing and recourse to drawing on reserves. By 1976 it was estimated that the Soviet Union and Eastern Europe as a whole owed some $45 billion; by the end of 1978 the figure had risen to $58 billion, of which nearly half was owed to western banks. The dramatic increase in foreign debt led to efforts by governments in the Soviet Union and Eastern Europe to introduce drastic measures to reduce the balance-of-payments and balance-of-trade deficit. Frank reported, on the basis of data relating to 1978 and 1979, that

> debt service has been eating up a quarter or more of foreign earnings and credits in most of Eastern Europe and over one half in Poland, and it has become necessary to make sharp cuts in imports to keep this burden from growing further. Poland, whose debt is estimated at $15 billion, has been obliged to reduce its investments and to announce increases in food prices again in order to answer its needs for increased imports of equipment and food. (*Frank 1980: 231*)

The economies of the Soviet Union and Eastern Europe were slowing down seriously during the late 1960s and 1970s. Attempts were made to counter this by foreign borrowing and the pursuit of expansionary strategies, while at the same time trying to reduce the level of state subsidies. These strategies not only served to deepen the economic crisis that was rapidly developing during the 1970s but also increased the level of dissidence and social unrest.

By the end of the 1970s, there were clear indications in many of the "older" state socialist countries of a significant rethinking of socialist theory and practice. In China, the four modernizations, in Vietnam, the economic reforms, in the USSR the beginnings of efforts to streamline and restructure the economy (*perestroika*), were all significant developments. These developments were driven essentially from above. In other, "younger" state socialist countries also – e.g. Vietnam, Mozambique, Ethiopia – the 1980s saw an increasing preparedness to consider economic reform (involving liberalization) as necessary. During the latter part of the 1980s, the attempt at controlled economic reform gave rise to increasing social discontent and political unrest, which culminated in "the revolution" of 1989 (see chapter 9).

The explanation for the increasing revisionism of "socialist" governments is controversial. For some, ever closer integration with the capitalist West and capitalist South obliged economic restructuring and political compromise (e.g. Frank 1980). For others, the limits of extensive primitive accumulation under early socialism having been reached, a drive for modernization and intensification led to rising imports, especially of advanced technology, from the West. But whether the impulses were initially from outside or inside, the economic reforms of the late 1970s and the 1980s created new tensions and precipitated political as well as economic crises. An essential element in the economic crises was the burgeoning foreign debt and growing pressure for more radical reforms. Since 1989, and the collapse of state socialism in Europe and across the world, what was once referred to as the Second World is now increasingly integrated within the global capitalist political economy and subject to broadly similar forces for change. And, as in other parts of the developing world, the international agencies and developed capitalist states are actively promoting policies of economic reform – of stabilization and structural adjustment – to encourage liberalization and privatization, and the development of market forces.

3   THE END OF THE THIRD WORLD

Towards the end of the 1960s, as the developed capitalist economies began to move into crisis the developing countries as a whole appeared to experience a period of growth. International capital and commodity markets continued to boom and, as the World Bank noted in 1987,

> some developing countries liberalized their trade regimes in the mid-1960s, became exporters of manufacturers, and gained directly from the expansion in world trade. Most of the others benefitted from rising demand for raw materials and foods. So, in one way or another, the developing countries that participated in the expansion of world trade experienced high output growth. (*World Bank 1987: 14*).

In the early 1970s, accumulation in the developing countries as a whole was close to the 5.7 percent rate achieved in the advanced capitalist countries; by the end of the 1970s it was running at about twice the 4 percent a year of the advanced capitalist countries. While real GDP growth in the advanced capitalist countries was 4.7 percent in the period 1965–73, it slumped to 2.8 percent between 1973 and 1980; in the same period the developing countries as a whole recorded GDP growth rates of 6.5 percent and 5.4 percent (Mosley, Harrigan, and Toye 1991: 5). The share of world capitalist investment in developing countries went from 16.5 percent in 1973 to 23.25 in 1979 (Armstrong, Glyn, and Harrison 1984: 353).

It was on the basis of such data that some argued against what they termed "The Illusion of Underdevelopment" (Warren 1980) and for the progressive development of the Third World during the 1960s and 1970s; and indeed, significant rates of growth were recorded mainly by a select group of newly industrializing countries whose performance was taken by "the optimists" as indicative of a general process of development and by "the pessimists" as challenge to the supremacy of the developed world. The NICs and the OPEC countries together certainly experienced a very considerable growth; and discussions of a new international division of labour surfaced in the mid-1970s together with a call for a New International Economic Order (NIEO), at a time when the action of OPEC appeared to hold out the prospect for a real challenge from the developing countries to the prevailing dominance of the developed countries.

But for most developing countries, the 1970s were more difficult than the 1960s. It rapidly became clear during the second part of the 1970s that, not only were the developed countries becoming less prepared than ever to open themselves to a new international order as signs of recession began to increase, but the increase in oil prices achieved by the OPEC countries had generally adverse effects on the majority of non-oil-exporting developing countries. For many developing countries, particularly those strongly committed to a "nationalist" development strategy built around import substitution, foreign exchange was a major constraint; commodity prices held up in the wake of the first oil-price increase and many developing capitalist countries began to borrow heavily (OPEC surpluses channeled through western banks). This created the conditions for what was to emerge rapidly as "the debt crisis," to which the response of the international financial institutions was "stabilization" and "adjustment." For a time the high import demand of these countries provided much needed markets for western commodities. But by the end of the decade this was no longer the case. While the OPEC producers and NICs surged ahead during the latter part of the 1970s, most other developing countries began to experience growing indebtedness, declining terms of trade and increased balance-of-payments problems.

This resulted in increasing differentiation within "the Third World" and the beginning of "the end of the Third World" (Harris 1986): different regimes of capital accumulation and different state forms, following different policies and different trajectories. Generally, those countries experiencing strong economic growth were better able to provide the conditions under which "vulnerable" social groups could survive and defend their living standards; those whose economic crisis only deepened during the 1980s experienced the full severity of adjustment.

If, even in the 1970s and 1980s, the developing countries as a whole performed well, in terms of various economic-performance indicators, in comparison with the industrial capitalist West, there was considerable variation within "the Third World." East Asia and South

Table 1.1   Regional patterns of growth, 1965–2000

Region	Growth of real per capita GDP (percent)			
	1965–73	*1973–80*	*1980–89*	*1989–2000*
Sub-Saharan Africa	3.2	0.1	−2.2	0.5
Latin America and Caribbean	3.7	2.6	−0.6	2.3
Middle East and Mediterranean	5.5	2.1	0.8	2.1
Eastern Europe	4.8	5.3	0.8	1.5
South Asia	1.2	1.7	3.2	3.2
East Asia	5.1	4.7	6.7	5.1

Source: World Bank 1990: 11, 16

Asia showed the highest rates of real GDP growth, growth in exports and growth in domestic investment. The poorest performance was that of sub-Saharan Africa, with Latin America and the Caribbean, North Africa, and the Middle East little better. If growth of real per capita GDP is taken as an indicator of economic performance, it is easy to see the difference between the Asian region – particularly East Asia – and the others (see table 1.1).

But, increasingly through the period under consideration, it was the size and "burden" of its foreign debt that came to characterize the severity of the crisis for any developing economy. The deepening recession in the West and the effects of increasing oil prices on the economies of oil-importing countries in Africa, Asia, and Latin America began to have their impact, and loans for development turned increasingly into debts. In the 1970s, the global economic crisis was characterized particularly by a financial crisis, with growing international financial instability and international debt. Indeed, one key aspect of the global crisis with which this book will be particularly concerned is that of the so-called "debt crisis," which developed rapidly during the second part of the 1970s and surfaced in an acute form at the beginning of the 1980s.

It was in large part in response to the growing balance-of-payments problems experienced by an increasing number of countries, that the International Monetary Fund began to intervene more systematically in the fiscal policy of developing countries in particular with loans conditional on various "stabilization" measures during the late 1970s. The perceived need to take these measures still further and to "adjust" macro-economic policy as a whole to meet the "new" circumstances of a world in recession led to the introduction (by the IMF in collaboration with the World Bank) at the beginning of the 1980s of the various programmes of "stabilization" and "structural adjustment" that came increasingly to characterize the decade.

4 THE DEBT CRISIS AND STRUCTURAL ADJUSTMENT

Already by the mid-1960s the burden of debt carried by the developing countries was considerable and the debt-servicing requirements worrying. According to the Pearson Commission (Pearson 1969) by the mid-1960s debt service was eating up 87 percent of new lending to Latin America and 73 percent of new lending to Africa. *Business Latin America* reported in 1968 that the average debt-service ratio for Latin America was at least 14 percent in 1966, while the Inter American Development Bank estimated 20 percent. But though the governments of Latin American countries were criticized by bankers as "deadbeats" who "year after year have had to come back to Washington for bail-out loans and foreign 'stretch-outs'" (Payer 1989: 10), the bankers were evidently prepared to consider lending money to these "deadbeats" with debt crises. In the period between 1955 and 1970, 7 developing countries – all regarded as countries with considerable economic development potential (Argentina, Brazil, Chile, Ghana, Indonesia, Peru, and Turkey) – were involved in 17 debt reschedulings. There were also some debt reschedulings for low-income countries, including India, but these were designed to provide additional finance when official lenders could not increase new lending. The private bankers did not fear rescheduling, as long as they could continue to collect market rates of interest; indeed, the first reschedulings of bank debt in the late 1970s and early 1980s made these loans even more profitable. Also, it is clear that, in the case of default, the banks confidently expected a government rescue.

Thus, even before 1973 and the first dramatic increase in oil prices, many developing countries had heavy debts and had experienced specific debt "crises." But the commodity price boom of the 1970s and the reassurance that ultimately there would be no "bad debts" among the governments of developing countries encouraged western banks to increase their lending. Indeed the most eager lending-was to oil-exporting countries with large populations and sizable markets (e.g. Venezuela, Nigeria, Indonesia, Mexico).

Between 1973 and the early 1980s the principal source of external finance had become the private commercial banks offering nonconcessional loans. But the international agencies appeared to speak for all when they argued (as did MacNamara in his 1977 Presidential Address) that the large growth in private commercial lending to developing countries did not make a debt crisis inevitable, and that it could be staved off by appropriate corrective actions. In 1977, the Bank was "even more confident today than ... a year ago that the debt problem is indeed manageable" (cited in Mosley, Harrigan, and Toye 1991: 22). Indeed, throughout the 1970s the Bank had not been much concerned about adjustment and did not oppose large-scale commercial borrowing to maintain high economic-growth rates. In fact it saw high growth as the guarantee of the continuing credit-worthiness of developing countries and it had repeatedly soothed fears about the sustainability of the recycling operation. It was not until after the second "oil shock" in 1979–80 that the Bank publicly revived "questions about the international financial system's ability to recycle enough funds ... to maintain import levels and economic growth rates" (World Bank 1980: 3).

However, as trade deficits and balance-of-payments problems increased during the 1970s, an increasing number of developing countries – including the so-called "miracle economies" (e.g. Brazil, South Korea) – were obliged to borrow in order to cover their oil-import bills and deficits. From 1970 to 1984, the total external indebtedness of developing countries rose from $64 billion to $686 billion, with the proportion of that debt owing to private banks rising from one-third to over one-half and the share of total new flows rising from 15 percent in 1970 to 36 percent in 1983 (World Bank 1985: 2). During the 1970s international bank capital expanded dramatically owing to the growth of petrodollar accounts and capital flight from advanced capitalist countries like the United States. Enormous accumulations of international bank capital encouraged an unprecedented rise in lending of private bank capital to Third World governments. At the same time, debt reschedulings became more common: an average of three developing countries a year rescheduled their debts during the 1970s (World Bank 1985: 4).

On every measure, the debt-servicing abilities of developing countries deteriorated, particularly after 1974, as their debt increased. Between 1974 and 1981 the developing countries as a whole ran twice as big a balance-of-payments deficit as the advanced capitalist world. Their debts represented the cumulative effect of these deficits. The borrowers were hit by rising interest rates and shrinking markets for their exports, as well as by deteriorating terms of trade. Increasingly, non-oil-developing countries were forced to run massive balance of payments deficits if they were to expand. The coincidence in the late

1970s and early 1980s of rising interest rates (resulting in part from the strict monetary policies of rightwing governments in the United Kingdom, the United States and the Federal Republic of Germany) and further oil-price rises helped create the deepest recession since the 1930s. Under the impact of the recession in the advanced capitalist countries and the increased oil prices, the terms of trade for most developing countries deteriorated rapidly, as did their balance-of-payments situation. As their financial and economic situation deteriorated, more and more developing countries were obliged to seek new loans or to reschedule their existing debts. The number of debt reschedulings rose to 23 in 1981–2, and to 65 in 1983–4. A global debt crisis was developing.

The debt crisis was a direct consequence of the decision by the developed countries to leave the intermediation of the large OPEC balance-of-payments surpluses, caused by the oil-price rises, to the private banking system. The recycling of these surpluses was believed, wrongly, to be a profitable (riskless) form of lending because the borrowers were mainly Third World governments who would never willingly default on sovereign debt. But the end of the 1970s saw not only a significant rise in real interest rates – as rightwing governments, convinced of the need to limit the money supply as the key to reducing inflation, came to power in the United Kingdom, the United States and the Federal Republic of Germany in quick succession – but also another even more dramatic increase in the price of oil. The deflationary effect of these developments precipitated a world slump in 1979–80. For countries which had borrowed heavily in the 1970s, the combination of a rising nominal interest rate and a falling rate of inflation created an alarming increase in the cost of borrowing. At the same time, the price of almost all developing-country exports began falling and the terms of trade, which had remained broadly favourable during the 1970s, began a sharp decline. Declining terms of trade combined with higher financial outflows for debt service constituted sources of acute pressure on balance of payments. The widening payments deficits either had to be financed, by more borrowing, or else their economies "adjusted" to bring demand for foreign exchange into better balance with the decreased supply.

The growing debt crisis surfaced visibly and unavoidably in 1982 when Mexico threatened default. Certainly borrowing continued, with the middle-income economies as a whole increasing their debt/GNP ratios from 36.1 in 1980 to 46.1 in 1989 (with the lower middle-income economies rising from 37.7 to 67.7) and low-income countries other than China and India increasing their indebtedness (in terms of debt/GNP) from 27.0 in 1980 to 71.0 in 1989. But much of this borrowing was now conditional on adopting IMF and World Bank approved stabilization and structural adjustment programmes. The debt crisis, however, had a number of different dimensions. For the western bankers and the international financial system as a whole, it was the big debtors that appeared most threatening and for whom specific "rescue packages" were devised; but within the developing world, it was often those with smaller debts but a higher debt ratio that appeared in deepest difficulties.

For once the debt crisis surfaced in 1982, private lending dried up overnight for all developing countries that were already highly indebted; and by 1986, private lending had fallen back to a third of its 1980 level. The banks had expected the US and other governments, and the IMF, to bail them out; and indeed the IMF and the World Bank did devote billions of dollars to rescue packages, while the Bank for International Settlements and the United States provided some "bridge" financing; but it became rapidly apparent that the banks would effectively have to bail themselves out.

For many of the smaller debtors, particularly those in Africa where the bulk of the foreign debt was owed to governments and official agencies rather than to private commercial banks, the situation was exacerbated by significant reductions in official lending. Government aid was also experiencing cut-backs as western governments emphasized "restraint" and the flows of official aid overall showed no increase, despite a substantial rise in Japanese government aid expenditure. "In the 1980s, then, the global economic context placed a premium on finding ways of bringing down balance of payments deficits to the level that could be financed by stagnant aid flows and rapidly dwindling private lending" (Mosley, Harrigan, and Toye 1991: 9): global adjustment, in other words, focused particularly on the adjustment of the developing countries. It could be argued that the international debt crisis signaled a watershed in relations between the developed and developing countries: western banks now became less concerned with pouring capital into developing countries than with recovering their existing debts. The role of the International Monetary Fund during the 1980s largely reflected the concern of western governments and private banks to ensure debt repayment virtually at all costs. Developing-country governments were publicly criticized for failing to recognize the need for structural adjustment during the 1970s; the fact that the World Bank itself had only just arrived at this conclusion was not discussed. "Structural adjustment" came to be synonymous with economic reform during the 1980s and became the "only acceptable strategy for development," according to the international financial institutions that were to dominate the economic policy of the developing world throughout this decade.

In April 1979 at an UNCTAD meeting in Manila, Robert Mac-Namara announced a new move on the part of the Bank to make long-term non-project assistance available to countries which were prepared to embrace economic policies which the Bank regarded as necessary for development (Mosley, Harrigan, and Toye 1991: 34). In 1980 the World Bank formally introduced structural adjustment, with loans for four countries (Kenya, Bolivia, the Philippines, and Turkey, which accounted for nearly half of the total value). In 1981–2, 10 new countries undertook debt reschedulings, more than in the whole of the 15 years between 1956 and 1970. But the reschedulings had strings attached. In return for loans, reductions in government deficits, limits to money supply growth, currency devaluations, etc., to improve trade prospects and reduce expenditure were demanded. Structural adjustment loans (SALs) were needed, the Bank argued, "to assist countries ... prepared to undertake a programme of adjustment to meet an existing or to avoid an impending balance of payments crisis" (World Bank 1988a: 22).

There was some uncertainty within the Bank as to whether the crisis of 1979–80 marked "a permanent change in the world economy, not ... some temporary phenomenon which will later automatically reverse itself" (MacNamara in his 1980 Presidential Address) or an essentially temporary phenomenon associated with a structural transition (as emphasized in several subsequent World Bank *World Development Reports*). It seems that MacNamara espoused the former; but arguably the latter view informed much of the Bank's policy thinking of structural adjustment during the first half of the 1980s.

In the new political-economic climate of the early 1980s, the Bank, like many western governments, also shifted its general view of what constituted appropriate economic policies for recovery and growth. As has been remarked "during the Clausen Presidency (1981–86) the MacNamara interpretation of the world was largely swept aside" (Mosely, Harrigan, and Toye 1991: 23–4). If, during the 1970s, external finance had been used as a substitute for structural adjustment, now it was to be used to support structural adjustment. Looking back over "the past dozen years," the World Bank in 1985 argued that

> foreign finance can promote growth through higher investment and technology transfers. It can allow countries to adjust gradually to new circumstances in the world economy. But it can also be misused, so that countries end up with more debt but no corresponding increase in their ability to service it ... Countries that ran into debt-servicing

difficulties ... were countries that had borrowed and failed to adjust
or had not tackled the problems with sufficient urgency. (*World Bank
1985: 6*)

Adjustment was presented as the key to debt management.

Between 1980 and 1986, a total of 37 SALs were negotiated:
activity built up slowly in the first three years of operation, reached
its height in 1983 and fell away rapidly between 1984 and 1986.
What was stressed initially was that the SAL was a response to a
once-and-for-all, exceptional crisis in the balance of payments, albeit
one that would require assistance over a longer period than that for
which IMF Stand-By finance was available. Such assistance was to
be confined to countries both willing and able to make progress on
policy reform.

By 1983, however, SALs were increasingly defended as a means
of persuading more governments to *change* their economic policies
– these being given a greater prominence than external factors as
causes of poor performance: "the past dozen years have underlined
... the crucial role of domestic policies in determining the performance of developing countries – particularly in the use they make
of foreign finance" (World Bank 1985: 6). Reforms were increasingly
sought in areas (e.g. institutional arrangements) which, even if
successful, would have little immediate impact on the balance of
payments. Instead of providing balance-of-payments assistance to
countries willing to undertake structural adjustments, the Bank increasingly saw itself as using SAL funds to facilitate the countries'
decision to adopt a broad programme of economic reform (Berg and
Batchelder 1984: 23–4). Conditionality was now imposed less to
maximize the probability of repayment of the loan than to enable the
borrower to remove what the lender sees as fundamental policy-
induced obstacles to economic recovery and growth. Conditionality
on the part of the Bank, as opposed to that applied by the IMF was
applied across a wide range of policy areas: a high percentage of
SALs included conditions relating to 19 typical policy measures, while
the average SAL had conditions in 10 of these 19 areas. A particular
SAL could have as many as 100 separate policy conditions (the
second SAL for Thailand boasted over 100 conditions). Only by
responding rapidly and rigorously implementing these policies of
"adjustment," it was suggested, could developing countries receiving
SALs expect to make the necessary "transition" and achieve the conditions required for renewed growth and a resolution of their debt crisis.

Coordination between the IMF and the World Bank became a
matter of increasing concern through the 1980s. In early 1989, two

important innovations were introduced designed to improve IMF–
World Bank coordination: the Policy Framework Paper (PFP) and
the New Concordat. The PFP is a document drafted by the IMF,
and amended and agreed by the Bank and the borrowing government, which sets out a joint understanding of the economic situation
of the borrowing country and the policies necessary for "successful
stabilization and adjustment." Furthermore, cross-conditionality between the Bank and the Fund, although formally it does not occur,
in practice has now become reality. This arises because Bank adjustment lending normally requires an IMF stabilization loan to be in
place; and if the conditions of both loans are then coordinated through
a PFP – and if bilateral donors, and other multilateral donors like
the European Development Fund, then follow suit by making their
aid subject to the conditionality of the Fund and the Bank being
observed (as has increasingly been the case during the 1980s) –
then the borrower's freedom of action becomes extremely limited.
Furthermore, as some commentators have remarked, "since the Bank
from 1986 has begun to speak publicly of the political aspect of structural adjustment lending, and has acknowledged its efforts to build
up internal coalitions in borrowing countries in support of its policies,
it is perfectly clear that the tightening of cross-conditionality has direct
political implications for the countries concerned" (Mosley, Harrigan,
and Toye 1991: 55), not only restricting the room for maneuver for
governments but giving explicit support to those within the country
whose interests coincide with those of the IMF and the Bank.

5 SOCIAL CRISIS AND POPULAR UNREST

Studies which showed a tendency for poverty in developing countries
to worsen under adjustment were circulating within the UN "family"
of organizations from 1983. However, it was not until the mid-1980s,
when the social costs of the recession and of adjustment measures
were becoming undeniable, that UN agencies like UNICEF and
the International Labour Office (ILO) openly argued for "adjustment
with a human face." One indication of how far policies for aid and
development had shifted towards a neo-liberal consensus during the
early 1980s is provided by the fact that the UNICEF report was
widely regarded as quite radical when it was published (UNICEF
1987) although in fact most of its proposals were borrowed from the
World Bank's *World Development Report, 1980* (World Bank 1980c) and
it accepted most of the fundamental premises of those arguing for
structural adjustment. The debate in international circles triggered

by the UNICEF report coincided with a change of leadership within the Bank (from Clausen to Conable) and a greater concern for interdonor consensus than had been evident previously. In particular, Conable seems to have been attracted by certain of the compensatory measures advanced in the UNICEF package. The Bank's first venture was its involvement in 1987–8, with UNICEF and others, in the design and funding of the Program to Mitigate the Social Costs of Adjustment (PAMSCAD) in Ghana, one of the first African countries to adopt and pursue an adjustment program under IMF and Bank auspices (started in 1983). PAMSCAD came to provide a model for one strand of a broader policy which the Bank launched later in 1987 (together with the United Nations Development Program (UNDP) and the African Development Bank) called "Social Dimensions of Adjustment" (SDA). The SDA program has been strongly criticized both by other agencies and by independent social analysts as inadequate and ineffective. In practice, by the end of the 1980s, despite considerable discussion of adjustment with a human face and a more explicit concern with poverty alleviation (see the World Bank's *World Development Report, 1990*, which is focused on "poverty"), relatively few examples of effective mitigation of the social costs of adjustment by combined government and agency action could be identified.

Whatever the stated concern of the Bank with compensatory programs and poverty alleviation towards the end of the 1980s and into the early 1990s, the general argument of the Bank has consistently been that early and rigorous implementation of structural adjustment effectively reduces the social costs of adjustment and ensures better economic recovery. This is, in effect, an argument for adjustment without a human face insofar as it implies greater benefits to a "short, sharp shock" in the long run than to a gradual and more cautious approach.

In fact, in many developing countries today the combination of the recession and specific adjustment and austerity measures has been devastating. Rapid social change has been a feature of the past half-century, to be sure, and the process of class formation and transformation, the rural exodus and the growth of urban areas, has generated enormous social changes. But social change in times of prosperity generates less effective tension than change under duress in conditions of economic stringency and austerity.

By the 1980s, as the world recession turned into a global slump, the process of restructuring which accompanied the crisis and aimed to restore the basis for capital accumulation in the industrial capitalist countries increasingly affected the rest of the world. In parts of the

Third World this restructuring has been accompanied by a continuing economic crisis – notably in sub-Saharan Africa, North Africa and the Middle East, and Latin America; elsewhere – notably in East Asia – relatively high rates of growth have helped overcome or postpone economic problems. In former Eastern Europe and the Soviet Union also, global restructuring has had its impact. Insulated to some extent during earlier periods from the crises (and booms) of the capitalist world, from the 1960s onwards the state socialist economies became increasingly drawn into the rhythms of that wider world to experience their own parallel crises during the 1970s and 1980s. With the collapse of state socialism in the "revolution" of 1989 and the subsequent disintegration of the Soviet Union, the so-called Second World has become, in effect, an integral part of "the developing world," experiencing a broadly similar process of transformation and similar forms of external intervention in the shaping of economic policy.

One effect of greater integration and synchronicity within the world economy is a greater degree of simultaneity and similarity in what might broadly be referred to as "class struggles" around the process of capital accumulation and around government measures to resolve crises in that process and to promote renewed accumulation. It becomes less surprising then that a "wave" of popular protest accompanies the process of structural adjustment and government austerity measures as it takes place across the developing world (and even the developed world) during the last two decades.

For the contemporary global crisis of capitalism is not only a financial-economic, but also a political-economic crisis; it is also (although this is less considered by the economists who dominate the debates on "the world in transition") a social and cultural crisis. In the last 20 years, the world has been turned "upside down" and a process of fundamental restructuring of social relations, ideas, and values has taken place. Increasingly, since the late 1970s, economic reforms and restructuring have been accompanied, in the West, South and East, by far-reaching changes in the nature of the state and in the definition of state–civil society relations – the very nature of politics and the significance of "democracy" has been subject to redefinition. Rapid changes in the structure of social relations, taking place particularly at a time when the relationship between the state and civil society is undergoing fundamental restructuring and reconsideration, have given rise to new social divisions and solidarities and to new forms of identity and morality. New certainties (fundamentalisms of various kinds) have emerged just as old certainties or faiths have crumbled.

Not only economic and political structures but the very relationship between state and society have been substantially redefined as new forms of integration and disintegration have developed to lay the foundations for the world of the 1990s and beyond. Popular protest is an integral part of that process. This is not to say that the world of the 1990s and beyond will be entirely different from that of the "postwar period," but it will be qualitatively different, not least in the degree of economic integration which will ensure that developments taking place within states will be increasingly conditioned by global forces. At the same time, resistance to certain aspects of those developments will continue to be associated with various forms of open struggle and protest.

In our view, then, it is the crisis and process of reconstruction of global capitalism that began in the late 1960s and early 1970s that has generated the economic policies of liberalization and austerity that have themselves given rise to the upsurge of popular unrest across the developing world with which this book is broadly concerned.

2

Food Riots Past and Present

<hr/>

For developing countries around the world, the last two decades present an engaging historical problem: the reappearance of food riots and associated forms of popular protest. Since the mid-1970s, an international wave of price riots, strikes, and political demonstrations has swept across the developing world in a pattern at once historically unprecedented and reminiscent of classical food riots best documented in European social history. Modern protests, however, are fundamentally a product of the international political economy.

Like their predecessors, the contemporary insurgencies occur in a distinct temporal cycle (e.g. Kamen 1971; Rudé 1964; L. Tilly 1971) and reveal coherent political purposes rather than mob rule, "a highly complex form of direct popular action, disciplined and with clear objectives" (Thompson 1971: 78). Yet the recent protests are also unprecedented. Taken together they are analogous to an intra-national strike wave (Shorter and Tilly 1974), occurring now as coincident events of essentially similar form across a large number of countries. Modern food riots occur in response to a new and ever more integrated global system. Their specific origin lies in the inter-national debt crisis and a regimen of institutionally coordinated austerity policies or "structural adjustment" programs. Poor and indebted nations have been subjected to a relatively common set of neo-liberal reforms, urged on them by international agencies in vary-ing degrees of forcefulness according to the debtor's integration into the world economy and domestic political complexion. The purpose of this chapter is to explore these historical contrasts with particular attention to theories of classical protest, their application to recent events, and the contribution of both to a broader explanation of collective action.

Two observations focus this comparison. First, the history of food riots is not confined to Western Europe. Popular uprisings in response to dearth and distributional practices have been documented in other societies from Asia to Latin America (Meade 1989; Rogers 1987; Wong 1982; Wright 1973). Indeed, David Arnold's (1979) study of grain riots in South India in 1918 notes their "broad similarity with eighteenth-century European food riots" (1979: 112). The present study mainly relies on the European experience because it has inspired more research and the major theories of popular protest that frame the comparison. Second, this analysis is concerned with the wave of austerity protests spawned by recent stabilization policies, a phenomenon distinct from episodic communal riots (see, e.g. Lubeck 1985) and local price disturbances (see, e.g. Banton 1957; Epstein 1958; Kearney 1979) that have also plagued developing countries.

Our comparison will be drawn more strictly between bread riots in Western Europe during the period of modern state formation and capitalist development, on one hand, and austerity protests since the mid-1970s in connection with the debt crisis on the other. Contemporary austerity protest is the object of explanation as a dramatic phenomenon in its own right and because, we shall argue, it signals a new phase in the development of the global state system. In general, the chapter argues that modern food riots in the developing nations are generated by processes analogous to economic liberalization policies that produced classical food riots, but today's transformation is taking place at the international level. Neo-liberalism simultaneously affects all Third World countries in much the same fashion as *laissez-faire* policies within nations once affected particular towns and regions, although the two processes are distinct in other ways.

The argument is elaborated in several steps. First, we review classical studies of food and price riots in an effort to identify the best available explanatory ideas. Next, we describe modern austerity protests, noting similarities to bread riots of the past, distinguishing features of the contemporary phenomenon, and reviewing the evidence about its structural causes. Third, looking behind the empirical correlates and expressive forms of austerity protest, we explore the conditions of urban social organization that may support popular mobilization and legitimating traditions of the moral economy. Finally, the broader determinants of austerity protest at the level of state policy and international economic restructuring are explored and integrated in a theoretical explanation linking past and present.

1 EUROPEAN BREAD RIOTS

Popular protests over food shortages have a long pedigree in European history. Peter Clark's (1976) study of disturbances in Kent begins in the mid-sixteenth century and Buchanan Sharp (1980) dates the incidence of rioting in the west of England from 1586. English historians agree that the long evolution of the food riot reached its apogee in the eighteenth century or, more precisely, "the second half of the eighteenth century, particularly the crises of 1766, 1795 and 1800, [that] was the golden age of food rioting" (Bohstedt 1983: 212). Across the channel, Louise Tilly (1971: 24) observes that "the market riot was an old phenomenon in France, but the late seventeenth century saw a great increase of such riots" as well as the appearance of new forms which became common throughout the eighteenth century and continued until the 1850s, somewhat later than in England. "One variety or another of the food riot prevailed in most European countries until well into the nineteenth century" (C. Tilly 1975: 385).

Popular uprisings over food prices and shortages did not occur in isolation, but represented one species of the practice Hobsbawm calls "collective bargaining by riot" (1964a: 7), stretching from the mid-sixteenth to the mid-nineteenth century. Riots occurred over disputes concerning religion, enclosures, elections, labor, and military exactions. During these years, riot was the most common form of popular protest and uprisings related to food were the most common form of riot. Stevenson's (1974: 33) observation about eighteenth-century England applies to much of Western Europe: "the most persistent and widespread riots were those associated with food, for it has been calculated that two out of every three disturbances in the eighteenth century were of this type" (see also C. Tilly 1976; Rudé 1964).

Food riots took several forms: (a) the *blockage* or *entrave* that prevented the export of grain from an area in which shortages existed; (b) the *price riot* or *taxation populaire* in which food was seized by protestors, a just price set, and the lot sold; (c) the *agrarian demonstration* in which farmers destroyed their own produce as a dramatic protest; and (d) the *market riot* in which the crowd took retributive action against commercial agents (e.g. bakers, millers) or local magistrates in the form of looting or "tumultuous assembly to force dealers or local authorities to reduce prices" (Stevenson 1974: 33. For similar typologies see L. Tilly 1971; Rose 1961; Rudé 1964, C. Tilly 1975).

Although bread riots appeared in distinct forms across time and space, they also combined with other protest tactics, particularly in later years as new methods of political organization developed.

> Even in the shortages of 1795–96 and 1800–1 there was some overlap of [riot and industrial strike] forms. Strikes were common in both years and occasionally they merged with attempts to reduce the price of provisions. Thus in 1795 when the Chatham shipwrights struck work on some naval vessels, they assembled that evening in the market to reduce the price of provisions. In the period 1811–13, food riots and frame-breaking took place side by side. (*Stevenson 1974: 62*)

Moreover, the actions of rural producers and urban consumers were sometimes joined. "[T]own and country were often closely connected ... townsmen took a remarkably active and leading part in so-called peasant risings, and agricultural labourers were a potent force for discontent in towns" (Kamen 1971: 331). The early nineteenth century was a historical divide that saw both the transformation and steady decline of riot politics. "Some aspects of this change in the nature of popular protest [include] the greater organization and planning by 1800, the increasing use of handbills to advertise riot and co-ordinate rioters, and the use of threat tactics on a broader scale" (Booth 1977: 100). Organized protests related to food were incorporated into other forms of action, such as labor disputes, and increasingly politicized. The "mob" was giving way to the industrial working class. (Hobsbawm 1959: 110).

Analysts differ on the conditions that produce food riots and those differences, of course, are linked to implicit and explicit theories. The varied empirical claims will be surveyed before turning to competing theoretical explanations at the end of this section. The most fundamental difference concerns whether riots resulted from objective conditions of hardship, social constructions of injustice, or some combination of the two. In the first group, certain historians have stressed depredations stemming from harvest failures, increasing food prices, trade slumps, industrial depressions particularly in the cloth trades, unemployment, or the coincidence of two or more of these conditions (Stevenson 1974; Sharp 1980). R. B. Rose (1961: 291), for example, argues that "to a large extent the existence of such [price-fixing] riots was a function of harvest fluctuation, but also of trade fluctuation." Hard times foster protest in this parsimonious and unmediated interpretation of riot causes.

Conversely, other historians and many social scientists agree with Charles Tilly (1976: 389) that conflicts "occurred not so much where men were hungry as where they believed that others were unjustly depriving them of food to which they had a moral and political right" (1976: 389). Within this second theoretical family, however, writers differ concerning the locus of ideas about injustice and the conditions that activated those beliefs. One approach focusing on public policy attributes rioting to the repeal of traditional statutes protecting consumers against grain shortages and speculative price rises (Beloff 1938; Rose 1961; Williams 1984). Louise Tilly (1971, 1983) extends this theme arguing that riots were a form of political conflict generated by the intersection of state centralization and market expansion. The fundamental change centered on the repeal of paternalistic consumer safeguards such as laws against withholding grain from the market for speculation, priority for small buyers before millers and bakers, official measurers, and enforcement of such protections by local magistrates (L. Tilly 1971). As a result ordinary citizens were left prey to unregulated markets. Edward Thompson's (1971) analysis of the moral economy of the poor begins with state and market changes, but argues further that their effect on popular mobilization is mediated by traditional judgments about legitimacy fashioned in local communities. In combination, Thompson and Tilly argue that the sea change beneath the riotous eighteenth century is the movement from pre-industrial society with its protections against privation to the *laissez-faire* policies of an emerging commercial and industrial capitalist society. In this view, the empirical conditions precipitating popular protest are changes in law and economic organization (e.g. enclosure, centralized marketing).

Despite these differences concerning the conditions that generate protest, the research literature demonstrates some consensus about the locations, participants, targets, and aims of rioting. Protests occurred in a variety of geographical settings and not merely in rural areas of production and shipment. There were, of course, major agrarian uprisings such as the East Anglia riots of 1816, although "the agricultural labourer was always the last to bestir himself ... and when he did so it was a real indication of the deplorable conditions prevailing at the time, whether they were political, social, or economic" (Peacock 1965: 11). In France, George Rudé (1964: 21–2) notes, "the food riot remained as the typical and constant expression of popular discontent; and this was true of the village as it was of the city and market town." In more exacting statements, however, writers avoid terms such as "agrarian" protest which might imply that their causes lay in the realm of agricultural production rather than in national politics and markets. Roger Wells (1977: 740), for example, stresses, that these "were not *rural* riots." Agricultural regions were generally not affected unless and until shortages became epidemic on a national level (Clark 1976).

Food riots were most common in towns, particularly industrial localities specializing in textiles and mining, as well as in distributional centers such as ports and market towns. Location reflected function; "riots resulted from market expansion and ... erupted in productive areas from which the grain was drained by metropolitan, military, or overseas demand, and in large cities" (L. Tilly 1971: 26). Different types of food protest had their characteristic locations. "Blockages tended to occur in rings around port cities or metropolitan centers, but at some distance from them ... [T]he city, however, preferred the price riot" (C. Tilly 1975: 387–8). And there were national differences, with price riots occurring regularly in Paris from the revolutionary years onward, but rarely in London (Rudé 1964; Rose 1959; Bohstedt 1983). The pattern changed over time as urbanization accelerated and growing constituencies such as town workers became more organized. By the late eighteenth century the modal location of riots was shifting to manufacturing towns (Stevenson 1974: 45ff.).

As one would infer from the geographical pattern of disturbances, riot participants represented a variety of social categories. Agricultural labor and the lowest ranks of the urban poor were least represented, if not unknown, in contemporary accounts or arrest records (Rudé 1964; Stevenson 1974; Booth 1977). Artisans were frequent participants, particularly in the earlier periods (Sharp 1980; Clark 1976), although their predominance steadily gave way to a broader representation of the working class. Speaking of eighteenth-century English food riots, Rudé (1964: 37) notes "the large number of industrial workers that took part in these disturbances." Various writers agree with Thompson's (1971: 115) observation that "initiators of the riots were, very often, the women" (c.f. Sharp 1980; Booth 1977; Stevenson 1974). Women were better acquainted with the marketing practices of food dealers, more apt to detect unjustified shortages and price rises, quicker to mobilize within the community, and less likely to be treated roughly by authorities called in to quell disturbances. "Another special group of rioters," according to Clark (1976: 377), were the teenagers "like the Leicester 'children' who pulled down the town gibbet in 1607 in support of the Midland rebels, or the London apprentices who provided the rank and file for many metropolitan riots." In addition to these particular segments, however, protests generally involved a cross-section of the working population.

The most clearly established proposition about food riots is that they were not chaotic or violent spasms of irrational crowds, but organized and purposeful political actions. Nowhere is this interpretation better illustrated than in the selectivity of riot targets. Protestors did not rampage indiscriminately, but focused their wrath on particular individuals and institutions whom the crowd held responsible for unjust practices. Typically, it was not the producers or retailers of food but the middlemen who were seen as responsible for shortages and price rises: the grain dealers, wholesalers, speculators, and mills. Grain shipments by wagon, ship, and canal barge were seized and distributed among participants or sold at a just price. Warehouses were raided with similar results. Textile workers in 1770 Rheims "seized the town's markets ... proceeded themselves to sell all grain in the markets at three-quarters of the current price. They then turned their attention to the warehouses and to the granaries of the numerous religious houses which they treated in a similar fashion" (Rose 1959: 434). Grain dealers and millers were set upon at their places of business as well as at their homes, which were stripped of property and even burned. Farmers were not exempt, however, particularly large-scale operators who were involved in speculative practices such as withholding food from the market. Similarly, shops that were sometimes exempted or "only raided as an afterthought, a token gesture" (Booth 1977: 95), were included in the larger conflagrations. "In London a whole series of attacks took place from September 13th [1795], lasting almost a week, in which the shops of bakers, food wholesalers, and the houses of men convicted of monopolistic offences were attacked" (Stevenson, 1974: 59). Thompson (1971: 107) shrewdly observes that in the midst of attacks on grain dealers and millers, "the crowd clearly selected its own targets, deliberately by-passing the bakers" who were known within the community. In France, Rudé (1964: 21) notes repeatedly that "shopkeepers, millers, farmers, and merchants" were either attacked by the crowd or compelled to sell food at lower prices. If middlemen were the most common target, farmers and shopkeepers were close behind in popular assessments of responsibility.

The aims of food riots were modest: to solve short-run problems of supply and price, restore normality to markets, activate relief measures by local officials, or remind merchants of their obligations to consumers. As Clark (1976: 378) notes, "the rioters' objectives were usually conservative, limited, and deferential." Prior to the French Revolution, ideas of liberty and popular sovereignty played no part in bread riots, "there was no question of overthrowing the government or established order, of putting forward new solutions, or even of seeking redress of grievances by political action." By the nineteenth century, however, this was changing as the supply and price of food were absorbed into labor issues and political struggles such as Chartism (Booth 1977; Wells 1977; Bohstedt 1983). Yet, even within their earlier limits, popular uprisings frequently succeeded in bringing immediate relief, if not the reversal of deeper causal currents. Bread riots "often worked in the short run; crowd action brought prices down, forced stored grain into the public domain, and impelled the authorities to greater efforts toward assuring the food supply" (C. Tilly 1975: 386; c.f. Rose 1961).

Rudé summarizes and compares classical, eighteenth-century bread riots in England and France.

> In both there was the same quick response to the rising price of bread and wheat. In both, the main center of activity was the market ... In both, the target of the crowd's hostility was the grain factor or the farmer, though in England, at least, the former was more strikingly so than the latter. In both, a central feature was the forcible reduction of the price of food by riot ... In France, this *taxation populaire* almost always took the form of compelling farmers, bakers, and merchants to reduce their prices; in England, as often as not the crowd itself conducted the sale ... The differences between the two movements, although not so remarkable, are also worthy of note. The French grain riots of 1775 were a "snowball" movement, spreading in a series of consecutive eruptions from one market to another. The English riots lacked this unity; though having a common origin and purpose and linked in time, they appear rather as a series of separate eruptions ... The composition of rioters of 1775 and 1766 were not the same. In France, apart from Paris, they were mainly peasants; wine-growers, farm labourers, and village craftsmen. In England [they] were weavers, tinners, colliers, bargemen, or merely "the poor" ... For all this, both movements were of the same popular tradition. (*Rudé 1964: 44–5*)

To Rudé's useful summary, we should add the provisos already discussed. Protest patterns change over time, according to the type of riot and its urban or rural setting. In the nineteenth century, particularly, the pattern was shifting toward a conflation of classical food riots and demonstrations related to labor and political issues.

2   THEORETICAL EXPLANATIONS

Four general theories have been proposed to explain the origins, timing, and changing forms of food riots: rational response, moral economy, community, and state and market.

Bohstedt (1983) uses the term "rational response" to identify explanations that assume, implicitly or explicitly, that riots vary directly with hard times. Harvest failures, trade slumps, industrial depressions, unemployment, military exactions, and related events that produce either rapid price rises or distributional imbalances predict the occurrence of popular protest without the necessity of positing intervening mechanisms. Disadvantaged social groups respond rationally and proportionately to dearth by seizing food from those who have it, by appealing to those in authority to reduce prices, or by imposing just prices themselves (Rose 1961; Stevenson 1974).

Rational response theory is no theory at all because it fails to explain the process in which people decide when and how to act. Its empirical shortcomings stem from the frequently documented absence of any direct relation between hardship and protest. As Clark (1976: 377) observes, "in general there was no close correlation between the incidence of riots and national indices of dearth and distress ... the points of ignition were to be found less in high prices *per se* than in price discrepancies" between the town and countryside or between the fair-price notions of producers and consumers (see also L. Tilly 1971: 24). Repeated inquiries have shown that riots do not occur in regions of the greatest suffering, at the depths of economic slumps, or at the highest price levels (e.g. Booth 1977; Bohstedt 1983; Hobsbawm 1964b; L. Tilly 1971; Snyder and Tilly 1972). Reflecting on trends throughout the eighteenth century, Charles Tilly (1975: 385) notes that "conflicts over the food supply became more widespread and virulent toward the end, despite the fact that the productivity of agriculture was increasing, the threat of death-dealing famine dwindling." These studies should not be interpreted to mean that hardship is inconsequential as a condition of protest, but only that it is not a sufficient cause. The role that hardship may play is debated, some claiming that it is one among several factors in a causal combination, and others insisting that it makes no necessary contribution after other confounding factors are specified.

In the second theoretical approach, Edward Thompson's (1971) well-known essay on "The moral economy of the English crowd" develops perhaps the most convincing explanation of the social mediation of economic hardship and political protest. People rallied against food shortages, price rises, and marketing malpractices not as some spasmodic reaction to dearth, but out of a sense of injustice. Popular action was based on a

> legitimizing notion ... the belief that they were defending traditional rights and customs ... supported by the wider consensus of the

community ... a consistent tradition of social norms and obligations, of the proper economic functions of the several parties within the community, which, taken together, can be said to constitute the moral economy of the poor. An outrage to these moral assumptions, quite as much as actual deprivation, was the usual occasion for direct action. (*Thompson 1971: 78–9*)

The explanatory contribution of moral economy has been widely acknowledged by students of European popular uprisings (L. Tilly 1983) and of Third World peasant rebellions (Scott 1976).

Thompson's critics, nevertheless, find a number of limitations in the concept of moral economy. Sharp's (1980) study of English popular uprisings in the late sixteenth and seventeenth centuries found

little indication of any moral economy governing the behavior of food rioters in the earlier period ... Too much emphasis on the notion of a moral economy of the crowd can lead to an overly sentimental view of the life and behavior of the poor and can obscure the reality of the pain, desperation, and anger they felt in times of depression and scarcity. (*Sharp 1980: 33*)

Sharp concludes that the moral economy observed by Thompson in eighteenth-century political actions was itself a product of governmentally initiated consumer protections in response to earlier protests. In separate but equally vigorous critical studies, Craig Calhoun (1982) and Dale Williams (1984) maintain that the moral economy as construed by Thompson is a backward looking cultural response that does not accurately characterize English dissenters who were fully involved in modern market practices and rebelled against current conditions with timely remedies, rather than attempting to reclaim the past. Others argue that, although the moral economy provides the general backdrop of eighteenth-century protest, as an explanatory concept it fails to address social class and regional variation in the incidence of rioting (Wells 1977; Booth 1977).

The third theoretical approach focuses on local communities as the relevant context of popular protest. Community theories typically begin with an appreciative review of the moral economy argument, but go on to discover fundamental flaws in that approach, particularly its emphasis on social classes as the locus and agency of popular action. Calhoun (1982) and William Reddy (1987) argue that political protest in eighteenth- and nineteenth-century Europe was mounted not primarily by working-class constituencies – as opposed to artisans, outworkers, and small farmers – and that classes themselves were not politically coherent or unified groups. On the contrary, political movements drew their vitality from traditional communities in which questions of status honor and the disruption of established ways of life by capitalist industrialization were greater incentives to mobilization than any chimerical class interests. John Bohstedt (1983) pursues this line in a study of riots and community politics in England and Wales around the turn of the nineteenth century. Rioting characterized those communities that stood between agrarian and rapidly growing urban-industrial society. "Riots were community politics" (Bohstedt 1983: 26); the distinctive form of political struggle successfully practiced by cohesive communities when they were threatened from the outside (by press gangs, armies, wage-cutting and labor-saving industries, grain speculators) and still able to activate the claims of local patronage politics.

> Riots were frequent in towns like Devon's because they were successful local politics, in part because their discipline enabled the common people to exert maximum pressure on particular targets while the "protocol" of riot precluded direct challenges to the authority of the local gentry that would raise the costs and lower the prospects of success. And they were disciplined in large part because of solid conventions born of frequent practice, and because the rioters' heritage of success gave them confidence that local politics might once more satisfy their claims and reaffirm their role in the community. (*Bohstedt 1983: 202–3*)

The community theory of food riots is persuasive for its attention to political detail and fine-grained explanation of variation in the location, timing, and mobilization of protest support. Equally important, this approach raises strong empirical challenges to the precision of explanations based on moral economy and class conflict. Any general explanation of food riots must be consistent with the collective results of studies at the local level and important mechanisms of protest mobilization may be revealed only to the close observer of community action. Yet it is also true that a full explanation of food riots must look beyond local actions to discover their causes in the economy and state organization which appear in community theories simple as "external threats." The peculiarities of local politics, in Devon for example, do not explain cycles of protest over time and space. Food riots are generated at the intersection of local grievances and national or even international forces of economy and politics. A complete explanation must address both community and societal conditions as well as the form of their interaction.

The fourth theory of food riots based on state and market is the logical complement to community theory. Here the hypothesized causal conditions work at the national level and affect local settings to the extent that communities reflect broader processes. Louise Tilly (1971: 25) summarizes the approach:

> The large-scale political and economic changes which I believe were crucial to the increased importance of food riots as a form of political conflict were: (1) a two-directional movement in French political centralization and concentration on the national level of policy decisions concerning economic matters, then toward a modification of the traditional paternalistic economic policy; and (2) the formation of a national market, also under the influence of state action.

The political shift from paternalistic to *laissez-faire* policies, seen as central by Tilly and others including Thompson, involved the repeal of laws regulating the grain market and the abdication of public responsibility for ensuring an adequate food supply at fair prices: the abandonment of protections against hoarding or speculating on crop futures and of laws ensuring bread prices "fixed" to the cost of grain, public granaries, sale of grain on the open market with priority given small buyers, and so forth. Food riots were a direct response to state reforms that eliminated interventionary protections for consumers and promoted free markets.

In this epic shift to economic liberalism, the state was more than a mere regulator. State expansion accompanied market centralization, itself requiring changes in the food supply available to those armies, bureaucracies, and urban populations increasingly in the service of the state. Older paternalistic models operating at the local level and assuring "a plentiful supply of necessaries at a low price" (C. Tilly 1975: 428) were undermined by new national policies aimed at greater efficiency and market regulation. Spanning a century and more, the policies included such varied activities as enclosure, land concentration, capital intensification of farming, proletarianization, grain export, taxes, tariffs, and other governmental efforts to regulate the food supply. Price riots were simply one expression of popular grievances stemming from this broader change. "In the last analysis, the food riot was only an epiphenomenon. Below the surface raged a long struggle by builders of states to secure the survival of people most dependent on them and most inclined to serve their ends, a struggle to wrest the means of subsistence from a fiercely reluctant peasantry" (C. Tilly 1975: 392).

Criticisms of state and market theories parallel those of moral economy and community. First are questions of location and timing. National trends in market expansion and state formation say little about when and where rioting will occur except in so far as particular localities experience more numerous or intense external pressures. Bohstedt (1983: 211–12) claims "food riots [cannot] be explained as local reactions against the growth of a national market system. The chronologies of food rioting and of capitalist market development do not match. Most of the riots were not reactions to new market pressures ... So far from promoting food riots, the growth of the national market was beginning to make them obsolete by 1800." Although the timing of food riots and market expansion is an open question, Bohstedt's criticism is not all together apposite because the theory argues not that protest grows steadily with markets, but that it prevails during the period of transition from paternalism to *laissez-faire*. A second and more general criticism of state and market theory is its preoccupation with structural factors to the neglect of the meanings and processes that animate protest action. On such questions, the theory tends simply to endorse moral economy and move on to broader issues of societal change with little concern for linking these levels.

With few exceptions, the various theories of food riots are complementary rather than opposed. They operate at different levels of social organization and explore different correlates with models that rarely allow assignment of causal priority to one factor, such as the vigor of local tradition, over another such as the exactions of state formation. Indeed, they are more often eclectic. Community theories, for example, recognize the changing environment of economic policy while state and market theories acknowledge moral economy as the normative base on which new practices are imposed. At least one important theoretical challenge is to develop these linkages in explanations that move across levels and dimensions.

A suggestion of greater consensus among the theories appears when they turn to explanations of change, particularly, the decline of food riots during the nineteenth century. Theories agree that riot as a political strategy steadily disappeared in the 1800s, that the organization of popular protest shifted to labor unions and social movements which were more effective at engaging centralized states and bourgeois interests. "[M]ost protests about food in the late nineteenth and early twentieth centuries take new forms: they are sponsored and carried out by formal organizations; they operate through planned meetings and demonstrations; and they are often indirect, channelled through struggles about wages and standard of living, rather than about food *per se*" (L. Tilly 1983: 341).

Each theory cites its own set of reasons for the change, yet those reasons often describe one general process from different standpoints.

Thompson (1971: 128–9) argues that 1800 was a watershed; the paternalistic model and moral economy are giving way to a still indiscernible liberalism.

> We are coming to the end of one tradition, and the new tradition has scarcely emerged. In these years the alternative form of economic pressure – pressure upon wages – is becoming more vigorous; there is also something more than rhetoric behind the language of sedition – underground union organization, oaths to the shadowy "united Englishmen". In 1812 traditional food riots overlap with Luddism ... The forms of action which we have been examining depended upon a particular set of social relations, a particular equilibrium between paternalistic authority and the crowd.

Hobsbawm (1959: 124) takes a similar view with more pointed emphasis on how the mob gave way to the industrial working class; "the classical 'mob' has declined ... industrialization has substituted for the *menu peuple* the industrial working class."

On behalf of community theory, Bohstedt (1983: 223) suggests two related reasons for the decline of food riots: expanding markets led to reduced prices and fewer shortages while the efficacy of community politics was eroded by new "vertical" relations. "Riots were the mode of conflict in the framework and patronage politics. In this period patronage politics was beginning to break down and class politics was forming." Reasoning from the standpoint of state and market theory, Charles Tilly also notes improvements in food production and distribution and, even more decisively, the maturation of the capitalist state. The change involved winners and losers:

> state-makers and merchants succeeded in dissolving most of the framework of peasant life throughout the continent, in encouraging the emergence of cash-crop producers oriented to national markets, and thus in destroying the bases on which the peasantry resisted and had the capacity to resist ... The dissolution of the peasant community removed the chief defenders of those rights. The food riot vanished as the peasants lost their struggle against the penetration of capitalism into the countryside. (*C. Tilly 1975: 389–90*)

In summary, the classical food riot disappeared from the European scene for three closely related reasons. Improvements in production and distribution simultaneously lowered prices and reduced the likelihood of famine. State expansion shifted the terrain of politics away from the local village and paternalistic arrangements as it simultaneously introduced more effective forms of repression in the anti-Jacobin spirit of the early nineteenth century. And industrialization, coupled with state centralization, realigned politics by shifting its axis to national class struggles over wages and working conditions.

The theory is convincing for both the unanimity with which it is held and its empirical fit with changing forms of political conflict in Europe. Yet some writers press the theory further to infer a universal pattern in which "primitive" forms of protest such as the bread riot are permanently superseded by industrialization (Hobsbawm 1959) and state centralization (C. Tilly 1986). According to these interpretations, food riots should not reappear in the late twentieth century, at least not in countries that have undergone industrialization, unionization, creation of political parties, and modern state formation.

Yet from the mid-1970s onward, austerity protests in the form of price riots and popular uprisings have swept across the developing countries, including many of those in Latin America (e.g. Argentina, Brazil), Eastern Europe (e.g. Poland), and Africa (e.g. Zambia) that rank among the world's most industrialized economies, possess vigorous traditions of labor organization, and provide prototypical forms of centralized, "bureaucratic-authoritarian" states (O'Donnell 1978, 1988). Strictly speaking, modern food riots do not contradict theories of collective action designed for the historical experience of western European countries. They do, however, cast doubt on general evolutionary interpretations of shifts in protest styles and, perhaps more important, they provide the basis for a comparative history capable of explaining why certain forms of protest reappear under new conditions that prove analogous to earlier transformations.

3   MODERN AUSTERITY PROTEST

For good reason the food riot is considered a thing of the past. Until recently, research on popular uprisings in the developing countries centered on peasant disputes over tenancy and commodity prices (Paige 1975; Scott 1976), or industrial wage disputes (Banton 1957; Epstein 1958). Although occasional reports of bread and price riots appear in the historical literature (Arnold 1979; McFarlane 1982; Meade 1989), these events are described as rare, isolated, and a product of unique national circumstances. Although our own canvass is limited, we have encountered only one clear antecedent to modern austerity protests: Ceylon's *hartal* disturbance of 1953 that arose in response to the government's decision to abolish a consumer subsidy for rice, resulting in a three-fold price increase.

> The hartal not only closed business places and government offices but also produced widespread riots and disorders and extensive damage to transportation and communications facilities throughout the southwest corner of the island. Railroad tracks were blocked by trees and boulders, telephone lines were cut, and vehicles and buildings were set afire. A state of emergency was declared, and at least ten persons died in clashes between police and rioters. (*Kearney 1979: 258*)

The infrequency of riot in countries accustomed to severe economic hardships and fiscal austerity is puzzling. In an essay about Latin American urban migration and politics during the 1940s and 1950s, Eric Hobsbawm (1967: 56) once wrote "it is remarkable how few riots – even food riots – there have been in the great Latin American cities during a period in which the masses of their impoverished and economically marginal inhabitants multiplied, and inflation as often as not was uncontrolled." For its time, the observation is both accurate and provocative. The question, then, is what changed? What accounts for the international wave of food riots that has appeared in recent years?

Popular protest stemming from austerity policies is relatively new for the obvious reason that the policies themselves appear on a broad scale only in the modern era of Third World development. With the exception of Ceylon's *hartal* of 1953, austerity protests *per se* were unknown until the debt crisis. Prior to the 1970s, popular uprisings over prices, unemployment, and scarcity followed the contours of the classical food riot. V. S. Naipaul (1991: 311) describes price demonstrations in West Bengal during the mid-1960s as following "hallowed tradition" and, indeed, the events recall scenes from eighteenth-century England.

> Since 1965 prices of rice and other foodstuffs had soared to unheard-of heights. Kerosene disappeared. Factories closed. Retrenched workers committed suicide. Even qualified engineers and doctors couldn't find jobs. In West Bengal there was a great uprising ... The people started off by confronting retailers in markets and insisting that they take their prices down. In places they looted godowns where grain was being hoarded illegally. When the government used the police against them, there was resistance by the demonstrators. From stone-throwing to setting public places and transport on fire – this has been a hallowed tradition of protest since British times. When someone sets a bus on fire, you know that now he means business. (*Naipaul 1991: 311*)

In the early months of 1974, India also experienced a series of interrelated food riots, protest demonstrations, and strikes in the states of Gujerat and Bihar. The unrest stemmed from conflict among the political parties and widespread allegations of official corruption which coincided with food shortages and price rises (Frenkel 1978). Although these events anticipated in outward form the austerity protests that would appear in other countries later in the decade, they did not arise directly from structural adjustment measures fashioned by international institutions and adopted by the central government of India in response to foreign debt.

Modern austerity protests begin in the mid-1970s, first in Peru and then Egypt. We shall define *austerity protest* as large-scale collective actions including political demonstrations, general strikes, and riots, which are animated by grievances over state policies of economic liberalization implemented in response to the debt crisis and market reforms urged by international agencies. Because "structural adjustment" policies were devised and implemented by the International Monetary Fund, the violent protests that frequently ensued have come to be known as "IMF riots." The popular phrase, however, should not be taken to mean that the IMF has singlehandedly forced austerity measures on defenseless states or that certain domestic economic and political interests are not served by these policies.

Austerity protests January 1976–October 1992 (N = 146)

	Country	Date of first protest	Number overall
1	Peru	July 1976	14
2	Egypt	January 1977	1
3	Ghana	September 1978	1
4	Jamaica	January 1979	3
5	Liberia	April 1979	1
6	Philippines	February 1980	4
7	Zaire	May 1980	4
8	Turkey	July 1980	1
9	Morocco	June 1981	3
10	Sierra Leon	August 1981	2
11	Sudan	January 1982	3
12	Argentina	March 1982	11
13	Ecuador	October 1982	5
14	Chile	October 1982	7
15	Bolivia	March 1983	13
16	Brazil	April 1983	11
17	Panama	October 1983	2
18	Tunisia	January 1984	1
19	Dominican Republic	April 1984	3

20	Haiti	May 1985	6
21	El Salvador	May 1985	4
22	Costa Rica	August 1985	2
23	Guatemala	September 1985	1
24	Mexico	February 1986	2
25	Yugosiavia	November 1986	7
26	Zambia	December 1986	2
27	Poland	March 1987	6
28	Algeria	November 1987	3
29	Rumania	November 1987	3
30	Nigeria	April 1988	2
31	Hungary	August 1988	2
32	Venezuela	February 1989	7
33	Jordan	April 1989	1
34	Ivory Coast	February 1990	1
35	Niger	February 1990	1
36	Iran	August 1991	1
37	Albania	February 1992	1
38	India	February 1992	3
39	Nepal	April 1992	1

Austerity protests are a direct result of the growing external debt of developing countries that became socially defined as a crisis in 1982, leading to the implementation of a series of stabilization policies thereafter. During the 1970s, many international banks lent freely in a scramble to put their burgeoning petrodollar reserves into profitable loans. Developing nations, in turn, borrowed aggressively to finance domestic consumption, a stable currency, state enterprises capable of competing with multinational corporations, and all of the politically calculated appearances of economic development. Although causes of the crisis run deeper, by the late 1970s many smaller nations began to feel the strains of insolvency as a result of a worldwide recession, successive oil-price shocks, declining world commodity prices, and accelerating debt service obligations (Block 1977; Brett 1983; Moffitt 1983; Wood 1986). Pleas for help from these countries were dismissed as individual cases of fiscal mismanagement until 1982 when Mexico's threatened default dramatized the structural crisis facing even the industrialized oil exporters of the Third World.

The IMF responded to balance-of-payment problems of debtor countries by renegotiating the terms of their loans and rescheduling debt payments. Because new loans depended upon private-bank financing, the IMF became involved increasingly as both a policy adviser and a credit rating service. Once the Fund approved a stabilization program for the borrower country, private-bank capital for refinancing the debt followed. IMF certification, however, usually required that the debtor country accept various conditions affecting the national economy. This, in turn, led to growing external and private-capital pressures on domestic economic policies. IMF "conditionality" typically involves implementation of market-oriented policies aimed at economic stabilization. The purpose of economic stabilization programs is to discipline Third World economies in which inflation, price distortions, excessive demand, industrial protection, and profligate government spending are alleged to cause the debt problem. Reforms that correct these practices are the presumptive means necessary for economic recovery and debt repayment (Honeywell 1983; Cline 1983; Williamson 1983).

Austerity programs include stern measures or "shock treatments" that trigger market mechanisms to stimulate export production and increase government foreign-exchange reserves. So, according to the theory: currency devaluations make Third World exports more competitive in international trade; reduced public spending curbs inflation and saves money for debt repayment; privatization of state-owned corporations generates more productive investment and reduces public payrolls; elimination of protectionism and other restraints on foreign investment lures more efficient export firms; cuts in public subsidies for food and basic necessities help to "get prices right," benefiting domestic producers; wage restraints and higher interest rates reduce inflation and enhance competitiveness; and import restrictions conserve foreign exchange for debt servicing (Killick 1984; Cline and Weintraub 1981).

These programs embody clear distributional implications. The urban poor and working class are affected by a combination of subsidy cuts, real-wage reductions, and price increases stemming from exchange-rate devaluations and elevated public-service costs. A reduced share of national income for labor and greater income inequality are frequently documented ill effects. Domestic price increases may benefit rural producers, depending on their size and the degree of dependence on imports. The middle classes are hurt, especially public employees facing the elimination of their jobs. Consumer prices rise and shopkeepers' sales volume suffers from diminished demand. Finally, certain sectors of the national bourgeoisie are adversely affected: businesses and factories that rely on imports, domestic borrowers, and enterprises that depend on mass consumption. Among the few beneficiaries of austerity programs are the firms and social classes connected with export production, foreign investors and transnational firms, large agricultural interests, and state managers (Bernal 1984; Cline 1983; Diaz-Alejandro 1981; Foxley 1981; Frenkel and O'Donnell 1979; Pastor 1987; Sutton 1984; UNCTAD 1989b; UNICEF 1989).

The political implications of austerity are rich and intricate. Because stabilization works a hardship on the majority of the population, albeit on classes with little political power, strong governments are necessary to implement the policies effectively, reinforcing the "bureaucratic-authoritarian" state (O'Donnell 1978; Kaufman 1986; Sheahan 1980). But austerity regimes are inherently unstable because they depend on results to sustain themselves while at the same time generating elite factionalism and popular revolt (Frenkel and O'Donnell 1979; Petras and Brill 1986; Seddon 1988). It may be generally true, as Paul Lubeck (1990: 4) suggests about Nigeria, that "ironically, the turn toward military authoritarianism during the 1990s, so necessary to implement the neo-liberal SAP [structural adjustment program] designed by the World Bank, actually mobilized and strengthened democratic forces within Nigerian civil society to a degree unimaginable before."

In most countries, these new policies have met with stiff opposition, including mass political demonstrations, strikes, and riots. In fact, a wave of austerity protest has occurred in 39 of the approximately 80 debtor countries. Between 1976 and late 1992, some 146 incidents of protest occurred, reaching a peak from 1983 to 1985 and continuing to the present without attenuation (figure 2.1). These mass protests have challenged class-biased stabilization as a solution to the debt crisis, deposing regimes or modifying their policies in some countries, suffering repression in others, but generally raising the political costs of measures that would stabilize the global political economy at the expense of large sections of the populations of Third World countries.

Austerity protests are overwhelmingly urban actions. The characterization "mass" protest is justified by the numbers. Thousands joined street riots in Cairo and São Paulo; ten and sixty thousand, respectively, held demonstrations at government headquarters in Lima and Kingston; hundreds of thousands participated in national strikes in Argentina, Yugoslavia, and India. In many instances, protests begin with official announcements that subsidies are to be eliminated and prices allowed to rise as a condition for new and rescheduled loans. In other cases, the changes appear suddenly as they did to Caracas bus riders confronted one Monday morning with fare increases that sparked a fierce conflagration – the crowd burned buses and moved on to loot stores in a week of rioting. Protests initiated in the capital city commonly mobilize sympathetic actions that spread to 3 (Dominican Republic), 9 (Tunisia) or even

16 (Venezuela) other cities. Demonstrations and riots typically target specific institutions perceived as responsible for the depredations. Marches and protesting crowds converge on major thoroughfares and government buildings such as the treasury or national bank, the legislature, or the presidential palace. Looters attack supermarkets and clothing stores. Where fuel and transportation subsidies are part of the austerity package, buses and gasoline stations are burned. The international dimensions of austerity are recognized symbolically in attacks on travel agencies, foreign automobiles, luxury hotels, and international agency offices. Protests take varied forms, often appearing as classic food riots (e.g. Morocco, Brazil, Haiti) and at other times as protest demonstrations that turned violent (e.g. Sudan, Turkey, Chile) or as general strikes (e.g. Peru, Bolivia, India). Frequently, however, protest initiated with one of these tactics is transformed to another – demonstrations turn to riot, spontaneous violence is rechanneled in political organization. In most instances, demonstrators demand lower prices, restored subsidies, compensatory wage increases, jobs, and even repudiation of the foreign debt.

Participants usually include a cross-section of the urban poor (shantytown dwellers, unemployed youth, street vendors) and working class (unions). In most instances, these low-income groups are allied with other affected segments of the population: students in Liberia, teachers in Guatemala, public employees in Bolivia, shopkeepers in

Figure 2.1 Austerity protest by year and consumer prices[a], 1976–1991, N = 122

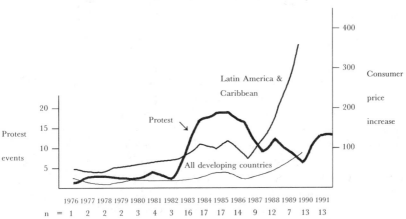

[a] Percent change over previous year.
Source: International Monetary Fund 1990.

the Dominican Republic, and professional groups from physicians to pilots in Sudan. Middle-class consumers have supported demonstrations in Chile and business organizations were part of the opposition in the Philippines. Church groups and Christian base-community organizations have coordinated protests in a number of Latin American countries. Once mass discontent is made evident by these coalitions, political parties may take up the anti-austerity cause in successful bids for national office (e.g. Peru, Dominican Republic). In several countries austerity protests initiated political crises that sooner (e.g. Sudan, Turkey) or later (e.g. Philippines, Haiti, Poland) toppled the national government.

Figure 2.1 illustrates the timing of austerity protest and its association with inflation. Although consumer price increases in Figure 2.1 are not standardized on wages, other evidence shows that the great majority of protest countries have suffered losses in real income from 10 to 40 percent during the 1980s (*World Economic Survey 1990*). The figures demonstrate an imperfect association between protest and hardship; the trend lines are roughly parallel until the mid-1980s and then depart. In a quantitative study of austerity protests, Walton and Ragin (1990) have shown that both the occurrence and the severity of protests are explained by overurbanization (i.e. urbanization rates beyond levels expected for the degree of industrialization) and the extent of international involvement in the national economy (i.e. "IMF Pressure" operationalized by the conditions associated with borrowing over IMF quota limits, loan renegotiations and restructurings). A number of other potential predictors such as the debt burden, inflation, level of economic development, and export dependency contribute little to the explanation of protest events beyond what is explained by IMF pressure and overurbanization. Generally, in a large-sample comparison the statistical evidence indicates that the causes of austerity protest are hyperurbanization and the involvement of international agencies in domestic political-economic policy. Countries with large, poor, and underemployed urban populations experience protests when governments impose policies with regressive social class consequences in the interests of serving foreign debts (Walton and Ragin 1990).

Turning from aggregate statistical indicators to case-level evidence about the conditions of protest, a pattern emerges that suggests parallels with historical studies of food riots. If the countries that have had austerity protests are rank-ordered on both protest severity and overurbanization, the top ten cases are: Peru, Chile, Bolivia, Tunisia, Morocco, Egypt, Brazil, Dominican Republic, Argentina, and Zambia. We suggest that the mechanism linking overurbanization and protest is a well-developed organizational infrastructure capable of mobilizing political action. The research literature shows a high degree of urban social organization, particularly in working-class communities, in these countries. Peru, for example, is one of the countries in which the social integration and political activism of squatter settlements was initially discovered (e.g. Mangin 1967) and frequently analyzed as a style of popular organization compatible with the political system (e.g. Collier 1976; Dietz 1976; Leeds and Leeds 1976). Similarly, Chile has had a strong tradition of union and urban community organization (Goldrich, Pratt, and Schuller 1967; Portes 1972), and the evidence for local mobilization in voluntary associations is repeated for the other Latin American cases (Portes and Walton 1976).

If this pattern comes as no surprise to students of Latin American cities, unexpected corroboration comes from the North African cases that rank high on the list. Recent work on Tunisia and Morocco, for example, demonstrates a distinctive yet analogous pattern of communities actively organized in labor unions, occupational associations, opposition parties, student groups, and Islamic brotherhoods (Burke 1989; Seddon 1988). Finally, the seemingly incongruous case of Zambia also fits the pattern because austerity protests occurred in the nation's copperbelt towns where miners have been organized for many years in trade unions that are key among other supra-tribal groups in community politics (Epstein 1957; Zuckerman 1986). Our interpretation is that the particularly explosive combination in these cases lies in the depredations of austerity politics visited upon the urban poor and working classes who are already organized and oriented to political action.

Hobsbawm's observation about the absence of a tradition of popular protest in Latin American cities during the 1940s and 1950s may have been true in a time when roughly 20 percent of the population lived in urban areas and states were just beginning to assume responsibility for social welfare. Yet three contemporary developments suggest that the alleged quiescence was neither universal nor lasting. First, recent comparative research suggests that urban uprisings, strikes, and food riots did occur in the developing countries during the nineteenth and early twentieth centuries with some regularity (e.g. Arnold 1979; Beinart and Bundy 1987; Burke 1989; Meade 1989; Rogers 1987). Second, as levels of urbanization have risen rapidly worldwide in the mid-twentieth century, from 20 to over 60 percent in Latin America for example (Gilbert and Gugler 1982), cities have become increasingly the locus of social protest. Third, states have responded to the twin challenge of urban unrest and social-service needs with policies designed to incorporate the new urban groups. Through political efforts to ameliorate grievances states extended protections to their growing urban constituencies and these welfare policies soon became the bases for a new moral economy.

Hobsbawm attributed the anomalous quiescence of Latin American cities to rapid urban migration and the apolitical mobility aspirations of heterogeneous former peasants. The new urbanites, moreover, were allegedly susceptible to cooptation by populist regimes such as those of Vargas in Brazil or Perón in Argentina. "[T]he experience of populism reflects the relative passivity and lack of initiative of the urban masses, much more readily mobilized by an existing and sympathetic power from above" (Hobsbawm 1967: 63).

Yet, from 1890 to 1917, the urban masses of Rio de Janeiro organized popular movements in tandem with labor unions. Repeated uprisings during these years, including food riots, were aimed precisely at the inequities of rapid urban development: slum clearance, prices and routes of public transportation, uneven provision of services such as electricity and lighting, and cost-of-living increases generally. "[P]opular protest cannot be divided into the neat categories of pre-modern street riots and modern trade unionism ... Carioca street protests prior to 1917 were part of a developing system of political ideology, representing a facet of the popular classes' culture that was no less 'modern' than the trade union movement that was developing along side it" (Meade 1989: 242). Nor were such urban protests unique to Latin America. Burke (1989: 45) has shown that in the Middle East from 1750 to 1914 "there were two major causes of urban protest ... subsistence food crises and exorbitant fiscal demands" both of which drew militant crowds to the principal mosque where reforms were demanded on behalf of an "Islamic moral economy."

Rapid urbanization in the developing countries, notably from 1950 to 1970, had at least one unambiguous political consequence. Whether for progressive or opportunistic reasons, governments began to implement policies designed to meet the employment and subsistence requirements of the new urban groups, both poor and middle class. In a more acute analysis than Hobsbawm's pessimistic rendition of populism, Cardoso and Faletto (1979: 129–31) argue that import substitution industrialization (ISI) was pursued by a new "developmentalist alliance" composed of commercial agriculture, state bureaucracy, national industrial capital, urban merchants, and the urban middle and working classes. If elite groups and their middle-class retainers reaped the greatest rewards of the new policy, it was nevertheless a regime of "developmentalist populism" by virtue of the social wage guarantees that it conceded to the urban masses in the form of price subsidies and public services. Pacification of the urban crowd that had demonstrated its disruptive muscle earlier in the century was essential to the social pact:

> industrialization was the result of a policy, agreed upon by the various sectors, that reconciled the developmental needs of a type of economy that not only created an economic base for the new groups *but also offered opportunities of socio-economic incorporation to the popular groups which because of their numbers and presence in the cities might otherwise alter the system of domination*. (*Cardoso and Faletto 1979: 131; emphasis added*)

The policies of this developmentalist alliance produced an "urban bias" in their distributive consequences, as critics have correctly noted (e.g. Lipton 1977). Yet the same critics, by arguing for policies that would reverse the bias and favor rural producers, miss the social-class dimensions of the broader strategy. Developmentalism was less a policy benefiting some unalloyed urban interest than it was a class coalition of industrial and export interests that paid the price of social peace with concessions to the urban masses. "Urban bias created the basis for the populist coalition between state, the urban classes, and industrial capital, whether foreign or local. The urban middle and working classes were junior partners in these coalitions, but compared to the rural population they received substantial benefits in health and educational services and through food and other subsidies" (Roberts 1989: 672). Peasants suffered from this bias, particularly as a result of arrangements that assured cheap "wage foods" for the working classes. As de Janvry has shown for Mexico and Latin America in general,

> The large capitalist farms are the producers of exports, raw materials for industry, and luxury foods for the domestic market such as coffee, fresh fruits, vegetables, cotton, and wheat. The peasants, by contrast, are primarily producers of the basic wage foods – corn, beans, and rice. These last three crops are the staples of the Mexican diet, but they are unattractive to capitalist farmers because of the low profitability of their production, which results from state controls on the prices of wage foods ... Price suppression of wage foods comes about through free trade, concessional imports, overvalued exchange rates, and direct state control of price levels. (*de Janvry 1981: 125, 155*)

To complete the argument we need only add that the mechanisms de Janvry cites for supporting a policy of urban bias came to rely heavily on foreign borrowing during the 1960s and 1970s.

Policies for the provision of cheap wage foods, nevertheless, represent only one area in which developmentalist regimes established a social pact with the new urban groups. "This alliance could be maintained only by creating and expanding employment opportunities for the masses" (Cardoso and Faletto 1979: 143), including middle-class employees of state-owned enterprises and public bureaucracies in the fields such as health and education. Finally, and most dramatically, states catered to potentially restive elements of the urban poor with a series of urbanization programs that became increasingly popular, not to say necessary, in the 1960s and 1970s. Militant squatters were pacified with land titles and basic services (e.g. water, streets, sanitation, transportation). Public or publicly assisted housing and low cost sites-and-services programs were conceived as methods of defusing popular grievances.

The critical feature of all of these programs was that they implied a bargain between the state and the urban poor. Public assistance was provided in exchange for political loyalty. The new urban groups were expected not only to refrain from embarrassing protest demonstrations, but to turn out in support of the state on ceremonial occasions and election day and to channel their demand-making through the instrumentalities of government or the ruling political party (e.g. Barnes 1986; Cornelius 1975; Khuri 1975). Although these "patron–client" arrangements are sometimes dismissed as politically ineffective or oppressively paternalistic, close observers of Third World urban politics have shown the great ingenuity with which the poor are able to extract benefits from this system while simultaneously using it to protect themselves against repression (Leeds and Leeds 1976). Just as Thompson characterized the moral reciprocities of eighteenth-century English paternalism, the urban poor in today's Third World regard the developmental guarantees of the state as legitimate rights and express their protest in terms of injustice when the social pact is violated.

The moral economy of the urban poor looks backward to rights guaranteed in the developmental pact, but also forward to the objectives promised in developmental ideology. It defines the rightful expectations of the urban poor and their own obligations as citizens. The moral economy, as Scott (1976: 3) observes in the context of peasant society, is constituted by "their notion of economic justice and their working definition of exploitation – their view of which claims on their product [are] tolerable and which intolerable." In Latin America, ideas of economic justice draw upon Roman Catholic traditions of patrimony as the reward of the faithful and on liberation theology's preference for the poor. The liberal state of the nineteenth-century independence movement is embraced in popular forms of democratic participation and a basic acceptance of the market economy. People expect jobs for the able-bodied and a living family wage, rather than charity or control of the means of production. The migrant culture of cities expects progress, if not for one's self then for one's children – particularly through education. Exploitation is labor compensated below the level of intergenerational improvement. The urban poor are organized in church groups, migrant clubs, neighborhood associations, small-business groups, labor unions, sports clubs, and many more vehicles of civil society. Under symbols of the cross and the national flag, squatter invasions demand legal recognition and physical incorporation, and they offer in return self-governing, law-abiding communities ready to work for the economic advancement of their members (Mangin 1967).

In Africa, the moral economy draws upon tribal and ethnic bonds refitted for the urban setting and on colonial forms of "native" self-government, housing, and community development (Iliffe 1987). Muslim cultures expect alms-giving from the affluent and modest jobs for members of Islamic Brotherhoods. "In addition to petty-income opportunities, the moral economy of the *gardawa* [Koranic students] depends upon charity in the form of housing in the entryways of houses" (Lubeck 1985: 380). Urbanization has produced a complex blend of detribalization in the form of fading rural customs and re-tribalization along lines of occupation, trade unionism, residential community, and local government (Epstein 1957; Leys 1975). Local organizations resemble their Latin American counterparts: religious sects, tribal and kinship associations, migrant clubs, friendly societies, unions, and dance groups. In Latin American and African cities, a new form of civil society has emerged from the period of rapid urbanization to provide the locus in which an evolving moral economy has fashioned the developmental social contract.

The developmental state was able to sustain and shape the moral economy during rapid urbanization as long as economic growth and foreign lending ensured fiscal prosperity. In the mid-1970s the social pact collapsed. The debt crisis resulted not only in the elimination of artificially supported levels of domestic consumption (e.g. subsidies and overvalued exchange rates), but also in the abrogation of many customary guarantees such as housing, public employment, education, and health care. When austerity protests responded to internationally prescribed market reforms, no doubt was left about the moral economy that animated the perceived betrayal. Crowds from Rio to Rabat crying "Out with the IMF!" demanded a restoration of food and transportation subsidies, employment, and wages commensurate with inflation. Governments were blamed for sacrificing their own citizens in the interests of foreign banks. Protestors demanded that the state meet its responsibilities to the people who, during the decades of patron–client politics, had upheld their end of the bargain.

4   CLASSICAL AND AUSTERITY RIOTS COMPARED

Classical food riots and modern austerity protests reflect a number of striking parallels as well as some critical differences which we shall summarize and endeavor to explain. By contrast to certain traditions of comparative history, our interpretation is neither that riots constitute elementary forms of collective action that recur episodically as indicators of social strain, nor that popular insurrections appear regularly across societies as pre-modern paroxysms destined for replacement by the evolution of the interest-group politics of industrialization (cf. Rule 1988). Rather, we shall argue that riots and demonstrations over the cost of living are common occurrences in market societies; forms of popular protest that change in interaction with the state and economic organization, but also persevere as a result of recurring moral and material forces.

In both the classical and contemporary periods, riot politics are introduced by far-reaching policy changes that promote free-market economies at the national and international levels respectively. Riots respond to the elimination, in different ways, of "paternalistic" consumer protections understood by the populace as legitimate rights. Yet there are important differences in scale and organization of the two periods. Policy changes in the classical period, though influenced by foreign trade, were implemented in the interests of an expanding national state and deepening market system. In the contemporary period, changes result from a closer integration of the global economy with the international state system coordinating the reorganization through agencies like the IMF. In both periods, moreover, riots produce short-term success in the presence of rescinded measures and palliative solutions to price rises, but long-term depredation and socio-economic restructuring. Finally, in both periods the food riot appeared in combination with other forms of protest (e.g. strikes, political demonstrations) and incorporated related grievances (e.g. unemployment) in appeals for popular justice.

Modern austerity protests operate on a much broader canvass, involving not simply a few (European) neighboring countries but a vastly larger set of developing nations sharing a common dependence on the trade, aid, and investment of advanced industrial societies. This constitutes both a quantitative difference in the scale on which protest is acted out and a qualitative difference in the organization of protest. Austerity protests are predominantly urban risings, unlike the town-and-countryside events of the eighteenth century, and characteristically they spread quickly and contagiously through a national network of cities during any given protest episode. The pattern is closer to Rudé's description of coordinated French riots than to the more segmented English style. But, again, there is a qualitative difference. Modern protests, that may involve the capital city and anywhere from 6 (Morocco) to 16 (Venezuela) major urban centers, are clearly national urban uprisings.

This difference in scale, of course, is connected with the distinct and international conditions that precipitate austerity protests. Famine and distributional inequities that played at least some role in classical food riots are absent in today's unrest. It is not the availability of goods that is at issue, but their price — a fact that accounts for the characteristically modern pattern of looting. Austerity protests, moreover, respond to a variety of price increases (food, petroleum, transportation, and school fees) that stem directly from government policy changes rather than from the actions of a number of private sellers. These differences are related to a more broadly based pattern of protest that is also clearly focused on responsible parties. The modern urban masses are developmentally literate, well aware of the public underpinnings of the social pact and the international origins of austerity — as their protest slogans and placards demonstrate.

The targets of austerity protests differ in interesting ways. Owing to the complexity of modern markets, angry crowds fix responsibility on the retailer rather than the middleman — supermarkets, clothing, and appliance stores rather that grain merchants and speculators. Authorities are still important targets, but now as perpetrators of hunger rather than as protectors of the people too slow to act in their expected capacity. Modern targets also include institutions such as government buildings (the treasury or national bank), buses, gasoline stations, and symbols of foreign affluence like travel agencies and imported automobiles. Where classical food riots petition local magistrates for redress, austerity protests appeal to the national government.

Given enormous changes in social structure over 200 years, riot participants naturally represent different social strata and occupational groups. In the modern period, the urban poor, working class, informal-sector workers, and sometimes middle-class government employees, students, shopkeepers, and professionals comprise the typical cross-section of protest participants, replacing artisans, miners, workers in town industries, and agricultural laborers. As Thompson noted about the eighteenth-century English crowd, women are active participants in austerity protests. Generally, austerity protests incorporate a wider cross-section of the national population – and, more specifically of the urban population which represents a larger and more diversified fraction of the national population. This follows from the broader effects of structural adjustment programs which penalize, for example, national capital, middle-class salaried employees, professionals in state-owned enterprises, public-sector workers (teachers, doctors), and students, in addition to the urban poor.

Burke's (1989b) study of classical and modern Islamic protest movements complements our results. Austerity protests call upon the traditional moral economy, but foster new tactics and participants.

> I.M.F. riots do not follow . . . the classic patterns. . . . [T]hey occurred in scattered districts, instead of in the core of the old city. They appear to have no central spatial focal point. The slogans chanted by the crowd, where these are known, appear not to involve the old language of Islamic protest. The protestors appear to have been drawn chiefly from students and recent urban migrants, mostly unemployed young men . . . [W]hat is striking is not the reassertion of the old repertoire of Islamic collective action, but the contrasts: one looks in vain for the ulama-led demonstrations, processions from the mosque to the citadel. At the same time, the behavior of these crowds does not fall into the patterns of the old secular political style of collective action. It is not entirely fanciful to suggest that just beneath the surface one can detect a residue of the old Islamic moral economy: the targets of the crowd's wrath appear to have been selected with an eye on their place in the web of power relations which prop up Middle Eastern regimes. They include local government agencies, luxury hotels and restaurants. They represent visible and flagrant transgressions of culturally grounded notions of justice: international consumption styles, corruption, and gross inefficiency. (*Burke 1989b: 52*)

Food and price riots occur throughout the history of market societies, typically in conjunction with other non-violent forms of protest, when severe economic hardship is socially defined as the result of public policies that betray the moral economy. Concretely, these policies involve the abandonment of consumer protections in the free-market reforms that serve the centralization of capital and state power. Specific protest incidents are triggered by visible and abrupt exactions which simultaneously generate palpable hardship, a clear perception of responsible agents, and a sense of injustice grounded in the moral economy of the poor. Riot and street demonstrations are the natural means of redress for popular assemblies mobilized by a sense of immediacy, betrayal, and the need for autonomous action. Popular protests understandably distrust conventional forms of political participation, the failure of which typically defines the immediate crisis, and therefore resort to means at their own disposal. Demographic and social structural changes generate new groups vulnerable to market reforms, groups that shift over time from rural to urban locales and national to international political arenas. Targets, methods, and rallying cries of protest change. Yet, in other ways, an essential class struggle perseveres, first at the level of national markets and centralized states, now at the level of a global economy and state system.

5   CONCLUSION

Contrary to the evolutionary assumptions that pervade theories of collective action, the complex form of popular protest that we conventionally refer to as the "food riot" continues to provide aggrieved assemblies with a means to express politically their claims to unjust treatment. As a vital element of the protest repertoire of modern urban populations, violent demonstrations against price hikes recur in societies with long traditions of industrialization, unionization, and democratic government. The food riot, and its associated styles of protest, obeys the rhythms of hardship, moral economy, and state entitlements. Just as the so-called "race riot" continues to bedevil cities of the advanced industrial world (Washington DC, Brussels, and Los Angeles most recently), so the food riot recurs when its structural causes recombine in history. Recognizing that comparative history must proceed with methodological caution, we urge bolder interpretations of collective action. "Riots have meanings as well as causes. To discover what they mean, we must learn to read them, scanning across centuries for patterns of behavior and looking for order in apparent anarchy that explodes under our noses" (Darnton 1992: 46).

Modern bread riots, like their eighteenth-century predecessors, arise at the intersection of state and economic reorganization, now determined primarily at the international level. Third World states are increasingly dependent upon technical agencies and financial institutions of the international economy for loans, investment, and, reluctantly, for policy choices that affect domestic society. Political sovereignty in the poor nations is challenged through the process of debt management. The key links between international demands, state action, and protest include: an "overurbanized" or large urban population not absorbed in formal sector and industrial employment and so more likely to experience the pains of austerity; cities that are socially and politically organized in a strong civil society (e.g. in unions, political groups, community associations, churches); and a moral economy that provides ideological legitimation for popular protest based on the social pact previously negotiated by developmental regimes.

Although many of the general interpretations of food riots based on the experiences of eighteenth-century Europe mistakenly relegate to the past this "primitive" form of collective action, the same theories, nevertheless, provide vital insights about the current period of international restructuring. Today's neo-liberal reform of the international economy duplicates in some key respects the depredations created by earlier national forms of state centralization and market integration. State and market theory applies to these developments and provides an explanation for the timing and form of the new cross-national wave of austerity protest. Moral economy gives meaning to the abrogation of the social pact established between developmentalist regimes and rapidly urbanizing populations. Structural adjustment eliminates precisely those resources that support patron–client arrangements in which the political loyalty of the masses is negotiated for subsistence guarantees. Community theories, finally, capture the link between hyperurbanization, urban social organization, and the civil society that carries on, and reinterprets, traditional moral economy. Each of the theories provides a key ingredient, but all of them need to be reformulated in a new synthesis. Popular protest is fashioned in civil society by groups struggling, on one hand, with the exigencies of redistributive state policies and attempting, on the other hand, to mobilize on the basis of culturally defined rights. State and culture provide the general elements of a theory of collective action.

The food riot as a means of popular protest is a common, perhaps even universal, feature of market societies – less a vestige of political-industrial evolution than a strategy of empowerment in which poor and dispossessed groups assert their claims to social justice. In the modern system of states and international economic integration, the explosive point of popular protest has moved, with most of the world's population, to the cities where the processes of global accumulation, national development, and popular justice intersect.

Part II

Case Studies

3

Fighting for Survival: Women's Responses to Austerity Programs

Victoria Daines and David Seddon

1 INTRODUCTION

In this chapter we consider the role of women in popular protest and collective struggle on a comparative basis across the developing world and conclude that women's involvement in such forms of political action has been widespread and significant, despite the tendency of commentators and analysts to ignore it. We show that women have not only supported but also participated in and even initiated demonstrations of resistance and protest against adjustment programs and austerity measures. Generally, however, the involvement of women in austerity protests has been seriously underestimated. As a consequence, not only the role of women in these protests but also the very character and significance of the protests themselves have not been properly appreciated.

Women's responses to austerity measures, where they have been considered at all, have all too often been seen only in terms of the "survival strategies" of the "victims" of adjustment. We suggest that, although women have suffered disproportionately in their confrontation with austerity, they have also, in their struggles to defend their living conditions and those of their families, developed forms of cooperative and collective activity of very considerable significance for our understanding both of popular protest and of social movements. Women's involvement in the more dramatic forms of collective austerity protest is deeply rooted in these every-day forms of resistance against those who threaten their survival (and the lives of those near and dear to them) and in everyday forms of collaboration and mutual support with those – generally other women – who share their difficulties, their struggles, and their ideas of social justice.

We develop, therefore, a framework which, while distinguishing between different forms of action, emphasizes both the ideological continuity and the practical interrelationship between them. Consequently, we reject the sharp distinction, often made by those considering women's struggles, between involvement in "public" popular protest on the one hand and participation in "private" action on the other and between "political" and "non-political" activities.

Finally, we suggest that, although women's involvement in popular protest against austerity has a long history (albeit one only now beginning to be written), there is growing evidence of the emergence in the developing world over the last two decades of an increasingly self-conscious, if often highly heterogeneous, women's movement. This adds a new and significant element (both organizational and ideological) – capable in specific instances of drawing together women of very different social backgrounds in protest and resistance – to the forces associated with the mobilization of the urban poor against austerity and adjustment.

2   WOMEN AS "VICTIMS" OF STRUCTURAL ADJUSTMENT

In the 1970s and early 1980s, stabilization and structural adjustment programs concentrated on macro-economic issues and were little concerned with problems of equity. Consideration of the specific effects of such programs on the poor and other vulnerable sections of the population (e.g. women, children, and the elderly) is recent and still not effectively integrated into their design and conception. As Pinstrup-Andersen has observed, "until recently, and with a few notable exceptions, short term effects on the poor have usually been ignored or given low priority in the design of adjustment programmes unless they were perceived to threaten political stability" (Pinstrup-Andersen 1989: 90). The inherent gender bias of structural adjustment programs is systematic (Elson 1991a, b); but this too has not been fully appreciated or else has been ignored.

Evidence has been accumulating rapidly over the last five years, however, to confirm the view that poor women have generally suffered particularly from the austerity measures associated with stabilization and structural adjustment programs. Cut-backs in public expenditure (particularly in the areas of health, education, and social welfare) have restructured and reduced the social services available, while economic liberalization and deflationary measures have increased un-employment in both the public and private sectors and squeezed real wages, so that family and household incomes have suffered sub-stantial reductions in many cases. All of these consequences of adjustment have hit poor women and their young children particularly hard (cf. Alexander 1990; Bolles 1983; Commonwealth Secretariat 1990; Cornia, Jolly, and Stewart 1987: 2; Ghai and Hewitt de Alcantara 1990; Green 1989: 36; Pinstrup-Andersen 1989: 91; and Selby, Murphy, and Lorenzen 1990).

In the second half of the 1980s, the social costs of adjustment and economic liberalization were increasingly emphasized by some inter-national agencies, and the costs to women and children considered as matters of grave concern. In the name of "adjustment with a human face," UNICEF and others began to suggest that adjustment had come to involve "a reaction too far" (Killick 1990), although they tended to accept that adjustment itself was itself necessary and inevitable. Towards the end of the decade, even the World Bank began to recognize the social and the political implications of the harsh austerity measures adopted as part of the adjustment package and to urge the need for "compensatory programs" (see World Bank 1990). But even these, when actually introduced, often failed to provide effective protection for the most disadvantaged against the rigors of adjustment (see Alexander 1990, on PAMSCAD in Ghana).

Increasing attention is now being paid to the effects of adjustment on women, and to ways in which women might be protected and women's concerns incorporated more effectively into the process of adjustment. Many of the recommendations, however, (particularly on the part of the international agencies) remain patronizing and prescriptive. The argument for "adjustment with a human face" has tended in practice to "focus attention mainly on women as victims, thus deteriorating into paternalism. It also tends to focus only on women in low-income households, and mainly on the detrimental impact of adjustment on women, and not on the contribution that women can make to effective adjustment" (Elson 1989: 71). Even some of the more recent studies with a specific concern for women in adjustment (e.g. Commonwealth Secretariat 1990), focus more on what development agencies can do for women rather than what women can do for themselves and how they may be supported and encouraged in their own initiatives and struggles.

3   WOMEN'S RESISTANCE AND PROTEST: FORMS OF STRUGGLE

A concern with women's subordination in the context of adjustment is both appropriate and valid, but, as Rowbotham remarks, with respect to women's struggles in the West, "the idea of oppression is both vague and rather static. It fixes people in their role as victim rather than pointing to the contradictory aspects of relationships which force the emergence of new forms of consciousness" (1980: 31). In the developing world, as in the West, women have not simply experienced subordination and oppression or suffered passively the efforts of international agencies and national governments to implement economic reforms but have struggled in the face of austerity and adversity.

Usually women's struggles have been categorized as involving essentially individual "coping" or "survival" strategies of different kinds (see section 4); often, however, their struggles have involved collaboration and cooperation with others – usually other women – to reduce the pressures and to increase the "room for maneuver" in the face of austerity. To see women only as the "victims" of adjustment programs and austerity measures is to ignore this. In many instances, furthermore, women's resistance has taken the more visible and overt form of collective struggle, whether in the workplace, in the community, or on the streets. And if the involvement of women in such forms of political activity has often not been recognized, it is largely because the definition of what constitutes "politics" has been narrowly conceived and because "political analysis ... bypasses or fails to address many activities and concerns precisely because the political has so often been arbitrarily severed from 'moral', 'social' or 'economic' issues" (Siltanen and Stanworth 1984: 204).

Women's involvement in collective forms of direct action – such as strikes, "bread riots" and political demonstrations – should be seen not as an extraordinary and exceptional intrusion of women into public politics but as part of a range of activities undertaken in response to government policies and state-induced austerity, all of which have a moral, social, and economic dimension and all of which have political significance. The crucial continuity between these different forms of struggle needs to be emphasized.

Poor women everywhere, and particularly in the developing countries during periods of recession and austerity, live lives of struggle. This struggle is often associated with what have been variously called "everyday forms of resistance" (Scott 1976, 1985) and "hidden forms of consciousness" (Cohen 1982). Scott, who used the term "everyday forms of resistance" to describe peasant struggles in Malaysia and elsewhere, suggests that

> most of the forms this (prosaic but constant) struggle takes stop well short of collective outright defiance ... These ... forms of class struggle have certain features in common. They require little or no coordination or planning; they often represent a form of individual self-help; and they typically avoid any direct symbolic confrontation with authority or with elite norms. (*Scott 1985: 29*)

Such forms of resistance have much in common with the various forms of so-called "passive resistance" characteristic of many situations where open protest, defiance, or resistance might prove suicidal (see Harper 1968, on lower-caste resistance in India; Cohen 1982, on "resistance and hidden forms of consciousness among African workers"; O'Hanlon 1988, on forms of struggle and resistance among "subaltern groups" in Third World societies generally; and Mason 1981, on workers' opposition in Nazi Germany). However, it is striking that Scott, while explicitly drawing attention to "some of the feminist literature on peasant society" (Scott 1985: 33) – which argues that informal and covert resistance often makes possible certain immediate *de facto* gains for those undertaking it, in order to indicate parallels between the "everyday resistance" of peasants and that of women – nevertheless fails to develop this brief observation further in his analysis.

Women's struggles – like the struggles of all subordinate groups – do tend to be directed towards very concrete and often immediate objectives. As Piven and Cloward have observed, "people experience deprivation and oppression within a concrete setting, not as the end product of large and abstract processes, and it is the concrete experience that molds their discontent into specific grievances against specific targets" (Piven and Cloward 1977: 20). Women's protest and resistance against austerity are also directed at very specific targets and with specific aims. Even when the forms of resistance and protest develop beyond the individual to the cooperative and even collective, this concern with tangible results and gains remains crucial, although in collective struggles the potential for a more comprehensive vision of the sources of exploitation and oppression, and the feasibility of seeking wider and longer-term objectives, are greater (as we shall see below).

The idea, however, of a simple evolutionary progression – from individual to collective struggle, associated with the development from "less conscious," "limited," and "less organized" to "more conscious," "wider," and "more organized" – implicit in much of the literature on forms of struggle (e.g. Cohen 1982, 1991; Scott 1985) is problematic, and although the structure of our own discussion indicates our broad sympathy with the idea that cooperative and collective forms of direct action have greater political impact than do individual forms of struggle, we have serious reservations about the some of the underlying assumptions implicit in such a schema. First, it tends to distinguish sharply between "private" and "public" forms of consciousness and resistance and to privilege the latter as somehow "higher" (i.e. more significant or advanced), effectively ignoring the fact that easy distinctions between "private" and "public" politics may themselves constitute a form of oppression rendering literally invisible, and therefore implicitly insignificant, the less conventional forms of struggle (see Siltanen and Stanworth 1984). Second, it tends to privilege certain forms of political organization (i.e. the hierarchical, in which a leadership galvanizes and amplifies the consciousness and actions of those imprisoned within a "lower" form of consciousness – for example, Cohen 1982: 257, 1991: 108) as against others (i.e. the egalitarian, in which cooperative and collective forms of action stem from specific circumstances – objective and subjective – of oppression and subordination as and when those circumstances permit, and consciousness is raised in part through participation in action – see Rowbotham, Segal, and Wainright 1980).

A different approach – more appropriate in our view to the analysis of women's resistance and protest – would emphasize the normality of the coexistence of different forms of consciousness and action, and stress the pervasiveness of those structures of oppression and subordination which permeate women's lives and generally permit only limited room for maneuver or space for the more overt, conventional forms of "public" struggle, resistance, and protest. Such an approach would emphasize the fact that "women make history, but not under conditions of their own choosing'; it would thus recognize both the potential for challenging structures of exploitation and oppression and the real constraints on direct action. It would also leave open for investigation, without prejudice, the question as to whether there are "distinctively female (or feminine)" forms of organization and action, as many commentators, including feminists, often suggest or imply. It would recognize the plurality of "languages" of protest as well as of forms of action and include within the scope of analysis a range of forms of political activity without prejudging their "priority" in terms of effectiveness in bringing about change.

In her discussion of women's struggles and direct action, Carroll stresses the importance of considering not only "the most spectacular or heroic examples," but also "the widely dispersed local actions, unnumbered and innumerable, of small groups of women at the grass roots" (Carroll 1989: 21). We agree, but what is also required, however, is the recognition that "everyday forms of resistance" may provide the ground from which, under specific circumstances, more overt and visible forms of struggle may grow (Cohen 1991: 108). That everyday forms of resistance and dissidence may constitute the seedbed for an apparently sudden burgeoning of open forms of conventionally recognizable "public" politics has been demonstrated frequently throughout history, and never more clearly than over the last two decades in Africa, Asia, Latin America – and Eastern Europe. The same is true, we would submit, of women's struggles. We would agree with the proposition that in general, women's struggle or direct action "has a more extensive history and has been more influential in the history of political action for social change than is generally recognised" (Carroll 1989: 3). However, women's involvement in collective – and more openly "political" – forms of resistance and protest generally has its roots in preexisting forms of collaboration and cooperation and in shared ideas about fairness, justice, and legitimacy. Only an adequate appreciation of the evolving social and cultural matrix within which the various forms of women's resistance and protest are embedded and generated will enable one to understand their "outbursts" of anger and outrage in such dramatic forms of protest as "bread riots" (see Caldeira 1990).

Finally, as Tripp points out, in her analysis of "quiet everyday forms of non-compliance and resistance" in Tanzania, "redefining political struggle to include non-organised and non-self-conscious action adds new dimensions to the meaning of politics and the processes of political change" (Tripp 1989: 3); and the concept of "everyday forms of resistance" is valuable in emphasizing that protest and resistance as forms of political struggle may exist even where they cannot easily be distinguished from everyday economic and social activities. It helps also to dissolve the always arbitrary distinction between "private" and "public" and to emphasize the fact that "the boundary between private and public arenas does not mark the limits of the political, and indeed is itself constructed through political process" (Siltanen and Stanworth 1984: 208; see also West and Blumberg 1990: 4–5).

4   SURVIVAL STRATEGIES

On the basis of a study carried out in the mid-1980s, Cornia argued that "for the majority of low-income households ... adjustment entails a variety of adaptations – known as survival strategies – in the creation and use of resources" (Cornia 1987a: 90). He suggested that

> little is known on [sic] the mechanisms and strategies allowing poor people to survive under conditions of extreme deprivation. Even less is known on the adaptations made in recent years in those countries where the army of the poor has been swollen by the ranks of those forced out of the formal sector by dramatic falls in production and employment. (*Cornia 1987a: 91*)

A study of coping with poverty in India, however, noted that, "while the poor families have as a single unit the objective of ensuring their survival, the coping responses to urban poverty of the individual members of the family need not all be the same. It is expected that their spheres of individual activity, age, gender and work status are likely to determine the nature of the coping response" (Kalpagam 1985: 2); in practice, "while the burdens of survival [for the family] are enormous, those of the women are even greater" (Kalpagam 1985: 18).

There has been increasing attention paid over the past five years to the way in which women, as key figures in households and families, struggle to ensure their own survival and that of their families. However, these struggles are usually identified as essentially defensive, providing little potential for changing the circumstances within which individuals and households (the usual "unit" of analysis for such studies) struggle. Jiggins has suggested, for sub-Saharan Africa, that "women's primary concern is first with survival and only thereafter with livelihood security" (Jiggins 1989: 956), while Pryer sees many of the activities of urban-slum women in Bangladesh as "struggles for survival rather than solutions to the problem [of deprivation and malnutrition]" (Pryer 1987: 140). Elson also considers that "there is a difference between survival strategies and activities that can form the basis for sustained growth and development both on a personal and a national level" (Elson 1989: 69). The same point is made, even more forcefully, by Selby, Murphy, and Lorenzen who argue that what are referred to as "survival strategies" are simply ways of "organizing for self-defence" and point out that survival is by no means guaranteed by such activities – in many cases, "people are *not* surviving" (Selby, Murphy, and Lorenzen 1990: 70).

We recognize that, in many instances, economic recession, structural adjustment, and austerity measures adopted by governments have combined to undermine preexisting cooperative structures and reduce the room for maneuver, making the securing of livelihoods increasingly difficult and often obliging women to adopt more individualistic strategies. Thus Jiggins argues, for sub-Saharan Africa, that "women's attempts to ensure and maintain an adequate livelihood for themselves and those in their care have been undermined during the 1980s. Deteriorating economic conditions, high levels of open unemployment, and the increasingly urgent need for cash to buy basic necessities impact on women's efforts to earn a livelihood" (Jiggins 1989: 969). Beneria also argues that the need to reduce expenditure on, for example, travel and transport, meant that households in Mexico City were less able to maintain their networks of relatives and friends outside the local community and emphasizes the effective "privatization of survival strategies" (Beneria forthcoming: 24). Many others make the same point and emphasize the ways in which "survival strategies" often involve women working longer hours, enduring increased exploitation and oppression, and experiencing greater isolation.

We accept the force of these arguments and much of the empirical evidence upon which they are based (see Daines and Seddon 1991: 12–15). But the sharp distinction between "defensive" survival struggles, which focus on "adaptation" and "coping", and effectively reduce the scope of social interaction, and "offensive" strategies, which aim at extending the room for maneuver and enhance livelihood security through development of social networks and mutual empowerment, is somewhat misleading. It should be recognized that "there is a danger, of dismissing the radical element in the struggles by the deprived which seek to change the present political and socio-economic framework in which they are enmeshed" (Blaikie, Cameron, and Seddon 1979: 56). We would urge a recognition of the fundamental point that even "defensive" struggles have the potential, under the right circumstances, to develop into more extensive forms of struggle with a greater capacity for expanding the room for maneuver and changing the conditions within which struggle takes place.

5   WOMEN'S NETWORKS

Much of the literature on "survival strategies" focuses on what may be termed "individual" or "household" strategies; but it is clear that much of the activity undertaken, by women at least, to defend their livelihood and that of their families involves cooperation with others outside the household. Cornia (1987a: 91) signals the widespread importance, in "survival strategies," of cooperation and collaboration between households, extended families and wider kinship groups; while Raczynski observes, of Chile in particular, that "households are not isolated, they are rooted in social networks and have links of support and solidarity" (Raczynsky 1989: 82). Women's activities and women's lives extend beyond the household and the labour market to a network of community and even wider social relationships.

In Chile,

> households are not isolated, they are rooted in social networks, and have links of support and solidarity. The support network includes exchange of goods and services, information, moral support, loans, and child-care, as well as the extended family. In the woman's case this is formed mainly by neighbours ... The woman's network deals mainly with domestic chores, loans of food and small amounts of money, utensils, child care, washing laundry, information, advice, etc.
> (*Raczynsky 1989: 82*)

Serrano, also referring to Chile, remarks that women are able to stretch scarce resources through exchanges of goods and services among kin and neighbors (1987, cited in Nash 1990: 344); while Safa, writing about Puerto Rico, reports of families (and particularly of women) in the shantytowns, that there is extensive mutual aid, involving borrowing and lending of goods and services and sharing in childcare, food preparation and other activities (Safah 1979: 452). In Jamaica, the operation of domestic networks of exchange by women was a major strategy adopted in response to the IMF economic-reform program adopted in 1978 (Bolles 1983: 150–2). In Tanzania, during the economic crisis of the late 1980s, urban women relied heavily on their networks within the informal sector to survive as small-scale entrepreneurs (Tripp 1989b: 616–18).

But the strength of women's networks often lies in the fact that "individually, each appears to be marginalised, but together they can spread costs, pool savings, and diversify enterprises without the risks and uncertainties of dependence on menfolk" (Jiggins 1989:

958). Thus, in her discussion of "work, consumption, and author-ity within the household" in Morocco, Maher observes that given the subordination of women within the household and their struc-tural economic dependence on men, "it is difficult to exaggerate the importance of networks of relations among women, based on kinship, patronage or both, which help women to escape, to some extent, the canons of consumption which the patriarchal society would impose on them and their children" (1981: 133). Evidently, women's networks can provide women with support which may under-mine the importance of marriage as a source of emotional and eco-nomic security, increase the scope for women's autonomous action beyond the household, and threaten the break-up of the household itself.

Certainly, as pressures on the household and family increase in times of crisis and hardship, the centrifugal forces also tend to increase. As Safa reports, of Puerto Rico, "economic instability is the most frequent cause of marital breakdown. There is no strong con-jugal bond in the shantytown household to hold a man and his wife together in the face of economic adversity" (Safa 1979: 450). At the same time, however, women's involvement in networks of relations outside the household and family may also serve to increase the resources available to the household and family, thereby improving its chances of survival as a unit, as well as benefiting its individual members. Clearly, women's networks can provide women with support of several kinds which, by their very existence and nature, tend to increase the scope for new forms of cooperation and mobilization. These may also contribute to the restructuring of households and the incidence of different household types (e.g. increase in female-headed households).

6   COOPERATIVE AND COMMUNITY ACTION

In their study of the defensive strategies adopted by poor Mexican households, by contrast with the evidence presented by Beneria, Selby, Murphy, and Lorenzen suggest that households were not being undermined by self-seeking despite their need to devise new methods for defending themselves. Furthermore, although they suggest that "the only resource the ordinary Mexican household has ever had is itself ... [and] ... its ability to exploit itself by organizing income-pooling, saving, and consumption" (Selby, Murphy, and Lorenzen 1990: 116), it seems that families "sought security in numbers and kinship" and even improvised on the "complex household" model by adding to the extended-family pattern a new kind of household collective "made up of multiple small families" (Selby, Murphy, and Lorenzen 1990: 170–71, cited in Walton 1992).

Elsewhere, in Africa and Latin America notably, strategies involving cooperation between households may include private income transfers (usually within an extended family or kinship group) and voluntary labor exchange for such activities as house repair and construction. In Tanzania, during the second half of the 1980s, as wage employment declined, incomes slumped and prices soared, urban women dramatically increased their involvement in the informal economy as "petty entrepreneurs," joining an *uptato* (rotating-credit society) in increasing numbers: "women had for many years pooled clothes, food and sometimes money, but those interviewed during 1987–8 reported that *uptato* membership had increased to an unprecedented extent" (Tripp 1989b: 614). Of the over 90 percent of women who owned their own micro-enterprises, half worked with one or two other women (Tripp 1989b: 616).

Economic crisis and the austerity that has accompanied adjustment, have undoubtedly made it more difficult for women to find time for cooperation and collaboration; all too often, the increasing burden of work has intensified demands on women's time to such an extent that isolation is actually increased. However, cooperative forms of activity may be able to overcome some of the weakness of individual action and actually strengthen women's capacity to go beyond survival to improve their welfare and that of their families, and develop the basis for more sustained, collective forms of activity and struggle. As the pressures on individuals and households increase, it becomes rational to take advantage of economies of scale and the social and even political advantages of cooperation.

Forms of cooperation that extend beyond limited interhousehold collaboration are well documented, particularly for Latin America. Many commentators refer, for example, to the experience of the "popular canteens" (*comedores populares*) which developed in Lima in Peru after 1979, as a response to a seriously deteriorating economic situation (Andreas 1989). Groups of women from between 15 and 50 households jointly carried out bulk purchase and preparation of food; poor households were either temporarily exempted from payment or given the meals on credit, so that the *comedores populares* became, to a limited extent, instruments of redistribution in favour of the poor (Commonwealth Secretariat 1990: 71). Communal food preparation also freed women on a regular basis for other activities, either productive and income-generating or supportive (e.g. childcare), of direct value to the households involved.

The importance of the Peruvian *comedores populares* as a widespread cooperative response to increasing austerity was considerable. Although precise data are lacking, "some of the most reliable sources point to the existence in this capital city of 1,500 popular dining rooms, with almost 50 members each, and 6,500 glass-of-milk committees, composed of more than 100,000 women" (Vargas 1990: 22). These activities clearly represented something more than local cooperation by individual households and by the women of those households; they represented the basis for more extended cooperation between women with potentially far-reaching implications. The glass-of-milk program began as a functional organization which women joined to obtain and distribute a daily glass of milk for all children under eight; it became one of the most centralized cooperative organizations run by women, with a substantial capacity to mobilize its members. Both the glass-of-milk and the *comedores populares* were coordinated at district and departmental levels. According to Vargas, their leaders became increasingly committed to women's issues, and considered the autonomy of their organizations a principal feature to be maintained. The organization of these consumption cooperatives is significant also: in the *comedores populares*, "women take weekly turns in buying food and cooking. They have assemblies, in which the members elect their leaders, information about how the facilities are running is imparted, and other activities are coordinated, like taking part in mobilisations" (Vargas 1990: 22).

In Brazil, women have formed groups to combat the difficulties created by the economic crisis (against rises in prices, in favor of better transport services, etc.); poor women have also participated in grassroots ecclesiastical communities, mothers' clubs, and mutual-aid groups. There are instances of community action, in which women have played a leading part, to cut the cost of basic foods and provide cheaper and nutritionally more balanced meals. In São Paolo, UNICEF reports that communities, helped in this case by government, organized themselves to purchase basic food from the central wholesale market where prices were 40 percent lower than at retail outlets, and in some cases groups bought food centrally at controlled prices and transported it to resell in local markets (Commonwealth Secretariat 1990: 71).

In Chile, Raczynsky has identified various forms of cooperative and collective forms of association "aimed at collectively facing the survival problem and the satisfaction of basic needs ... called 'popular economic organisations' (*organicaciones economicas populares*)" (Raczynsky 1989: 83). Such forms of association are not new (they existed under Allende), but they apparently proliferated during the late 1970s and early 1980s as the economic situation deteriorated. Some of these OEPs were locally based, others based on shared religious or political beliefs or having worked for the same employer. The more common associations were: (a) basic consumption organizations, such as community kitchens, purchase and supply associations, and self-help groups; (b) productive workshops – small units with 3 to 15 people producing and selling goods and services such as bread, clothing, knitting, laundry, carpentry, etc.; (c) organizations for the unemployed; (d) organizations related to housing problems, such as housing committees, water, electricity and mortgage committees, and committees for the homeless; (e) diverse organizations aimed at health, education and entertainment needs (Raczynsky 1989: 83). Women were involved heavily in most of these.

Beulink suggests that such cooperative responses by women to increasing austerity enabled them to "[take] charge of their own destiny, finding forms of organization that made them collectively stronger and individually more self reliant, hereby also considerably enhancing their self-esteem" (1989: 92). Of particular significance in this regard were the *ollas comunes* (communal kitchens, literally "shared stewpots") whose growth in numbers coincided with the economic crisis associated with the government's "free market" policies (in Santiago, there were 34 *ollas comunes* in 1982, 41 in 1984, and 232 by 1985, according to Scarpaci 1991: 4, 15). These, in Chile (and in Bolivia) as in Peru, involved groups of women pooling their resources to prepare meals. Also significant were the *arpillera* ('sackcloth' or 'coarse fabric') sewing collectives, which provided a context for women's empowerment and were often self-consciously "political." As Scarpaci reports, "*arpillera* workshops are more than just a place for sewing and exchanging materials. Teresita, the coordinator for sewing supplies and *arpillera* sales, says that the workshop is 'a place where women can find out about themselves'. It serves as a women's forum" (Scarpaci 1993: 11).

But the wider political significance of these cooperative ventures can also be considerable. In Peru, for example, as the *comedores populares* "have assumed an ever more visible role in maintaining the physical well-being and promoting the collective strength of *pobladores*, the recognition of women's importance as political actors has been immeasurably advanced" (Andreas 1989: 21). More generally, it has been argued, for Latin America as a whole, that the mobilization of poor urban women during the recession of the 1980s provided a grassroots base for the emerging women's movement:

in response to the economic decline, urban poor women were forced to rely on their own resources to ensure the survival of their families. The formation of communal kitchens and neighbourhood committees for infant nutrition and basic health care attracted the interest a number of groups with varying political objectives, including political parties, the Church, and international foundations and donor agencies. Although women's involvement in neighbourhood organisations is not new, the degree of coordination among local groups, the formation of "federations" of groups with similar interests and the linking of neighbourhood groups to other strands of the women's movement put this new phase of community organization in a new and more powerful context. (*Jaquette 1989: 6*)

7 FROM COMMUNITY ACTION TO COLLECTIVE PROTEST

Often it is hard, particularly in the case of community-based action, to distinguish the point where cooperative activity ends and collective resistance and protest begin. As Blondet has argued, for Peru, "the primary basis for mobilisation is the neighbourhood, where women join with men in fighting for water, health clinics, wood, kerosene, and schools. Mothers' clubs and communal dining areas are sites for women's collective action" (cited in Nash 1990: 345). It is clearly misleading to characterize these various forms of cooperative activity by women simply as concerned with welfare, consumption and basic needs, and thus as merely "social". Cooperative and community-based struggles, which may be all too easily dismissed as "survival strategies," may also provide the basis for more conventionally recognizable forms of collective action.

As Ghai and Hewitt de Alcantara remark,

the challenges posed by recession and adjustment lend momentum to other kinds of family and neighbourhood cooperation which go beyond simple "survival strategies" and create centres of dialogue and mutual assistance within an incohate civil society. Some, like neighbourhood soup kitchens in urban areas, draw families together in cooperative efforts to reduce the costs of subsistence; others grow out of broader urban grass-roots organizations in which the neighbourhood not only presents collective demands to local authorities but may be further integrated into a hierarchy of federations or confederations with the capacity to make itself heard at the national or international level. (*Ghai and Hewitt de Alcantara 1990: 24*)

But many commentators, particularly those writing on Latin America, tend to identify community and neighborhood associations and struggles as concerned above all with questions of consumption. They argue that "members are drawn together to protest unacceptable living conditions, the elimination of subsidies on such public goods as utilities or transport, the lack of credit for housing, the sudden rise in food prices or environmental problems. Their demands are not generally framed around issues of employment or remuneration, that is, around conditions of production" (Ghai and Hewitt de Alcantara 1990: 24). This analysis is, at first sight, not too different from that of Manuel Castells regarding urban protest movements in general (which he suggests develop essentially around demands focused on collective consumption – Castells 1977, 1978, 1983). But, they go further to suggest that "the kinds of civic organisations springing up in many urban areas of Latin America and Africa as a result of the crisis tend to involve a large number of women, for the obvious reason that women are most likely to be concerned with difficulties arising in the sphere of consumption" (Ghai and Hewitt de Alcantara 1990: 24). Others also share this perspective which tends to distinguish, in our view too sharply, between struggles around "consumption" and struggles around "production," and appears to associate the former with women (and presumably the latter with men).

Eckstein, for example, remarks that women's "isolation" within the home and their "economic marginality" have allegedly contributed to quiescence on their part, but argues that one consequence of this economic marginality is that they have often been in a better position to sustain struggles around the home and in the neighborhood. She observes that

> in Mexico City, for example, women in the city's largest shanty town have protected their community against land developers attempting to evict their families and against police who attempted to arrest participants in a local organization that used militant tactics, including physical violence, to defend local interests (Velez-Ibanez 1983: 119–22). In São Paulo, in turn, women in charge of household consumption were the main force behind the Cost of Living Movement and efforts to form communal shopping groups in the late 1970s (Singer 1982). (*Eckstein 1989: 25*)

She goes beyond this empirical demonstration of women's involvement in specific kinds of protest and resistance to argue that gender may, analytically, be of consequence in two distinct ways: as a social base of mobilization and resistance and as a set of issues around which men as well as women can press for change . . . From an analytical perspective, the women's mobilizations in defence of housing and other consumer claims, as well as in defence of "the disappeared" [in Argentina], call for another important revision of orthodox Marxist thinking. [For] women's non-involvement in the production process has made it easier for them to defy the established order. (*Eckstein 1989: 26*)

Women's collective protest around "consumption" issues is seen as derived from their "economic marginalization" which in turn makes defiance easier.

Eckstein's argument is flawed, not least because of her apparent acceptance of the idea that women are "economically marginalized" and not involved in the production process – an idea amply contradicted by numerous studies (e.g. Perlman 1976) – and the tendency to assume that women's struggles are *naturally* about "domestic" and "community" issues because they tend to "remain in their neighbourhoods during the day while their men work elsewhere" (Eckstein 1989: 25). Somewhat similar assumptions are made by Ghai and Hewitt de Alcantara, who suggest that

particularly in Latin America, where women have traditionally been far more restricted to the sphere of the "home" than in Africa, neighbourhood organizations are drawing women out of isolation and into organisations which must deal with the state, not necessarily because women have been originally concerned with politics but because they have been preoccupied with guaranteeing the future of their families. (*Ghai and Hewitt de Alcantara 1990: 24*)

As the Association of Salvadorian Women put it: "when the private, domestic realm is altered from the outside, Latin American women come out of their homes and take to the streets" (Association of Salvadorian Women (ASW) 1982: 17). Again, a simple distinction is implied, between women's normal "private" isolation and their exceptional involvement in "public" politics, and between "welfare" issues and "political" issues, which we find unacceptable. (For a general critique of these distinctions, see Siltanen and Stanworth 1984.)

Such an approach, while clearly intended to emphasize the undoubted importance of women's involvement in community politics and the relevance of "domestic" concerns to wider issues, runs the risk of identifying struggles around collective consumption issues as peculiarly "womanly" without adequate analysis of the ways in which women, by their own struggle and various forms of resistance and protest, redefine and convert "private" and "non-political" issues into "public," "political" issues. As Villavicencio and her colleagues remark, in the case of Peru, "popular women's groups *ruptured* the division between public and private worlds, politically broke the patriarchal order and let their power be felt" (Villavicencio, Olea, and Vargas 1990: 157; our emphasis).

In the case of Brazil, the almost seamless web of local community action involving women of the urban poor, more general forms of organized protest at deteriorating economic and social conditions, and wider political opposition to government policies – woven as women active in all these areas joined together to generate a broad women's protest movement – is well documented. Thus,

> women of the popular classes were among the first to protest the authoritarian regime's regressive social and economic policies. They organized against the rising cost of living, demanded adequate day schools, day care centres, running water, sewers, electrification, and other urban infrastructural necessities, and clamored for their "right" to adequately feed their families, school their children, and provide a decent life. Community mothers' clubs provided the organizational base for several political movements that expanded into citywide, and even nationwide political campaigns. (*Alvarez 1989: 21*)

The Feminine Amnesty Movement, the Cost of Living Movement and the Struggle for Day Care Movement were three such women's campaigns which drew strength as protest movements from the grassroots clubs and associations. Although the Amnesty Movement and the Cost of Living Movement were absorbed by the political opposition after the 1978 elections, the Struggle for Day Care Movement continued to grow and popular women's organizations proliferated throughout urban Brazil (Alvarez 1989: 38–45).

Women have undoubtedly been strongly associated with community action and urban protest movements concerned with issues of collective consumption; but this is not to say that they have not also been involved in other forms of protest, in the workplace and over employment conditions, as well as in the community and in the streets. To overemphasize women's involvement in struggles around collective consumption, and to ignore their involvement in other struggles would be misguided, as would any sharp distinction between "consumption" and "production" in an analysis of the political economy of urban protest.

8 PROTEST AND RESISTANCE IN THE WORKPLACE

Over the past two decades, women – in Latin America as elsewhere – have increasingly been drawn into the labor force (including paid employment), both as a result of the growing demand for cheap, casual labor on the part of employers seeking to reduce their costs of production, and of the pressure on household incomes as redundancies and falling real wages have taken effect (see Standing 1989). In Uruguay, for example, "the participation of women in the workforce rose from 38.7 per cent in 1981 to 44.2 per cent in 1984 as the lack of employment for men forced more women to enter gender-segregated jobs. The jobs paid only one-half to two-thirds of men's wages in a stagnating economy" (Nash 1990: 343). But as women became increasingly involved in the wage labor force – mainly in low-paid jobs in the informal sector – those already in paid employment suffered disproportionately from job cuts. In Chile and Uruguay during the 1970s and in Brazil and Costa Rica during the early 1980s, for example, the supply of women's labor increased significantly in the years of greatest economic contraction, but formal jobs for women did not and unemployment among women workers rose sharply (Leslie, Lycette, and Buvinic 1986). Similarly, in Barbados, where in 1983 women accounted for some 46 percent of the labor force (White 1986), unemployment among women rose from 15.1 percent in 1981 to 24.1 percent in 1985, compared with 7.4 percent and 13.0 percent respectively for men (Massiah 1988).

The great majority of women workers are employed in the informal sector, where trade union and other forms of collective organization remain weak, but, insofar as women have come to represent a significant, albeit still small proportion, of the paid labor force in the formal sector and a presence in the organized labor movement, their role in trade-union activities and direct industrial action has increased in importance. It has been argued recently that "as member and officials of trades unions, women are fighting in many countries for better wages and working conditions despite their lower level of unionization than men" (Commonwealth Secretariat 1990: 45). But, in general, their numbers in the trade-union movement have re-mained small, particularly in positions of influence, relative to their male counterparts. Furthermore, in virtually all countries, women have faced discrimination, harassment, and oppression, in their work situation not only from their employers, but also from their male colleagues (see, for example, Mahfoudh 1988; Pittin 1984). Women's branches or sections of trade unions remain rare; formal proportional representation, let alone positive discrimination, within unions is extremely rare. Often, as in the West, women are involved in trade-union activities and in industrial action mainly in a supportive role.

Women within the organized labor movement are fighting for change, and in some countries significant changes have been taking place. In Peru, for example, women have historically faced strong opposition within the trade unions; but despite this, women have now established special "women's comittees" within the Central Union of Workers (CGTP) and have undertaken within their own unions a struggle for their most pressing demands. There were, for example, important mobilizations around the Women Workers' Petition of 1986, their primary objective being to make sexual harassment illegal. Also, despite opposition from many union officials, women from the slum areas, with support from feminists and some non-government organizations (NGOs), have held meetings and workshops to discuss the similarities and differences in their respective situations and to draft collective proposals.

It remains the case, nevertheless, that women's struggles in the workplace tend to be based on their own initiative, rather than as part of formal trade-union action. It is widely claimed, by employers and governments seeking investment and even by supposedly objective commentators, that "women are docile workers," cooperative, and easy to control (see Anker and Hein 1985: 85–6). Male workers and trade unionists also often argue that "women are backward" when it comes to trade union or other collective action (Anker and Hein 1985: 82–5). But, "women are never completely docile or subservient. They learn to survive within constraints, and many are quick to subvert oppressive situations to their own advantage" (Bandarage 1988: 67). As Elson argues,

the supposed compliance of women workers is very deceptive. Women are experts at outwardly complying with authority, especially male authority, while inwardly rejecting its legitimacy. Women have had to learn to be patient, to bide their time, in their dealings with male authority in the home, so it is not suprising if this response is transferred to the factory. But the evidence from many cases suggests that when women workers are aroused to take militant action, they are tenacious in pursuit of their goal. Women textile and garment workers around the world have shown that they are capable of sustained resistance to unfair management practices; to closure threats; to refusal to recognize their grievances. (*Elson 1983: 9*)

In Tunisia, for example, where from April 1972 a policy of liberalization was adopted, women workers in the textile, confectionary, and even electronics industries began from 1975 onwards to protest their declining wages and deteriorating working conditions with unofficial strikes and demonstrations; and as workers' protests became more widespread and vociferous during 1976–8, women factory workers were very much involved.

Not only textile and garment workers, but also women in the micro-electronics industry (notorious for its superexploitation and oppression of women workers) as well as in the footwear, and food-processing industries have demonstrated their capacity to organize and act collectively on many occasions, despite harassment and obstruction by the male-dominated trade unions, employers, and the state. Particularly in the Export Processing Zones and Free Trade Zones established in many developing countries as part of the drive to economic liberalization and export-led industrialization (e.g. the Dominican Republic, El Salvador, Honduras, Hong Kong, Korea, Malaysia, Mexico, the Philippines, Puerto Rico, Singapore, Sri Lanka, and Thailand), where the proportion of female workers is generally high, women have responded to attempts to reduce their wages and increase restrictions on their working conditions as a consequence of government austerity measures with collective action.

In the Philippines, for example, where government policies of adjustment under Marcos led to severe austerity measures and restrictions on workers' rights, fewer than 50,000 women were registered union members in 1982. Despite this, the Philippines has seen some of the most extraordinary examples of women workers organizing: "the highly-organised alliance of unions in the Bataan Export Processing Zone has few parallels, and courageous struggles elsewhere in the country have debunked the foreign investors' myth of the docile Filipina workers" (Women Working Worldwide 1991: 179). The formation in 1985 of the Women Workers' Movement (KMK) – which has an estimated 20,000 members – has subsequently strengthened the position of women workers in various industries, and in the agricultural sector, through its representation on the Labour Advisory Consultative Council (LACC).

More generally, the detailed examination of women's struggles at work "explode[s] the myth that women are passive and pliant in the hands of their employers. They are often the first to protest at the possible relocation of their factory and are fearless in their attempts to save their jobs" (Women Working Worldwide 1991: 203). In Sri Lanka, "[b]eneath the veneer of subservience and docility most Sri Lankan women are tremendously resourceful. They embody a fighting spirit" (Bandarage 1988: 80). Thus, the strike at the Polytex garment factory in 1982, was conducted totally by 700 women in the face of state emergency regulations, police intimidation, and threats by the factory management: "by sticking together and by working in solidarity with local residents, other trade unions, and feminist organizations in the country, the Polytex women workers finally won the right to a union in January 1983" (Bandarage 1988: 69). But, the constraints on overt and collective protest are often considerable, in the Free Trade Zones in Sri Lanka, according to women workers interviewed by *Voice of Women*, restrictions did not even permit the mentioning of the words "trade union" (Bandarage 1988: 69). Even so, spontaneous unorganized stoppages were not infrequent.

If women generally adopt forms of "everyday resistance" for the most part (in common with other oppressed groups, including workers according to Cohen 1982), this clearly does not preclude more overt and collective, even dramatic, forms of protest and resistance on occasion. Often, however, when they do act collectively, the action is undertaken "spontaneously," not as a result of trade-union prompting but rather through the informal structures of association developed by women working together. Action is frequently triggered by a sense of outrage at some gross injustice or infringement of their perceived basic rights as workers and as human beings. The example of action at the Mostek micro-electronics plant – which employed predominantly women workers – in Penang (Malaysia) in 1985 is illustrative of a more general pattern.

In April, the Mostek management carried out a "voluntary resignation" exercise, which cost 500 workers their jobs; a smaller plant elsewhere in Malaysia was closed. Despite repeated questioning by the remaining workers regarding their own prospects, the management consistently stated that there would be no further retrenchments and that their jobs were safe. This reassurance continued right up to the time the management posted a notice at the end of September requesting workers to clear their lockers and take a one-week holiday. Some workers fell for this ploy; others were not sure. Again, the management reassured them. The next day, many of the workers received letters of termination, and over the next week a thousand had been sacked. The women were shocked. "It was like I had been cut with a sword. I just sat on the floor and cried," said one woman. "I had been working for seven years. I enjoyed my job. The company had been good to me, I don't mind saying. But I could never describe how I felt that morning I got my letter. It was as if the world had ended for me. I have two children, my husband is dead. I couldn't imagine how I was going to feed them," said another.

The women were outraged, as much at the way in which they had been treated as at the fact of redundancy. They decided to respond. "Some of us got together and decided that there was no point in keeping quiet. If we were going to be retrenched we wanted to know why. We all felt hurt and angry. I remember telling my friend I felt like rubbish in the dustbin," reported one woman. The women's response took their employers, and others, by surprise. They initiated a picket of the factory, which lasted for over a month. "My husband asked me why I wanted to go and join the picket every day. I told him: every day for the last four years I had worked hard in the factory. When the management wanted us to do overtime, we would. When they had to make an order, we would help them. We slogged for them, really worked our hearts out. But when we needed their help ... they didn't even have the decency to tell us to our face," said one of the "activists" (Commonwealth Secretariat 1990: 58–9). It was largely as a result of the women's collective action in the face of the Mostek management's "sell-out" that the Women Workforce Action Group was established in Penang to support women workers coming to the Free Trade Zone (Women Working Worldwide 1991: 134–6).

Elson has argued that "it is clear from the many instances of militant action by Third World women workers, that they do have the self-respect to challenge their exploitation. But in many, many cases, they have to make their challenge in confrontation with a heavily armed, undemocratic state" (Elson 1983: 10). Despite their justified fear of repression and retribution, however, women have shown themselves prepared, on occasion, to transcend everyday forms of resistance and organize more openly. If women workers are clearly prepared to protest collectively at what they regard as unfair treatment by employers, they are also prepared to take action of a more openly political kind in protest at what they regard as unfair and illegitimate government policies and state intervention when this threatens their livelihood and that of their families. Women workers, from both private and public sectors, have joined in political demonstrations and strikes called by the trade unions in response to the introduction of austerity measures by governments in a wide range of instances in Africa, Asia, and Latin America; and, despite the likelihood of a violent response by the state, they have also been involved, as have women working outside the formal sector, in the more dramatic forms of "spontaneous" popular protest, including "bread riots," in many countries over the past two decades.

9   WOMEN AND POPULAR PROTEST

Elizabeth Fox Genovese has argued that, historically, "the under-valuation of women has led to the underestimation of their parti-cipation in all forms of collective protest and resistance to exploitation and oppression" (Fox Genovese 1982: 28). Much the same point is made in the special issue of *Women's Studies International Forum* on women's direct action when Carroll suggests that "women's non-violent direct action has a more extensive history and has been more influential in the history of political action for social change than is generally recognised" (Carroll 1989: 3). As Feijoo and Gogna observe, of Argentina,

> from a historical perspective, feminist, feminine and/or women's strug-gles date back – with differing character, composition and objectives – to the end of the 19th and beginning of the 20th century ... These struggles were fragmented, dispersed and conjunctural, and they left a more or less permanent and diverse impression on women's memory. We know little about them in terms of scientific knowledge, but more from personal experience and self-examination. This relative per-manence within the subjects themselves combines with the "public" absence of these struggles when it comes to research, analysis and retrieval, as feminist historiography has so often shown ... The re-appearance of the women's movement on the political scene between 1981 and 1984 must by necessity refer back to these issues. (*Feijoo and Gogna 1990: 80*)

In the contemporary period, women's involvement in social move-ments and urban protest has also gone generally unremarked; as Jelin observes,

> [the woman] is not seen when she stays at home, tied to domesticity and the sphere of private life. Nor is she seen socially when she leaves the house to take part in collective action of a public nature, and this is what has to be rescued from oblivion. In fact, the theme of social movements, even *new* social movements, hardly identifies the gender of the participants or asks how gender influences the nature of par-ticipation, collective practice or the meaning of action. (*Jelin 1990: 6–7*)

The point is made even more strongly and developed further by Caldeira with respect to women's involvement in social movements in Brazil. Her argument is worth reproducing at length:

Anyone who has followed the development of social movements in the city of São Paulo since the 1970s either directly by observing daily life in the surrounding shanty towns, or indirectly through the newspapers, will know that these movements are in the main constituted and led by women. It is women who form the mothers' clubs and who are the major participants in the Christian Base Communities (CEBs). They have mobilized around specific demands such as health care, nurseries or the needs of the shanty towns and it is women who go around these popular neighbourhoods collecting signatures in support of different petitions. It was women who thought up, implemented and in the main directed the Cost of Living Movement. And basically it is women who make up the demonstrations that leave one or other of these marginal neighbourhoods almost daily for the Town Hall to express some protest or demand about the precarious conditions in their neighbourhoods . . . .

With all the evidence available in the recollection of the participants, from researchers familiar with these movements and from what has appeared in the newspapers, it is incredible that information on women's participation is absent from the analysis in almost all studies on these social movements. In the majority of cases the protagonists of these movements are described using general categories, such as the "inhabitants of peripheral areas", the "popular classes", the "people", the "poor", and so on, with no reference whatsoever to their gender.
(*Caldeira 1990: 47*)

Even Castells, whose work has been so influential on research into urban protest and urban social movements, paid only scant attention in his earlier works to the involvement of women and "the politics of gender." Throughout the more recent *The City and the Grassroots* (Castells 1983), however, women are described as having a special place in urban struggles and in the historical case studies women are seen as mobilizing on behalf of their families" needs in the context of the evolution of urban-based class and power struggles (Lowe 1986: 53). Furthermore, gradually accumulating – albeit still partial and patchy – evidence from the developing world over the last two decades shows that women's involvement in various forms of collective protest and resistance has been considerable, even if it has often gone unremarked. Among the most dramatic of these are the "austerity protests" in response to government policies of adjustment and economic liberalization adopted so generally across the developing world during the 1970s and 1980s.

Examination of the social base of these instances of popular protest reveals the central involvement of the working class in its broadest sense, and particularly those sections of the working class most seriously affected by growing unemployment and declining incomes

– the urban poor. In an earlier study of austerity protest in 22 countries up to 1986, Walton concluded that, in general, "workers and the urban poor contribute the largest number of participants, but public employees, students, churches, unions, and small businesses are frequently represented and sometimes the vanguard" (Walton 1987: 20). Walton's discussion is, however, silent on the gender composition of the crowds who launched and sustained these movements of popular protest. This is not surprising; reports of austerity protests rarely include reference to such matters, and it is extremely difficult, even when the specific object of enquiry is the role of women in popular protest, to find the necessary evidence (Daines and Seddon 1991).

Consequently, in most descriptions and analyses of popular protest against austerity and adjustment, although frequent reference is made to "the social composition of the crowd," little mention is made of women. There is nothing new in this "invisibility" of women, but it is in striking contrast with the importance now generally assigned by social historians to women's involvement in popular protest in eighteenth- and early nineteenth-century Europe and the very considerable literature that has developed around the issue (cf. Bohstedt 1988).

The fact that particular attention to the gender composition of the crowds involved in contemporary popular protest has rarely been paid means, however, that the evidence is still very partial and patchy. While women's involvement is undoubtedly significant, its scale and full extent is difficult to determine, largely because most reporters share the (questionable) view that the women involved are generally "as anonymous in their public presence as they are ignored in the literature. They make up the banner-carrying crowds that fill the squares and public administration offices. Rarely, however, are they the spokespersons of these demonstrations" (Caldeira 1990: 54). Even in Latin America, where perhaps the most serious consideration has been given to women's involvement in politics, protest and social movements during the last two decades (e.g. in Eckstein 1989; Jelin 1990; Jaquette 1989), there is still remarkably little literature concerned explicitly with women's involvement in popular protest and there are few studies of their participation in the kind of events which constitute our main concern in this book.

Certainly this is not because women have not been involved; indeed, historically, they have been a crucial element in several major instances of a related kind – as in the case of the Movimiento Inquilinario which started with a rent strike in Veracruz, in Mexico

in 1922 (and which came to be known as "a woman's rebellion" –
see Castells 1983: 37–48). In that case,

> it was women who spontaneously started the rent strike; women who
> organized the committees of *patios* (tenements); women who resisted
> the eviction by clashing with the police; women who organized them-
> selves in a network of groups that would come in support on hearing
> the signal of a whistle; women who were the ones most often arrested;
> and women who took to the streets against the army when the moment
> came in July 1922. (*Castells 1983: 46*)

Significantly, the situation of Veracruz in 1921–2 "was characterized by an economic crisis which was dramatically lowering employment and income, an accelerated process of urban growth, and
a massive transfer from commercial capital to real estate investment
to take advantage of the predisposition of the newly established
political power towards private capital's initiative" (Castells 1983:
43). Elsewhere in Latin America, historical research is only just
beginning to reveal the importance of women's involvement in popular protest (as in the case of Peru, where the first Assembly of Women
organized the first "women's march" around the issue of the high
cost of living in 1919); but the evidence remains patchy.

Only careful and specific investigation on a comparative basis
across the developing world of the involvement of women in popular
protest – from a subjective as well as an objective point of view
– would provide an adequate basis for a full appreciation of the
significance of women's participation in public collective protest.
But the limited evidence available so far reveals that even where
popular protest has taken the dramatic and most "public" forms
– those of street demonstration and "riot" – women have been
actively involved. Furthermore, an examination of a selection of
more recent urban social movements reveals "the decisive role of
women in several of the urban movements we have studied" (Castells
1983: 68).

10 CASE STUDIES OF WOMEN IN
POPULAR PROTEST

In Latin America, we can take Argentina as a revealing first case
study for which good documentation is available (see Feijoo and
Gogna 1990). Between March 1982 and August 1985, there were at
least six distinct instances of major urban austerity protest (Walton

1989b). Women's protests were an important and integral part of the broader protest movement.

Protests by women began in early 1982, when, as "housewives," they instigated "purchasing strikes" in several districts on the outskirts of Buenos Aires, and organized demonstrations to protest against the high cost of living in Quilmes and the cities of Cordoba and Rosario. In July 1982 the National Housewives Movement — which was to organize a national campaign against indiscriminate price rises in a situation of rapid deterioration of living standards — was formed in a middle-class neighborhood in San Martin. Towards the end of the year an upsurge of popular protest spread through the various districts of Greater Buenos Aires as the imposition of additional taxes sparked of a massive response. Women participated in considerable numbers in the demonstrations, which often brought together as many as 20,000 people and reports of public protests in Avellaneda indicated that "many women took part in the meeting and many of them berated the mayor with their fists raised, while they sang along with the men to football-stand music" (*Clarin*, November 19, 1982, cited by Feijoo and Gogna 1990: 96).

In some cases it was the housewives' groups or committees that called for or attended meetings outside the town halls (in Avellaneda, Lanus, Lomas de Zamora, Tres de Febrero); in other cases, representatives from the local groups within the National Housewives' Movement or the Argentine Women's Union debated with local-government authorities. According to eyewitness accounts, by making their presence felt in these main squares the protestors were expressing their moral outrage and rejection of a policy that was cutting the living standards of the Argentinian people. Whether women were representatives of groups and organizations, or had just turned up at the demonstrations, their statements followed a comon pattern: they emphasized that the protest was "not political"; they spoke of the need to dispel their fear and participate; they stressed the justice of their collective demands and voiced support of a strategy of organization and unity — in other words, they distinguished their undeniably political protest from "politics", representing it as involving "ordinary women" concerned with basic rights and welfare (see Feijoo and Gogna 1990: 95–6). A few days after the wave of neighborhood protests, women from almost the whole of Greater Buenos Aires gathered for a meeting in San Martin. They formulated a petition demanding measures to halt the rise in the cost of living, which was delivered to the Economy Ministry after a meeting in the Plaza de Mayo in December. Among other demands, the petition requested a reduction in the price of food, the elimination of taxes on medicines, and a freeze on the price of bread, milk, and meat. Protests continued throughout 1983 and 1984, but on a reduced scale. At the beginning of 1983, women supported a demonstration in front of Lanus town hall against an increase in taxes and charges for services. In September the same year, the Tucuman Housewives Movement (which had just been established) organized a 15-minute blackout to publicize their protest at the exorbitantly high cost of living. At the same time the movement made an appeal to the "goodwill" of the authorities and asked them to be flexible regarding the demands of the trade unions, while also entreating the unions to seek ways of protesting that would not paralyze the country (Feijoo and Gogna 1990: 96–7).

Even after the successful installation of a constitutional government in Argentina, women continued to protest against price rises. In March 1984 the National Housewives Movement called for a 48-hour purchasing strike, aimed at those sectors "which cause destabilization with exorbitant price rises while unemployment and low incomes are still rife in most Argentine homes" (Feijoo and Gogna 1990: 96–8). In May, the movement, together with the Union of Argentine Women and other groups, drew up a document which called for the defense of democracy and constitutional order with the full participation of citizens, and requested a number of key measures, including: price controls for the top 100 companies and the large meat producers; affordable prices for basic food staples and subsidies for bread, milk and meat, and free school dinners for the children of low-income families. The document obtained 25,000 signatures, but the campaign came to an end in October 1984 and the movement as a whole appears to have begun to disintegrate during 1984 and 1985.

In Africa and in Asia, where popular protest against adjustment and austerity is well documented (see chapters 5, 7, and 8), the evidence relating to the active involvement of women is still sparse; women remain largely "invisible" in the crowds otherwise so vividly described, although we know that they have participated actively in popular protest. In Africa, certainly,

> in the face of heightened threats to survival, women workers and peasants have and will become increasingly militant. In mining towns of Zambia in 1981, for example, women demonstrated against higher prices of maize meal and its unavailability and they encouraged the miners to strike. In 1981 Tanzanian women in Dodoma also demonstrated over the poor distribution of fuel needed to keep grain mills going, which led to a redistribution of fuel. Women workers have engaged in independent strike actions. (*Mbilinyi 1985: 182*)

But, despite these passing references, the bulk of the literature on women's responses to structural adjustment in Africa focuses on "survival strategies" and individual responses, with passing reference to forms of cooperative or community activity; there is little, as yet, on women and popular protest.

In Asia, despite the documentation of popular protest against austerity measures associated with economic reforms in several countries (e.g. Sri Lanka, India, the Philippines, Nepal), there is only limited evidence of women's participation available. Scattered examples include that of the Anti Price Rise Movement which developed in Bombay during the early 1970s and mobilized women to protest against inflation and put pressure on the government to make essential commodities available at low prices through state-controlled ration shops (Gandhi 1990a). For further discussion, see chapter 7.

But, even in the Middle East and North Africa, where cultural restrictions on women's activity in public places are often particularly severe, we know that women have been openly involved in street demonstrations and "riots" against government economic-reform policies and the austerity measures associated with them, as well as in other less "visible" forms of resistance and protest.

In an analysis of popular political movements in Iran, for example, de Groot points out that women were actively involved in the demonstrations against the Shah as well as in the various less overt forms of political activity. High inflation and the austerity policies of the Amouzegar government during 1977 and 1978 "had created favourable conditions for the rise of protest on economic grounds" (Moghadam 1992: 24); and, as de Groot points out, "the hardships of life in the [late] 1970s could well be especially sharp to women, with their responsibility for household provision and welfare" (de Groot 1989: 219). The political significance of the involvement of women, and particularly poor urban women, in the popular movement to overthrow the Shah was considerable. Furthermore, despite the often culturally reactionary and restrictive policies of the subsequent regime towards (particularly middle-class) women, Afshar points out that "Ayatollah Khomeini has been careful to retain the massive support of those impoverished women who both took to the streets in the movements against the Shah and have voted for him in subsequent elections" (Afshar 1985: 260).

In Turkey, the deepening economic crisis of the late 1970s precipitated a political crisis in which open violence between contending political movements and factions grew ever more common, until martial law was declared and in September 1980 a military coup brought a change of regime and the intensification of the program of "economic reform" introduced by the previous civilian government. In the general strike and massive demonstrations a decade before, which had precipitated an earlier coup, women had been actively involved. When in Istanbul more than 100,000 workers and unemployed went out into the streets, many were women; and when clashes with the security forces led to the deaths of several demonstrators, women were active in the reprisals that followed; Guzel (1989: 173) refers to the lynching of a policeman by a group of women demonstrators. Given this experience of involvement in popular protest, it was not surprising that women participated actively in the popular struggles that took place, in part over government policies of adjustment and austerity, in the late 1970s, and many were arrested and jailed for their role in these struggles. In the more recent upsurge of popular protest, at the beginning of the 1990s, with miners and other workers increasingly striking and involved in demonstrations, women have been actively involved.

In Morocco, where on a number of occasions between the mid-1960s and mid-1980s government cuts in public expenditure and other austerity measures generated large-scale popular protest (in 1965, 1978–9, 1981, and 1984), women from both the public and the private sectors were actively involved (see Seddon 1989a: 240–52). Although references to the participation of women are limited for the earlier protests, there is good evidence in the case of the 1984 "bread riots" to show that many of the protestors were women. Clement refers to female high-school pupils, students, and professionals (lawyers and doctors) in his analyses of the pattern of arrests and the subsequent judicial proceedings (1985, 1986); accounts of the protests in the northeast of the country refer to women's active involvement in the street demonstrations as well as to their vocal support from houses and rooftops (see Seddon 1989a: 249); while women in the northwest were reported to have actively supported the demonstrations with shouting and screaming, shouting slogans, and calling for the replacement of King Hassan by a president "like in Algeria," and some women were even shot by security forces (see Clement 1986: 38).

In Tunisia, when a wave of popular protest broke out in January 1984 (shortly before that in Morocco), in response to government austerity measures, women in the southern towns where the demonstrations originated were reported to have supported the demonstrators by shouting and screaming from their houses. In one small southern town, Al-Mabrouka, women factory workers, the majority of them between 16 and 25, marched from the textile factory where they worked to Al-Mabrouka itself, chanting slogans against the decision to double the price of bread. As they passed the main cafe of the first poor quarter to be built in Al-Mabrouka they were first harangued then joined by the men sitting there; as they went past the high school they were joined by students. Gathering men, women, and even children from the poorer quarters as they went, the demonstrators eventually stormed the police station, as well as the local party headquarters, the town hall and the headquarters of the National Guard (the most prominent government buildings). During the demonstrations and attacks on the buildings, security forces fired on the crowd and several people were killed; many others, including numbers of women, were injured. In his detailed discussion of this event, Zghal draws attention to the crucial role played by women in the starting of the protest and suggests that the involvement of the men of Al-Mabrouka in the demonstration "was partially due to the women's provocation" (Zghal 1989: 17). As the demonstrations and "bread riots" spread from the south throughout the country, they were met with increased state force. In Tunis itself, when police tried to intervene, thousands of demonstrators gave battle. "Barricades went up everywhere. Again and again, troops opened fire on the crowds with automatic weapons. Tanks and armored personnel carriers rumbled through the streets, often firing on anything that moved. Many protestors were killed, and many more wounded, including women and children" (Paul 1984: 4).

State repression against protestors, including women, is well documented; it is also, demonstrably, unable in all instances to quell the upsurge of anger and outrage that fuels such popular protest. Even in Sudan, where the level of repression under President Numeiry had been such as to effectively silence all organized opposition, including the trade-union movement, women were actively involved in the "bread riots" which broke out in March 1985 and rapidly evolved into mass protest and political opposition to the Numeiry regime. Despite very real fears of heavy state repression, hundreds of women took to the streets of Omdurman in greater Khartoum at the end of March to protest against rising prices, government policies, and the intervention of the IMF (see Seddon 1988: 189). Within a few weeks, the al-Numeiry regime had been overthrown.

In Algeria, when, after several years of mounting social unrest culminated in major urban riots in October 1988, the state responded with unprecedented violence, it shocked the Algerian people with its savage repression of the protest movement. Security forces in large numbers used live ammunition against the crowds and thousands were arrested. Women and children were among those arrested and brutalized in the aftermath of widespread confrontations between the security forces and the demonstrators. Torture of those arrested, including women, was common.

This is not to say that women take to the streets ignoring the possibility of reprisals and repression; simply that, on occasions, as in the case of men from similar backgrounds and under similar circumstances, their anger and outrage moves them to collective action.

11   WOMEN'S RESPONSES, STATE REPRESSION

It has been argued (of Britain), that "in the history of policing there have been far fewer confrontations between women and the police than, for example, between the police and strikers, the unemployed and in public order confrontations. Women have featured in these struggles, but usually in support of men, and they have rarely been considered 'dangerous' by the state" (Radford 1989: 42). The author suggests that "the exceptions are interesting: the Greenham women, like the suffragettes, have been heavily and violently policed. It is, apparently, when women have acted autonomously as women, that they have been the targets of heavy policing. A similar point can be made with respect to the policing of prostitution in the nineteenth and twentieth centuries" (Radford 1989: 42; see also Young 1990). Certainly throughout the developing world, women have been widely subject to "heavy policing" as members of various protest groups and as participants in various forms of resistance and protest. They have suffered the harassment, physical violence, and arrests generally meted out to protestors and demonstrators. But women have also been subject *as women* in distinctive ways to state repression when they have been identified as politically threatening − usually in ways associated with sexual harassment and violence (see, for example, Amnesty International 1991).

The general physical repression of popular protest by state security forces and legal repression by the judicial process is well documented; less considered, however, is the specific response of the state to women in protest (for an important exception, see Booth 1987). It could be argued that women involved in forms of protest that can be identified as clearly "political" often experience much the same indiscriminate repression and state violence as do men involved in the same activities. In Chile, Scarpaci argues,

> the most active volunteers of these neighbourhood organisations were
> the first to be sought out after the bloody coup d'état that desposed

Salvador Allende. Few have forgotten the house-to-house searches for community and political party leaders ... and the massive civil and human rights abuses which followed. Perceived as "enemies of the state" these local leaders were rounded up, detained, tortured, murdered, or sent into exile. State terror under military rule was *gender blind. (Scarpaci 1993: 21—2, our emphasis)*

We would suggest, however, that responses to women in protest are more complicated than this. Even in Scarpaci's text, a woman volunteer in the *olla commun* he studied, while speaking of women's very real fears of violence against them as participants in neighborhood organizations by the state security apparatus after the coup, refers, with evident irony, to the way women were treated by the state: "in all these years the dictatorship has treated us like naughty little girls. We've been scolded, even disciplined to a certain extent" (Scarpaci 1993: 22). It is suggested by some commentators that women may have a kind of special dispensation insofar as their protest is not generally taken as seriously as it might be, either by employers or the state, or by their male colleagues. Alvarez, for instance, suggests that

the ingrained belief that women are indifferent to politics may have led the military rulers of Brazil to believe that anything women do is intrinsically "apolitical." Thus, even when women began organizing campaigns against the rising cost of living or for human rights in Brazil, the military seems to have allowed women's associations greater political leeway than was granted to militant left, student and labor organizations, which were seen as more threatening to "national security." (*Alvarez 1989: 25—6*)

But even in those cases where women are given apparent immunity from the usual state response to protestors and demonstrators, this rarely lasts long. For example, when in February and March 1989 an extraordinarily violent series of riots swept across Venezuela following the announcement of a structural adjustment program which included the elimination of price controls on basic goods and foodstuffs, it was reported that, initially at least, looting by women and children was officially tolerated. "A pact was reached. Men remained above, behind some barricades. Only women and children could loot. But in an orderly and cultured way. Under the watch and direction of police who yielded to the situation" (cited in Walton 1989b: 27). Shortly, however, the military police moved in with tanks and teargas and the violence escalated. Women were no longer treated "differently" from men. In Morocco, in 1984, once the demonstrations had been brought under control and dispersed, women, even in the shantytowns from which the majority of the demonstrators had come, offered tea and cakes to the army, but spoke of their fear of reprisals and repression (Clement 1986: 40).

It seems to us that when women protest against government economic policies explicitly as *housewives, mothers of children, and "victims" of austerity*, they deny that their actions are "political" in the narrow sense of the word, and make their claims in the name of common justice and welfare, while at the same time by their very public protest making welfare a profoundly political issue. Given the ambiguities surrounding forms of political action by women that explicitly claim to be "non-political," the state's response to such forms of protest is likely also to be ambivalent. When, however, they deviate from this terrain, or "go further," and participate in actions more easily definable as "political" (like street demonstrations and riots) they either become effectively "invisible" as women and merge indistinguishably into the crowd or the mob, against which state violence is felt to be broadly legitimate, or else are identified as threatening in a distinctive way as deviants from the image of women as "non-political" and become subject to specific forms of harassment and repression – usually associated with sexual violence of some kind. Female militancy is threatening of "social order" in a variety of ways, and tends to be met with extreme responses by those who see themselves as the guardians of law and order.

In other words, if women protest in conformity with their "proper role" (peacefully, modestly, in defense of family and community, welfare, and related issues), they may be tolerated, up to a point; if, however, they protest actively, thereby denying their willingness to remain within their socially constituted "proper role," they will tend to be treated either simply as protestors (their gender becoming largely irrelevant) or as "wild women" (their gender becoming highly visible and "threatening" – see Young 1990: 41–88). Where women, whether protesting *as women* or as part of a wider movement of the exploited and oppressed, threaten the existing social order, however, the response is generally likely to be violent and repressive (see Booth 1987: 35–6).

12   CLASS, GENDER AND "POPULAR" PROTEST

In discussing women in popular protest against austerity, this chapter has generally referred to women from the working classes in the broadest sense. When economic policies threaten livelihoods, it is among the urban poor that the threat is most acutely felt and, arguably, the anger and outrage greatest. But it is evident, even from the partial and patchy data presently available, that women from different social backgrounds are involved, albeit often in different ways, in austerity protests and movements in opposition to cuts in public expenditure on welfare and increases in prices. It has even been argued that it is precisely the specific character of the issues around which women's struggles are often organized – broadly, welfare issues – and the way in which they are often characterized (both by the state and by the women involved themselves) as "nonpolitical" and "womanly," that makes possible the "transcending" of class divisions and the emergence of "a women's movement." As the socially defined "private" guardians of welfare, it has been argued, women generally (from whatever social class) tend to accept this special role, which explains their preparedness to act collectively against the state as the "public" guardian of welfare when it is seen to betray its trust by cutting subsidies and increasing prices, for example, and by abandoning its role as protector of the poor.

We cannot agree that the involvement of women from different social backgrounds in popular protest necessarily constitutes "a transcending of class divisions." The evidence suggests strongly that what we have referred to as popular protest involves essentially women of the urban poor, even if middle-class and professional women, and feminists, are sometimes also involved and may on occasion play a leading role in organizing and orchestrating other forms of protest and resistance. Equally, however, the significance of what appears to be an increasing tendency for popular struggles to be supported by and even, on occasion, integrated within an explicitly "women's movement" should not be underestimated.

Vargas (1990) argues that in Peru at least the "women's social movement" as a whole consists of three different elements – that of poor women in squatter settlements, that of liberal (bourgeois or "middle-class") women, and that of the feminists – which cooperate and collaborate in certain areas and over certain issues, but which are also distinct; while Villavicencio, Olea, and Vargas (1990: 164) suggest that "the three stream thesis applies, not only to Peru but to Chile, Argentina and Uruguay." Such a distinction also appears generally valid outside Latin America. In some cases, these different elements may, of course, have conflicting interests.

In Sudan, for example, while "there is no doubt that women played an active role and were instrumental in bringing about the downfall of the [al-Numeiry] dictatorship" (Bashir el Bakri, et al. 1990: 179), a distinction is made by some between the involvement of ordinary women and "women of the leisured classes." Whereas the response of the former

> to the severe economic breakdown of recent years has been to try and find as many ways to generate income, in order to get by on a day-to day basis and to attempt to acquire [basic] consumer goods ... women of the leisure classes are engaged in a lifestyle of conspicuous consumption at all levels. Thus it is evident that in this period class differences among women and the class struggle became sharper. (*Bashir el Bakri, et al. 1990: 178–9*)

In Jamaica, in the period immediately after the implementation, by the democratic socialist Manley government, of an IMF economic-reform program, women of different political persuasions and from different social classes were mobilized with different and conflicting objectives.

> Two demonstrations held in January and February 1979 were part of the effort to destabilise the Manley government. Poor women, organised by a faction of the conservative element, marched through Kingston and in various other locations on the island, under a banner denouncing the Manley government for the rising cost of living. Another group of women, pro-Manley and anti-conservative, held a counter-demonstration, calling for greater self-reliance to overcome an inherited set of problems. Finally, a third group of women, led by progressive forces, demonstrated calling for an end to US imperialism and decrying the IMF, in solidarity with international progressive movements. (*Bolles 1983: 156*)

However, while women from the working classes broadly conceived have always a more direct and immediate involvement in protest movements associated with the defense of living standards than those from more affluent social backgrounds, there is no simple link between popular protest, social class, and political orientation. Austerity protests by the urban poor, we suggest, are directed against policies which are seen both to threaten living standards and to challenge preconceived and preexisting "social contracts" between state and people (and against the governments that introduce and implement them), whatever the ideological and political orientation of the government concerned. In the case of the Manley government, cited above, it seems that women from the urban poor were protesting against the policies implemented by a socialist government, not for narrow "political" reasons (even if their protest was orchestrated by the conservatives), but from basic self-interest and a concern for survival. Such actions have often been taken to exemplify the inherently "conservative" and "backward" character of women in politics or alternatively to emphasize the distinction between gender-based politics and class-based "politics." Austerity protests, however, are essentially spontaneous, pragmatic responses to government policies seen to threaten basic needs and basic rights. As such, they are not inherently ideological, nor "political" in the narrow sense, but represent in effect social movements in opposition to what is perceived as the illegitimate dismantling of a historically negotiated contract between state and people; such movements are, however, political in a broader sense – with their central concern for social justice and "the moral economy," they constitute a distinctive form of populist movement.

Women's involvement in such movements tends to derive from their class position (as members of the urban poor and working classes broadly conceived), and from the acute threat to their livelihoods and those of their families posed by unemployment, inflation and cuts in public welfare services; at the same time, however, whether in the factory, the neighborhood or the street, women also take part, often explicitly, as women, making use of the cultural ambiguities surrounding women in public action to draw attention to the issues of social justice associated with austerity policies imposed upon the vulnerable and the disadvantaged. Increasingly, and very significantly in our view, women also take part in response to and resistance against, their gender subordination and oppression. As Reddock observes,

> to a large extent the militancy of women during labour and political disturbances has been a reflection of their needs based on their positioning within the sexual division of labour ... [their responsibility] for the social and economic welfare of themselves, their children and relatives is what often motivate[s] them in their struggles for social and economic survival. (*Reddock 1990: 66*)

Popular protest can be channeled and directed, on occasion, by more "politically" motivated groups to give it a distinctive "political" orientation. One of the consequences, however, of participation in movements of resistance and protest is frequently a heightened consciousness and greater openness to "political" ideology. Many women have been "politicized" by their involvement in popular protest over the last two decades. In some cases this has meant a greater awareness of the possibilities and limitations of everyday resistance, community action and essentially "spontaneous" protest movements and has led women into new relationships with political movements, trade unions, and the state; in some, it has generated a greater awareness of the strengths and weaknesses of action by women *as women* and has led to a rethinking of gender relationships and of involvement in "the women's movement."

Castells remarked, in his study of selected urban protest movements, that "in none of the cases observed were the gender relationships at the core of the conflict, in spite of the decisive participation of women in the movements" (Castells 1983: 335). There is, however, growing evidence that, increasingly during the period under consideration (that of the mid-1970s to the present), the influence of "feminism" as a specific political ideology has been felt even among the urban poor. In Brazil, for example, while the period from 1975 to 1978 was seen by many Brazilian feminists in the early 1980s as a time of very elementary, undefined feminism (Alvarez 1989), significant developments were to take place over the next five years. The 1978 International Women's Day celebration provided the basis for an emerging "women's political platform."

> Along with the gamut of issues concerning the "feminine" side of the Brazilian class struggle (women's important role in the struggle for democracy, political amnesty, the rising cost of living, improved social services and urban infrastructure, the need for a more just distribution of income, the lack of equal pay for equal work, and so on), the women's movement began calling attention to the politics of the private sphere, the politics of the family, and of reproduction. (*Alvarez 1989: 33–4*)

After 1978, many neighborhood women's groups began focusing on what Alvarez calls "gender specific" issues (such as day care and domestic labor) rather than on "gender related" issues (such as running water, sewage, etc.).

While it is probably premature to generalize, the Brazilian experience would appear to be not untypical as regards the developing world as a whole, where there is substantial evidence of the growth of the women's movement in general and of feminism in particular and of its increasing influence on women's struggles. Certainly the evidence from other parts of Latin America would support this thesis (Feijoo and Gogna 1990), as would the data available for south and southeast Asia (e.g. Omvedt 1986). Generally, we would agree that "if we survey the decade from the mid-seventies to the mid-eighties, women's voices were heard as never before, and women remained at the forefront of many of the most important progressive struggles of the decade" (Segal 1990: 296). At the same time, however, recognition of the heterogeneity of women's situations – and of the need for "the women's movement" to accept and draw on the experiences and struggles of women from different social backgrounds – has also been growing.

The issue of how women's popular protest, as discussed in this chapter, relates to the uneven global development of the women's movement is a complex one, which requires a more extended treatment not possible here (see, however, Daines and Seddon 1994; Rowbotham forthcoming; Wieringa 1990). Suffice it to say that female militancy, of the kind exemplified in the various forms of collective protest and resistance discussed above, while not the same thing as feminism (as "a social movement and body of ideas challenging the structures and power relations that produce female subordination" (Molyneux 1990: 32)) and while clearly having its roots in the anger and outrage of the urban poor and their demands for social justice, also effectively challenges the prevailing structures and power relations and thus constitutes a significant dimension of the women's movement, whether recognized as such or not. Recognition of the extensive involvement of women in popular protest will certainly oblige many women – and others – to reconsider the political significance of women "fighting for survival" and encourage them to reconsider and redefine the role of women in politics, and hence in the promotion of economic and social change.

4

Latin America: Popular Protest and the State

John Walton and Jonathan Shefner

On January 15, 1985, hours after the Jamaican government announced an increase in the state-controlled price of petroleum products, protest demonstrations erupted across the Caribbean nation. Groups numbering 40 to 50 people blocked roads with automobiles and burning tires, halted rail and air service, and forced the closure of schools, government offices, and business establishments. A crowd of 1000 rallied in one of Kingston's poor neighborhoods while another contingent of 300 shouting demonstrators marched on the Prime Minister's office at Government House. The protest spread quickly to the provincial cities of Montego Bay, Ocho Rios, May Pen, and Negril. As police moved to reclaim the streets after three days of mayhem, at least 10 people were killed in gun battles between officers, snipers, and roving gangs. It was the worst civil violence since a similar incident six years earlier nearly to the day. This time, as previously, the political party in power – the Jamaican Labor Party (JLP) in 1985 and the People's National Party (PNP) in 1979 – blamed its opponents for instigating the riot in an effort to discredit the government. Prime Minister Edward Seaga explained that the 21 percent increase in petroleum (gasoline, propane, kerosene) prices was necessary to offset partially the 50 percent devaluation of the Jamaican dollar and that the devaluation was strongly urged by the International Monetary Fund as a condition for new foreign credits. The protests had no effect on government policy and opposing groups were temporarily stalemated. In June, yet another fuel price increase led to renewed demonstrations followed by a 3-day general strike called by six major trade unions, including the JLP-affiliated Bustamante Industrial Trade Union. This time the government proposed a 12–15 percent wage increase to compensate for the previous year's 30 percent rate of inflation, a gesture the unions regarded as inadequate. With his own party support eroding, Mr Seaga concluded "We have gone to the maximum as far as the social costs of devaluation are concerned." Before long, the Prime Minister was echoing the sentiments of his predecessor and principal antagonist, Michael Manley of the PNP, when Seaga proclaimed "I don't intend to let them [the IMF] add Jamaica to their tombstone of failures."

1   INTRODUCTION

Latin America has played a definitive role among Third World regions in the recent transformation from the postwar era of development to the "lost decade" of economic crisis. During the 1950s and 1960s, the countries of Latin America and the Caribbean enjoyed the highest average rates of economic growth. As a pattern of uneven development began to assert itself, Latin America was the birthplace of dependency theories, the inspiration for analyses of unequal terms of trade, and the research laboratory for developmental policies such as import substitution. In the 1970s, when international lending by banks, advanced-country governments, and multilateral agencies increased twelve-fold, Latin America and the Caribbean alone absorbed nearly half of the borrowed funds. Brazil, Mexico, and Argentina have consistently been the world's largest debtor countries ranked by the absolute size of their external obligations. In the mid-1970s, various countries in the region such as Peru and Jamaica provided the early warnings that the global economy was headed for a structural breakdown and the debt crisis was first publicly recognized in Mexico in August 1982. Latin America of the 1980s saw debtor countries attempt a regional political alliance to press for better terms of debt repayment with the Cartegena Consensus. Failing any amelioration of mounting hardship, the region has provided some of the most spectacular and sustained popular protests against structural adjustment programs. Owing to all of the preceding factors, Latin America has also been the principal test case for recent debt-relief programs.

Latin America, therefore, is the logical starting point for our analysis of debt-crisis politics and a rich source of hypotheses for comparative evaluation. The purpose of this chapter is three-fold: to describe the socio-economic setting in which a wave of popular austerity protests began in Latin America more than 15 years ago; to analyze the form and composition of these rebellious developments; and to develop an interpretation of the protest movement that integrates contributing influences at the local, state, and international levels.

Latin America may lead other world regions in yet another feature of the debt crisis, the sheer number of publications that treat the continent's economic problems and policy prescriptions. For example, several review essays which discuss up to a score of recent books and collections have recently appeared in the *Latin American Research Review* (Sachs 1988; Edwards 1989; Sheahan 1989; Golub 1991). Perhaps the most striking characteristic of this literature is its singularly economistic focus. Volume after volume examines the macroeconomic dimensions of the crisis, where the blame lies in comparisons of profligate global lending institutions and national economic mismanagement, the prospects for recovery under market-based reforms, and to a much lesser extent the shadowy issue of "political instability" as a possible consequence of austerity. Yet very little analytical attention has been devoted to the large majority of Latin Americans who are poor – how they have been affected by the crisis and how they have responded to it in their daily lives and political actions. With a few exceptions (Gonzáles Tiburco and Escobar Latapí 1991; Selby Murphy, and Lorenzen 1990), social scientists have analyzed the problems of debt and austerity exclusively from the standpoint of official actors.

This chapter attempts to integrate an analysis of popular responses to austerity with the constrained choices open to state policy and the pressures stemming from international sources. The debt crisis is treated as a problem of Latin America's political and moral economy. We are concerned less with the policy maker's justification of approaches to the crisis than with the experience and evaluation of policy actions expressed in varied ways by popular constituencies.

In brief, the argument claims that years of uneven economic growth and rapid urbanization in Latin America were beneficial for the growing city masses because they ensured some (e.g. rural–urban) mobility by providing people a modest place in the urban economy and sheltering them from the worst effects of growing inequality with compensatory social-wage policies (e.g. food, transportation, and housing subsidies). The broad implementation of austerity measures as a condition of structural adjustment and debt restructuring represented an attack on the very means that made urban life sustainable. Austerity led to popular protest in the times and places that combined economic hardship, external adjustment demands, hyperurbanization, and local traditions of political mobilization. The effects of protest are varied and combined with other domestic currents, ranging from negligible impacts on stalwart regimes (e.g.

Chile) to collapse (e.g. Haiti), electoral succession (e.g. Peru), and hastened return to democratic rule (e.g. Argentina, Brazil). In many instances popular movements have exerted pressure on states to temporize adjustment programs and demand more favorable debt-relief arrangements from multilateral agencies such as the International Monetary Fund. The IMF, banks, and advanced-country governments, in turn, have been forced to weigh the trade-offs between stringent repayment schedules and political instability in friendly debtor countries. In the end, this chapter argues that the political and economic crisis of the past decade in Latin America cannot be understood without a full appreciation of the manner in which the urban poor have played a role among the key actors in the unfolding future.

2   SOCIAL CONSEQUENCES OF STRUCTURAL ADJUSTMENT

Thirty years ago, the United Nations proclaimed the 1960s as the "Decade of Development." Today, the best that poor nations can hope for is an unforeseeable end to the drain on national resources. In 1970, the total external debt for all developing nations stood at $64 billion, with two-thirds of that held by other governments and international agencies. By 1984 the debt burden had increased tenfold to $686 billion, over one-half of that held by private banks. In five more years of policy efforts to control the crisis, the latter figure doubled to $1.2 trillion, most of that now in the hands of international banking syndicates grown leery of any further cash outlays to countries saddled with enormous burdens on their foreign exchange reserves. The World Bank reports that Third World countries experienced a net capital drain of $43 billion to the industrial countries in 1988, reversing a positive balance of $18 billion as recently as 1982 (World Bank 1989). Although neither the World Bank nor the private-bank syndicates think about such numbers in human terms, UNICEF's annual report for 1989 concluded that "more than a thousand children continue to die each day in Africa [alone] as a consequence of the economic witches' brew that flows out of low primary commodity prices, poor borrowings, high interest rates, [and] the remaining debt crisis" (UNICEF 1989a: 1).

So-called "structural adjustment" policies were well known to international agencies before 1982 when the debt crisis was publicly recognized with Mexico's current accounts bankruptcy. But austerity became the watchword of global policy in the years that followed.

Banks looked for evidence of "stabilizing" economic reforms before advancing new or emergency loans and the International Monetary Fund assumed a central regulatory role as economic planner and evaluator of national creditworthiness. Applied by the IMF with striking uniformity across debtor nations, structural adjustment required currency devaluation, increased interest rates, reduced imports, greater freedom to foreign capital, elimination of tariff protections, privatization of state-owned firms, and, above all, reduced public expenditures in the form of cuts in state subsidies for food, transportation, petroleum products, education, and health services. Countries as diverse as industrialized Brazil and agrarian Ghana required the same "shock treatment"; an abrupt domestic redirection toward free-market policies the net effect of which would be to generate income for debt servicing.

Austerity policies have had a number of dramatic effects, as we shall see below, but none of them included any general relief from or solution to the debt crisis. By 1989, UNCTAD concluded in its annual report that "austerity measures imposed on the poorest countries by the International Monetary Fund as a condition for new loans, have produced no results" (*UNCTAD Trade and Development Report* 1989b). On the contrary, the policies which produced an accelerating transfer of income from the poor to the developed countries simultaneously led to economic stagnation in the Third World. UNCTAD's report

> foresees a deterioration in their growth performance, particularly in Africa and Latin America and in the least developed countries of Asia ... Adjustment programme measures aimed at achieving balance in external payments, for example, often produce perverse effects. Thus, attempts at checking domestic demand reduce government income from taxes and import duties, which are often a major source of revenue; while currency depredations raise the domestic currency costs of government debt-service obligations and imports, thereby exacerbating inflationary pressures. (*UNCTAD Bulletin 1989: 7*).

Recent data show some improvement. In 1991, the ratio of interest payments to export earnings was at its lowest since 1982 and net capital flows returned to a favorable balance. But Latin American debt is still above the level that the World Bank regards as "critical." Indeed, despite the good news, Latin American and Caribbean debt is 78 percent greater than it was in 1980 (*Latin America Weekly Report*, January 16, 1992). The impact of more than a decade of austerity has had devastating impacts: income disparities have increased, real

Table 4.1   Socio-economic indicators for major Latin American countries (ca. 1970–1990)

	1 Population 1990 (×1000)	2 Percent urban 1965	3 1990	4 Total external public debt $ per capita 1988	5 Long-term public debt to export earnings (%) 1970	6 1987
1 Argentina[a]	32,322	76	86	1,529	88	552
2 Bolivia[a]	7,313	40	51	64	232	743
3 Brazil[a]	150,368	50	77	622	110	320
4 Chile[a]	13,174	72	86	1,075	162	240
5 Colombia	31,819	54	70	437	127	179
6 Costa Rica[a]	3,015	38	54	1,308	48	241
7 Dominican Republic[a]	7,170	35	60	466	75	165[c]
8 Ecuador[a]	10,781	37	57	926	75	379
9 El Salvador[a]	5,252	39	44	326	34	172
10 Guatemala[a]	9,196	34	42	245	30	200
11 Haiti[a]	6,504	18	30	108	174	156
12 Honduras	5,139	26	44	570	45	270
13 Jamaica[a]	2,521	38	52	1,467	28	208
14 Mexico[a]	88,598	55	73	970	109	278
15 Nicaragua	3,871	43	60	1,873	67	1,758[c]
16 Panama[a]	2,418	44	55	1,576	49	63
17 Paraguay[a]	4,277	36	47	523	125	213
18 Peru[a]	22,332	52	70	603	69	348
19 Trinidad/Tobago[a]	1,283	30	69	1,431	29	91[c]
20 Uruguay	3,218	81	83	953	92	184
21 Venezuela[a]	19,735	70	90	1,352	26	197

[a] Presence of austerity protest
[b] 1985 figure.
[c] 1986 figure.
[d] 1987 figure.
[e] 1988 figure.
[f] 1989 figure.

Sources: United Nations 1990; World Bank 1990;[b] International Monetary Fund 1990;[b] World Bank 1989.

minimum wages are two-thirds of 1980 levels, and informal economies, with their attendant uncertainties, have increased their prominence, especially in urban areas (PRELAC surveys cited in *Latin American Weekly Report*, January 30, 1992 and June 4, 1992). Table 4.1 summarizes these longitudinal shifts in economic growth, debt burden, and hardship for the major Latin American and Caribbean countries.

The significance of critical analyses coming from agencies like UNICEF and UNCTAD is that they confirm the assessment of

7 Consumer price index	8 Earnings per employee Average growth (1980=100)	9	10	11 Percent central-government spending Education	12	13 Health	14
1990 (1985=100)	1970-1980	1980-1988	1988	1972	1989	1972	1989
61,930[f]	-1.5	1.4	97	20.0	9.3	—	2.0
675	0.0	-10.3	46	31.3	20.3	6.3	6.6
87,722[f]	4.0	0.0	109	8.3	4.2	6.7	6.1
242	8.1	-1.7	105	14.3	10.1	8.2	5.9
305	-0.2	3.2	115	—	—	—	—
219	—	—	—	28.3	17.0	4.0	27.2
426	-1.0	-4.4[c]	79[b]	14.2	—	11.7	—
658	3.3	-1.3	95	27.5	23.4	1.5	9.8
288	2.4	-9.3	63[b]	21.4	17.6	10.9	7.4
190[f]	-3.2	-2.7	89	—	—	—	—
116	-3.3	4.6	157	—	—	—	—
151	—	—	—	22.3	—	10.2	—
185	-0.2	—	—	—	—	—	—
1,405	1.2	-5.2	72	16.4	12.3	4.5	1.7
—	—	-10	31[c]	16.6	—	4.0	—
102	0.2	3.2	123	20.7	19.1	15.1	19.8
249[f]	—	—	—	12.1	11.4	3.5	3.0
88,733[f]	—	-3.0	95[d]	23.6	15.6	5.5	5.5
159	—	—	—	—	—	—	—
1,794	—	1.0	118	9.5	79	16	4.5
480	3.8	0.1	98	18.6	19.6[e]	11.7	10.0[e]

concerned social scientists writing throughout the decade. Looking beyond aggregate economic indicators to social effects, a number of investigators have shown the regressive effects of structural adjustment policies. (Frenkel and O'Donnell 1979; Sheanhan 1980; Foxley 1981; Diaz-Alejandro 1981; Cline 1983; Sutton 1984). The middle classes, the poor, and especially the urban poor have suffered the greatest burden of debt servicing. Reduced government spending affects middle-class state employees, import restrictions hurt small commercial enterprises and national industries dependent foreign equipment, sale or closure of state-owned corporations eliminates jobs, and cuts in state subsidies of food and transportation often spell the difference between bare survival and destitution for the urban poor. What has been achieved by these sacrifices? Pastor (1987) has reviewed the major studies of stabilization policy effects and has separately examined the experience of Latin American "program countries" subject to IMF reform policies. He concludes that, with the exception of balance of payments assistance which is provided as lure for adopting austerity programs, all other effects are inconclusive or negative.

> The major findings are that: 1) program countries did experience significant balance of payments improvement but this was mostly due to increased capital inflow induced by the IMF's "seal of approval" and *not significant current account improvement*; 2) in contrast to IMF official goals, Fund programs in Latin America seem to be associated with *accelerating inflation* and not inflation rate reduction; 3) in contrast to the growth-oriented critique, Fund programs had mixed impacts on growth rates [i.e. some up and some down]; and 4) Fund programs were *most significantly and consistently associated with declines in wage share.* (*Pastor 1987: 249; emphasis added*)

A longitudinal study of poverty and inequality during adjustment in Peru conducted under World Bank auspices also demonstrates the failure of these policies to protect the poor (Glewwe and Hall 1992).

Table 4.1 provides an overview of socio-economic changes in the major countries (1 million + population) of Latin America and the Caribbean during the last 20 years or so. In a region already highly urbanized by Third World standards, the population living in cities has continued to swell (the averages of columns 2 and 3 have increased from 46 to 62 percent between 1965 and 1990). The total external debt per capita in 1988 (column 4) averaged $877, a figure roughly ten-times greater than in 1970 and equal in 1988 to the GNP per capita. Columns 5 and 6 demonstrate the growing debt burden from 1970 to 1987 by expressing long-term public debt as a percentage of export earnings, the source of foreign exchange with which external debts must be paid. Where the average total debt was once less than a country's annual export earnings, by the late 1980s it was three times that amount (columns 5 and 6 average 85 per cent and 331 per cent respectively). Inflation continued to increase at a rapid rate in 1990 (column 7). When the cost of living is standardized on the basis of wage increases, the data show that whereas real income gains and losses were small and roughly equal in number across countries from 1970–80 (column 8), during the 1980s most countries (10 of 16 where data are available) showed real wages declining by larger amounts (column 9). Certainly the pattern is varied. The real earnings index (column 10) shows a decline for 10 countries and an increase for 6. As governments have been obliged to meet external debt payments that represent a growing proportion of national income, the amount of money available for social welfare programs in fields such as health and education has also declined. Where columns 11–14 provide complete pairwise data, the percentage of government spending has decreased in 18 instances and increased in only 6.

Data from a variety of other sources confirm these results in a general pattern of economic deterioration with some variation across countries and indicators. Class polarization has moderated within some cities, if not all, and the general rate of urban primacy appears to be dropping as the large capital cities confront more severe problems than the still-growing secondary urban centers (Portes 1989). From 1980 to 1987, the rate of urban unemployment nearly doubled (PRELAC 1987). The informal sector expanded, but not enough to absorb the newly unemployed. On the contrary, "an expanding informal sector does not counterbalance a stagnant formal sector; rather, both sectors expand and contract together" (Portes 1989: 25). Where survey data are available, it appears that households adapted to the crisis in various ways including an increase in the number of jobs held by family members and, even more characteristically, through a variety of cost-cutting measures from reduced expenditures on food and other necessities to multiple occupancy of housing (Selby, Murphy, and Lorenzen 1990). The World Bank study of Peru from 1985–90 showed a 55 percent drop in household consumption (Glewwe and Hall 1992). In the case of Mexico, researchers suggest that as a result of these coping strategies significant declines in real-wage income may have produced greater relative impoverishment in the white-collar, wage-dependent middle class than among the more resilient urban poor – who, nevertheless, bear greater absolute income and social-wage losses (Escobar Latapí and Roberts 1991; Lustig 1990). A recent UNICEF study of Argentina shows a similiar pattern of downward mobility with 34.5 percent of the population in poverty, up from 20.6 percent in 1980. Although the number of those born into poverty decreased, "what increased dramatically, by 338%, was the number of those who were pauperised by the progressive erosion of their purchasing power" (*Latin American Weekly Report*, September 17, 1992).

3   POPULAR PROTEST

Beginning in the mid-1970s, a new phenomenon entered on the world political stage, a form of popular protest that initially went unremarked beyond passing journalistic note because it appeared a simple recrudescence of the time-honored food riot. In July 1976,

Peru, and shortly thereafter Egypt, experienced the first modern austerity protests characterized by mass demonstrations, strikes, street violence, and looting all expressed as retaliation against sharp price increases and cancellations of public subsidies for basic foods, gasoline, and education. In addition to providing the first austerity protest, Latin America experienced the highest rate of popular unrest with 16 of its 21 principal countries recording at least one uprising (table 4.1) and the continent as a whole contributing two-thirds of the worldwide total of protest events (see chapter 2).

Typically, austerity protests were precipitated by drastic, overnight price hikes resulting from the termination of public subsidies on basic goods and services, proclaimed by the government as regrettably necessary reforms urged by the IMF and international lenders as conditions for new and renegotiated loans. Five deaths in the first Peruvian protest began a pattern of violence. Peru remained a hotbed of austerity protest with students and workers demonstrating against increased food prices in 1977, followed in 1978 by a march of public employees over state layoffs. This protest, though cheered on by other public workers watching from surrounding office buildings, was dispersed by police tear gas. Other areas of early protest included Kingston, Jamaica in April 1977 where demonstrations against unemployment and price rises turned to looting (Girvan, Bernal, and Hughes 1980).

With increasing frequency in the late 1970s and early 1980s, IMF "conditionality" provided the test for bank lending of new money, which soon began to dwindle, and loan restructuring for the purpose of easing debt-service obligations through lower interest rates or extended repayment schedules. Debtor countries became the experimental subjects of "shock treatments" aimed at stimulating market mechanisms and export earnings through a combination of currency devaluation, reduced public spending, wage restraint, elimination of consumer subsidies, tariff reduction, import curbs, opening to foreign investment, and privatization of parastatal corporations.

Classical price riots are well known to European history and have occurred previously in modern Third World settings: India (Arnold 1979), Ceylon (Kearney 1979), Chile (Wright 1973), and Sierra Leone (Banton 1957). To the limited extent that disturbances of this sort have been studied, they are shaped wholly by national factors and occur in isolation. The case of Colombo, (then) Ceylon is typical of these modern price riots. A revolt rose in response to the government's elimination of subsidized rice prices and, although protests recurred in 1965 and 1966, this was an issue of strictly domestic politics, having no connection with debt or with protests in other developing countries (Kearney 1979 and chapter 8 of this volume).

The new style of rebellion that swept Latin America was different. It was a wave of coincident national demonstrations in which dissidents were often aware of events in neighboring countries. In their own words and actions, demonstrators were protesting against internationally prescribed adjustment policies – "Out with the IMF!" decried placards and street demonstrators in Santo Domingo. The foreign debt was imposed unjustly on the poor, as Panamanian protestors asserted when they broke into the legislative palace and spray-painted "Let the ones who stole the money pay!" Popular protest appeared in similar forms, and even coined the same slogans, in countries as far apart as Ghana, Zaire, Turkey, Poland, and Sudan. The symbols of protest showed the participants were unequivocal in their assessment of blame. In Chile, demonstrators opposed to the Pinochet dictatorship and its austerity policies carried banners attacking the IMF, international usury, and imperialism, as they chanted "Work, bread, justice, and liberty!" In Brazil, following several austerity protests carnival song lyrics were changed to say "Hey, IMF, give me some money." Before long, it was clear that the new phenomenon was an international protest wave – a recurring form consisting of large collective actions in opposition to state economic measures that stem from international pressures and aim at domestic market reforms to reduce foreign debt. In the vernacular, they were already well known as "IMF riots."

As coincident cross-national events stemming from a common condition of the international political economy, the wave of austerity protests followed characteristic patterns of timing, location, form, targets, and participants. In addition to such parallels, national political cultures gave a particular stamp to both the expression and the effect of social protest.

Timing

Following their appearance in 1976, the uprisings continued at a rate between 2 and 4 each year, until they escalated sharply in 1983 with the political recognition of the debt crisis that began in Mexico. The frequency of austerity protests reached a peak from 1983–5, declined through 1987, and then achieved a fairly steady state of recurrence up to the time of writing. It is premature to claim that the wave has come to an end. One of Latin America's most spectacular incidents of riot and looting on a national scale in Venezuela during late February and early March of 1989 came relative late in this period.

The last three years have seen ongoing protest in Venezuela, varying from street riots in Caracas involving thousands of students and workers in October 1991 leaving 12 dead, to nationwide strikes in May 1992. Failed coup attempts in February and November 1992 were explained as the army's response to three years of corruption and mismanagement. Popular support for the government was conspicuously absent after each coup and many observers considered the insurgencies as a reflection of popular preferences.

The 1990s also brought new riots in Brazil, marches and strikes in Bolivia over privatization of industry, and a two-month strike by health workers in Peru. Uruguay, previously unscathed by austerity protest, experienced a 36-hour national strike in response to deteriorating wages.

The immediate explanation for this chronology lies with the implementation of structural adjustment programs at the national level, programs which were themselves by-products of the number and timing of restructured and renegotiated loan arrangements. If the latter observation seems overly obvious, it nevertheless suggests evidence for the idea that protest results less from steadily worsening conditions throughout the period than from abrupt and palpable shocks – from the intersection of political action and economic hardship.

Location

The protests took place predominantly in cities, and spread through national urban networks, reflecting the locus of austerity reforms. Riots that erupted in Caracas spread to 16 Venezuelan cities during the first two weeks of March 1989. In a series of strikes and demonstrations of the mid-1980s, at least a dozen cities were affected in both Brazil and Peru. After several days of violence in the capital Port-au-Prince Haitian protests erupted in six outlying towns. Looting in the Santo Domingo, Dominican Republic spread to 17 cities (Espinal 1988). Although protest typically multiplies through a network of cities, it usually begins in the capital where mobilization is easier and government targets are at hand.

The spread of protest demonstrations is often rapid and spontaneous as news of violence in the capital reaches provincial cities. The spatial distribution of protest mirrors the location of aggrieved groups: the urban poor whose subsidized food and transportation are eliminated, industrial workers and civil servants who lose jobs in state budget cuts, university students whose educational subsidies are cut. Conversely, one of the objectives of structural adjustment is to stimulate agricultural production and export through higher prices. Instances of rural protest are exceptional and where they occur prove the rule owing to their connection with the closure of state-owned companies, as in the case of marches by Bolivian miners.

Form

Protests appeared in three distinct forms: strike, demonstration, and riot. Latin America's strong trade-union tradition has facilitated the mobilization of particularly affected segments of the working class and has ensured sufficient solidarity in labor confederations to permit the use of the general strike as a weapon against government austerity programs. In both the Andean and Southern Cone countries, general strikes of 24 or 48 hours have been called repeatedly in response to announcements of an impending devaluation or price hike. Political demonstrations are equally common and often sponsored by organized labor along with other groups such as opposition political parties, church groups, and neighborhood associations. A massive march through the streets of Rio de Janeiro in 1983 turned out several hundred thousand opponents of the military government's economic policy. In June 1985, six Chilean unions participated in a general strike, which included water and utility workers, air traffic controllers, prison guards, postal workers, and bank employees. A general strike in June 1984 against low wages idled an estimated 20 percent of the Argentine workforce. This followed an even more successful 24-hour shutdown of business, industry and transportation in December 1983. After 1976, a series of general strikes were called to protest austerity in defiance of the Peruvian military regime.

Riots involving the extremes of looting and violence are common. Groups do not gather and take to the streets with the intention of rioting. On the contrary, riots usually result from peaceful demonstrations gone awry as a result of police provocations or overzealous protestation. Indeed, it is so often the case that strikes generate demonstrations or demonstrations embolden looters that the three types seldom occur in pure form. In April 1983 a march of unemployed workers in São Paulo turned into a looting and window-smashing spree.

Under the heading of form we should emphasize that austerity protests are bloody affairs, particularly when they lead to riot. In both the Dominican Republic and Venezuela many hundreds were killed and thousands wounded or jailed, even according to official reports that seek to minimize the numbers of demonstrators. Although it is tempting to attribute state violence to authoritarian regimes such as Pinochet's Chile, democratic countries such as the Dominican Republic and Venezuela have experienced brutal repression in response to protests *cum* riots. The Dominican Republic saw angry demonstrations, bus burnings, looting of food stores and barricading of main roads in a 1987 wave of strikes and riots. Police action that followed resulted in hundreds of wounded, nearly 100 deaths, and an estimated 5,000 arrests in 17 cities (Espinal 1988). The official death toll in Venezuela reached 300 after 5 days of rioting in 1989, with over 2,000 wounded and as many jailed. And critics claimed that the government grossly underestimated casualties. In Argentina, just before the succession of President Alfonsín by the newly elected Menem, a week of riots and looting left at least 16 dead, 80 wounded, and thousands arrested after riot police opened fire on crowds numbering up to 1000. Another incident turned violent in Buenos Aires when a shoot-out between police and slum dwellers resulted from attempts to block roads and loot trucks in March 1990. Although most of the violence is due to crowd-control methods of the army and police, protestors have responded with sniping in Venezuela and bombings in the Dominican Republic, Peru, Ecuador, and Chile. Pitched battles were fought in Brazil in 1983 when 2 days of rioting left 200 stores looted, 48 houses invaded, and 125 cars and buses destroyed.

Targets

The targets of political demonstrations and riot violence reflect a good deal about the moral economy of the Latin crowd. Marches and rallies congregate in the major thoroughfares and public plazas. Targets symbolize agents of austerity policy and the international economy: government buildings, the treasury and national palace, the legislature. This was the pattern in the 1983 Chilean protests at government buildings in downtown Santiago. Panamanian protestors in the same year ended a march through downtown Panama City at the legislative palace where they chanted and spray-painted slogans on marble walls. More than 20,000 students and workers congregated in Mexico City's Zocalo in 1986. Peruvian protestors stoned the National Lottery Building, the treasury, and other government offices in 1976, chanting "Down with the Military government! Up with salaries!"

When protests take the form of violent direct action, crowds focus on their immediate grievances and local communities. Looting is aimed at supermarkets, clothing and furniture stores, gasoline stations, and banks. In Haiti a CARE warehouse was sacked and burned because participants claimed that donated food was being hoarded and privately sold by corrupt officials. In May 1989, Argentine shoppers began walking out of stores without paying for food as a protest against hunger and the action escalated into crowd assaults on shops. Private and foreign automobiles and travel agencies are attacked in clear linkages between local grievances, external debt, and the lending countries. Public transportation is widely subsidized in Latin American cities and precipitous fare increases regularly result in bus burnings. Chilean protesters not only targeted government buildings, but also participated in land invasions on the outskirts of Santiago in 1984 and in poor neighborhoods in 1985. Laid-off Brazilian workers showed their anger by destroying a factory assembly line in São Paulo.

Participants

Participants are characteristically drawn from a limited set of social categories. They are mainly the urban poor: slum dwellers, participants in the informal economy, and the unemployed. But the working class and labor organizations also play a key role. The class composition of protestors widens with participants motivated by public-service cuts: students, teachers, health-care workers, and other government employees. In some instances, other middle-class consumers (e.g. of petroleum) and shopkeepers join demonstrations. And occasionally, professional groups ally with broad movements for reform. Alliances are forged among participating groups. Protests may begin in the shantytowns or city streets, but neighborhood associations fashion protest coalitions with churches, political parties, and labor unions.

Labor has played a mixed role in austerity protests. In some cases it has initiated action as in the 1985 Chilean protests when a general strike was called by six major unions representing water and utility workers, air traffic controllers, prison guards, postal workers, and bank employees. Panama's largest union, the National Council of Organized Workers, led a 1985 protest march. Peronist labor federations called a general strike in 1983 and shut down business, industry and transportation for 24 hours. But labor lagged behind church and community protesters in the Dominican Republic. Except in cases where protest is expressed in strikes, labor unions have not played a prominent role among the popular groups opposed to austerity measures. One explanation is that the syndicates engaged in concessionary negotiations with governments in order to save some of their former benefits (see, e.g. Roxborough 1989).

The church has played an active part in political demonstrations and local mobilization. In the Dominican Republic, criticism of the government came from both church hierarchy and Christian base communities. Bishops attended a rally of Christian youth in May 1984 and Cardinal López Rodriguez challenged the government to a dialogue. "The situation is extremely difficult, much more so than many people imagine" (*Latin America Weekly Report*, May 11, 1984). Neighborhood priests criticized IMF policies and included attacks on government policy in Good Friday celebrations. In Brazil, bishops led 50,000 in an outdoor protest. Chilean church officials acted as spokesmen during the 1984 protests and five Peruvian Bishops asked the military government to end its repression of a month-long series of protests.

On some occasions political parties have organized and directed protests for their own aims. Much of the 1985 violence in Jamaica was the result of shoot-outs between rival gangs allied with the Jamaica Labor Party and the People's National Party. An Argentine rally in June 1984 was organized by youth groups of the major opposition parties.

Analysis of rank-and-file participation shows that austerity protests attract a cross-section of social classes and occupations. The urban poor coordinate with students and public employees (e.g. Guatemala), miners and church groups join forces (e.g. Bolivia), and general strikes mobilize the underemployed and consumers (e.g. Argentina, Peru, Chile). Shopkeepers, often victims of looting, have at other times joined in protest. Reacting to increases in food prices and imports mandated by the IMF, shopkeepers allied with the transport operators of Santo Domingo in response to fuel price increases. In a coordinated action, Brazilian taxi drivers blocked roads while 31,000 public employees staged a protest march. Reacting to cuts in the state sector, public employees frequently participate in general strikes. In June 1984, some 500,000 civil servants, including teachers, health-ministry employees and customs officials, protested in Peru.

Few austerity protests have produced permanent organizations or social movements (with rare exceptions such as Poland's Solidarity). Conversely, however, various Christian base communities (Levine and Mainwaring 1989) and housing movements (Eckstein 1990) have grown out of urban communities activated by austerity issues.

Mexico's Urban Popular Movement (CONAMUP) and National Front in Defense of Wages and Against Austerity and Scarcity (FNDSCAC) were among a variety of social movements that pressed political reform during the 1980s (Carr 1986; Davis 1990).

Generated inductively, the foregoing features of austerity protest demonstrate a distinctive form of collective action. Austerity protests capture many features of classical food riots and mass political demonstrations, but they also represent something unprecedented: an international protest wave orchestrated by global economic forces as they intersect with characteristic features of uneven development (e.g. hyperurbanization, aid dependency, patron–client politics, class domination of economic policy). Broad parallels in austerity-protest timing, location, form, targets, and participation help to establish that we have a coherent empirical object amenable to theoretical explanation. General similarities, however, do not mean uniformity. Protests take varied forms and, as we shall see, produce different political effects. Latin American countries differ in the number, style, and significance of popular uprisings – and a few have not experienced mass protest. A full explanation of austerity protest must comprehend the demonstrated regularities, sources of variation, and the fundamental causal mechanisms that produce the pattern and significance of these events.

4   AGGREGATE ANALYSIS OF AUSTERITY PROTEST

The cases of austerity protest in Latin America and the Caribbean lend themselves to quantitative and case-study methods. The first approach emphasizes systematic treatment of cases and potential generalization, while the second stresses difference and interpretation. Each approach illuminates a distinct surface of the phenomenon and a more complete understanding results from their combination (Ragin 1987).

Quantitative analysis of protest events relies on a relatively exhaustive search of journalistic and secondary sources which indicates that 16 countries in Latin America and the Caribbean have experienced austerity protests, some repeatedly producing a sample of 80 distinct events. The procedure begins by assembling all of the generally available accounts of austerity protests fitting the previous definition from sources such as the *New York Times*, *Latin America Weekly Report*, the *Economist* and various national periodicals such as *Proceso* (Mexico), *Veja* (Brazil), and *ABC* (Spain). Countries are first divided into protest and non-protest groups. For those that experienced one or more protest events, an index of "protest severity" was formed from four indicators: (a) an ordinal measure (with four categories) based on the number of reported deaths and arrests; (b) an interval measure of the number of separate protest episodes occurring between 1976 and mid-1989; (c) a dichotomous measure of the presence or absence of rioting; and (d) an interval measure of the spread of protest, based upon the number of national cities reporting major unrest. The severity index ranges from mild protest in countries such as Mexico and El Salvador, with only one or two events in the form of public demonstrations and brief strikes, to strong protests in countries like Venezuela, where extensive rioting occurred in 16 cities, or Peru where large demonstrations in many cities have occurred repeatedly.

Pursuing an explanation for the occurrence and severity of protests, a number of standard data sources were consulted for economic, political, and social indicators. Although far from definitive, particularly with small samples and crudely measured indicators, this procedure is useful for sorting out causal hypotheses deserving case-study examination, as we shall see. Most of the indicators are straightforward measures of debt burden, the extent of involvement with various debt-renegotiation programs and agencies, import and export partners as measures of trade dependency, urbanization, and so on. One measure was specially constructed. Statistical data on urbanization were transformed with a technique that "controls" for the close association between urban population increases and level of economic development (Bradshaw 1987) such that the variable may be interpreted as "excess" or "overurbanization" – the level of urban population concentration above and beyond what would be expected at a given level of industrialization or economic development.

Table 4.2 groups indicators conceptually in a manner that allows interpretation of various hypotheses which have been advanced to explain the presence or absence of "IMF riots" and their severity within protest countries (e.g. Bernal 1984; Girvan 1980; Moffitt 1983; Loxley 1984; Petras and Brill 1986; Kaufman 1986). The correlations in Table 4.2 for protest occurence and severity are consistent in direction and magnitude, but stronger on the severity variable. This is because the presence or absence of protest is scored as a (dummy variable) 0 or 1 respectively, resulting in a truncated range of variation on the dependent variable which reduced potential associations, particularly in a small sample. Protest severity, however, was measured on linear scale allowing much more variation and the opportunity for associations to emerge. The following discussion refers to protest in general, because of the consistency between the two variables, but is best confirmed by the second, severity.

The first group of indicators of IMF conditionality shows moderately strong positive associations and significant correlations between protest severity and the number of renegotiations and of restructurings (0.50 and 0.53). In general, the greater the involvement of international agencies in a country's debt-repayment policies, the greater the likelihood of protest and of severe disturbances within protest countries. Debt burden *per se does not* explain the association because the ratio of debt service to exports, for example, is more weakly correlated than the conditionality measures.

Contrary to much general theorizing (e.g. Bernal 1984; Frenkel and O'Donnell 1979; Honeywell 1983), the second group of measures of dependency is weakly associated with protest and, even at that, in the reverse direction from what is usually hypothesized. The modest negative correlations suggest that the less the dependency (e.g. lower trade concentration, MNC presence) the greater is the likelihood of protest. Third, indicators of economic hardship are positively correlated with protest *severity*, as one would expect (0.45 for the Consumer Price Index in 1983 and 0.50 for the yearly average rate of inflation). Fourth, various measures of social structure show a mixed pattern of association with protest. Level of development (GNP per capita) and the distribution of the labor force in services or manufacturing have no significant effect on protest. Higher levels of "tertiarization," for example, do not give rise to urban unrest as has been conjectured. Conversely, both urbanization and over-urbanization are *strongly* associated with protest. Similarly, evidence for the effects of potential bases of social mobilization is found in the strong and significant association of unionization and protest severity (0.65). Finally, the political indicators show few tangible or consistent correlations with protest, a fact of some interest given other research and theorizing — assuming, of course, that the measures reported here validly operationalize regime characteristics. For example, these results run contrary to the suggestions by Epstein (1989) that regime type affects protest and by Petras and Brill (1986) that legitimacy and state–civil links foster protest. One positive association between protest and "state sanctions" or repressive measures applied to earlier protests contradicts the view of O'Donnell (1978), Kaufman (1986), and Sheahan (1980) that bureaucratic-authoritarian states effectively suppress dissent. In this case, the "strong states" have more austerity protest.

Summarizing these results, measures of IMF conditionality, hardship, urbanization, and unionization are the best predictors of aus-

Table 4.2 Correlations of the occurrence and severity of austerity protest with selected indicators of economic, social, and political conditions in Latin America during the 1970s and 1980s

General category/indicator	Protest occurrence	N	Protest severity	N
Conditionality and debt dependence				
Number of renegotiations	0.13	19	0.50[a]	15
Number of restructurings	-0.06	19	0.53[b]	15
Loans/IMF quota	0.39[a]	19	-0.18	15
Average debt service/exports	0.14	19	0.22	15
Use of extended fund	0.24	19	-0.10	15
IMF Pressure Index	0.22	19	0.22	15
Trade and investment dependence				
Multinational penetration, 1973	0.14	18	-0.13	15
Export commodity concentration, 1980	-0.03	18	-0.32	15
Export partner concentration, 1980	-0.01	19	-0.43	15
Import partner concentration, 1980	0.02	19	-0.35	15
Raw material export, 1980	-0.26	19	0.30	15
Domestic investment/GNP, 1980	-0.19	18	-0.17	15
Economic hardship				
Consumer Price Index, 1983	0.18	18	0.45[a]	15
Average inflation, 1973–84	0.12	18	0.50[a]	15

Table 4.2 (*continued*)

General category/indicator	Protest occurrence	N	Protest severity	N
Social Structure				
GNP per capita, 1981	0.08	18	0.22	15
Urbanization, 1980	−0.05	18	0.47[a]	15
Overurbanization, 1980	−0.26	18	0.52[b]	15
Tertiary sector employment, 1980	0.05	18	0.19	15
Manufacturing employment, 1980	−0.05	18	0.08	15
Unionization, c. 1975	−0.11	18	0.65[b]	14
Political characteristics				
Protest events/population, 1948–77	0.17	19	0.36	14
State sanctions/population, 1948–77	−0.04	19	0.51[a]	15
Civil rights index, 1973–9	−0.33	19	0.19	15
Political rights, 1973–9	−0.35	19	0.23	15
Government revenue/GNP, 1980	0.19	18	0.21	15
Direct taxation/revenue, 1980	0.13	18	0.15	15

Significance levels: [a] $p < 0.10$, [b] $p < 0.05$

Source: This table is from a paper by Jon Shefner, entitled "Debt, austerity and resistance," that reanalyzes the data in Walton and Ragin (1990) using a larger, updated set of (35) protest countries as of 1990

terity protest. (See Walton and Ragin 1990 for a more complete analysis of these data on a global scale.)

In a more interpretive vein, these results suggest that international interventions in Latin American societies in the form of austerity programs combine with domestic structures that make vulnerable large numbers of people who are already organized in urban communities. The situation is aptly described by Cardoso and Faletto (1979: xvi) who conceive "the relationship between external and internal forces as forming a complex whole whose structural links are not based on mere external forms of exploitation and coercion, but are rooted in coincidences of interests between local dominant classes and international ones, and, on the other side are challenged by local dominated groups ... [an] 'internalization of external interests.'" If governments, banks, and interests connected with the export economy benefit from austerity, and help internalize external policies, then the urban poor, labor, and their middle-class allies have challenged those interests in dramatic ways. Although protest mobilization has come predominantly from the urban poor and their community organizations, labor has also played a role – sometimes in an alliance with other groups and, in a number of protest events as the initiator of general strikes focused on austerity issues (especially in Peru, Argentina, Ecuador, Bolivia, and Brazil). On other occasions, nevertheless, labor's role has been to follow the example of the political parties by using popular protest for its own opportunistic purposes. More nuanced patterns emerge from case studies of some of the better documented austerity protests.

5   PROTEST CASES COMPARED

The following case-study comparison treats four Latin American countries: Brazil, the Dominican Republic, Mexico, and Venezuela. The selection was guided in large part by the availability of published accounts of selected protest events and does not claim to be a representative sample. Nevertheless, the set does provide a cross-section of Latin American countries by size, geopolitical importance, debt magnitude, national wealth, and political regime (from democratic Venezuela to authoritarian Mexico and transitional Brazil). Comparisons based on any unique set will reflect a certain bias. For that reason the results of the case-study comparison will be integrated subsequently with aggregate analysis of all protest and non-protest countries.

Brazil

The first in a series of Brazilian austerity protests came in April 1983 and grew out of local issues in a working-class community. Following agreement on a letter of intent to the IMF in early 1983, São Paulo unions expressed concern about rumored legal changes that would cap wage increases in public-sector unions. Federal government employees in the state of Rio Grande do Sul struck until the government threatened to break the action with mass layoffs. Cuts in government spending drastically reduced state orders to industry, causing large-scale layoffs of factory workers (Sheahan 1991: 129). Unemployment in São Paulo reached 15 percent before the protests.

The São Paulo barrio of Santo Amaro is home to 1 million people, including 100,000 shantytown residents and 80,000 unemployed. Santo Amaro is a highly organized community and had mobilized previously around issues of housing and transportation. In 1981, squatters invaded a state farm and in March 1983 a militant crowd destroyed 27 buses belonging to a private company that locked out riders to pressure the government for a rate hike. In February, moreover, a 30 percent devaluation had begun to press meager incomes below the subsistence level. Within the community, 20,000 steel workers recently had been laid off and the Telefunken factory had moved to a tax-free zone taking away 6,000 more jobs. Concrete depredations related directly to austerity and unemployment were thus daily concerns of the barrio's 93 neighborhood improvement organizations, the active union movement (especially São Paulo's leftwing CUT), and the political parties ranging from the Brazilian Communist Party to the Workers' Party and the rising Democratic Movement Party.

On April 4, a demonstration was called by the local coalition Committee Fighting Against Unemployment which unified on the motto: "We won't die of hunger and be quiet about it." Two hundred demonstrators gathered in front of a popsicle factory that had recently attracted long lines of applicants for 5 advertised job openings. As the crowd moved to a nearby square to continue the demonstration and speeches, some took oranges from a delivery truck and soon began bombarding the surrounding commercial area. A 30-hour riot was underway that drew 3,500 participants; resulted in 2 deaths, 130 injuries, 560 arrests; and left 200 stores looted, 40 homes invaded, and 125 cars and buses destroyed. On the third day of the riot, organizers of the initial demonstration sought to refocus action on the employment issue and rallied a new march of 3,000 on the state governor's palace. When the governor sent the labor secretary out to meet the peaceful assembly, and palace guards tried to lure them within water-canon range, more mischief followed. An iron fence around the palace was torn down, symbolically perhaps as that led to an appearance by the governor, which offered no satisfaction. Demonstrators smashed buses provided to take them home and the police were finally set on the crowd. Prophetically, the governor who had been dining with his counterpart from Rio, remarked that this was only the beginning. Six months later, rioting broke out in Rio and featured looting of supermarkets and food warehouses.

Three more protests erupted between November 1986 and July 1987 as President Sarney tried to control inflation and wages with the Cruzado Plan which, he hoped, would win labor's support. After more violent demonstrations in Brasilia during November, the major labor confederations decided in December 1986 to call the first general strike in 21 years. The unions felt that they had been caught short in the wage and price freeze and that the government was unable to control rising prices on the growing black market. The effect of a call for wage freezes after a year in which inflation reached 255 percent added to labor's disaffection. From 1980 to 1985 the minimum wage fell 19 percent and the decline accelerated to 38 percent between February 1986 and June 1987. Nevertheless, the general strike produced disappointing results with an estimated 12 percent walkout (Roxborough 1989). Labor and the Sarney government found themselves deadlocked, each unable to press effective action through general strikes or the Cruzado Plan respectively.

In February 1987, Sarney temporarily gained support with the announcement of an indefinite moratorium on interest payments. Yet the minimum wage in 1987 provided little more than one-third of the minimum requirements of family survival while 30 percent of the economically active population earned less than the minimum wage (*Economist Country Profile* 1987). Popular protests once again filled the vacuum in late June when Rio rioters burned buses and even stoned the now unpopular president.

Dominican Republic

Dominican unrest began during Easter 1984 as President Blanco returned home to report on what he thought was a successful round of debt negotiations in Washington. In this second phase of structural adjustment, the conditions agreed upon in anticipation of a new $600 million IMF loan would preserve a concessionary fixed exchange rate with the dollar for oil imports, similarly protect certain imported foods, and avoid reductions in public spending. The bad news, however, was that all other imports would be subject to free-market exchange rates meaning a 200–300 percent increase in many commodity and food prices overnight. Immediately, business groups called for a 24-hour general strike on April 23, and the five labor confederations added their endorsement.

In the Santo Domingo suburb of Capotillo, a citizens' committee hastily planned its own 12-hour strike and attracted the support of three surrounding neighborhoods.

> The main influence in the strike committee [*Comite de Lucha Popular de Barrio Capotillo y Zonas Aledanas*] came from local *communidades de base* of the Catholic Church ... The organizers of the original protest in Capotillo were thus well-prepared. The mass meeting that decided to declare the strike appointed groups to contact the media, collect money and carry out door-to-door canvassing for support. The strike in Capotillo was totally successful, but it rapidly ran out of control of the organizers. (*Latin American Weekly Report, May 11, 1984*)

Street demonstrations by thousands in Santo Domingo and other cities looted stores and food trucks, burned banks, barricaded thoroughfares with burning tires and vehicles, and clashed violently with police. In just three days, 60 were killed, 200–300 injured, and 1,000 arrested.

The riot's ferocity surprised its organizers as much as it did the president. The co-sponsoring *Frente de la Izquierda Dominicana* "had no idea what was happening." The president's Revolutionary Democratic Party and Juan Bosch's opposition Dominican Liberation Party both scrambled for political advantage in belated and scapegoating denunciations of the IMF. Similarly, the *Central General de Trabajadores* (CGT) tried to capture popular mobilization by calling for a general strike that resulted only in the arrest of labor and leftist party leaders. Blanco's government retreated temporarily on price increases, but reimposed them in July after taking the precaution of arresting potential protestors. Austerity protests returned with a Santo Domingo shopkeepers' strike in February 1985 and a series of nine bombings on the eve of a general strike in July 1987 called to oppose "the policies of hunger of the government."

Organized labor's role in the Dominican protest was even more limited than in Brazil. Following the events of April 1984, the five confederations successfully pressed for a 40 percent increase in the minimum wage which, nevertheless, was quickly nullified by inflation.

As economic conditions deteriorated, the number of strikes and labor actions (e.g. strike threats, picket lines, demonstrations) dropped sharply.

> The April riots showed the capacity of popular forces to disrupt the system ... the spontaneity of the movement pointed to the weakness of organized labor. During the April riots, trade unions showed little control over the situation while unknown popular organizations, frequently claiming neighborhood representation, assumed leadership ... labor leadership showed little commitment to workers' causes, choosing instead to respond to their political sponsors ... Since April 1984, Dominican society has witnessed an important change in the forms of popular struggle. (*Espinal 1988: 23–4*)

Indeed, the same writer concludes that the future of Dominican unions depends on their ability to acknowledge and ally with these changes.

> Initially, organized labor backed these protest movements ... But as the assaults have turned more threatening and unmanageable, organized labor has opted for negotiation with business and the government, the Catholic Church playing a mediating role. But whether organized labor will stay at the negotiating table or back the more spontaneous explosions of the urban poor is crucial to the survivability of both the labor movement and the democratic prerogatives in place since 1978. If organized labor disregards popular demonstrations, it runs the risk of losing the limited credibility it has as a representative of workers. (*Espinal 1988: 29–30*)

Mexico

For a large, urbanized, unionized, and heavily indebted country that has been subjected to every form of IMF intervention and structural adjustment, Mexico has witnessed surprisingly few austerity protests. Several explanations account for the anomaly, the most obvious being a tradition of controlling press accounts of events embarrassing to the administration. Yet, despite censorship of news stories about protests, it is also true that the dominant political system has successfully contained the extent of protest that would be expected by economic considerations alone. The pattern is explained by a once powerful corporatist state that embraced peasant confederations, official labor unions, and "popular" organizations, rechanneling potential dissent through ameliorative measures. As the debt crisis worsened after 1982, and the government's eager endorsement of austerity resulted in a 40 percent drop in real wages, the old-regime methods of domination began to falter.

Prior to the crisis, Mexico's rapid economic development had created a highly unequal distribution of wealth which also provided improvement in the standard of living of the urban working and middle classes. Throughout the 1960s and 1970s, real minimum wages rose steadily while prices of basic foods declined. An extensive study conducted in the state of Jalisco in the late 1970s found that "over 50% of the industries surveyed ... paid wages high enough to allow their workers and their families to survive on a single wage" (Escobar Latapí and Roberts 1991: 98). Oil exploitation led to rapid growth from 1978 to 1981, the GDP expanding at an annual rate of 8.5 percent. In the same process, however, the domestic economy became more vulnerable to external influence with mounting debts incurred to develop the petroleum industry, greater dependence on oil-export earnings, and deterioration in the terms of trade for non-oil exports. "Rising interest rates abroad and falling international oil prices, as well as a large fiscal deficit and an overvalued exchange rate, sparked massive capital flight. In turn, the supply of new international loans dwindled, further aggravating the economic and financial crisis which began in early 1982" (Lustig 1990: 1326). Since 1982, the economy has been stagnant with negative economic growth rates in most years.

The real economic growth rate averaged −0.3 percent each year between 1982 and 1987 (Covington 1990) and the gross domestic product fell 14 percent from 1982 to 1989 (Tello 1991). Public spending as a percentage of GDP dropped from 32 percent (1981) to 19 percent (1986), as the "... share of public expenditures allocated to debt servicing rose from about 25 per cent in 1980−1 to about 40 percent in 1983−85" (Lustig 1990: 1334; Covington 1990). Food subsidies were cut by more than 80 percent between 1984 and 1986. "These and other government spending reductions resulted in a 100 per cent increase in the price of bread and tortillas, a 60 per cent increase in the price of gasoline and a 30 per cent increase in the price of natural gas and electricity" (Covington 1990: 6; see also Davis 1990). The food subsidies were changed to a two-price targeted system in which general population subsidies were eliminated and market prices prevailed, while a target population of the poor was provided subsidized food in government stores. With the shift from general to target-population subsidies government expenditures on food subsidies were reduced 43 percent (Lustig 1990).

The results of subsidy cuts became clear in a survey that showed "the majority of families with incomes lower than twice the minimum wage experienced a drop in consumption of all food products except tortillas. In addition, there was a clear substitution away from animal protein" (Lustig 1990: 1336; see also Cordera Campos and González Tiburcio 1991). By 1985, the price of a basic food basket as a percentage of the minimum wage had increased to 50 percent from 30 percent in 1982 (Lustig 1990: 1335). The reduction in government spending also resulted in a general decline in health, as well as a reduction in quality and quantity of public health services. "Government spending on health and social security in 1987 was lower than in 1970" (Cordera Campos and González Tiburcio 1991: 34).

Real wages in the formal sector declined 52 percent from 1980 to 1988 owing to a combination of inflation and wage-restraint policies (Covington 1990: 6; Tello 1991). Unemployment rose from 2.7 million in 1981 to 4.6 million in 1984. The 1980 unemployment rate of 6 percent doubled by 1988 (Lustig 1990: 1334; Tello 1991: 59). Rising unemployment was most acute in the cities where jobs in manufacturing and construction disappeared.

The state sector, both governmental and industrial, was also slashed drastically. By July 1985, 20 percent of the personnel in local and regional governments had been eliminated. The agricultural ministry cut 20,000 workers, the urban development and ecology ministry suffered staff reductions of 20 percent, and the nationalized banking industry was reduced by 40 percent. The number of state-owned enterprises was reduced by 41 percent through privatization and closure. "Altogether, 51,000 full-time jobs were eliminated due to cutbacks" (Gentleman 1987: 51). The state's power to dispense patronage was clearly on the decline.

Despite this dismal economic record, popular protest was episodic and easily controlled by the state until natural disaster and the electoral cycle provided moments of opportunity. Massive demonstrations in Mexico City's central Zocalo plaza began following the September 1985 earthquake and aimed its protest at government inaction on the plight of the homeless. In February and April 1986, thousands gathered to complain of the lack of housing and jobs: "there have been demonstrations and marches in recent weeks in protest of the government's failure to improve the economy or to deal with the growing unemployment. Police have dealt with the protests sternly in an effort to head off an explosion of violence" (*Chicago Tribune*, April 20, 1986). A May Day march 10 days later was crushed by riot police. Yet, the opposition was not to be suppressed and made its point with new strategies of collective action.

Two related initiatives began a remarkable change in Mexican political style. First, a variety of "social movement organizations" took up the cause of the working class and urban poor, particularly the housing question in Mexico City (Davis 1990; Eckstein 1990). In 1983, political groups on the "non-union left" formed a National Front in Defense of Wages Against Austerity and Measures in the Cost of Living (FNDSCAC), which was criticized as too economistic by one wing of the socialist party that established its own National Committee for the Defense of the Popular Economy (CNDEP) – an unfortunate rivalry which the sponsoring groups soon rectified in a merger that produced the National Worker Peasant Assembly (ANOCP). It was the ANOCP "which inaugurated a new tactic of popular protest, the *paro civico*" or, roughly, civic strike (Carr 1986). Emerging simultaneously were the *coordinadoras* "loose national associations [which] coordinate the activities and struggles of hundreds of local and regional centers of resistance to anti-peasant and anti-worker policies ... The *coordinadoras* and the ANOCP have been responsible for organizing a most dramatic and innovative response to the politics of austerity and economic stabilization. In October 1983 and again in June 1984, two civic strikes were held throughout the republic. The tactic consisted of activities ranging from work stoppages and non-attendance at work to meetings, marches. encampments outside public buildings, land occupations, roadblocks, hunger strikes, boycotts of public buildings, and power turn-offs" all of which drew the support of 1.5–2 million people (Carr 1986: 17).

Second, of course, has been the growing political opposition to the PRI organized initially by the coalitional Democratic Current movement and in the National Democratic Front Party of Cuauhtémoc Cárdenas which clearly defeated PRI and now President Salinas in the Federal District in the national elections of July 1988 – and, some suspect, in the nationwide plurality. Whatever the actual result, everyone including Salinas agrees that the old model of PRI hegemony has collapsed under austerity. In the years since 1988, Cárdenas's Democratic Revolution Party (PRD) and the rightist National Action Party (PAN) have mounted increasingly competitive campaigns. Three important gubernatorial victories by PRI have been reversed by the president because of the publicity generated by vigorous protests against official vote fraud. A political system based on patronage and power has little to recommend it when its fund of favors is nearly dry and its power has lost legitimacy. Yet the new administration presses forward on structural adjustment and the hope of debt reduction. After ten years of failed austerity policies, the Mexican political system appears headed towards dissolution of the one-party state.

Venezuela

Finally, the case of Venezuela is of special interest owing to its favored position among Latin American countries as an oil exporter, stable democracy since 1958, and presumed immunity to the pains of austerity. National complacency was shattered in late February and early March 1989 when an extraordinarily violent series of riots swept across Caracas and 16 other cities. In fact, the 1980s had been no less recessionary in Venezuela than in the rest of Latin America. As petroleum prices and foreign exchange earnings dropped, the country's foreign debt rose to $35 billion, one of the continent's highest per capita rates. Caracas and other large cities continued to grow in tandem with declining government revenues resulting in worsening conditions in housing, education, health, and transportation (Fadda 1986). "In 1981, 22.5 % of Venezuelans lived in acute poverty. Just six years later, that number was up to 54 %" (Ellner 1989). President Jaime Lusinchi, in the waning months of his administration, had reversed the nation's compliant stance on the foreign debt by suspending payments on the debt principal and petitioning the IMF for loan restructuring. Campaigning successfully for a second presidential term, Carlos Andres Pérez called the IMF a "bomb that kills people with hunger" and pledged to limit further payments to 20 percent of foreign exchange earnings.

The mood of rebellion was kindled when Pérez assumed office in March 1989 and seemingly betrayed his election promise. Pérez drafted a rigorous austerity plan of his own, presumably as a demonstration of national commitment of economic reform which would persuade the IMF to provide new loans and renegotiated terms of repayment. Labor unions replied by announcing their intention to fight for wage increases promised during the election campaign. Initial protests during the week of February 21 were generally peaceful, although gunfire erupted in a clash between police and students at the Central University of Venezuela in Caracas killing a university employee. On February 26, just three weeks after Pérez's inauguration, the government announced a structural adjustment plan which included elimination of price controls on basic foods and services; increases in the cost of gasoline and transportation; a public hiring freeze; national sales tax, income tax reforms; interest rate increases;

and currency devaluation. In addition to the perceived betrayal of campaign promises, "resentment in Venezuela's slums had been building for some time, particularly in response to illegal hoarding of products by merchants waiting for official authorization to increase prices. Foods such as spaghetti, sardines and corn flour, basic staples in the diet of the poor, disappeared from the shelves for weeks" (Ellner 1989: 8). These precipitating circumstances combined in a sense of injustice animating the crowd and directing its action. As a police inspector observed during the melee, "It's a popular uprising. There are riots everywhere. They are furious" (*Sacramento Bee*, February 28 1989). Although various authorities looked for scapegoats in "subversive elements," foreigners who had "penetrated the slums," and "loafers, thieves, and vagabonds" (Ellner 1989: 7), informed observers concluded with University Rector Luis Fuenmayor that "This is a popular protest by the people. To view it in any other way is to fool oneself" (*Time*, March 13, 1989).

The actual rioting began in the streets of Caracas on the Monday morning February 27 when commuters were greeted with rate hikes of 50–100 percent, well in excess of even the objectionable figure of 30 percent mentioned in the previous day's announcement (trips between downtown and working-class suburbs such as Guarenas and Guatire, for example, jumped from 10 or 12 Bolivars to 16 or 18). Reaction by the crowd was immediate. Shouting slogans against the price increases, several hundred protestors swelled to thousands who overturned and set fire to buses and automobiles, barricaded streets, threw stones, and began looting stores specializing in food, clothing, electronic equipment, furniture, and household appliances (*El Nacional* 1989). The initial phase of the riot was festive until constitutional guarantees were suspended and the army and police moved against the demonstrators. At first, the metropolitan police ignored the looting and, some claimed, even joined it saying that their own salaries had not been paid (*SIC, Centro Gumilla* 1989). Looters observed an ethic emerging in the situation. Unscrupulous merchants were denounced, but fellow pillagers were advised to take just two cans of sardines each and leave some for others. "A pact was reached. Men remained above, behind some barricades. Only women and children could loot. But in an orderly and cultured way. Under the watch and direction of police who yield to the situation" (*El Nacional* 1989: 37). The barrio of San Andres de El Valle held a fiesta with champagne, meat, and imported whiskey, products of the looting. (*SIC, Centro Gumilla* 1989). But the festive mood soon turned deadly as military police moved in with tanks and tear gas, shooting even innocent pedestrians, according to reporters on the scene. Three days of uncontrolled rioting gave way to a week of military occupation and sporadic gun battles in the barrios. In the end, 300 people died, 2,000 were injured, and another 2,000 jailed in the nation's most destructive urban uprising.

In the immediate aftermath of the riots, the government sought to restore confidence with emergency food airlifted to Caracas, price controls on a standard basket of consumer items, and a 32 percent wage increase which, nevertheless, was included as a delayed condition of the original austerity plan. Before long it became clear that the uprising would not deter Pérez from his policy of sacrificing the domestic standard of living for concessionary new loans and repayment terms from the IMF. During the latter years of the Lusinchi administration, organized labor under the leadership of the Venezuelan Confederation of Workers (CTV) had been moving gradually to a position of greater independence from the Democratic Action (AD) Party. The AD's once-guaranteed labor vote has been dwindling in the face of increasing illegal abstentionism (up from 12 to 22 percent in 1989) and opposition challenges, particularly from the *Causa R* independent labor movement (Ellner 1989). In the months leading up to the February riots, the CTV had been engaged in a protracted series of negotiations and new decrees on wage increases which failed to cover lower-income groups. The working-class majority whose standard of living was falling rapidly had little confidence that the CTV was representing their interests. As one labor leader admitted:

> The CTV could not confront and channel the protest because it had lost its capacity to rally the masses ... "I have always proposed that the CTV take the masses to the streets. If they [working people] had done that, the riff-raff would not have taken control. You have to give an outlet to the people's discontents and it is precisely the union movement which should play that role and has not. That is what we are paying the consequences for now." (*SIC, Centro Gumilla* 1989: 135)

The Pérez government and its austerity program never gained legitimacy. Although there was no recurrence of widespread rioting after 1989, resistance flourished in pilferage, sabotage, and clashes with the police (*New York Times* January 31, 1992). In February 1992, a military coup was foiled by forces loyal to President Pérez, yet the jailed colonel who led the revolt was soon named the country's most popular figure in opinion polls. A second coup attempt in November 1992 also failed for lack of any spontaneous support from the masses. Hoping for a sign that the public mood had shifted back in his direction, Pérez appealed for a heavy turnout in the state and municipal elections scheduled just nine days after the second coup attempt. Far from support, two-thirds of the voters abstained despite a mandatory voting law and those who did vote rejected candidates of the president's Democratic Action Party.

6 POLITICAL CONSEQUENCES OF AUSTERITY PROTEST

What have the Latin American popular protests accomplished? This straightforward question has no simple answer. On the one hand, the events described here are still unfolding and it will doubt-less require a long time before we are able to look back on the period that began in the mid-1970s and weigh its long-term signi-ficance. On the other hand, many of the actions embraced by a concise definition of austerity protest are inevitably embedded in deeper political changes making it impossible to separate discrete cause-and-effect relationships. Recognizing these difficulties, which after all characterize any assessment of agency and social change, certain effects can be identified and their interactive relationships indicated. Five types of effects are suggested by the foregoing dis-cussion and may be described in the order of their importance for political transformation.

In the first instance, it is undeniable that a number of protests have had no appreciable effect − at least no effect on ameliorating hardship. In some cases, such as Pinochet's Chile, protests were fiercely repressed, low-income barrios attacked, and suspected dis-sidents jailed and killed. In other cases, palliative measures were offered to quell disturbances, such as the São Paulo state govern-ment's decision to issue food stamps at one point. More important as a general pattern, countries such as Venezuela offered short-term concessions at the peak of popular unrest, only to slowly and strate-gically reintroduce austerity programs months later.

Second, however, a number of insurgencies successful blocked price hikes, at least for a time, and reduced the overall scope of the austerity package. Governments frequently retained the basic structural adjustment program, but attempted to compensate for cost-of-living increases with higher wages (e.g. Jamaica, Ecuador), public works and employment stimulation (Chile, Brazil), and price freezes (Guatemala). Although these concessions were palliative and usually temporary, they lent efficacy to the protest movement and put governments on the defensive. However opportunistically, ruling groups endeavored to disassociate themselves from IMF policies and the growing perception of lender exploitation. A new mood of debtor populism entered the political realm and became a valuable resource that groups struggled among themselves to claim. The sometimes insignificant material benefits stemming from official concessions must be understood in context with more important gains in the legitimacy of the protest cause.

Third, austerity protests contributed directly and indirectly to regime shifts that took place in several ways. In the most direct form, the state simply collapsed in Haiti where the long-awaited fall of the Duvaliers was expedited by a national uprising in several waves that focused on unemployment, food shortages, and corruption. Austerity protests began in Brazil and Argentine during the late phases of military rule and sped the transition to democracy in the early 1980s – in part because the generals wanted no part in the debt mess (MacEwan 1985). More generally, the pains of austerity have become central issues in electoral politics. National leaders such as Alan García in Peru and Michael Manley in Jamaica rode into office on a wave of popular hope that they would reverse the economic free fall – and were ridden out for their failure to do so. In a related vein, riots broke out in Caracas when President Pérez betrayed what was perhaps his most important campaign promise not to cut a deal with the IMF. Structural adjustment is a central and volatile issue in Latin American electoral politics, although it is not always clear who benefits from the manner in which the issue is exploited.

Fourth, regime changes are paralleled, and sometimes produced, by a changing structure of popular mobilization. The venerable pattern of patron–client urban politics is on the decline, not least because states no longer command the financial resources to provide cheap food and transportation, public employment, low-cost housing options, easy access to imported consumer goods, and all the mobility opportunities that go with influence-trading in a patronage system. This shift is beginning to appear in urban ethnographies (see Eckstein 1990; Gay 1990; Selby, Murphy, and Lorenzen 1990; Stokes 1991). Nowhere is the change more apparent than in Mexico where one-party rule suffered major challenges in the 1980s, both at the polls and in the realm of organizational control. In Mexico and Argentina, official unions are losing their following to unemployment, the inability to deliver benefits, and the democratic appeal of rival independents (Roxborough 1989). Similar disaffection plagues the traditional political parties, such as Mexico's PRI, and even Brazil's PMDB coalition that briefly held sway over the democratic transition. In the place of waning formal institutions a number of "new social movements" (Eckstein 1988) have captured the imagination of women, church-affiliated action groups, neighborhood groups, and independent labor. There is evidence, including the foregoing case studies, to support our claim in chapter 2 that a new kind of civil society is emerging in Latin American cities – a set of groups relatively independent from the state and formal economy that articulate the aspirations and culturally defined rights of the poor majority. It is easy to romanticize these developments and entertain wishful trends. In Mexico, for example, the gains of the 1988 "democratic revolution" were not repeated in 1991 national elections and neo-liberal policy is moving forward with a US free-trade agreement. Mindful of the contradictions, we nevertheless propose that the struggle over development policy increasingly will engage the forces of civil society and the liberal state – a state, that is, increasingly anxious to abandon its developmental and welfare responsibilities despite the claims of citizens. Ironically, the protest years have brought less of the feared "political instability" than invigorated democratic movements – a fearsome prospect for patronage politics.

Finally, the debt crisis in all of its antecedants and complexity has introduced a national political transformation in which global policy issues increasingly intrude on the state in Latin America. The consequences of this intrusion move in two directions. On one hand, as grudgingly implemented structural adjustment programs demonstrate, states have sacrificed political sovereignty to foreign banks, agencies, and governments in the interests of economic assistance. No doubt the pattern has historical precedent, but the scale has never been as great. On the other hand, states have been subject to forceful and contradictory pressures from below. The demands of their own urban poor have never been so outraged and violent. Domestic decline in the interests of foreign debt servicing offers the basis for populist appeals by varied political factions. States are forced to manage the contradiction. International agencies, moreover, are acutely aware of the new demands of the poor (whom the agencies have prided themselves on serving) and are highly sensitive to charges of "loan pushing" or the implications of "IMF riots." The Latin American urban poor, in short, have been heard at the fund, the bank, and the state house. Since the peak of austerity protests in the mid-1980s, debt relief, albeit conditional on domestic reform, has become the objective of a shifting policy or "aid regime" (Wood 1986). The two events are neither accidental nor directly related. Yet it is certainly true that the actions of the urban poor (even if understood as threatening "political instability") constitute one side of a three-handed game in which the state and international agencies also influence who will bear the costs of reform.

7   CONCLUSION

Fundamentally, austerity protests reflect in one dramatic form the changing conditions of communities, classes, and states within the global political economy. As Charles Tilly (1975: 392) remarked about earlier disturbances in Europe, "[I]n the last analysis, the food riot was epiphenomenal. Below the surface raged a long struggle by builders of states ... that struggle, rather than the food riot is the real concern of this essay." Austerity protests provide a strategic vantage on crucial changes over the last 15 years in relations between communities, social classes, and the state. At one level, the debt crisis pits rebellious slum dwellers and working classes against international financiers and their allies in the domestic economy (e.g. multinational corporate managers and exporters). The state, caught between powerful forces at home and abroad, is obliged to concede a decisive role in social policy to its international patrons in exchange for sustaining loans. In a deeper sense, however, states are actors with interests and conflicts of their own – interests in maintaining legitimacy and power while managing conflicts in their own ranks. The state incorporates the debt crisis in a special way, absorbing the tensions of its political environment and attempting to mediate them with declining material and symbolic resources.

The social crisis plays itself out differently in each country as a result of popular mobilization and the distinctive features of states. Because they enjoy less tolerance from their creditors and constituents, small democratic states are most vulnerable to the crisis, particularly if they defy interventionist policies. As Jamaican prime minister in the 1970s, Michael Manley insisted that the poor would not suffer in the interests of IMF-prescribed and regressive reforms, but it was Manley's government that succumbed to a credit squeeze and exploitation of economic hardship by the opposition party. It was a chastened Manley who returned to power in 1989. In the Dominican Republic, unrelenting adjustment programs have split the ranks of labor and the Dominican Revolutionary Party. Costa Rica is the only small and democratic state to receive favorable treatment on conditionality and new loans, perhaps because it provides the United States with a rare and stable ally in the troubled Central American region.

Large authoritarian and corporatist states have been more successful at implementing austerity programs. Mexico and the Southern
Cone states under military rule combined government acceptance
of structural adjustment with large sums owed abroad, circumstances that generated more concessions from international agencies.
Mexico has usually been the first country offered new repayment
arrangements, whether they were renegotiated interest rates initially
or debt relief more recently. With the transition to democracy,
however, Argentina and Brazil found themselves in a position closer
to Venezuela, needing to moderate austerity measures in the interests
of domestic peace (cf. Frieden 1991). Nations vary in the skill with
which they have negotiated with the IMF for loan concessions. Brazil
has maintained a good deal of policy autonomy while withholding
debt-service payments, but Peru got nowhere with this approach
and Venezuela has met with only modest success in trying to convince the IMF that substantial debt relief is necessary to avoid new
riots. There is no ready formula for predicting the outcome of these
negotiations which determine how heavy a burden debtor nations
will be required to bear. But these are the terms in which the negotiations are carried out; country-by-country political bargaining
rather than economic nationalism or any "debtor's cartel."

Latin American states will continue to face a dangerous dilemma.
On one hand, states are palpably threatened by popular mobilizations that demand an end to arrested development and regressive
reforms. Governments have been deposed and seriously weakened by
popular insurgencies. Official opposition to the IMF in some form
is almost a requirement for legitimacy. Governments and opposition groups have used the crisis for domestic political gain, including
by blaming the IMF for their own mistakes. On the other hand, the
keys to recovery, as everyone recognizes, include debt relief, new
loans and investment, and favorable trade arrangements. Governments have to take a middle course, as the once-populist regimes
of Peru, Argentina, Jamaica, and other countries have discovered.

From the standpoint of popular movements, the debt crisis has
generated an unprecedented wave of protest the result of which, ironically, is not instability but new pressures for democracy. In Latin
America the protest has been virulent precisely because governments
had borrowed to support a developmental model that guaranteed
capitalist expansion with welfare-state benefits. The moral economy
of the urban poor understood that political loyalty was proffered in
exchange for cheap food, transportation, self-built housing plots,
and jobs. As these began to disappear, countries that combined
economic hardship, excess urbanization, austerity pressure, and a

capacity to mobilize in labor and community groups were the most likely to rebel. Protest was expressed according to the political contours of particular societies, in street riots, demonstrations, and general strikes, but these forms also merged and engaged the passions of the urban poor, labor, and even elements of the middle class. In a variety of ways, the rebellion produced small successes if not a reversal of economic depredations. The protestors won some concessions, forced the issue into national and international policy debates, and created a general climate demanding more democratic participation in the reform process.

The Latin American social crisis is a watershed change in which the "bureaucratic-authoritarian" state and developmentalist model are being replaced by bourgeois democratic political systems with fewer welfare-state protections. The change poses many an irony and unpredictable outcome. Whether the reorganized democracies prove to be more than a constitutional framework for competitive internationalized capitalism, whether they will refashion the moral economy of development in a new vision of public responsibility and social welfare – all these depend on how the forces analyzed here, particularly the popular movements, fare in the continuing struggle.

5

Economic Adjustment and Democratization in Africa

Stephen P. Riley and Trevor W. Parfitt

1 INTRODUCTION

It has become commonplace to suggest that sub-Saharan Africa (SSA) is currently experiencing a second wind of change (e.g. *The Independent on Sunday*, June 2, 1991; Lancaster 1991; Riley 1992a). Whereas Macmillan's wind of change entailed the replacement of colonial administrations by indigenous governments, the current change of political weather involves either displacing or clipping the authoritarian wings of African regimes, many of which have held power continuously since the colonial withdrawal. Thus, Zambia's President Kaunda and Côte d'Ivoire's President Houphouet-Boigny, both head of their respective nations' one-party administrations since independence, have faced increasing pressure to concede democratic reforms in recent years. Both have been forced to accept the principle of multi-party elections in the face of growing opposition to their untrammeled rule. As we shall see, in Houphouet-Boigny's case he survived a competitive multiparty election in 1990 against a divided opposition with a low turn-out and amidst many allegations of electoral fraud. In the case of Zambia, the multiparty elections of October 1991 led to the overwhelming defeat of Kaunda and his ruling party (Mills 1992; Widner 1991). Kenya, which has been effectively subject to continuous one party rule by Kenya African National Union (KANU) since its independence, was also the site of growing agitation for free multiparty elections. In December 1991, Daniel arap Moi's government conceded. It agreed to revise the Kenyan constitution to allow for political pluralism. Multiparty elections took place in 1992, although the opposition was divided. Similar political trajectories are developing in Tanzania and Ghana, with political pluralism emerging and competitive presidential elections scheduled. In Ghana, Jerry Rawlings was elected to the presidency in November 1992 with 58 percent of the vote. He retains the central role he has played in Ghanaian politics since the early 1980s. Other states that have had to concede democratic freedoms include Mali, Benin, Togo, and Gabon. Even the most uncompromising dictatorships, such as those of Mobutu in Zaire and Banda in Malawi, are being forced to consider reforms that would previously have been inconceivable. Those rulers who wish to take an intransigent stance are being encouraged to reconsider their position by such examples as the overthrow of Traore in Mali and Mengistu in Ethiopia. The removal of these "strongmen," who refused to compromise with the growing democratic opposition to their rule, has shown that the apparently impregnable dictatorships that dominated many African states have suddenly become quite vulnerable. The upsurge of popular pressure for political reform has become so widespread that *Africa Confidential* can quite accurately state that "Not a single country in Africa in now untouched by the spirit of change which has made itself felt since 1989–90" (April 5, 1991).

It might be asked how this impetus for political change articulates with the process of economic change that has been taking place throughout SSA during the 1980s, which is often referred to as "structural adjustment." It might be argued that the structural adjustment programs (SAPs) that have constituted the conditionality for most western aid are complementary to the political reforms that the African populace are campaigning for. The SAPs are designed to bring overextended, inefficient, and corrupt state mechanisms under control by forcing them to reduce their wasteful interventions into the economy and to accept market discipline. This will to impose economic control on the state is mirrored by the desire of the African people to make their states politically accountable. Certainly, this is the view of the majority of western donors, including Britain's minister for overseas development, Lynda Chalker. She has recently argued that aid conditionality should be premised on a recipient's observance of human rights and principles of democratic accountability, as well as on the traditional concerns of SAPs: "Sound economic and social policies that allow free reign to market forces" (*The Sunday Times*, August 18, 1991; see also Chalker 1991; Riley 1992b). In other words, she sees the concerns of the African people to achieve democracy as being quite compatible with the concern of western donor states to ensure that African governments observe market principles.

This view as to the complementarity of democracy and the market can be traced back to liberal thinking. It is premised on the contention that a wide distribution of economic power brought about by market competition will be mirrored by a wide distribution of political power through the adoption of democratic principles. It is on the basis of this view that many of the largest aid donors, including the World Bank and the EC, seem to be moving towards a conditionality package designed to impose political and economic liberalism on Africa through enforcing political and market reforms (Nelson and Eglington 1992).

Leftists would argue that this liberal line of thought is intrinsically flawed. The natural action of the market brings about concentrations of economic power. These powerful economic groupings may then exert influence in the political arena to protect their own interests at the expense of the rest of the populace. This process will enhance tendencies towards differentiation in society and undermine the state's accountability to the weaker groups, whilst increasing the influence that powerful groups may have in governing circles. Such an analysis clearly undermines the liberal view as to the complementarity of democracy and the market. This chapter will examine the interconnections between structural adjustment programs and the movement towards democratization with a view to establishing how far market reform is likely to enhance or obstruct democratic progress.

2   THE POLITICS OF ADJUSTMENT

Structural adjustment emerged as the primary Western response to the African debt crisis. Sub-Saharan Africa's external debts climbed from under $6 billion in 1970 to over $80 billion by the mid-1980s, reaching more than $112 billion by 1989 (World Bank 1990). This growing debt was associated with a wide-ranging economic crisis, characterized by such factors as chronic balance-of-payments deficits, associated foreign-exchange shortages, hyperinflation, declining production, and fiscal imbalances. The Bretton Woods institutions

(BWIs), particularly the World Bank in the Berg Report (see World Bank 1981a) traced this crisis to such factors as overvaluation of the exchange rate, which had a depressant effect on domestic production and exports, whilst encouraging import growth; excessive state intervention, which helped to generate inflation and led to inefficient use of resources due to overextension of the public sector; and protectionism, which featherbedded inefficient industries.

Consequently, the BWIs designed structural adjustment to address these problems. Thus, most SAPs involve a devaluation with a view to correction of the balance of payments, tight fiscal policy in order to reduce the government deficit and bring inflation under control, and liberalization of the economy to enable the market to allocate resources efficiently. On the basis of a survey of 27 African states that mounted a total of 41 IMF programs during 1980–4, the World Bank observes that 85 percent of the programs limited government borrowing and expenditure; almost 90 percent of them entailed reduction of the government deficit as a proportion of the GDP; and sixteen of them (or over half of the programs outside the CFA (Communité Français Africaine) area) entailed changes of the exchange rate (World Bank and UNDP 1989). The question as to how far these reforms have resulted in the desired effects of stimulating domestic production and creating market conditions conducive to growth is a vexed issue that has been the subject of much debate.

However, even more salient to the concerns of this chapter is the question of structural adjustment's socio-political effects. It may be noted that efforts to reduce the fiscal deficits of debtor states often involve such measures as wage freezes, mass redundancies of government employees, tax increases, reduction or elimination of politically sensitive subsidies (often food subsidies), and reduction of spending in the social sector. Devaluation leads to price increases for imports, which can adversely affect industries or agricultural concerns that are import dependent, as well as putting pressure on those sections of the populace who may be dependent on food imports. A variety of analysts have noted that these tendencies exert a significant downward pressure on the living standards of significant social groups.

Organizations such as UNICEF and UNESCO have tended to focus on the effect of retrenchment in the social sector. UNICEF notes that during the 1980s "the proportion of government expenditure devoted to health has fallen in most countries of sub-Saharan Africa" (Unicef 1989a), whilst a UNESCO report points out that "government expenditure per primary school pupil is falling in 21 out of the 23 countries surveyed" (World Bank 1990) (18 of this sample were in sub-Saharan Africa and government expenditure was falling in 13 of them). UNICEF comments on these developments as follows:

> UNICEF's staff know from first-hand experience that in most countries the real cost of such cuts is being paid, disproportionately, by the poor and by their children. And since 1984, we have been concerned to draw world attention to the social consequences of adjustment policies and to warn that the worst was yet to come. (*Unicef 1989b*)

These observations drew a sympathetic response from the Managing Director of the IMF, Michel Camdessus, who commented that; "Too often in recent years it is the poorest segments of the population that have carried the heaviest burden of economic adjustment" (UNICEF 1989b) The Bank also has recognized that "dealing with shocks and excessive public debt often involves cuts in public spending, which may hurt the poor directly" (World Bank 1990). Its figures indicate that real per capita social spending in SSA has fallen 26 percent between 1980–5 (see table 5.1).

The Bank has attempted to respond to some of these criticisms by developing a limited number of social programs designed to counteract these adverse tendencies. Such programs have been initiated for Madagascar and Ghana in SSA, the best known of them being Ghana's Program of Action to Mitigate the Social Costs of Adjustment (PAMSCAD) adopted by the government in 1987. The Bank describes it as involving "twenty-three antipoverty interventions that cover public works, credit, training, low-cost water, health, drugs, nutrition, and shelter, all with a strong orientation toward community involvement and the participation of indigenous NGOs [Non-governmental Organizations]. (World Bank 1990). Although PAMSCAD may be a laudable attempt to address some of the social problems that have been exacerbated by structural adjustment, it

Table 5.1   Fiscal contraction and social spending in sub-Saharan Africa[a]

Real expenditure per capita	1980	1985	Change (%)
Total non-interest spending	96	64	−33
Social spending	85	63	−26
Social spending as a percentage of total non-interest spending	23	26	13

Note: [a] 1978 = 100%

Source: World Bank 1990: 116

has been criticized by observers such as Loxley and Green because it "was tacked onto the end of the body of the reform package as a reluctant afterthought, under pressure from UNICEF and concerned bilateral donors." As Loxley notes, "such considerations were not, and generally, still are not, built directly into adjustment programmes" (see Loxley 1990: 21; and Green 1991). In the event, PAMSCAD's efficacy has been severely limited by delays brought about by poor coordination between the various donors and indigenous organizations involved in the program (World Bank 1990).

It seems all too possible that the BWIs response to the question of poverty represents too little too late. This view becomes even more plausible if one considers how the austerity policies associated with structural adjustment programs have fed into the political climates of various of the states undergoing adjustment. There is considerable evidence to suggest that the declining standards of living that structural adjustment programs tend to impose on certain sections of the population can lead to political unrest and instability. Such unrest tends not to originate with those who were actually poor in the first instance (that is, before structural adjustment program policies began to bite), but, rather, with those who have been deprived of their stake in society by some aspect of an austerity program that has moved them towards or below the poverty line. Thus, workers and state employees who have been laid off, or whose real wages have declined due to wage restraints combined with price rises, seem particularly prone to becoming politically active in opposition to the policies that they see as disadvantaging them. One may cite a number of examples to illustrate this tendency.

3   AUSTERITY PROTESTS AND POLITICAL REFORM

The overall effect of the policies is often to destabilize the recipient states as key groups in the populace rebel against the combination of rising prices and declining wages and public services. As other chapters in this collection show, this has occurred across the world and not just in sub-Saharan Africa. In North Africa, for example, anti-IMF riots became common in the early 1980s. In Sudan, they took place when the bread subsidy was abolished, and in Tunisia and Morocco in the wake of IMF programs which involved the removal of food subsidies (Seddon 1984). In sub-Saharan Africa, similar protests have emerged as economic decline has taken hold and adjustment measures have been implemented. These austerity protests have pre-dated the more recent democratization pressures.

In Ghana, the reaction of the urban workers was at first generally very hostile to the structural adjustment program implemented from the early 1980s under the quasi-military regime of Jerry Rawlings. 25,000 labour redundancies were announced in 1984–5, and were followed by a further 32,000 layoffs in 1985–6. By the start of 1986 there was widespread dissatisfaction amongst the well-organized Ghanaian trade-union movement.

One incident illustrates this. Following the arrest of several trade union leaders who had voiced their opposition to the redundancies, workers gathered to protest outside the Hall of the Trade Unions (the headquarters of the Trade Union Congress) in Accra. They were faced by an estimated 1,000 policemen who – with armored cars – sought to control the protest (*Africa Events*, February 1986; Parfitt and Riley 1989). Not surprisingly given the commitment of the Rawlings regime to economic reform, the protests of the urban workers had little effect.

Elsewhere, the progressive policies of some states have been undermined. Both the Frelimo government in Mozambique and Roberts Mugabe's regime in Zimbabwe attempted to deliver educational and health services to the rural areas in the early 1980s. They sought to counteract the patterns of urban bias in such provision as had been provided by the colonial administrations. The cut-backs in Zimbabwe, for example, arising from the 1982 agreement with the IMF have had a markedly adverse effect upon child health. There was a real deterioration in child nourishment in 1982–4 brought about by the stabilization measures of those years (Davies and Saunders 1987). Broader surveys have also confirmed a deterioration in nutritional intake with a linked increase in infant mortality (Cornia, Jolly and Stewart 1987).

Such a deterioration in the quality of life has led to many austerity protests across Africa. A lengthy strike by teachers, and demonstrations by schoolchildren and students, took place in Liberia in the aftermath of the decision of Samuel Doe's government in December 1985 to cut public sector salaries by 25 percent. Doe's government was responding to increasing pressure from its external creditors, particularly the US government. In Madagascar in 1985 a protest movement against the Ratsiraka government emerged as a result of externally infuenced policy changes which included creating a free market in rice. Great hardship was in evidence in urban areas. There were reports in 1986 that poor families were selling their children in local markets as they were unable to feed them. During 1987 there was famine in the south of the country, rioting in the country's ports, attacks on Asian traders, and student strikes (*The Africa Review*,

1988). Widespread urban protests in Madagascar's main cities continued during the late 1980s and early 1990s. In Niger in the mid-1980s the bureaucratic and urban worker groups affected by austerity protested, despite increased external credit from the BWI's which was, it was claimed, being used to improve economic efficiency and develop the state's resources. One of Niger's civil servants provided a simple translation of this: it meant "more unemployment" (*The Africa Review*, 1987).

Freetown, the capital of Sierra Leone, was also the site of a series of organized, as well as "anarchic," protests concerning austerity in the period since 1978, when the national currency was delinked from sterling and a precipitous economic decline took place accompanied by a series of stabilization programs. Popular discontent at rising prices and shortages of basic commodities was fueled by the public excesses involved in Sierra Leone hosting the annual conference of the Organization of African Unity (OAU) in July 1980. On walls in the poorer parts of Freetown, a slogan was written: "OAU for you, IOU for we" (Riley 1984: 213). The escalating prices of the food staples, like rice and palm oil, for Freetown's urban poor contrasted sharply with the $200 million cost involved in hosting the OAU for three days. A newly constructed presidential village and conference center, new street lighting on its approach roads, and a fleet of new government Mercedes cars were all easily observed symbols of conspicuous consumption. As Green has pointed out, quoting a Ugandan commentator, the "wingless vultures in Mercedes" in many African states are one of the few social groups which have been left unscathed by the economic crisis (Green 1989).

In Nigeria and Sierra Leone there were general strikes in 1981 as a result of wage freezes and import curbs. In both states, public transport was brought to a halt, power cuts took place, and schools closed.

Subsequent strikes took place in Nigeria in 1982 and 1983, although the expulsion of approximately 2 million migrant workers in January and February 1983 "no doubt went some way to sublimate Nigerian workers' discontent" (Van Hear 1988: 72). In Freetown a series of more spontaneous protests continued to take place. These involved particularly schoolchildren, students, and the young unemployed who closed off roads in the capital with barricades and looted shops, offices, and vehicles (Riley 1984). Such protests were often quickly suppressed by the politically loyal paramilitary police, the Internal Security Unit (ISU).

Nigeria's structural adjustment program, which was introduced in July 1986, met with consistent opposition from the Nigerian Labour

Congress (NLC). The Babangida administration encountered particular difficulties in April 1988 when the World Bank and the IMF put on pressure for the abolition of Nigeria's fuel subsidy in exchange for a renewed structural adjustment program. The resultant 6 percent rise in the price of petrol precipitated a major riot in Jos between the police on the one hand and students, workers, and schoolchildren on the other. This resulted in 12 deaths and the burning of several government buildings In the wake of the riot, protests spread across the country with civil servants, hospital workers, tanker drivers, and others coming out on strike in defiance of a ban on industrial action.

One of the most interesting aspects of this particular outburst is that such violent protests were sparked by such a small price rise. However, it seems clear that this was in fact the culmination of growing discontentment with the rigors of Nigeria's structural adjustment program. Devaluation of the naira substantially raised the price of imported inputs and spare parts for Nigerian industry, resulting in numerous closures and cut-backs. In Kano, 19 companies were forced to close between May and October in 1987, whilst 60 percent of industries were operating at 20 percent and 25 percent of capacity. This had severe results for the living standards of workers who were either laid off, or put on short time. The results of austerity prompted the former head of state, General Obasanjo, to contend that the structural adjustment program had "drastically reduced the living standard of all productive workers except speculators and commission agents" (quotation from *Africa Confidential*, January 8, 1988; see also *Africa Confidential*, May 27, 1988). It has been argued that public discontentment with austerity was one of the factors that fed into the attempted coup of April 1991 (*Financial Times*, April 23, 1991).

In addition to this example, one might point to austerity-related unrest and protest in Sierra Leone, Niger, and Mozambique. Sierra Leone's IMF-backed program of 1986 entailed flotation of the leone, which brought about a collapse in its value from Le 5.02 to the US dollar on June 1, 1986 to Le 35.5 against the dollar on January 1, 1987. This, together with the removal of price subsidies, led to rampant inflation estimated at some 300 percent. Hoogvelt pointed out that in January 1987, the minimum required to feed a family of five for one day was Le 50, whilst the highest paid Sierra Leoneans were paid Le 1000 per month (Hoogvelt 1987). This raised considerable discontentment with the Momoh regime. Amongst the first signs of this were major student demonstrations in February 1987, which were prompted by dissatisfaction with the inadequacy of their food allowances in the wake of the structural adjustment program (*West Africa*, February 2, 1987). This popular discontent-ment was one of the factors underlying the attempted coup of March 1987 (*West Africa*, April 13, 1987). In Mozambique a four-year IMF/World Bank program involving devaluation, state retrenchment, and privatization prompted widespread factory strikes and protests at rent rises during 1990–1 (*Africa Analysis*, August 8, 1991). Niger has seen riots during this period prompted by a BWI program that has reduced the opportunities of Nigerian graduates to obtain skilled work (*Economist Intelligence Unit* 1990, Country Report; Togo, Benin, Niger, Burkina Faso, 1).

Even Ghana, which the IMF and the Bank were once wont to extoll as a success story for adjustment, has encountered popular resistance to the social privations resulting from its structural adjust-ment program. Devaluation of the cedi, combined with the removal of subsidies on health, education, and other social services caused the government to clash with the Trades Union Congress (TUC) (*Africa Confidential*, September 2, 1987).

Perhaps even more significantly, austerity also depressed living standards for the lower ranks of the armed forces, thus alienating what had traditionally been a bastion of support for the Rawlings regime. Tensions within the armed forces came to a head with a serious attempted coup in September 1989 led by one Major Quashigah, previously a strong Rawlings loyalist. He had retained the loyality of lower-rank soldiers who believed that he was "the only officer who had kept faith with them and cared for their welfare" (*Africa Confidential*, October 20, 1989: 3). Although the coup was thwarted, tensions were high in Ghana, not least because the minimum wage remained pegged at Cedi 216 as late as January 1991, whilst the daily expenditure for a family of four was estimated at over eight times that amount (*West Africa*, January 13, 1991: 3148). It may be noted that this remained a fundamental difficulty for most Ghanaians irrespective of PAMSCAD.

Interestingly, opposition to the regime has recently taken the form of popular agitation for the restoration of a multi-party democracy. In August 1990, the Movement for Freedom and Justice (MFJ) was founded, to work for this aim. The MFJ's support comes from the working and middle classes and a variety of other groups, including the TUC, New Democratic Movement, Kwame Nkrumah Revolu-tionary Guards, Ghana Bar Association, and the Catholic Bishop's Conference. Western donors, including the United States, have backed these demands for democracy, making their aid to the Rawlings regime conditional on political reform (*Africa Confidential*, April 19, 1991). Indeed, such pressure was been a major factor in forcing Rawlings to concede. Presidential and parliamentary elections were held in Ghana in 1992. This is an ironic situation, given that many of the elements of the MFJ initially based their opposition to Rawlings on their dislike of the austerity policies that were forced on Ghana in the form of aid conditionality. Apparently, Rawlings expressed concern that a new democratic government would abandon the policies of fiscal rectitude that have produced a succession of budget surpluses between 1986–9 (*West Africa*, January 13, 1991). Rawlings subsequently announced that he would be standing in the presidential elections – and won in November 1992.

These examples illustrate some of the complexitites that characterize the interrelationship of economic and political reform. The market adjustment deemed necessary to African economic health by the BWIs tends to lower living standards for significant sectors of the urban populace. These groups often respond to such developments by becoming politically active in opposition to the governments implementing BWI programs.

In the Ghanaian instance such opposition has taken the form of agitation for democratic reform. A similar course of events can be traced in Benin, where the Kerekou regime was replaced by a multiparty polity in 1990 in the wake of widespread strikes and demonstrations by teachers, students, and civil servants. These protests were initially prompted by economic dissatisfaction, notably over the failure of the Kerekou regime to pay substantial salary arrears. Whilst the new government promised to satisfy the basic demand for payment of arrears, it also agreed a new structural adjustment program with the BWIs that involved state retrenchment of employees and the abolition of price controls, both measures which have prompted opposition in other African states (*Economist Intelligence Unit*, Country Report, Togo, Benin, Niger, Burkina Faso, 1; 1990 and 2; 1990; see also Allen 1992). Clearly, this entails risking a further round of protests against the new regime. The Benin example can be supplemented by many similar past cases across the continent. Even under the more authoritarian forms of rule, a series of economically motivated protests developed in the 1980s. As the liberal academics Bratton and van de Walle have pointed out, "African populations have not been passive in the face of declining living standards and government malfeasance" and describe strikes, demonstrations, marches, and boycotts by principally professional, urban-based groups (Bratton and van de Walle 1991: 21; see also Bratton and de Walle 1992). But not all these forms of economic resistance took on a liberal political hue, and many protests had non-economic objectives as well. To the extent that adjustment underlies the political discontentment that has prompted the current moves towards multi-partyism in sub-Saharan Africa, there is no simple or direct complementarity between market reforms and democratic reform. Rather, they are more likely to prove contradictory.

In order to test this proposition, we shall proceed to case studies of Zambia, Côte d'Ivoire and Zaire. These cases have been selected due to their geographical diversity, their differential colonial heritage, and the variant (as well as serious) nature of the disturbances that have destabilized what seemed to be three of the stablest regimes in sub-Saharan Africa. The cases will examine how the state responded to the initial problem of debt with a view to identifying policy triggers that may have precipitated popular action. We will then identify the social origins of those involved in protests in order to examine why they became politically active. This will provide us with an insight into the aims of these newly active forces, and, importantly, it will enable us to assess the balance between their instrumental desires for satisfaction of their immediate economic needs and any more radical aspirations that they may express for a transformation of the political system.

The variant responses of the above states to the campaigns for democracy will be examined with a view to providing a prognosis as to whether or not the forces fighting for reform have made, or are likely to achieve, any substantive gains.

4   ZAMBIA: DEMOCRACY – THEN ADJUSTMENT?

During the 1980s, in Zambia there was continuing conflict over externally imposed austerity measures and persistent urban-based popular protest against growing hardship. Eventually the conflict and protest had an impact upon political life, including the fate of the dominant aging nationalist leader, Kenneth Kauda, and his ruling one-party United National Independence Party (UNIP) government. Kaunda's government vacillated over the implementation of economic adjustment while responding to protests and seeking to maintain its political hegemony. However, as a consequence of external pressures for political liberalization, and domestic opposition, Kaunda's government gradually lost control of the political situation as the 1980s progressed. In September 1990, after prolonged pro-democracy agitation and a precipitous decline in his own personal popularity, Kaunda finally conceded that greater political choice was needed. He announced that political pluralism would be allowed and the one-party constitution was revised to allow for competitive multiparty politics. Perhaps overconfidently, he expected to hang on to power by revitalizing the ruling party, using the state's patronage powers and hoping for a divided opposition. After initially refusing to accept external election observers from bodies such as the Commonwealth and the US National Democratic Institute for International Affairs (NDI), Kaunda changed his mind in the expectation that these observers would witness and legitimate a popular reaffirmation of his continued right to rule Zambia (Bratton, Bjornlund, and Gibson 1992).

The multiparty election of October 1991 proved otherwise. Kaunda, who had been president since 1964, received only 25 percent of the vote with the remainder going to Frederick Chiluba, the presidential candidate of the opposition Movement for Multi-Party Democracy (MMD). The socially diverse opposition represented in the MMD won an even more resounding victory in the legislative elections, receiving more than 80 percent of the votes and 125 out of 150 parliamentary seats (Mills 1992; Wiseman 1992). In some ways the MMD's majority was too large in that the ruling UNIP was almost completely replaced. Chiluba's party dominated political life. Seven other minority parties gained little support, and only in Kaunda's home area, the Eastern Province, did UNIP retain significant numbers of votes.

Chiluba took office in November 1991 after a graceful transfer of power (a somewhat rare occurrence in Africa) with significant international and domestic support. Despite this, his government soon ran into difficulties. He was faced with the contradictions mentioned earlier in this chapter: the new expectations of donors that African governments should simultaneously pursue both economic adjustment and political reform. The clear complementarity between these expectations was not so evident in the Zambian case after the 1991 elections.

Kaunda's government had vacillated over – and then delayed – the economic adjustment that Zambia's creditors expected and thought necessary to secure further credit and debt relief. Thus there were many competing expectations of Chiluba. The external donor view was that he would (and should) quickly implement the necessary structural adjustment measures. His domestic constituencies thought otherwise – and hoped for the general improvement in the quality of life that the MMD promised. It was perhaps naive to expect that newly enfranchised citizens voting in the first multiparty election for many years would vote for further austerity for themselves. The last election in Zambia in which there had been opposition candidates was back in 1968 in much easier economic circumstances. Amongst the donors, there was little sustained thinking as well as an inconsistency in approach regarding the implications of greater pluralism in Zambia. As we shall see, some states, such as Zaire, were treated relatively leniently by creditors; others, such as Zambia, fared less well.

Nevertheless, in response to external pressures and despite the warnings of the past, Chiluba did institute a series of economic adjustment measures which provoked 40 strikes in six months. Subsidies were reduced, with the subsidy for the food staple, maize meal, being withdrawn in January 1992. The national currency was devalued by 30 percent, thus adding fears of increased inflation which was already over 80 percent in 1991. The first post-election budget speech also emphasized the private sector and announced the sale of parastatals. Complaints about these policies were linked to a series of related criticisms of Chiluba's political style and appointments. A heated controversy concerned Chiluba's acceptance of an expensive luxury car from a South African businessman (*The Guardian*, May 4, 1992; Kibble 1992). There are thus doubts over the continued stability and purpose of the new MMD government, although the events of 1991 "reversed a trend of almost two decades in which power had become increasingly unrepresentative and coercive" (Baylies and Szeftel 1992: 90). In view of this, what were the social and economic forces behind the undermining and fall of Kaunda's government and how did it fail to maintain its political hegemony?

From the early 1970s onwards, the Zambian government was beset by increasingly severe economic difficulties. Many of Zambia's 8.5 million people suffered as a consequence of the decline in world prices for copper, one of Zambia's major exports. This dependence upon copper exacerbated the deteriorating terms of trade between Zambia's principal export and its imports – many of which were provided by a hostile South Africa. Zambia inherited a small external debt on independence – but this rose significantly afterwards. The state's external debt grew very substantially in the 1980s. The 1980 total external debt stock of $3.26 billion rose to $7.22 billion by 1990, with corresponding rises in the most significant indicators – such as the debt-service ratio (World Bank 1991c). By 1986 the annual interest payment on Zambia's external debt represented 40 percent of the government's budget, compared to 15 percent in 1980. Although Zambia's gross national product (GNP) subsequently fell substantially in 1990, the expected debt-service payment was still crippling. The debt-service ratio, when the debt was paid in the 1980s, was up to 100 percent of export earnings. External aid, to offset increasing debt repayments, was fairly meager, averaging

$315 million a year in the mid-1980s (Clark and Allison 1989). A number of debt repayments were also defaulted on from the mid-1980s onwards – decreasing the government's credibility in the eyes of the BWIs. As Zambia's external debt grew and negative current-account balances persisted, the economy was subject to a series of externally imposed stabilization and adjustment programs.

Seven of these programs were tried during the period 1975–86. All failed to meet the agreed "performance criteria." The measures that the BWIs sought to impose were familiar ones, including a reduction in subsidies and price increases, which fueled inflation and hardship. Popular responses were strong. In December 1986, for example, violent riots occurred when the price of maize meal was doubled as a result of cuts in subsidies as a part of an IMF austerity program. A number of people were killed by the security forces. Kaunda reversed the price increases and continued the subsidies – and blamed the BWIs for their callousness.

In this respect, the economic origins of pro-democratic agitation lay with both the BWIs and the government of Kaunda. The BWIs sought to secure economic recovery and reform (and debt repayment) through stabilization and adjustment. Kaunda's failure related to his regime's style of politics and the way in which economic hardship and austerity measures filtered through to the urban based groups with political clout. As is the case in many African states, internal inequalities inside Zambia are large – and grew significantly in the 1980s. Less than 70 percent of Zambians are literate, and the infant mortality rate is 120 per 1,000 live births. As Kibble also points out, only half the population has access to safe drinking water (Kibble 1992). A rural–urban dimension of inequality has inevitably structured the effects of austerity, with many Zambian economists arguing that the rural poor were relatively better off than the urban poor during adjustment. The rural population could at least grow food and operate in the growing parallel economy, whilst urban dwellers were engaged in formal occupations or in the highly competitive "informal sector" (MacGaffey 1988). This later took on an overt political dimension – as much of the pro-democracy protest in Zambia, as elsewhere in Africa, came from urban-dwelling professional groups such as lawyers, teachers, and public-sector workers. Such groups will expect their interests to be defended and promoted by the Chiluba government and the other new regimes, and this may mean that the needs of the rural majority will continue to be neglected (Riley 1992a).

When he realized the human costs, Kaunda did initially resist the external pressures for stabilization. There were periods of vacillation and a short "break" with the IMF (from May 1987). A New Economic Recovery Program (NERP) sought to provide an economic alternative to adjustment under the aegis of the BWIs. It was unsuccessful and was heavily criticized by external donors and possible investors for avoiding "tough" decisions. The national currency, the Kwatcha, was seen as overvalued. The development objectives were also viewed as unrealistic. Aid donors gradually withdrew their funding from 1987 onwards and as a consequence Kaunda's government started to implement some stabilization reforms.

Clearly some reform was necessary as Kaunda's political machine had created a huge and inefficient state sector with parastatals which became engulfed in the "spoils system" of rewarding political factions and supporters (Szeftel 1983). Whatever the justification, however, a series of partial economic reforms did take place from the mid-1980s onwards. From 1989, food subsidies were slowly reduced. In July 1989 the price of maize doubled. The price doubled again in June 1990 with a bag of maize meal (sufficient for a family for two weeks) rising to cost $7.40, compared to the average weekly wage of a low paid worker of $2.0 (*The Independent*, July 3, 1990). It is perhaps not surprising that food riots occurred in such circumstances.

Zambia's trade unions played a key role in focusing economic complaints towards Kaunda's government. Frederick Chiluba, as head of the Zambian Confederation of Trade Unions (ZCTU) sought to make it clear that the unions thought that Kaunda and UNIP was responsible for the growing economic crisis of the late 1980s. Zambia's business community also blamed them (Baylies and Szeftel 1992). Thus a link between governmental incompetence, patronage, and drift – and economic hardship – was established and became politically salient, whilst the broader responsibility of the BWIs was minimized.

Subsequent demonstrations over economic concerns thus became more politicized in that they also called for an end to Zambia's one-party state and the resignation of Kenneth Kaunda. During protests at Zambia's university in 1989 and 1990, students chanted "Kaunda must go," and, as an interesting variant, "Castrate Kaunda" (*The Independent*, June 29, 1990). Elsewhere, the political message was also taking hold. One journalist found a young person in the street who argued: "the government calls it a participatory democracy. The problem is we don't get to participate ... Anyone could do better than Kaunda" (*Observer* July 1, 1990).

Faced with a government that seemed unwilling to change its leadership and was held responsible for the country's economic plight, opposition political organization developed quickly in the late 1980s. The dominant opposition that emerged was a broadly based, seemingly non-ideological coalition that drew support from both the business community and organized labor. Initially the MMD appeared to be divided and poorly organized. It seemed to consist of many careerists as well as people with criminal connections (*Africa Confidential*, March 8, 1991). However, some of the factional disputes were soon resolved and it became much better organized and a highly effective popular communicator in all of Zambia's constituencies (Bratton, Bjornlund, and Gibson 1992). In 14 months it was able to develop from coming into existence as a newly constitutional political organization to being the power in the land.

The MMD's success has however presented it with diverse problems. The new president Chiluba claimed on November 2, 1991 that the hour had come "to build a new Zambia" (*The Guardian*, November 4, 1991). The form that this new Zambia would take was unclear from the political pronouncements made by his party during the election campaign. The new government was also unclear about its present objectives other than the need to secure further external credit. This is perhaps due to the uneasy coalition which now holds cabinet or ministerial positions, including trade unionists, business supporters of the MMD, and overt political appointees. As Baylies and Szeftel point out "the nature of the MMD itself seems to reproduce the structural conflicts and factional intrigues which transformed UNIP from one of Africa's most effective mass movements into a shell for transmitting presidential orders. In that way MMD seems to reproduce rather than replace UNIP" (Baylies and Szeftel 1992: 91).

The new government certainly faces many of the old government's problems – both in domestic policy and externally. Growing criticism of the new government's performance raises the specter of a return to power of the old UNIP government – perhaps without Kaunda, who has retired. The standard of living is declining under the new "democratic austerity" which seems scarcely less bearable than the old austerity of the 1980s. Chiluba's power base in Zambia's powerful unions is likely to grow less secure and there will be a greater challenge to the government unless it utilizes its patronage powers more. As Chiluba's halo begins to tarnish, the specter of greater urban dissent and protest becomes more likely.

Such domestic pressures count relatively little with governments when external creditors still expect debt repayment and policy reform. As we have seen, the new government has implemented a series of orthodox measures including currency devaluation and the removal of subsidies. It has yet to implement fully its program of privatization and to reduce government spending. The logic of political support and spoils politics would count against much progress on that front (Szeftel 1983). Economic adjustment is viewed by external creditors as the way to produce debt repayment. The alternative, substantial debt relief, has not been forthcoming for the new government. Chiluba's government expected a "democracy dividend" in the aftermath of his electoral victory – Zambia's creditors, principally the BWIs, the United Kingdom, and the United States, were initially thought favorably disposed. But little has transpired. Chiluba's government, an unlikely inheritor to Kaunda's, continues to remain so much in debt and so far from genuine participatory democracy. Only half of Zambia's registered voters turned out in the 1991 elections: perhaps a reflection of the limited choice on offer. The new government's complaisant acceptance of the BWIs suggestions of economic-policy reform may weaken the value of even that limited choice.

5 CÔTE D'IVOIRE: DEMOCRACY DEFERRED?

One commentator on post-independence Africa points out that "almost alone among African states, Ivory Coast ... [is] ... a story of apparent success after decolonization" (Fieldhouse 1986: 187). This "success," also called the "Ivorian miracle," rests upon two things: the iron grip of Ivory Coast's long-lived, unopposed leader, Felix Houphouet-Boigny, and the fluctuating world-market returns from the three principal export crops of coffee, cocoa, and timber.

The Ivory Coast (or Côte d'Ivoire) is a major world producer of cocoa. Its fortunes are therefore intimately linked to world commodity prices, although there has been some agriculture diversification away from this principal crop. Cocoa production increased from 94,000 tons in 1960–1 to over 240,000 tons in 1974–5, and went up to 590,000 tons in 1986–7 (*The Africa Review*, 1988). Cocoa production has continued to grow, although the farmers and the Ivorian state have been hit by the decline since 1986 in world cocoa (and coffee) prices. Houphouet-Boigny claimed that his export commodity-based regime represented "state capitalism" and generated a higher average income for Ivorians than for citizens in any other state in sub-Saharan Africa. Accordingly, by 1991 coffee and cocoa production in the Ivory Coast represented 41 percent of GDP. But cocoa exports fell to 712,500 tons that year, from a high of 780,500 tons in 1990 (*The Africa Review*, 1992). Despite Houphouet-Boigny's boasts, cocoa farmers have experienced the grimmer side of "state capitalism." From 1990, there was political unrest among farmers because they were receiving lower prices for their produce and the arrears they were owed by the state marketing board remained unpaid.

Presumably the president was also suffering from this downturn in prices as he was a major cocoa farmer himself. Born with the century, 93-year-old President Felix Houphouet-Boigny has been the force behind Ivorian development and a key factor in Ivorian political life since independence in 1960. The son of a Baoule chief, he became one of the small minority of francophone African leaders who played a significant role in metropolitan politics in France in the 1940s and 1950s. He was a deputy in the French National Assembly from 1946. This political base enabled Houphouet-Boigny to influence pro-foundly nationalist politics. As a result, he and a small elite group supporting him, have been at the center of Ivorian politics since 1952.

Houphouet-Boigny's development strategy has been the country's development strategy. He has presided over an Ivorian model of agriculturally based development which has as its roots a strong pea-sant agriculture, a receptive attitude to foreign investment, especially from the former colonial power, France, and a relatively benign form of personalized rule. However, explanations of Ivorian political life should not exaggerate the influence of Houphouet-Boigny. They should also pay attention to the unified Ivorian political and commercial class that has been central to the political economy since independence (Campbell 1978). It has also been argued that the Ivorian system involves a reasonably efficient and politically auto-nomous form of administrative system (Crook 1989).

As Crook explains, in the Ivory Coast there has emerged

> a strong state which overpowers, indeed is out of all proportion to, civil society, but which is able to maintain a strong disciplined state machine capable of maintaining the conditions for extraction of revenue from the peasant and mercantile economy. The Ivorian state has been virtually autonomous; a unified elite was able to use foreign factors of production to create its resource base and foreign personnel to give itself continuing control over administration (through restricted re-cruitment) and over the private sector. (*Crook 1991: 235*)

The Ivorian "strong state" is supported by a political system which operates in a cooptive and usually subtle manner. It has sought to incorporate most of the diverse elements of Ivorian life, while being based upon the cocoa producers and with significant support from France. The Ivory Coast has been relatively stable politically since independence despite several attempted coups, notably in April 1980. The regime also weathered a series of urban protests in the 1980s which came from principally professional and unionized groups such as teachers, doctors, transport workers, and civil servants. Ever since independence, the political scene has been dominated by Houphouet-Boigny's political party, the Democratic Party of the Ivory Coast (PDCI). The PDCI's position in Ivorian politics has been unchallenged until recently.

However, in the late 1980s a sustained threat to the PDCI's continued rule developed. Pro-democracy and anti-austerity protests were frequent. Houphouet-Boigny was eventually forced to open up the political process and hold multiparty elections in 1990. Although he remained president and the PDCI is still in power, much uncertainty now surrounds the succession, the future of the ruling party, and the commercial interests tied to it. Speaking at a press conference, and responding to calls for his retirement, the president said: "I'm refusing to grow old so that I can serve my country. The Ivory Coast will have the best successor to Houphouet because God will help me to give him to you" (*Africa Economic Digest*, March 12, 1990: 6).

Even with God's help, whoever presides over the Ivory Coast after Houphouet-Boigny finally retires or dies will be faced with a series of acute economic policy dilemmas. Even more severe forms of adjustment will be required by the state's major overseas creditors. Although a series of austerity measures have been implemented, in many respects the current leadership has been trying to avoid the political consequences of its own economic misjudgments since the late 1980s. The "Ivorian miracle" ran into major difficulties in 1987. But even as early as the 1970s it was evident that external debt was increasing rapidly. Total external debt stocks stood at just $256 million in 1970. This had risen to $8.3 billion by 1987, making the Ivory Coast one of SSA's most indebted states. It thus featured in a list of the world's top 17 indebted states identified by one debt "rescue package" of the 1980s, the Baker Plan.

Debt repayments were suspended in May 1987 for the first time in 26 years of independence (Parfitt and Riley 1989). Without this suspension, debt-service payments would have amounted to $1.15 billion in 1987, mostly on commercial loans contracted at high rates of interest. Debt-service payments were an average 35 percent of export earnings in the late 1980s. Ivory Coast's decision to suspend debt repayments was very significant. It was viewed favorably by western investors and creditors who supported the model of development that the Ivorian case represented. Writing about the suspension of debt repayments, *West Africa* magazine commented: "Some saw such a move by a hitherto model debtor and exemplary economic manager as a graphic illustration of the economic crisis facing governments throughout the continent; others saw it as a political manoeuvre by one of Africa's most esteemed leaders to secure a fairer deal from the west for the continent's governments in distress" (*West Africa*, January 11, 1988: 16).

With the benefit of hindsight, May 1987 was the month when the Ivorian miracle finally started to crumble – with significant political consequences. Judged from the point of view of the planter elite, as well as the wider society, subsequent economic and political developments have not been favorable. The Ivorian model had always involved the use of a stable statist regime which sought to boost export agricultural productivity by price incentives, and relied upon securing economic growth by exploiting the cheap land and labor that was available. The state, and its splendid capital of gleaming skyscrapers in coastal Abidjan, was thus dependent upon an attempt to plan statist development based on fluctuating world commodity price-based revenue.

A series of debt and austerity crisis were the consequences of the drop in commodity prices. The regime tried to reduce its external debt repayments and its creditors sought economic reform. Adjustment, rescheduling and political crisis have been features of the Ivorian political economy ever since. The regime has sought to trade upon its international creditability with the principal creditors. After all, the availability of such high levels of credit for the Ivory Coast in the 1970s and early 1980s was one indication of the way in which Houphouet-Boigny's government was viewed by the OECD countries. Like Zaire, it was seen as having a conservative, pro-western government which pursued an economically rational development policy in close concert with France, the former colonial power. Unlike Zaire, it was also seen as a suitable politically stable site for western investment as well.

Much of the overseas investment in the Ivory Coast came from France, although Germany is the main destination of exports. Some of the related political relationships are obscure, others are the more visible pillars of indirect colonialism. French troops are stationed in the Ivory Coast and extensive French military assistance has been given to the Ivorian army (Joseph 1976; Staniland 1987).

France has enhanced its relationships with its former colonial possession post-independence with the main impetus being trade, although, more generally, "the exercise of power in Africa was vital if French status in Europe was to be maintained" (Chipman 1989). Up to the end of the 1980s, strong elements of continuity have existed in French relations with Africa. Forty years ago, colonial policy was determined by Francois Mitterrand as the relevant minister in the Fourth Republic (Chafer 1992). Forty years on, Mitterrand as president still retains a close control over French policy in Africa. His son, Jean-Christophe, was until recently his adviser on African affairs (*The Africa Review* 1992). Whilst there are elements of continuity, a change in the French stance on Africa took place at the end of the 1980s. French politicians increasingly saw francophone Africa as an economic liability. Much criticism focused upon the ossified one-party structures in the core francophone states, such as Ivory Coast. Accordingly, France also pressed for political liberalization. It was dubbed "Paristroika." This external pressure coincided with growing domestic dissent at the social and economic costs of the Ivorian model.

One major source of popular protest against austerity in the Ivory Coast appears to have been the student population of the capital. Abidjan's university population of 25,000 are squeezed into university buildings designed to hold 8,000. In February 1990, a series of electricity cuts just prior to mid-term examinations sparked off the first significant protests. Student protestors were joined by public-sector workers in the power industries, public transport, and in the all-important artery of the port. Strikes were also staged by the country's transporters of goods and by taxi drivers. Initial threats of action became major public protests on the streets, spreading to the areas of the luxury hotels, and executive residential districts. Students were joined by their lecturers. Civil servants also joined to protest against possible salary cuts (Bratton and de Walle 1991). An important grievance in early 1990 was the so-called "Solidarity Tax." In addition to tax increases, job cuts were made.

Demonstrators were also protesting about high-level corruption. It was perhaps unfortunate for Houphouet-Boigny's political fortunes, if not for his soul, that he was at that time supervising the completion of the Notre Dame de la Paix, a huge Roman Catholic basilica in his home village of Yamoussoukro that copied the style of St Peter's in Rome. Substantial public and private funds were spent on its construction; a total building cost of at least $300 million is a widely accepted figure. In early 1990, anonymous pamphlets were also circulated containing details of the alleged corruptly acquired wealth of senior members of the ruling party. Students staged a general strike, and rioted. They were joined by schoolchildren carrying placards denouncing the president and the ruling party. The austerity protests thus acquired a specific political focus.

In March 1990 the president had defended the one-party system by using the standard argument that it minimized ethnic conflict. Multiparty politics, he argued, would be tribally divisive. However, two months later, responding to these widespread demands for political change (and economic-policy reversals), he announced that he had accepted the suggestion of his ruling party's political bureau that multiparty politics be legitimized again (Widner 1991). Accordingly, multiparty legislative elections were held on October 25, 1990. Houphouet-Boigny's new democratic credentials were tarnished by many allegations of malpractice and intimidation by the ruling party. The PDCI retained 163 of its 175 seats but the opposition parties won some representation. A Workers' Party candidate won the parliamentary seat where Houphouet-Boigny lived. Ivorian pluralism had created 26 opposition parties prior to the elections, but only 19 parties actually contested (*Africa Confidential*, November 23, 1990).

Divisions in the opposition, fraud, patronage politics, and intimidation also affected the presidential elections on October 28. Opposition parties had little time to seek political support. They found it expensive to travel about the country to campaign, "as a litre of petrol cost more in the Ivory Coast than it did almost anywhere else in the world" (Widner 1991: 58). Houphouet-Boigny faced one other candidate, Laurent Gbagbo who led the Ivorian Popular Front (FPI). Gbabgo was an unpopular candidate who had lived in exile in France from 1982–9 but unofficial estimates suggested that he had gained up to 40 percent of the vote, despite much massaging of the figures by the ruling party's supporters in the bureaucracy (*Africa Confidential*, November 23, 1990). Officially, Houphouet-Boigny won 82 percent of the vote, although 39 percent of those on the electoral register abstained. The president was returned for a seventh term of office – until 1995.

The unsuccessful challenge to Houphouet-Boigny and the PDCI did not end popular protest. It has continued, with a leading role being played by students and the new major opposition party, the FPI. The FPI has sought to develop a long-term strategy looking to the next elections in 1995, whilst the other opposition parties, and the students, continue to stage street protests against the regime and its policies. In May 1991 a student-organized march with 20,000 participants sparked off army involvement to crush the demonstration. Further demonstrations took place in early 1992 when the government rejected the findings of the Yopougpon report into the army action which had found that allegations of rape, brutality and theft were sustained (*The Africa Review*, 1992). In February 1992 marchers burned cars and rioted in the capital's center whilst demonstrating over the report's findings. The government subsequently arrested over 100 people, including the opposition leader Laurent Gbabago and human rights activists. They are currently serving prison sentences, after being convicted of inciting the riot. The government's actions were masterminded by Alassine Quattara, the prime minister, whilst Houphouet-Boigny was overseas in France. The arrests and prison sentences drew widespread criticism from a range of sources, including western governments. They also cast doubt over the character of the leadership that would replace Houphouet-Boigny, although the constitutional successor is not Quattara, a former IMF official who is continuing to implement the adjustment program, but Henri Konan Bedie, the president of the National Assembly.

Quattara's appointment in 1990 was aimed at providing a new technocratic gloss on a decaying regime. Although three IMF programs have conspicuously failed since 1987, the government still has a limited financial credibility left. Some debt relief has occurred with the official creditors rescheduling $800 million in 1991. This was announced in tandem with a reform of the commodities marketing board. Further slow progress on economic liberalization can be expected as the total debt stock of $17.96 billion at the end of 1990 gives creditors great leverage (World Bank 1991). The financial gap at the heart of the Ivorian political economy now necessitates continued economic liberalization but the political costs must surely endanger the future of the existing Ivorian polity. The PDCI leadership lost its political hegemony in the conflicts of 1989 and 1990. Continuing the liberalization program is likely to spark off further domestic challenges from urban-based groups despite its recent resort to arrests and intimidation.

6   ZAIRE: THE PATH TO DEMOCRACY OR CHAOS?

Until recently, western leaders have been wont to justify Mobutu Sese Seko's dictatorship of Zaire in terms of his ability to maintain the peace in that huge country. Indeed, Mobutu's accession to power in 1965 brought to an end the political crisis that threatened to break the country apart in the early 1960s and he has maintained at least a measure of order for most of the ensuing period. However, political order has been kept at the cost of the Zairean economy. Mobutu's rulership has been secured through his skillful use of patronage, which has entailed the development of an elite that owes its power to his. Virtually all positions of state influence are in Mobutu's gift and so advancement is dependent on loyality to the leader, or Guide, as he prefers to be known. Such advancement has been made particularly attractive by Mobutu's utilization of state resources to finance patronage for his political elite. It is accepted that appointment to office carries with it the right to misappropriate any resources associated with that position. Consequently, corruption has run completely out of control in Zaire. One commentator noted that corruption "reaches an intensity in Mobutu's Zaire that goes beyond shame and almost beyond imagination" (Delamaide 1984: 23). According to one estimate, some 20 percent of the budget was lost yearly to corruption (Korner *et al.* 1986). Mobutu himself took a lead in encouraging this pillage of state coffers, his personal holdings in Swiss banks being estimated at some $5 billion in the early 1980s.

The development of this patronage system has had deeply adverse effects on the Zairean economy. Whilst the copper price remained fairly buoyant, the country could earn sufficient resources to finance the corrupt activities of its parasitic elite. However, in the wake of the OPEC oil-price hike of 1973, the collapse of the copper price and the onset of world recession, Zaire's debts began to emerge as a problem. In 1975, Zaire stopped paying any principal or interest on its commercial bank debt, which then amounted to some $700–800 million. This prompted the first of a succession of IMF interventions in 1976 with a fairly typical stabilization program involving such measures as reduction of state spending and corruption. Mobutu treated the fund's conditionality with typical cynicism, making an initial agreement to gain access to the first tranche of assistance, only to ignore any commitments he had made once the funding had been delivered. This behavior eventually led the IMF to send in a team to run Zaire's economy in 1978, a measure that led to outright conflict between members of the Zairean elite and the IMF staff. The leader of the IMF team, Erwin Blumenthal, was intimidated to the extent that by the end of his year-long stay in Kinshasa, he was sleeping with a shotgun under his bed. He later concluded that the Zaireans had no intentions of paying their debts. Despite this, the IMF continued to make agreements with Zaire. The unusually tolerant line owed much to Mobutu's careful adherence to US foreign policy objectives in sub-Saharan Africa. Thus, he was one of the first African leaders to recognize Israel, he has sent forces into Chad to fight against Libyan incursions into that state, and he has consistently provided logistical support for American opposition to the Marxist MPLA regime in Angola. Such actions led the United States to exert a restraining influence on those zealots in the Fund who wished to take a stiffer line on Mobutu's economic profligacy.

These circumstances allowed the Zairean debt to run out of control to the point where it stood at nearly $5 billion in 1983. This may have been a factor behind Mobutu's apparent change of heart in that year, for not only did he agree yet another IMF program, but he actually began to observe conditionality demanding cuts in government spending, tighter budgetary control, and devaluation of the Zaire. For a time Zaire became the Fund's model pupil in sub-Saharan Africa. However, it is notable that stabilization was implemented in such a way as to minimize the effects on the Zairean elite, whilst the lower echelons of society suffered disproportionately from the privations of austerity. The 1983 devaluation sent the prices of staple foods soaring upwards by some 200–300 percent, whilst wages were restrained and thousands of workers in the public sector were laid off. Highly paid state officials tended not to be affected, whilst social services such as health and education were severely cut. It is worth pointing out that the element of IMF conditionality that Mobutu resisted most fiercely was that which demanded abolition of corrupt parastatals from which many members of his elite gained their illicit incomes.

This unequal division of the burdens of austerity roused discontentment amongst workers and other groups that had been disadvantaged by IMF stabilization, as evidenced by the strike of workers at Matadi Harbour on the Zaire river during January 1985. They brought all commercial traffic to a halt in support of their demand for a 50 percent wage rise, which breached the 25 percent wage limit agreed with the Fund. Mobutu was clearly aware of popular resentment of the austerity program, commenting to one western minister that Kinshasa was a powder keg. These tensions came to a head in 1986 when Mobutu limited debt-service repayments to 10 percent of export receipts and raised public-sector wages by up to 150 percent according to grade. This represented a clear break with the IMF. However, Mobutu also engaged in intensive diplomacy with the Reagan administration, particularly stressing his role in helping the Americans to supply arms to UNITA in Angola through allowing them to use the Kamina air base near the Angolan border. The United States applied pressure on the Fund to modify its terms for Zaire, prompting one senior IMF official, C. David Finch, to resign in protest. Nevertheless, Mobutu won his new stabilization program with relaxed conditionality. Once again he used Zaire's strategic value to the Americans to win US support and reluctant IMF backing for his corrupt rulership. (For a more detailed account of the period to 1986 see Parfitt and Riley 1989: ch. 4.)

Mobutu's apparent immunity to IMF strictures lifted any restraint that there might have been during the 1983–6 period when Zaire had observed its stabilization programs on at least a superficial level.

The economy began to run-out of control with an estimated one-third of the coffee crop being lost annually through smuggling, whilst the illegal gold trade was actually larger than the official trade (*Africa Analysis*, June 9, 1989). In February 1989, the then prime minister, Kengo Wa Dondo, claimed that only Gecamines, the mining para-statal, was remitting any money into the state treasury. Zairean production of diamonds and petroleum did not appear in the state accounts (*Africa Confidential*, December 7, 1990). Nor was Gecamines immune to misappropriation. During negotiations for an IMF loan in 1989, it was revealed that $400 million had gone missing in copper-export earnings. This amounted to some 30 percent of a year's revenue. The Fund also questioned increased spending by the presidency and other political institutions that accounted for about half of state expenditure. Despite the plentiful evidence of extensive corruption, the Bush administration put pressure on the IMF to accord Mobutu yet another agreement, which resulted in a program being agreed in June 1989 (*Africa Analysis*, June 9, 1989). This was at a time when Zaire's economic disorganization had contributed to an expanding debt amounting to $8.8 billion and to consumer price inflation running at 104.1 percent (Economist Intelligence Unit 1990, Country Report; Zaire, Rwanda, Burundi, 4). The living standards of significant sectors of the populace were coming under increasing pressure, with an average civil servant earning 20,000 zaires a month, or some $25, whilst a soldier earned only a third as much (*Africa Confidential*, April 20, 1990).

It was in this context that Mobutu decided to embark on the experiment of sounding out popular opinion as to Zaire's political situation and what should be done about it. His motivation in launching this initiative is mysterious, one possibility being that his confidence in his own leadership was such that he believed he could not be challenged. Another quite feasible explanation is that he may have anticipated that opposition was bound to emerge given developments in neighboring states and sought to preempt it by initiating a process of symbolic reform that would remain under his control. In the event, his invitation that traditional leaders, associations, and individuals should make their views known unleashed a deluge of criticism of his rule. Explicit demands were made for Mobutu's resignation; for the dismantling of Zaire's only legal party, the Mouvement populaire de la révolution (MPR), this being one of the central vehicles for Mobutu's rulership; and for the establishment of a multiparty democracy. If Mobutu's declaration of *glasnost* had been designed to prompt opposition it had failed. Instead it had created a popular expectation of political change and Mobutu's failure to announce any reforms after an eagerly awaited cabinet meeting of April 5, 1990 was the signal that started extensive student rioting in Kinshasa (*Africa Confidential*, April 20, 1990).

This finally prompted Mobutu to take action on April 25, when he declared Zaire's Third Republic, which was to be characterized by a multiparty system. The number of parties was to be limited to three, with the long-banned Union pour la democratie et le progrès social (UDPS) being legalized and the MPR being split into two, the "moderates" and the "hardliners." (Mobutu did not bother explaining the significance of these soubriquets.) The legalisation of the UDPS did not prevent the authorities from violently repressing a demonstration by UDPS supporters on April 29. On May 3, Mobutu revised his plan for democratization, announcing that the MPR would not be split into two and that it would compete with the UDPS and a third unspecified party for power. These haverings were greeted with public contempt. The popular consensus was that Mobutu was trying to hang on to power by ceding only a symbolic form of muitipartyism (which was dubbed multi-Mobutism), whilst retaining actual control himself (*Africa Confidential*, May 18, 1990).

This growing opposition to Mobutu led directly to the Lubumbashi Massacre of May 11–12, 1990 in which a number of oppositionist students were killed. Mobutu despatched a unit from his crack Division speciale présidentielle (DSP) after students had beaten four soldiers they suspected of spying on them. The DSP killed large numbers of students using considerable brutality (estimates of the fatalities vary from 19 to over 100). Despite a news blackout, it emerged that the massacre had sparked serious clashes between students and government forces in other towns, including Kisangani, Bukavu, and Mbanza-Ngungu *Africa Confidential*, June 15, 1990; and *Africa Analysis*, May 25, 1990).

The Lubumbashi Massacre represented a turning point in Zairean politics for two reasons. First, it prompted many of Mobutu's external guarantors to begin to distance themselves from him, with Belgium breaking off diplomatic relations and the Americans criticizing the brutality of his regime. The end of the Cold War made Mobutu expendable to the states that had previously supported him as a reliable anti-communist ally, regardless of his excesses. Second, the massacre prompted a wave of political protest and strikes by civil servants, nurses, medical staff, and teachers. The civil servants were on strike from July 10 to October 1 demanding increases of up to 500 percent for the lowest paid. Although the strikes' demands were essentially instrumental, their demonstrations did have political overtones, one of their favourite slogans being "Mobutu voleur"

(Mobutu thief). The civil servants strike was ended when they were promised 100 percent pay rises. However, these were soon eaten up by hyperinflation. A correspondent for *Jeune Afrique* visited Kinshasa in late December 1990 and found that a bag of rice cost Z110 thousand ($70), whilst a bag of the staple, manioc, cost Z50,000 ($32). Prices were rising by the hour. Even a minister received only Z750,000 a month, amounting to barely $300. These conditions provoked food riots in Kinshasa, Lubumbashi, Bukavu, and Mbuji Mayi in December (Economist Intelligence Unit 1990, Country Report; Zaire, Rwanda, Burundi, 4; 1991, 1; and *Africa Confidential*, December 7, 1990).

Throughout this period Mobutu continued his manipulations with a view to maintaining his grip on political power. He encouraged the proliferation of parties with a view to dividing the emergent opposition forces. Mobutu also began to make belated preparations for a National Conference to design the new constitution for the Third Republic that had been declared a year before. Mobutu initially sought to ensure that the National Conference and its preceding organizing Commission would be composed of his own political supporters. He also tried the familiar tactic of coopting elements of the opposition, offering the prime ministership to Etienne Tshisekedi, leader of the major opposition party, in July 1991. Tshisekedi refused (*Africa Confidential*, August 9, 1991).

This unsuccessful gambit left Mobutu with no option but to go ahead with the National Conference, which finally got under way on July 31, in an atmosphere of high tension. The tension broke on September 22, when troops began to riot, sacking the warehouse at Njili International Airport. This was the signal at Kokolo Camp for troops to comprehensively loot Kinshasa. Throughout the last week of September 1991 civil order effectively broke down and this prompted French and Belgian forces to intervene to evacuate foreign nationals trapped in Zaire. There was much suspicion in Kinshasa as to Mobutu's role in prompting the riots. It was noted that the troops did not attempt to execute a coup, even though the rioters at the airport could easily have taken over Njili's control tower and the troops at Kokolo were less than 500 meters away from the main state radio and television transmitter. Mobutu for his part did not attempt to intervene to stop the disturbances until he called for a curfew on September 26. To many observers this was suggestive that Mobutu was behind the riots. Certainly, the breakdown of order could be seen as advantaging Mobutu, inasmuch as it led to the suspension of the National Conference and it created conditions in which Tshisekedi felt obliged to accept the renewed invitation to take over as prime minister (*Africa Confidential*, October 11, 1991).

It seemed as though Mobutu had succeeded in coopting Tshisekedi when they agreed to form a cabinet that was numerically dominated by opposition ministers, but in which MPR loyalists retained the key posts of defense, foreign affairs, and planning (*The Guardian*, October 15, 1991). However, economic conditions were so desperate by this time that many Zaireans simply would not accept the idea of a continuation of Mobutu's rule. In the wake of the riots inflation had increased to some 10,000 percent and civil servants and soldiers were openly contemptious of Mobutu's offer of a pay rise variously reported as 1000–2000 percent. There were even some doubts as to whether or not the government could print the money given that the German company that prints Zairean bank notes had canceled deliveries because of non-payment of printing bills. Nor did the government have any prospect of raising money since Gecamines, the only productive parastatal, had ceased payments to the state treasury in early 1991 (*Africa Analysis*, October 18, 1991).

In these circumstances Tshisekedi continued to battle with Mobutu for control of government, even though the rule of law had broken down. His obstinacy provoked Mobutu to sack him on October 21, a move that precipitated demonstrations by oppositionists estimated to number 15,000 (*The Guardian*, October 22, 1991) Mobutu appointed another member of the Union Sacre to replace Tshisekedi, one Mungul Diaka. This prompted yet more demonstrations and riots in Kinshasa and Lubumbashi (*The Guardian*, October 25, 1991). Tshisekedi responded by refusing to accept the legitimacy of his dismissal and by forming his own parallel government. He called on the armed forces to revolt against Mobutu's leadership (*The Guardian*, November 2, 1991). Mobutu demonstrated his own determination to hang on to power by postponing the presidential elections scheduled for December 1991. This prompted popular protests, but the army revolt that Tshisekedi called for failed to materialize (*Africa Analysis*, December 13, 1991).

By the end of 1990, Zaire's total external debt had reached a total of over $10 billion, with outstanding long-term debt at $8.85 billion (World Bank 1991). Despite this, Mobutu continues to exasperate his creditors. In February 1992 the National Conference was suppressed and further pro-democracy demonstrations were put down violently. The National Conference was subsequently revived. It may be that Mobutu's 28-year-old regime will finally collapse. A leaked cable from the Belgian ambassador to Zaire is reported to have said: "It is impossible to continue with Mobutu" (Riley 1992a:

116). At the time of writing, however, Mobutu continues to cling on to power in his bankrupt and chaotic country, clearly oblivious to the suffering of his people.

The Zairean decline into political chaos may be attributed in part to the venality and corruption of the Mobutu regime, but it also derives from the support given to this regime by the Western powers, inclusive of the IMF. Mobutu always knew that he could obtain external funding to bolster the patronage system that underwrote his rulership. Even when the IMF was allowed by the United States to take a relatively harsh line with Zaire, the main burden of austerity was inflicted on those at the bottom of society whilst Mobutu's elite was allowed to continue its illicit accumulation process. There is some evidence to suggest that this caused certain sectors of the urban populance to become politically active, notably students and public-sector workers. When Mobutu launched his misguided sounding of popular opinion, it was these groups in particular that made their opposition to his rulership known, forcing Mobutu to make the unprecedented concession of allowing the existence of opposition parties. However, Mobutu has had much experience of surviving challenges to his rule and by a variety of stratagems he has been able to prevent democratic elections from taking place that would remove him from power. Instead, he continues to preside over a bankrupt nation in which civil order has broken down.

7 THE POLITICS OF THE AFRICAN CROWD

The 1980s were a period in which economic reform, seen in countless stabilization and structural adjustment programs, became the rhetoric of state action across Africa. The fiscal crisis, unpayable debt burdens and limited room for maneuver of most African states meant that they had to try to implement an economic reform agenda in accord with the *laissez-faire* logic of the BWIs. A great neo-liberal project was initiated which involved reducing the role of the African state and its welfare functions and reconstituting African development to base it on market principles. (For a discussion of some of the ambiguities of neo-liberalism and its political consequences, see Colclough and Manor 1991; Lawrence and Seddon 1990.)

As we have seen, some African states such as Ghana have implemented the reform agenda thoroughly; other states, including Zaire and Zambia in the late 1980s, have partially implemented stabilization or adjustment programs. Ghana was heralded as a World Bank "success story" in Africa and has secured a disproportionately large share of external funding as a result. In other cases, the BWIs have been less pleased. After the Ivorian "miracle" of an export-agriculture high-growth economy turned into a mirage in the 1980s, several IMF support programs failed although the government has belatedly introduced liberalization measures. Zaire has continued to confound its creditors and supporters in the West. It finally started to thoroughly implement adjustment measures such as devaluation and government spending cuts in the mid-1980s but in a way in which the costs of such measures would be avoided by the kleptocratic class surrounding Mobutu. Zambia's government under Kaunda was made clearly aware of the human and political costs of adjustment in December 1986 when many were killed in foot riots. Kaunda is reported to have said that he hoped that the IMF would in future try to design an adjustment program which would avoid such deaths (Baylies and Szeftel 1992).

The efficacy of the neo-liberal strategy has been the subject of much intense politically charged debate. Here, our intention has been to assess the effects of economic adjustment and its relationship to the process of democratization. Implementation of adjustment has been uneven, partial and with immense human costs. Not surprisingly, as the measures took hold in some states and the damage to the social fabric became clearer, subtle changes appeared in the policy stances of the BWIs. Adjustment was now to have a "human dimension." It was to take into account the poorest and try to cushion them against its harshest effects. In addition, the reform agenda would have to be widened as the expected results of adjustment were not immediately forthcoming. A series of political and administrative restrictions upon economic reform were identified. What was viewed by the BWIs as economically rational reform was being hindered by political pressures and constraints within Africa. A major factor was the character of the African state and the styles of politics associated with the authoritarian leaderships in power. Thus both a "human dimension" and some political reform became a necessary adjunct to economic adjustment.

As Christopher Coker has pointed out, "political pluralism has been sold to the region by the West on the evidence of Eastern Europe alone" (Coker 1991: 119). Crude political solutions were insisted upon by donors, such as Britain and the United States. They assumed the complementarity of market liberalism and political pluralism. With rather more subtlety, the BWIs focused upon the mechanics of government rather than the niceties of popular participation. What was needed was not liberal democracy, but "good governance": a mixture of less corruption, more open decision-making, managerial efficiency and some limited degree of political pluralism (World Bank 1991). These governmental reforms would assist the neo-liberal economic reforms. Popular participation could do the reverse.

In response to the economic adjustment measures that were implemented in the 1980s, African peoples have adopted many diverse strategies to challenge, deflect, or avoid bearing the costs of the austerity involved and to seek a political alternative to the governments and politicians they hold responsible. Some African governments, such as Tanzania under the leadership of Julius Nyerere, have tried to lay the blame for austerity on the BWIs or the inquities in the wider world economy. In the mid-1980s, Nigeria's military government staged a debate on the desirability or otherwise of accepting an IMF loan and the conditionalities associated with it whilst at the same time effectively implementing the required economic reforms (Parfitt and Riley 1989). However, whatever the appropriate location of responsibility and blame, African governments have been the targets of popular protest as the plight of their citizens worsened. Popular protests have become frequent events in national capitals.

This chapter has charted some of the aims and strategies of what can be characterized as the "African crowd." Following the arguments of Walton and the historian E. P. Thompson, the African crowd's moral economy can be described as involving a range of objectives, including an end to corruption, the replacement of particular political figures, democracy, ethnic secessionism, class-conscious action, and more specifically instrumentalist austerity protests (Walton 1989). Many social groups have been involved though they have primarily been in urban locations. Lawyers, students, copper miners, organizations of rural women, urban workers and the unemployed, journalists, clergymen and others have all been active in struggles for justice.

However, a series of differing responses to austerity can be identified. The African crowd also initially had contradictory aims. As will be appreciated, not all the protests that have been discussed in this chapter were exclusively concerned with the effects of the BWI's austerity programmes. In Togo at the end of January 1992 several thousand women demonstrated on the streets of the capital to give, as they said, "a last warning to those opposed to democracy" after a prolonged struggle between the aging authoritarian President Gnassingbe Eyadema and his opponents (*Africa Analysis*, February 7, 1992: 6). There were violent strikes in Benin's capital city throughout 1989 as civil servants protested against the failure of the government to pay their salary arrears (Allen 1992). The sudden and unexplained death in 1990 of a leading opponent of President Omar Bongo of Gabon led to "public rage" on the streets of Libreville, with the sacking of shops and public buildings (*The Independent*, May 25, 1990). In Kenya a radical Presbyterian preacher called for multi-party elections and street riots resulted, the first stage of a prolonged struggle (*The Guardian*, September 11, 1990). Dozens of people at a football match were shot dead by the bodyguards of the former president Mohammed Siad Barre of Somalia because they shouted anti-government, anti-austerity slogans (*The Independent on Sunday*, July 8, 1990).

The relationship between austerity protests and the democratization pressures in Africa is thus complex and locally conditioned. In some African states, such as Benin and Côte d'Ivoire, a relatively clear sequence of first, austerity protest, and then broader political agitation can be seen. In other cases, austerity protest accompanies pro-democracy agitation. It has been claimed that, in South Africa, Burundi, and Uganda, civil strife has "acted as the midwife of democratisation" (Lemarchand 1992: 11). Austerity protests are thus part of a broader picture of opposition to the prevailing modes of rule in many African polities. The locale does determine the modality of protest and its consequences. This appears to be consistent with the situation more globally, as Walton and Ragin suggest: "striking miners in Romania and food rioters in Zambia's copperbelt towns respond in locally conditioned ways to the common experience of austerity measures implemented by states facing a towering international debt" (Walton and Ragin 1989: 172).

Moreover, it is by no means self-evident that the "wind of change" will blow right across Africa and produce even effects and create democratic politics everywhere, despite much talk or Africa's "second liberation" or "second independence" since 1989. Austerity protests have contributed to political change in states such as Benin in 1990, where multiparty politics now operates. But elsewhere, as in the Ivory Coast, Africa's authoritarian leaders have survived the political challenges for now although the austerity continues. Despite the prolonged protest over political and economic grievances in Togo, Eyadema currently still retains his grip upon power helped by ethnic divisions and a supportive army.

There are also questions concerning the character and the social base of those who have assumed power in the democratizing societies. Chiluba in Zambia is unusual in that he has emerged out of the trade-union movement, although his movement is likely to be unsupportive of the adjustment measures that have been implemented from 1991 onwards. Other new leaders have a more technocratic and managerial background. The new president of Mali, Souman Sacko, used to work for the UNDP and President Nicephore Soglo of Benin was an international banker. They have been described as "techno-politicians" (*New Statesman and Society*, June 14, 1991: 19). Such new leaders will more adept at negotiating with external creditors, and more sympathetic to the BWI's point of view, than at responding adequately to the economic grievances of their own people. The social base of the new democratic politicians is in middle-class or aspirant middle-class urban, professional, and public-sector groups. This is to be seen with most clarity in states such as Benin, the Congo, Gabon, and Niger in 1990 where such groups were behind the protests that led to the formation of the National Conferences (Lemarchand 1992: Lancaster 1991). Their complaints concerned tax levels, redundancies, the inefficiency of public utilities, the level of student grants, late payment of the salaries of teachers, and moral condemnation of corruption. Their interests are likely to be promoted by the new leaderships; but these interests are not congruent with the aims of the broader austerity protests.

In addition, across Africa as well as in the Zairean case discussed above, the army remains a potent political actor working behind the scenes to defend its own interests. It can intervene in a positive way – for example in ousting Moussa Traore in Mali in March 1991 and Joseph Momoh in Sierra Leone in April 1992. Both interventions were a product of economic grievances and democratization pressures, coupled with specific complaints against the personalities involved (*Africa Analysis*, September 20, 1991; *The New Democrat*, June 1992). The strength of austerity protests and democratization pressures may continue to be outweighed by key political actors, such as the military. The political leaderships that have assumed power in the newly democratized societies, such as Zambia, may also continue to be sympathetic to, or may not be able to avoid, further doses of structural adjustment. If a primary cause of the democratization pressures was austerity protest, then the success of that protest in contributing to democratizing the polity may be negated by further adjustment.

Such a likely possibility raises the question of the character of democracy and sovereignty in structurally weak states. Zambians in 1991 voted for a democratic change to UNIP and Kaunda, not for further externally imposed austerity. Chiluba identified UNIP, Kaunda and his policies as being primarily responsible for Zambia's misfortunes – although the responsibility is wider. If popular pressures produce national political change and economic expectations that are reversed by the BWIs, then the genuinely democratic credentials of the new regimes can be questioned. This may be inevitable, however, due to the crippling external debt most African states have and the leverage that this gives their creditors. As Dunn points out, "What particularly marks Africa out amongst the areas of the modern world is not the clumsiness of its rulers. It is the combination of its historic economic weakness (and its consequently painful susceptibility to misgovernment within the modern international political economy) with the comparatively weak institutionalisation of its civil society at the level of the territorial state" (Dunn 1986: 160) However, irrespective of the limited room for maneuver that African states have, across the continent there is a convergence of widespread aspirations for democracy with popular protests against the wrenching economic adjustment of the 1980s. Neo-liberalism requires a minimal role for the state; the many popular protests have been seeking an end to austerity. They have also been demanding a more efficient and accountable state which would deliver on its promises to provide welfare services for the majority. Popular movements for change such as those in Zambia, Côte d'Ivoire and Zaire have seen some advances towards those goals, despite the survival of the malign kleptocracy in Zaire and the longevity of Houphouet-Boigny. Austerity protests have been successful in creating a popular wave of dissent which has toppled some African leaderships. Such protests are likely to continue across the continent as the more pluralist political leaderships of the 1990s come to terms with persistent domestic unrest over further austerity. In Africa, as perhaps globally, "Democracy cannot sustain the debt; the debt cannot sustain democracy" (Smith 1991: 616).

6

The Middle East and North Africa

1 INTRODUCTION

On at least 25 occasions, in at least 9 countries, over the past $2\frac{1}{2}$ decades, major outbreaks of social unrest have swept through the cities of the Middle East and North Africa. Manifesting itself in a variety of forms – including strikes and marches, street demonstrations, and "riots" – this wave of popular protest has been generated by widespread outrage at the austerity measures implemented as part of government economic reforms. Only the "desert states" of the Gulf, Libya, and Mauretania, and the Ba'athist regimes of Syria and Iraq so far remain little affected (see table 6.1).

In virtually all cases, significant increases in the cost of basic goods and services (or the threat of these) have preceded and effectively precipitated the outbursts of popular unrest. The price of bread and other food staples appears to be particularly significant, in part because of their importance in household expenditure, especially for the urban poor, but also in part because of their symbolic value (particularly so for bread).

The riots and street demonstrations that constitute the most dramatic forms of popular protest have almost always involved the unemployed and those working in the informal sector; students have

Table 6.1   Austerity protest in the Middle East, 1965–1992

Country	Date(s) of major protest				
Algeria	1987,	1988,	1990		
Egypt	1977,	1986,	1987,	1989	
Iran	1978–9,	1991,	1992		
Jordan	1989				
Lebanon	1987,	1992			
Morocco	1965,	1978,	1981,	1984,	1990
Sudan	1979,	1982,	1985		
Tunisia	1978,	1984,	1987		
Turkey	1978–9,	1980,	1990		

often initiated the protests or joined in early on; in many cases, organized labor and "the working class" in the classic sense have been involved, as have public-sector employees or "white-collar" workers. In some cases, popular protest of the kind described has involved the professional and middle classes, although it is more usual for these to participate in less dramatic forms of protest and opposition. While popular protest through street demonstrations and "riots" is, not surprisingly, a predominantly male activity, women have also been involved, not only in support of men but in direct action themselves (for further details, see chapter 3). Popular protest, therefore, while predominantly an activity of the working classes broadly conceived, may encompass a wide spectrum of social forces.

Given that the urban poor are most dependent on basic goods and services, it is not surprising that they are universally involved. It is also relevant, however, that they constitute the sections of urban society with the least support from, and representation by, organized groups and institutions, and thus have few alternative means of expressing their grievances. The trade unions generally represent workers in the relatively protected areas of the economy, while the professional and middle classes tend to enjoy the support of their own associations. Political groupings and movements may claim to speak and act on behalf of the ordinary people, but they tend to rely primarily on activists from relatively privileged backgrounds and often fail to articulate or represent the interests of the urban poor. This is probably less true for the Islamic groups that have emerged so significantly over the past decade, although they too tend to be led by educated cadres.

The austerity protests have been largely "spontaneous" (not planned or organized by political movements or trade unions), although they have often followed or preceded more organized forms of protest. Street demonstrations and "riots" may be distinctive, but they are not isolated from longer-term movements or other forms of protest. They often simply constitute the most dramatic expression of protest and opposition in a series of less visible actions taking place over months or even years. They may be seen as the vivid manifestation of deeper currents of dissent and social unrest which "break out" at a particular conjuncture or when a precipitating event occurs.

The first of these protests took place in 1965 in Morocco following the government's introduction of austerity measures in response to a deepening economic crisis. Strikes by dissatisfied teachers led to large-scale demonstrations as they were joined by students and unemployed workers. Clashes between protestors and security forces left hundreds dead and the King responded by dissolving parliament and declaring a state of emergency, which was to last, in effect, until 1977 (Seddon 1989a: 240–1).

For a decade, the Moroccan incident appeared to be an isolated case, but from the mid-1970s onwards such austerity protests became more common. In January 1977, the decision by the Egyptian government to raise food and petrol prices by over 30 percent, as part of a program of financial stringency and economic reform designed under the auspices of the IMF, provoked long and fierce rioting in several major Egyptian cities. In the last few years of the decade, four other countries (Morocco, Tunisia, Turkey, and Iran) were to experience similar instances of massive urban protest, leading in the last two cases to a military coup and a revolution respectively. In the 1980s, many states in the region (Sudan, Tunisia, Morocco, Egypt, Algeria, Jordan) were shaken by outbreaks of popular protest against the effects of economic reforms, with significant political consequences in several instances (overthrow of the regime in Sudan, political reforms in Tunisia, Algeria, and Jordan). Even Lebanon, in the midst of a civil war, was affected when demonstrations took place in Beirut in 1987 against the effects of devaluation. As the decade of the 1990s advances, it is already clear that austerity protests will continue; in Morocco, Algeria, and Turkey in 1990, in Iran in 1991 and 1992, and in Lebanon in 1992, large demonstrations have already taken place against the effects of government economic-reform measures.

Generally, from the mid-1970s onwards, the reforms have been undertaken under the auspices of the IMF and the World Bank, with the former in particular emphasizing the need for draconian measures – which is why the protests have come to be referred to often as "IMF riots." By 1984, Egypt, Iran, Morocco, Syria, Tunisia, and Turkey had entered into a total of 14 IMF Stand-By arrangements for stabilization programs; and in the first half of the 1980s, Turkey, Egypt, Morocco, Tunisia and Sudan were all struggling with World Bank and IMF sponsored, structural adjustment programs. The dramatic increases in the price of basic goods and services which resulted from the austerity measures associated with these programs provided a trigger for urban protest, giving rise to epithets such as "bread riots" and "hunger uprisings," although a wide range of concerns, broadly associated with rapidly increasing inequality combined with relative and often absolute social deprivation, fueled the social unrest that underlay the demonstrations.

Increasingly, in the region, austerity protest has become more closely associated with demands for political reform; and in Tunisia (after 1984), in Algeria (after 1988), and in Jordan (after 1989), significant political reforms have indeed taken place, partly in response to such demands. During the Gulf War (1990–1), massive demonstrations throughout North Africa in support of Iraq and against the US-led "coalition" also criticized the continuing austerity measures associated with economic reforms and called for political liberalization at home (Seddon 1991).

From 1979 onwards, after the Iranian revolution, the relationship between popular urban protest and the dramatic rise of Islamism, with its explicit objective of overthrowing "illegitimate" regimes, became a matter of major concern to many governments, while commentators persistently drew attention to the revolutionary appeal of Islamism and to the increasing strength of the Islamic movements, particularly among the urban poor and disadvantaged in a period of rapid and traumatic economic and social change. Certainly, Islamic movements have been actively involved in many of the instances of urban popular protest during the 1980s. Interestingly, however, during 1991 and 1992, there have been signs of increasing popular protest in the Islamic Republic of Iran, following the introduction of reforms designed to liberalize the economy. Any simplistic theory of popular protest in the region as inevitably associated with Islamist opposition is therefore misleading, although there is little doubt that the Islamic movements, with their distinctive politico-religious appeal, continue to be able to capitalize on popular discontent and social unrest.

2   FRAMEWORK FOR ANALYSIS

The broad framework adopted in this chapter is that developed in Chapters 1 and 2. There we have argued that austerity protests are part of a general political response to the global restructuring of the period from the early 1970s to the early 1990s. They are to be explained largely as a reaction, by those sections of society which feel themselves to be adversely and unreasonably affected, to the domestic political and economic changes consequent upon the implementation of specific government policies in response to economic crisis.

A Chronological Framework

For the Middle East in particular, we accept Burke's general periodization for the analysis of popular protest movements. In his view (and ours), contemporary protest movements in the Middle East and North Africa − which have a long history − are broadly linked to the process of the region's integration into the capitalist world system and the transformation from pre-capitalist to capitalist society that began in the middle of the eighteenth century. The "long nineteenth century" (which coincides with the colonial period broadly conceived) may be divided into three periods of unequal length: (a) 1750−1839; (b) 1840−80; and (c) 1880−1925 − each one characterized by particular forms of popular protest and resistance (Burke 1986).

The "first wave" of protest (centered in Syria and Egypt) was predominantly urban; this represented a change from the older style of grain riots (see Shoshan 1980) to more politically focused challenges to the Mamluk system. The "second wave" comprised essentially rural protest and affected more of the region. The social movements of "the third wave" were of a more varied character:

> in the cities, as the old social forms and economic structures came to be supplemented by new ones, the old styles of urban protests, which had been linked to the mosque as a gathering point and the *'ulama* as key spokesmen and intermediaries, gave way to forms of collective action linked to the European working class movement: strikes, boycotts, and other forms of worker militancy. Most importantly, as portions of the Arab world came under European domination, experiments with new forms of social identity and political cohesion, notably secular nationalism, began to develop. (*Burke 1986: 21*)

A "fourth wave," associated initially with the struggle for national independence and latterly with the construction of the new post-colonial state, can also be identified – extending broadly from the 1920s to the early 1970s. Popular protest initially took forms demonstrating a continuity with the "third wave" and contributed crucially to the national liberation struggle; in those relatively few instances where popular protest continued after independence, it was generally mobilized around resentment at inadequate integration into the newly independent states (e.g. the Berbers in the Maghreb) or else around movements for regional or ethnic/national autonomy (e.g. the Kurds), and may be seen as an inevitable part of the contradictory political process of state formation. The later phases of this period were associated with a process of state-led national, economic, and political reconstruction and development, giving rise to various forms of state capitalism; the state also became a major source (through public expenditure) of welfare provision. Importantly, as we shall argue below, there developed "a widespread acceptance among people of the Middle East of the legitimacy of an interventionist state" (Richards and Waterbury 1990: 184).

If the fourth period may be characterized as one of "nationalist development" with the state playing a crucial economic and social role, the fifth period is that of *infitah* – from the early 1970s to the 1990s. *Infitah* is a generic term for "liberalization" ("opening up," in Arabic), involving shifts in state economic policy toward increased emphasis on the private sector and greater reliance on market forces, reform of public-sector decision-making, and opening up to the international economy. In varying ways, at different speeds, and with different degrees of commitment, the majority of states in the region "adjusted" in this direction during the period in question; even states historically strongly committed to playing a major role in the construction of new national identities and forms of development initiated economic reforms of a broadly similar kind (e.g. Egypt in the 1970s, Algeria in the 1980s, Iran in the early 1990s). An explanation for this general change lies in part in the development of internal contradictions and associated conflicts within the state, and in part with the pressures exerted by virtue of its deeper integration within a global political economy itself undergoing "structural adjustment."

This fifth period can be identified as a major period of transition in the Middle East and North Africa, from nationalist development under state capitalism to an emphasis on private capital accumulation under a regime of economic liberalism and *infitah* or internationalism. This transition has generated new economic and social contradictions and divisions and given rise to new patterns and forms of popular protest, to constitute a "fifth wave" of protest: "since the mid-1970s, the forms of urban collective action have once again begun to shift. Food riots have reappeared for the first time in years" (Burke 1989a: 10).

Approaches to the Analysis of Popular Unrest

We have attempted in earlier chapters to draw on a number of existing theories and intellectual traditions to develop a distinctive and coherent approach to the analysis of popular protest and social unrest in the contemporary period. In the case of the Middle East and North Africa, we must recognize, however, the prevalence of a distinctive tradition of historical and social analysis based on the notion that there is something so distinctive about societies and cities whose populations are Muslim that they can be characterized (at whatever period in history and in whatever particular part of the world) simply as "Islamic." This "orientalist" tradition has been subjected to devastating criticism (e.g. Said 1978, 1985; Al-Azm 1981), but remains strong, particularly in the analysis of urban economy and society; it pervades much of the writing on urban protest, both historical and contemporary.

For the orientalist, "the Islamic world" today remains essentially pre-modern in its values, culture and social structures, confronting "the modern (western) world" with hostility and conservatism. Given this emphasis on continuity in "Islamic society," it follows that it is the contradiction or clash between "traditional" and "modern" structures and values that generates the distinctive patterns and forms of popular protest in contemporary 'Islamic societies'. Order is maintained by force and by the notion of the *'umma* (religious community). Between the rulers and the masses are the *'ulema* (clergy), and only religious ideology and practice (embodied in the *'ulema*) hold "the Islamic city" together. The crowd is seen as a simple agglomeration of individuals, whose collective action is the result either of purely spontaneous urges or of manipulation; all that the ordinary people share is their existence as "the masses" and their membership of the *'umma*. Today, as in the past, popular involvement in politics in "Islamic cities" is to be seen, according to the orientalists, essentially in terms of "the mob" (the ordinary folk have no "truly collective life" – Lapidus 1967: 107); thus, "all that Lapidus' crowd, commoners, common people, or mob can do is plunder, as befits its character and suits those who manipulate it" (Al-Azmeh 1976: 7).

The conception of urban society in the Middle East and North Africa as essentially timeless and constituted through religious beliefs and practices, and of the urban population as a mere agglomeration of individuals mobilized only as a mob is a gross misrepresentation of the complex economic, social, and political structures and dynamics identified by recent historical and social-science research. It is a caricature, however, which has proved popular not only with orientalist scholars but also, all too often, with governments attempting to control and contain popular dissent and unrest, and with Islamists and other political activists trying to turn it to their own ends. Furthermore, it contains crucial elements which have all too often been ignored in the justifiable criticisms leveled at the orientalist paradigm – in particular, the idea of a distinctive Islamic conception of community and social justice.

In his introduction to *Islam, Politics and Social Movements*, Lapidus emphasizes the significance of the relationship between religious mentality and political action in Muslim countries (Lapidus 1988: 3) and refers specifically to "an Islamic moral vision" and "the Muslim moral economy" (1988: 11, 15). While critical of many aspects of orientalism, his co-editor Burke also invokes the notion of the "Islamic moral economy"; he refers to the view that "the moral vision of workers and artisans in Muslim societies was shaped by peculiarly Islamic notions of justice," shared by several contributors to the volume, and suggests that "taking a cue from [E. P.] Thompson, one can even refer to an 'Islamic moral economy' as a shorthand description of the culturally patterned ways this sense of justice was invoked by crowds throughout the Islamic world" (Burke 1988: 22). He recalls that "Thompson has argued that eighteenth century English bread rioters were guided by a 'moral economy', a religiously-grounded sense of justice which not only propelled them into action but also provided the rituals of rebellion (such as the 'setting of the price') according to which their actions were patterned" and admits that "it is tempting to see the actions of Muslim crowds as being similarly directed" (Burke 1988: 22). Indeed, he has argued more recently that, in the most recent wave of popular protest, "beneath the surface one can detect a residue of the old Islamic moral economy" (Burke 1989b).

Burke does, however, distinguish two rather different approaches to the study of popular protest involving what even he insists on referring to as "Muslim crowds" in "the Islamic or Muslim world." The first focuses on the religious ideas that have inspired and to a degree shaped popular movements, thereby identifying them essentially as Islamic movements; the second, instead of privileging ideology as the central analytical category ... focuses on the movement (regardless of the cultural idiom in which it expresses itself). Such an undertaking begins with a consideration of the patterns of collective action – what the rebels did, where they gathered, the slogans they chanted, the targets of their wrath. But it is ultimately concerned with tracing the connections between changes in the patterns of protest and the changing structures of the society. (*Burke 1988: 26*).

This is essentially a strategy of the social sciences.

We shall adopt this approach, and consider "Islam" as a set of historically and socially constructed beliefs and practices capable of very considerable variability depending on the precise economic, social, and political context, and on the particular needs and objectives of different social groups and institutions. The importance, however, of ideas about justice and legitimacy in regard to relations between state and society – many of which are inevitably expressed in terms of "Islamic" precepts – must not be underestimated.

Undoubtedly, austerity protests constitute one element in a more complex process of growing popular dissent and unrest associated with changing relations between state and society across the region, and a growing sense of social injustice. Significantly, dissent and unrest have been fueled not only by the effects of government economic policies but also by the various forms of state oppression deployed to support the implementation of those policies but now increasingly seen as illegitimate and in contradiction with basic notions of social justice and human rights. Consequently, austerity protests have come, increasingly during the last decade – and particularly since events in Eastern Europe in 1989 – to be associated with broader movements for social and political reform as well as with immediate economic demands. It is arguable that this development marks the beginning of a new, "sixth wave" in the chronology of popular protest in the Middle East and North Africa, in which secular democratic movements and Islamic movements vie with each other to recast politics in the region in significantly new forms.

For among those now calling for radical political change and social justice are the Islamists, who draw on widely recognized social and cultural values to condemn not only the policies of existing regimes but often the regimes themselves. While two years ago we would not have agreed with those (like Richards and Waterbury 1990: 295) who argued that "urban violence now is taking a predominantly religious form," the political significance of Islamic ideology and Islamist movements has undoubtedly become very evident. It remains to be seen whether the popular claims of "the moral economy" and demands for social justice that have constituted such an important feature of popular protest against austerity and social deprivation in the 1980s will become more or less closely associated with the Islamist movements during the 1990s or whether the secular democratic forces will be able to forge an organization and a political ideology sufficiently appealing to the popular masses to gain their support and their commitment to a democratic state.

3   FROM NATIONALIST DEVELOPMENT TO *INFITAH*

The Contradictions of Nationalist Development

In the Middle East and North Africa, as elsewhere in the developing world, the achievement of national independence was succeeded by an even more difficult task – that of initiating national economic and social development. Throughout the region it was recognized that, even if desirable, reliance on the private sector was unlikely to provide an adequate basis for such development; even in those countries where there existed a significant indigenous urban bourgeoisie (Morocco, Egypt, Syria, Iraq) it was expected that the state would actively provide the framework for private capital accumulation. The state's role in national defense, internal security, social welfare, and justice was paramount and unchallenged. In general, the interventionist role of the state was facilitated and reinforced by the monopoly (or predominance) of a single party over the political process.

An early example was that of Turkey, where from 1923 onwards political independence was succeeded by far-reaching economic and social change, constituting what has often been referred to as "a revolution from above." In 1931, Mustapha Kemal "Ataturk," former military leader, nationalist and now head of state, issued a manifesto containing six principles that were to provide the basis for the 1937 Constitution: the Turkish state would be republican, nationalist, populist, secular, etatist, and revolutionary. While supporting private enterprise the ruling Republican People's Party (the only party) prescribed state intervention in every area of economic and social life. In 1934, Turkey became one of the first developing countries to conduct an experiment in planned development with its first Five Year Plan. At virtually the same time as Turkey embarked on its distinctive "modernization" program, Colonel Reza Khan of the

Persian Cossacks effectively took over the Iranian state. He planned to proclaim a republic, have himself made president, and build a "developmental state" like that of Ataturk in Turkey; but the Shi'ite clergy were strongly opposed to a republic and persuaded Reza Khan to proclaim himself shah in 1925 and found the Pahlevi "dynasty." During the 1930s and 1940s, while neither populist nor revolutionary, the Iranian state established itself as the central force for economic development, much as it had in Turkey. Its first national plan was launched in 1944, and in the postwar years, Reza Khan's son, Mohammed Reza Shah, further consolidated the state's control over the direction of economic development. After 1953, following the nationalization of the Anglo-Iranian Oil Company, strong state intervention in key areas of the economy was combined with a professed economic liberalism and commitment to the promotion of capitalist development. The objective, as in Turkey, was "a revolution from above."

During the 1950s and 1960s, the governments of several newly independent Middle Eastern states (Egypt, Syria, Iraq, Sudan, and Algeria) adopted strategies for national economic and social development broadly resembling the Turkish model but using the term "Arab socialism" to designate their objectives. Many of these governments were also formed by military officers who had taken power in the name of the popular masses. Towards the end of the 1960s these were joined by the new regime of Colonel Qaddhafi in Libya. What all of these essentially radical populist regimes had in common was a commitment to rapid economic and social transformation with the state as a dynamic force for "revolutionary change" on behalf of and in the name of "the people." Under regimes of this kind, the role of the state is to dominate the commanding heights of the economy in order to direct a process of state (or "public") capital accumulation. Iran since 1979 has, despite its self-presentation as something quite distinctive, followed broadly this strategy, although there have been indications in the last few years of a degree of economic liberalization, culminating in the reforms under President Rafsanjani in the early 1990s. Despite effective criticisms of their "socialist" credentials, and a degree of liberalization since the late 1970s, Iraq and Syria have both adhered by and large to this model of economic and social development, under the strict control of the Ba'ath party, since 1963, while Libya has probably gone further, since 1975 in particular, than any state in the region (apart from the Marxist Peoples' Democratic Republic of Yemen), to "strangle" the private sector (although recently, some liberalization has taken place even here).

In a number of cases, however, the explicit role of the state has been actively to protect and nurture private capital accumulation. It has been suggested (by Richards and Waterbury 1990: 215) that one can see this "handmaiden" role in operation generally in Morocco and Jordan, in Turkey since 1950, in Iran between 1963 and 1979 in particular, in Tunisia since 1969, in Sudan since 1972, and in Egypt since 1974. In some of these cases, however, a rhetorical commitment to "liberalism" and "private enterprise" has obscured the crucial interventionist role of the state.

Through the decade of the 1960s and into the 1970s the vast majority of Middle Eastern and North African states could be characterized broadly as "state capitalist" and their strategy for economic development as essentially that of import substitution industrialization. That there were significant variations within this general pattern is undeniable; but in virtually all cases, the state came to be, and to be seen by the population as a whole to be, a key element in the process of national economic and social development. In all of the states of the region there was also a public commitment to social development and social welfare, even if the benefits of increasing public expenditure and the growth of the state apparatus were by no means equally distributed. Whether the dominant political ideology of government was "liberal," "socialist" or "Islamic," a form of social contract between state and people was forged, in which the state was identified as the guarantor of basic welfare as well as the promoter of economic and social development. Although political power was highly concentrated, with opportunities for political expression limited and in most cases the effective monopoly of a single ruling party (Turkey provides an exception and Morocco a partial exception), the government claimed to act on behalf of the people as a whole and, by and large, that claim was not widely challenged.

Economic Crisis and Economic Reform

During the 1970s and 1980s, a series of global recessions and the process of international restructuring affected the states of the Middle East and North Africa as much as any part of the world. At the same time, government policies of adjustment and austerity, adopted to respond to the deepening economic crisis, themselves generated new contradictions and conflicts.

It may be argued that the very strategy of economic and social development widely adopted in the region (as elsewhere in the developing world during the preceding period) itself generated structural contradictions whose resolution would in any case have required significant revisions and adjustments (Richards and Waterbury 1990: 217). And, while we do not ascribe the same weight as do these commentators to domestic policies alone, there can be no doubt that government macro-economic strategies (often adopted it must be said under considerable political pressure) were partly responsible. Growing import bills coupled with stagnant exports, resulting in part from the nationalist development strategy and in part from secular changes in the international terms of trade and protectionism by the advanced capitalist states – which discriminated against primary producers (except oil producers) in favor of manufactures – led to rapidly increasing trade and balance-of-payments deficits. Many governments continued to invest significantly more resources than were saved domestically; as a result many states came during the 1970s to rely heavily on external sources of investment capital and began to accumulate large external debts.

Particularly in countries where revenues from oil exports did not exist, or were insufficient to provide (potentially at least) a cushion against growing economic and social tensions, governments were faced during the second half of the 1970s with a painful dilemma: either to attempt to maintain the nationalist development strategy by further external borrowing or to implement austerity measures as part of a program of economic reform aimed at liberalizing and "internationalizing" the economy. The first alternative risked the disapproval of the major lending agencies upon whom most states had become heavily reliant; the second risked domestic unrest in response to rising prices, declining real incomes, and the evident withdrawal of the state from its previous commitment to safeguard its citizens' basic economic and social welfare. While the majority of Middle Eastern and North African states experiencing major social unrest during the last 25 years were not major oil producers, events in Egypt (1977), Iran (1979) and Algeria (1987 and 1988) suggest that even oil producers were not immune.

Generally, after the mid-1970s, the oil-exporting countries were in a better position to avoid large-scale external borrowing, but many states – Sudan, Morocco, Tunisia, Egypt, Syria, Turkey – developed substantial "resource gaps" (investment minus domestic savings) and associated external debts. The deep world recession of the late 1970s and early 1980s significantly worsened these problems, and the burden of debt undoubtedly increased the pressures to introduce economic reforms; the reforms, however, failed in most cases to

Table 6.2   External public debt in selected Middle Eastern countries

Country	External public debt ($ billion)			External public debt as percentage of GNP		
	1970	1981	1988	1970	1981	1988
Algeria	0.9	14.4	23.2	19.3	35.2	46.6
Egypt	1.6	13.9	42.1	23.8	43.7	123.4
Iran	2.1	–	–	20.8	–	–
Jordan	0.1	1.4	3.9	22.9	38.7	94.0
Morocco	0.7	7.9	18.6	18.0	52.4	88.8
Sudan	0.3	4.8	8.0	15.8	59.3	71.3
Tunisia	0.5	3.1	5.9	38.2	38.0	61.7
Turkey	1.8	13.8	31.1	14.4	23.4	45.3

Sources: World Bank 1983b, 1990

resolve the problem of indebtedness, which continued grow throughout the 1980s (see table 6.2).

Government measures to promote economic reform, often adopted under the auspices of the IMF and the World Bank as preconditions for further lending or for debt rescheduling, began to be implemented by several governments during the second half of the 1970s. But the reforms introduced were often less stringent than external creditors and the international financial institutions – or indeed often the government and certain fractions of domestic capital – would have liked; the program actually implemented usually represented an attempt to respond to increasing external pressures without giving rise to major political dissent and social unrest. Three examples – those of Egypt, Turkey and Morocco – clearly illustrate the powerful constraint applied by the threat of social unrest.

The Politics of Adjustment

In Egypt, the "open door" (*infitah*) policy adopted by President Sadat in the early 1970s encouraged private capital and promoted liberalization both in international trade and within the national economy; cuts in public expenditure, particularly on subsidies, were also part of the new economic policy. But foreign capital failed to respond to the incentives provided, as did domestic private capital; by the middle of the decade, the government deficit and domestic inflation were growing apace, the public sector was stagnant and state enterprises making substantial losses, the country had fallen into arrears on payments on its commercial debt and foreign creditors were pressing ever harder for action. Attempts to negotiate the rescheduling of Egypt's debts led to the design of a program of financial stringency and economic reform, including major reductions in subsidies on basic goods. In the spring of 1976 Egypt entered into a Stand-By arrangement with the IMF.

In November, however, Sadat faced Egypt's first openly contested parliamentary elections since 1952; he postponed action on subsidy cuts until January 1977, after the elections. When the price increases were announced, three days of rioting ensued in Cairo, Alexandria, and other Egyptian towns. Sadat was obliged to revoke the price increases, and the stabilization program was shelved. Growing fears of major domestic unrest were heightened by Sadat's assassination by Islamists in 1981 and a state of emergency was declared. Despite the restrictions of the state of emergency, the first half of the 1980s was marked by persistent outbreaks of unrest involving low-paid workers in the private and public sectors for the most part. On occasion, these instances of popular protest involved key personnel in the state's own security forces. In 1986, for example, thousands of urban security police demonstrated against their working conditions and low pay; the demonstrations evolved into riots as the police struggled with the national guard and other security forces.

The Egyptian government under Mubarak remained unwilling to consider major economic reforms, despite growing pressure from its foreign creditors, until early 1987, when an agreement was again concluded with the IMF. But the government proved unable to adhere to the conditions of the agreement, mainly out of concern for the potential domestic repercussions, and the program collapsed. In May 1988, the state of emergency was extended for a further three years, but even so there were signs of increasing social unrest; in August there was serious trouble in the popular and working-class district of Ain Shams when local members of the radical Islamist group Gama'at al-Islamiya clashed with the security police, leaving six dead and and several hundred injured. In September, Mubarak told a rally, "we need economic reform, but I've told the IMF that this reform must be in line with our social and economic situation and the standard of living." With an estimated 40 percent of the population on or below the poverty line, and prices rising by an estimated 30 percent during 1988 alone, the government was unwilling to risk the political consequences of the far-reaching measures demanded by the IMF. Mubarak publicly likened the IMF to an unqualified doctor who prescribes life-threatening dosages of medicine.

Less than a year later, clashes between workers and the police at the Helwan Iron and Steel Works left several dead and injured. More than 600 were arrested after thousands of police stormed the steel works, using teargas, electric batons, and live ammunition to break up a sit-in. The action was in support of wage demands and in protest against the dismissal of colleagues who had attempted to organize a strike for pay increases in line with inflation and to compensate for rises in food prices after cuts in government subsidies. As was reported by Amnesty International in October 1989,

> Egypt's public sector workers have been hard hit by cuts in subsidies introduced as austerity measures to tackle Egypt's burgeoning foreign debt ... Economic pressure forcing down the living standards of public sector workers was a factor in earlier public sector strikes in the textile industry, on the railways and elsewhere. It is likely to contribute to continuing industrial unrest. (*Amnesty International 1989: 22*)

For the next two years, until Egypt's support for the US-led "coalition" in the Gulf War radically changed its fortunes, the government attempted ineffectively to combine limited economic reforms along the lines demanded by the IMF with the maintenance of political stability (Seddon 1991). Major efforts were made, in particular, to crush the various Islamist groups for whom support appeared to be growing particularly in the poor quarters of the major cities. By 1992, when Egypt eventually concluded a new agreement with the IMF, "the Islamic threat" had reached alarming proportions.

In the late 1970s, Turkey found itself in one of the region's gravest crises. For several years it had been governed by fragile and changing coalitions, none of which could risk actively promoting economic austerity for fear of the political reaction. Despite the adverse effects of "the oil crisis" and related external developments, "instead of relying on upon internal adjustment to promote balance of payments improvement, the various coalition governments pursued expansionary policies, while allowing a decline in marginal savings ratios, and negative import substitution in the energy and manufacturing sectors" (Celasun 1983: 11). This is partly explained by the fact that "from the mid-1970s, an increasingly militant and organized working class movement became a major obstacle to the success of the governments' crisis management policies" (Margulies and Yildizoglu 1988: 145). Industrial action, however, was unable to prevent a decline in real wages and a deterioration in living standards for large sections of the urban population. The general economic situation worsened: inflation climbed from 30 percent in 1974 to reach 64 percent by 1979; the foreign-trade deficit stood at $2.8 billion, having been reduced from $4 billion in 1977 by simple inability to pay for imports; servicing the foreign debt of around $13 billion had become a major burden, and the debt itself had to be rescheduled in 1978.

Eventually, in 1979, the social democratic government resigned in favour of the conservative Justice Party, which introduced a stringent economic-reform program with the support of the IMF and the benefit of martial law. In the short term the program involved devaluation, the abolition of stamp and import duties, and export promotion combined with tight monetary control, restrictions on wage increases, and the elimination of subsidies; in the longer term the objective was a substantial restructuring of the economy, transforming it from one based on import substitution to an export-oriented one. The response from abroad (from the IMF and World Bank, the commercial banks and western governments) was very positive: fresh loans were obtained, existing debts were rescheduled and Turkey obtained a net foreign-aid inflow of over $1.5 billion in 1980. At home, however, the result was powerful opposition from a broad spectrum of interests, expressed variously in parliament and within the state bureaucracy and in a massive increase in public social unrest and political violence. The first nine months of 1980 witnessed the largest strike wave in Turkish history and widespread popular unrest as real daily wages (already down from TL 27.07 in 1977 to TL 20.54 in 1979) slumped to TL 15.34 and consumer prices rose by 100 percent (Margulies and Yildizoglu 1988: 145).

In September 1980, the army intervened, suspended parliament, and banned all political parties, student organizations, and trade unions. With a state of emergency declared and major restrictions on civil liberties imposed, the new military regime was able to implement far-reaching economic reforms, pursuing virtually the program initiated by the Justice Party government. Despite the implementation of rigorous austerity measures over the next decade, state repression (continuing after the nominal return to civilian government in late 1983) was able to prevent any but the most limited protest; it was not until the next decade, with a slackening of state repression, that social unrest burst out once again.

In Morocco, after more than a decade of state repression since the first austerity protests of 1965, the government felt confident enough by 1978 to introduce a limited three-year stabilization program. The program introduced stricter import controls and cut public expenditure. But the austerity measures, although relatively mild, were met by a wave of strikes and a significant growth in trade-union opposition. The strikes – involving mainly organized workers in both private and public sectors – continued throughout 1978 and into 1979. Rallies and marches were frequently dispersed, often with considerable brutality, but the actions gained limited wage concessions and the unrest was contained. At the beginning of the 1980s, however, the Moroccan government faced growing pressure from its international creditors to implement more far-reaching measures to reduce public expenditure, encourage private enterprise and investment, and promote greater efficiency in the allocation and use of resources. But when attempts were made to cut public expenditure and reduce subsidies on basic commodities, the resulting social unrest was widespread and severe. In June 19811 major price increases in sugar, flour, butter and cooking oil provoked general strikes by the main trade-union federations and in Casablanca the strike developed into a more general demonstration against the effects of government economic policies as workers in both the private and public sectors were joined first by small shopkeepers and then by students and the unemployed. The riots brought special police units, the national guard and finally the army into action; in two days of clashes throughout the city 600 people were killed and many more injured. Faced with such opposition to the austerity measures, the Moroccan government hesitated to push ahead with more stringent policies, thereby incurring the disapproval of the IMF and World Bank and the withdrawal of their support (Seddon 1989a: 247).

For the next year or so, the government was mainly concerned to prevent political dissent. But by 1983, with confidence in its ability to contain opposition once again restored, and with the economic crisis deepening, the government was prepared to initiate (in August) a program of stabilization, involving a 10 percent devaluation, fiscal and credit restraints, cuts in public expenditure, and reductions in the level of food subsidies. With the experience of June 1981 a vivid memory, these measures must have been implemented with some trepidation; but the price increases of between 20 and 35 percent produced no immediate visible response. The measures adopted did, however, encourage Morocco's external creditors to provide effective support in the form of debt relief and rescheduling. A second round of price increases affecting basic commodities was implemented in December, while the draft budget for 1984 contained proposals for further austerity measures during the year. The cumulative effect on the cost of living – in the five months between July and October 1983 the cost-of-food index rose 10.6 percent and the general cost-of-living index by 8 percent – combined with the prospect of more to come proved too much to bear. In January 1984, massive demonstrations of popular protest broke out in towns and cities across the country. In the two weeks that followed, as many as 400 people were killed in clashes between demonstrators and security forces, while an estimated 9,000 people were arrested for their part in the unrest.

Despite the evident risk of provoking popular unrest, the deepening economic crisis experienced by many Middle Eastern and North African states in the second half of the 1970s, and the combination of external forces and pressures from powerful domestic interests, obliged governments to take increasingly drastic measures to restore the basis for capital accumulation. In the majority of cases this meant economic reform, adjustment, and austerity, usually under the auspices of the IMF and the World Bank. First "stabilization" and subsequently "structural adjustment" programs became increasingly the standard response of governments in the region during the 1980s. The stated objective of these reforms has been to overcome the deepening economic crisis experienced ever more generally during the second half of the 1970s and the 1980s and to restore the conditions for renewed capital accumulation and development (see El Naggar 1987). Renewed growth, it has been generally argued, both by the reforming governments and by the international financial institutions themselves, is the precondition for the adequate provision of social welfare.

In fact, however, renewed growth has proved elusive and problematic even under the most stringent of economic reforms implemented in the most draconian fashion by the most repressive of "strong governments" (e.g. Turkey after the coup). At the same time, the effects of the reforms themselves have directly threatened the livelihoods and welfare of large sections of the population, notably the urban poor, and have generated widespread and bitter anger and resentment at what has been seen as a betrayal of the state's obligations and an assault on the very foundations of that relationship between state and civil society that is widely regarded as the prerequisite for the fulfillment of social justice and basic needs. The reforms themselves, designed to promote growth and development but all too often failing to do either and at the same time deepening inequalities and withdrawing support from those who have most need of it, have come to constitute a key element in the creation of what might be termed the preconditions for social unrest. The anger and resentment widely felt at the effects of economic reforms has manifested itself in a variety of forms, of which general strikes, political rallies and marches, "spontaneous" street demonstrations, and "riots" have been the most dramatic and visible. These manifestations of popular discontent have themselves, we shall argue, affected government policy and even national politics in a broader and more lasting sense.

But in order to appreciate the extent and significance of popular protest it is necessary to consider it systematically on a comparative basis for the region as a whole.

4 ANATOMY OF POPULAR PROTEST

Scale and Significance

The scale of austerity protests discussed in this chapter is substantial; often tens of thousands of protestors are involved, in numerous demonstrations, usually across several towns and cities. In several cases, popular protest has had significant and far-reaching political consequences. Indeed, after eastern Europe, this region provides the best indication of the political potency of austerity protest.

In the case of Iran, where it is even more difficult than usual to dissociate popular protest against government economic policies and deteriorating economic conditions from other more obviously political issues, it has been estimated that during 1978 there were nearly 2,500 mass demonstrations and urban riots, involving some 1.6 million people, and over 1,200 strikes; more than 3,000 people were killed and over 12,000 injured (Ashraf and Banuazizi 1985: 22). Clearly, this was quite exceptional; but elsewhere also, the scale of popular protest has been substantial.

In Turkey during 1979 and 1980, over 100,000 people participated in nearly 350 separate strikes, while tens of thousands took to the streets in the major cities of western Anatolia. Some 2,000 people died in clashes between protestors and security forces and in interfactional violence during the seven months from February to September 1980 alone, with many thousands arrested and jailed, before the scale of civil unrest precipitated a military coup. In Morocco, in 1965, as many as 200–300 people may have been killed in clashes with security forces and many more hurt, while "hundreds" were reported to have been arrested; tens of thousands of workers took part in the strikes of 1978–9; tens of thousands again participated in the general strikes and mass demonstrations of 1981, and over 600 people died in Casablanca alone. In 1984, huge crowds took to the streets in most of the major cities and clashed with security forces – a total of 400 were conservatively estimated to have died during the two weeks of protest, with many more injured and thousands (estimates vary between 2,000 and 9,000) arrested. In 1990, mass demonstrations followed a largely successful general strike (involving hundreds of thousands of workers) called to demand better pay and working conditions and to oppose the government's economic-reform policies; in Fes alone, some 20,000 demonstrators clashed with workers who refused to strike and with "blacklegs" brought in to operate the public services, as well as with the security forces. The final official death toll was 65, but local estimates suggest well over 100.

In October 1988, Algeria was rocked by the most serious unrest since independence in 1962. The demonstrations began in the poorer quarters of Algiers and the shantytown areas, but soon spread widely through the city; popular protest also was reported from other cities, including Oran and Annaba. The state responded to the unprecedented social unrest with unprecedented violence; security forces in large numbers used live ammunition against the crowds and arrested thousands of protestors. Probably tens of thousands were involved in all and clashes with security forces – the brutality of whose attempts at repression were extraordinary – left several hundred dead in the six days of rioting. Even when the protest was crushed in Algiers, there continued to be clashes in other, smaller towns, like Tiaret. In Tunisia in late 1977, growing dissatisfaction with economic conditions led to a wave of strikes which effectively brought whole sectors of the national economy to a standstill. The army was called in to deal with the strikers; and in response, the Union Général des Travailleurs Tunisiens (UGTT) called a national strike, which was observed throughout the country in January 1978. Hardliners in the cabinet voted for the repression of the strike movement with a view to destroying the power of the trade-union movement; and when disturbances broke out in Tunis during the general strike, the army was given *carte blanche*. Estimates of the number killed vary between 46 and 200; some 800 people were arrested immediately and thousands of trade unionists sentenced subsequently by summary courts.

In Egypt, in 1977, demonstrations involving between 2,000 and 4,000 protestors were reported in Cairo, with numerous "large" protests in other cities. The government imposed a curfew in Cairo and ordered the security forces to shoot anyone breaking it. Several explosions were reported and demonstrators fought police after nightfall in two densely populated suburbs, adding 13 to the death toll which, according to *Al Ahram*, eventually reached 43 (with 600 injured) in Cairo alone. At least 600 people were arrested in Cairo during the demonstrations and many more detained in other cities. The final official death toll (widely considered extremely conservative) was 73.

In cases like these, the very size and scale of the protest and of the violence was such that they could not be ignored. In some cases, however, although the numbers actually involved and the scale of violence were substantially smaller, the political repercussions were considerable because the popular protest gave rise to more organized forms of protest and opposition involving an even wider spectrum of social forces. In the case of Sudan, for example, the initial "bread riots" in Khartoum in March 1985 involved only around 1,000 people, while the mass march on the US embassy on the second day, which provoked the use of teargas and shooting by the security forces, was estimated only at "up to 2,000." Five people were reported killed in Khartoum and some hundreds injured after two days of clashes; the final death toll was probably no more than 20 to 30. But this demonstration of popular protest was only the prelude to the development of a more substantial, organized movement of opposition, involving strikes and a campaign of civil disobedience by professional and middle-class associations and student organizations as well as organized labor and public-sector workers. By the beginning of April, the number of those detained by the security forces had reached over 5,000. On April 3, "thousands of middle class Sudanese protestors flooded the city of Khartoum ... Diplomats estimated about 20,000 in the centre of the city. In contrast to the destruction during food riots the previous week by students and unemployed street dwellers, the demonstration was mainly people in their 30s and 40s and peaceful, if vociferous, and extremely well planned" (Seddon 1989b: 122). When the crowd of some 20,000, led by the professional associations (doctors, lawyers, engineers, and accountants) and joined by bank workers, shop staff, academics, and students, began to march on the presidential palace, a civil rebellion was declared. Meanwhile, large numbers of workers and salaried employees joined those already on strike. Shops and offices were closed and transport, telecommunications, electricity and water services were all seriously affected. Over the next two days the scale and extent of the demonstrations and civil disobedience increased, and a state of emergency was declared. On April 6, the army took power; the regime of President al-Numeiry had been overthrown (see Abdelkarim, el-Hassan, and Seddon 1985; Seddon 1989b: 120–4).

In Jordan, in 1989 demonstrations in response to price rises broke out in the small southern town of Ma'an and led to the deaths of around 10 people; some 50 or so were injured. Within a day or so, however, the rioting gave way to an orchestrated campaign to apply political pressure on the government not only to reconsider its economic strategy but also to introduce political reforms. Popular anger was directed largely towards Prime Minister Zaid al Rifai, who was blamed for the government's economic policies and the deteriorating economic situation. On the second day of the protests, local community leaders produced a petition outlining what were to become nationally endorsed demands: the resignation of al Rifai and his government and the formation of an "honest and strong nationalist government"; the revoking of the austerity measures, including the price increases and the formulation of a "national economic program" taking into consideration the plight of the lower classes; the punishment of officials convicted of corruption and embezzlement; the amendment of the current electoral law to provide a democratic, pluralist parliamentary representation; and the reestablishment of political freedoms and a free press. These demands were subsequently extended to include a call for the trial of al Rifai, the lifting of martial law (in operation since 1967), and financial support for small farmers.

Support for these demands gained momentum when the Amman-based leaders of the national professional associations backed the call for reforms and the resignation of al Rifai in a message to Crown Prince Hassan (temporarily in charge while King Hussein visited Washington). On the king's return he dismissed al Rifai and appointed a new prime minister together with three deputies known to be critics of the government's policies; he also nominated several experienced economists to key government posts. The government remained bound to a program of "economic reform" if it was to obtain the promised $250 million IMF Stand-By loan required to facilitate the rescheduling of Jordan's foreign debt; but political reforms were immediately introduced. By September, campaigning for the country's first general elections was under way; during September and October 1989 virtually all of those arrested during the April demonstrations were released; and in December a new government was formed with a program which included significant civil- and human-rights reforms.

In these instances, popular protest on a relatively small scale either gave rise to an orchestrated movement for political change or obliged the government itself to initiate political reforms to prevent the emergence of a more threatening and better organized opposition.

Geography of Protest

It has been suggested that "overurbanization" is a significant variable in the comparative analysis of contemporary austerity protest (Walton and Ragin 1990), and certainly, urban growth in the Middle East and North Africa has been extremely rapid. Shantytowns have sprung up and spread around the major cities of the region, while pressure on the inner areas of the "old cities" has increased dramatically. In many of the instances of popular protest considered, urban living conditions (infrastructure, housing and transport) have clearly been as important a source of discontent as the more frequently cited living costs, unemployment, and low incomes. In Cairo in 1977, in Algiers in 1988, and in Fes in 1990, for example, there is little doubt that population pressure and the extreme deterioration of the very fabric of the city contributed significantly to popular unrest.

Urban employment has failed to keep pace with the supply of labor, just as the development of the urban infrastructure has signally failed to keep up with the increasing demands of a growing urban population. The expansion of the informal sectors of urban economies has been particularly marked. Rapid urbanization has also resulted in the formation of new urban social classes and groupings; the massive expansion of the informal sector has led to a huge increase in the number of the various social categories that together constitute the urban poor. Urban population growth, the growth of the informal sector, and growth in urban inequality have gone hand in hand across the region. High levels of unemployment, low and unreliable incomes, and miserable living conditions have combined to create a massive problem of urban poverty and deprivation affecting not only the major cities but also smaller urban centres.

Contrary to what one might expect, austerity protests have not always started in the major cities or the capital, but in some cases began in smaller towns in historically disadvantaged but politically significant regions. Certainly, in the majority of cases, the mass demonstrations have begun and continued in the largest urban agglomerations, where the rapid growth of shantytowns and the overcrowding in the slums of the old cities and poor quarters ensure a "critical mass" of the urban poor who constitute the major source for "spontaneous" popular protest. But in Tunisia in 1984, the unrest started in the small towns of the semi-arid Southwest, in Morocco in 1984 the most violent demonstrations were in the underdeveloped north of the country, and in Jordan in 19891 it was unrest in the small town of Ma'an in the South that sparked off a wave of protest throughout the country.

In Tunisia in 1984, social unrest following price increases began in the Nefzaoua, a semi-arid region in the Southwest (historically the poorest region of Tunisia), and then spread to other parts of the South. The southern interior generally has a high unemployment rate, and many men leave the area for work in the more prosperous towns on or near the coast; some 60,000 were employed as migrant labor in Libya in the early 1980s. The region also suffered considerably from the drought of 1983–4 which substantially reduced the local harvest. After the outbreak of mass protest in January 1984, a local observer in Kebili (one of the small southern towns where violent demonstrations took place) remarked that "it was not for bread that the young demonstrated, but because they were the victims of unemployment." But this was not all. The south was an area where "Libyan influence" was felt to be considerable and where political opposition to the government had been openly expressed in the recent past. The governor of Kebili, declared that "foreign-inspired agitators" were involved in the demonstrations; in Gafsa, "capital" of the South, the governor identified "Libyan- or Lebanese-trained Tunisians" leading the demonstrations.

In Morocco, in 1984, the earliest demonstrations also occurred in the south (particularly in Marrakesh), where the drought of 1983–4 had seriously affected food availability and the cost of living. But the region where mass protest developed on the most significant scale and generated the greatest violence, was the North. This region, which had remained seriously underdeveloped under Spanish occupation until 1956, suffered acutely during its subsequent integration with the rest of Morocco between 1956 and 1960. Furthermore, the North, and particularly the Northeast where popular protest in 1984 was most severe, has been the source of open opposition to the regime since the 1920s and is still regarded as a politically volatile region. During 1958 and 1959, largely in response to the economic and political marginalization of the North, there was serious social unrest and even a major rebellion. Throughout the next two decades the region remained economically as well as politically marginal despite efforts to invest in agricultural development, and the majority of the population depended on remittances from migrant workers in Europe and elsewhere and from smuggling. In the late 1970s and early 1980s, the small towns of the region experienced a dramatic growth in population without a corresponding increase in jobs; unemployment was high and remittances were declining as the recession deepened in Europe. It came as no surprise to those familiar with the region's history and contemporary problems that when popular protest broke out the North and Northeast were particularly affected (Seddon 1981; 1989c).

In Jordan, in 1989, less than 48 hours after the government announced price increases for fuel and other basic commodities as part of the IMF economic-reform program, demonstrations in a small town in the south sparked off a wave of popular protest across the country. It was the fact that anger exploded first in Ma'an and then other small towns in the south that transformed a protest against price increases into a nationwide struggle for a fairer distribution of wealth, social justice, and political reforms. For it was the town of Ma'an that the late King Abdullah chose as a base when he first came to Transjordan; and since then, the south has been the bedrock of support for the regime. This bond was strengthened by the large-scale recruitment of young men from the region in the administration and the army. When public expenditure was slashed, many of them lost their jobs; in addition to its reliance on public-sector employment, the south is also heavily dependent on incomes from other activities hard hit by the economic reforms. The price increases were simply "the last straw." Unlike the cases of Tunisia and Morocco, however, the south of Jordan was politically significant not because of its economic marginality and tradition of political opposition, but precisely because of its economic dependence and its identification with the regime.

Whether starting in small towns or major cities, it is rare for major cases of popular protest to be confined to a single urban center — as in the case of the Casablanca riots of 1981 in Morocco. Generally, if protest is limited to a single center, it remains limited and may not be recognized as part of a wider protest movement. Often, however, while demonstrations take place in several centers, one in particular experiences major riots. This was the case in Morocco in December 1990, when a general strike gave rise to demonstrations across the country but the city of Fes experienced particularly serious disturbances.

Wherever the protest initially breaks out, in virtually all cases it subsequently spreads widely to other towns and cities. Sometimes this is because protestors themselves actually take their protest from one place to another; more frequently, the news spreads or the same factors trigger off a simultaneous protest in several places. In Egypt in 1977, for example, the demonstrations started in the industrial town of Helwan, where steel workers stoned cars and buses before ordering truck drivers to take them into Cairo. While Cairo then experienced the largest concentration of protestors and every railway line between Cairo and Alexandria, Suez, and the South was torn up in Cairo's suburbs, there were also large demonstrations in many other major cities, including Alexandria, Aswan, Kena, and Menia, where a new textile factory was badly damaged. In Sudan, in 1985, although Khartoum and its suburbs constituted the major focus of popular protest, other towns also were involved: there was rioting in Nyala, al-Fasher, and al-Geneina in the West; at Atbara in the north; and in Port Sudan in the east. In Turkey, when 50,000 coal miners in Zonguldak on the Black Sea coast went on strike in December 1990 – to be followed in January 1991 by hundreds of thousands of workers in other industries – the striking miners and their wives actually marched on the capital, Ankara, to press their demands for better working conditions, improved pay, and the resignation of Turgut Ozal, the architect of the government economic-reform program, and his government. They were stopped outside Bolu on their 150-mile march only by a massive display of strength by the security forces.

The Faces in the Crowd

In the majority of cases, the street demonstrations or riots have involved predominantly unemployed and casually employed young men, usually from the shantytowns and urban slums; the strikes have involved workers in the private and public sector, and the marches and petitions the more organized groups, including trade unions, professional associations and their members; while students may be involved in all three kinds of protest. There appears to be a very general tendency for the involvement of the more organized groups and of the middle classes to follow the "spontaneous" demonstrations of the urban poor, taking advantage of these to orchestrate more systematic and coherent opposition. Such tendencies are, however, very general, for it is clear from the instances presented above, that popular protest may have a complex dynamic or "bandwaggon" effect, so that those social groups initially involved may be joined by others, or even replaced by them as the protest finds new forms and patterns of expression. What starts out as a strike or march, may turn into a demonstration or riot, what starts out as a street demonstration may give rise to more orchestrated and organized forms of protest. Furthermore, several forms of protest involving different social groups may take place simultaneously.

The complexity of the process is exemplified well by the case of Iran prior to the revolution of 1979, where a combination of forms of protest, ranging from petitions and meetings, to rallies and strikes, marches and street demonstrations, involved student organizations, political groupings and the clergy, workers, shopkeepers, and the unemployed, men, women, and children. As Halliday remarks,

> the social forces that responded to the movement varied: in the first clashes of 1978 the main components were theology students and bazaar merchants, but these groups, far more in touch with the population than the secular parties, were able to call on the urban poor who formed the foot-soldiers of the major demonstrations in the latter part of the year. Parallel to these protests the students and parties continued their actions, and in the final weeks of the regime it appears that significant numbers of middle-class people also joined in the demonstrations. (*Halliday 1988: 44–5*)

If, as Walton has pointed out, "protest forms are mutable," it is also the case that "the faces in the crowd" may change as the protest evolves and changes. However, even in the case of Iran, "we do not yet have the detailed information necessary to establish who were 'the faces in the crowd' that made the Iranian Revolution, that is, a precise evaluation of the social forces behind the revolution" (Halliday 1988: 59).

Nevertheless, in most cases it seems clear that the majority of those involved have been the unemployed and casually employed from the shantytown and slum areas. As was said of the Tunisian protests of 1984:

> the disturbances were caused mainly by the young unemployed, a section of society who until now have been largely ignored by both President Bourghiba's government and political analysts ... right until the moment when President Bourghiba made his *volte face*, cancelling the increases, it was the rage of the unemployed which dominated the protest, and it was they who alarmed the government. (*The Times, January 7, 1984*)

In all cases, the rioters are mainly young, with the majority probably in the 15–25 age range; in some instances, observers have reported youths of between 12 and 15 involved in stone-throwing and other activities. But, on the basis of reports of those injured or killed (where such details tend to be highlighted), it also appears that the crowds often include the elderly. The majority of those involved in all forms of protest, and perhaps particularly in the street demonstrations and riots, are male; but there is sufficient evidence to suggest that women are also involved to an important extent, usually in "supportive" roles (e.g. shouting from the roof-tops) but sometimes more actively (for a more detailed discussion, see Chapter 3).

The physical pattern of protest within the towns and cities, while evidently linked to the social origins and location of those who took part, is difficult to generalize. Use of the phrase, "the Arab street" (Brumberg 1991: 186) or "the Muslim street" (Piscatori 1991 11–17) to refer to the social milieu of popular protest obscures the complexity of the social constituents and physical locations of popular protest. Frequently, however, demonstrations begin in the poorer quarters and shantytowns and then spread to other areas of town. In Algeria in 1988, for example, the riots started in the Bab el Oued, a slum district of Algiers and in the neighboring Kasbah, and in the Peripherique on the outskirts of the city where the major shantytowns are situated. In Algiers, a city designed for 850,000, the population now numbers over 3,000,000, and it is not surprising that the riots broke out first in the poorer, overcrowded parts of the city. But other factors are involved. The people of Bab el Oued, for example, have a long tradition of defying authority; it was the center of some of the fiercest resistance against the French. There were also major demonstrations in El Biar, the district of diplomatic and government residences, and in Hussein Dey, an eastern industrial area, and Jouba Qadim, areas which are known as Islamist strongholds. If the demonstrations are not orchestrated, they were not without distinctive socio-political "roots." Often, however, if the protest has its origins in the backstreets, the major demonstrations take place in the streets and squares of the town central areas, where the government buildings, office blocks, luxury shops, and hotels that are the major targets of the crowd tend to be concentrated.

Targets of the Crowd

The demonstrations of popular protest are, in most cases, spontaneous, in the sense of not being orchestrated or previously organized by established groups or movements; but the actions of the crowds in the streets are by no means random. If violence against property is common, and some immediate targets – such as places of work, vehicles in the street and shops – are almost routinely identified, more substantial destruction is usually directed towards the symbols of affluence (banks, luxury hotels, airline offices, expensive stores) or towards the offices of institutions representing the state or the party. In many demonstrations, explicit reference is made to the IMF or the World Bank; in some, open criticism of government policies or of the regime itself and the political leadership is expressed.

Looting is common, and often explicitly justified in the language of "the moral order." Reference to "hunger" is frequently made to underline the justice of the protests, and as a rallying cry. In Algiers in 1988, one of those in the crowd that gathered outside the burned-out Monoprix supermarket after the rioting, when the building had been stormed,-looted and put to the torch, claimed that "the kids did it … because they are hungry" (*The Independent*, October 10, 1988). In Cairo in 1977, when riot police opened fire on crowds marching towards the National Assembly, this did not deter the crowds, who replied by shouting in unison: "We are dying of hunger now, so go ahead and shoot us, Sadat" (*The Times*, January 20, 1977).

In many instances, there is explicit criticism of the regime and the political leadership, and reference to "alternatives." In Cairo, during the protests of 1977, one Helwan steel worker climbed on the National Assembly railings, his blue coat torn open at the elbows and his shoes held together with string. He waited a few seconds and then bellowed: "Lets bring this government down." Shortly after this, riot police arrived and drove the crowd towards Liberation Square, already crowded with over 3,000 demonstrators. As clouds of teargas covered the square, thousands more students marched through the main shopping streets, shouting "Nasser, Nasser" and "There can be no liberalization without food" (*The Times*, January 20, 1977).

In several cases, hostility towards "the one-party state" is demonstrated by attacks on the local authorities and the offices of the party itself. In Egypt in 1977, for example, in Alexandria, crowds of dock workers burned shops and two cinemas, and then went on to set fire to the Arab Socialist Union building. In Sudan in 1985, demonstrators smashed shop windows and car windshields, overturned vehicles and set them on fire, and blocked the streets with chunks of concrete and other heavy objects. Three buildings suffered particularly heavy damage: a branch office of the official Sudanese Socialist Union (the only party permitted under al-Numeiry), the Faisal Islamic Bank (preserve of the Muslim Brotherhood), and the luxury Meridien Hotel (Seddon 1989b: 120). In Algeria in 1988, in Kouba district to the east of Algiers, the mayor's office was burnt down; while in Oran, the Front de Liberation National (FLN) party headquarters was set on fire.

In many instances, elements in the crowd recognize the significance of external forces behind the austerity measures. In Sudan in 1985, students chanted, "We will not be ruled by the World Bank, we will not be ruled by the IMF," as the unemployed urban poor in the crowd protested at the increasing cost of living (Seddon 1989b: 120). "In Omdurman town, a part of greater Khartoum, hundreds of women took to the streets in a large demonstration to protest against rising food prices: many were shouting, 'Down down with the IMF'" (Seddon 1989b: 122). The role of external agents in the repression of the demonstrations themselves was recognized in the protests in Egypt in 1977: one group of demonstrators chanted anti-American slogans, claiming that all the teargas came from the United States; and indeed many of the empty canisters retrieved bore the label "CS 518 Federal Laboratories Inc. of Saltsburg Pennsylvania" (*The Times*, January 19, 1977).

Spontaneous Protest or Organized Opposition?

To argue that the many instances of popular protest discussed in this chapter were essentially spontaneous, in the sense of not having been planned or organized beforehand, does not mean that the actions of the crowd were random or irrational, or that no organized interests or groupings were involved. The evidence of a widespread moral indignation and anger directed towards specific targets has already been discussed; this suggests a concern with social justice and with broad social and political issues beyond the simple matter of cost of living and prices. Furthermore, elements in the crowd were clearly prepared openly to criticize the regime and the political leadership and to draw attention also to the external forces behind government policies.

The involvement and influence of more organized political group-ings cannot be denied. In many cases, "leftist" organizations were involved, and in almost all instances, there is evidence that Islamic groups participated in the demonstrations. In the case of Tunisia in 1984, some commentators suggested that "growing Islamic funda-mentalism" enabled agitators to encourage violence against property representing the symbols of luxury, corruption and foreign influence, and to adopt such slogans as "There is but one God and Bourghiba is the enemy of God"; and it is true that Islamist pamphlets were circulated during the demonstrations and that minarets were used to chant *allah u akbar*. Generally, however, there is evidence that the Islamic groups, like the opposition political parties and trade unions, were often taken by surprise by the outburst of popular protest and surprisingly slow to respond. In Algeria in 1988, some reports sug-gested that Islamic groups may even have played a significant part in attempting to limit the protest and avert violence. Despite the manifest involvement of political activists from opposition groups in most of the instances of popular protest, there is little support for the notion that they played a key role in orchestrating the social unrest. They – like so many others – were usually taken by surprise by what were essentially popular uprisings.

Some such groups claimed responsibility. In Tunisia in 1984, for example a group calling itself the Tunisian National Opposition Movement (MONT) claimed responsibility – from Brussels – for the demonstrations, and denounced "the repression by the Tunisian security forces of the hunger rioters." In Algeria in 1988, a group calling itself the Peoples' Movement for Algerian Renewal claimed responsibility for the popular protest – in a telephone call to a news agency; it demanded the government's resignation, the dissolution of parliament, the abolition of the FLN, the election of "peoples committees," the revision of the constitution, and an end to martial law. The movement was thought to be linked with anti-government groups within the FLN associated with the former Communist Party and strongly opposed to the government's economic policies, who used the riots, and the earlier strikes at Rouiba and in Algiers, to bring pressure to bear on the government to revise its economic strategies or stand down. But the recognized leftwing parties (officially outlawed but tolerated) clearly intervened only after the outbreak of mass protest, and then only to call on the government to resolve the crisis. The Tunisian Communist party, for example, wrote to the prime minister demanding that there be consultations with "all national forces" to find a solution to the situation, and otherwise confined itself to condemning the violence. The Social Democrats (MDS) and the Communist Party both criticized the deployment of the army and laid the responsibility at the door of the government, but did little else.

5   THE CONSEQUENCES OF POPULAR PROTEST

Immediate State Responses: Repression

The usual immediate state response to popular protest is to deploy the security forces, while at the same time denying that the unrest is anything other than the work of small groups of "agitators" or "enemies of the people." The latter claim is used to legitimize the former action, and to try to avoid the impression that the protest is general and that the state is moving to repress its own people.

In Egypt in 1977, even before the demonstrations had ended, government officials were blaming "communist agents" for engineering the protests; by the second day of the demonstrations, Cairo radio was interrupting its broadcasting every five minutes to inveigh against "communism." Neither the government-controlled press nor the radio gave information about the rioting, referring only to vague reports of "sabotage by leftists" and quoting claims by government that "communist-recruited elements" were agitating the crowds. On the evening after "normality" had been restored in Cairo, the minister of the interior announced that the authorities had uncovered a plot to burn down the city, adding that the violence was "an engineered Marxist plot aimed at damaging the country." In Tunisia in 1984, official explanations played down the doubling of bread prices and stressed the role of "foreign-inspired agitators." The governors of Kebili and of Gafsa, towns in the south where the protests started, both referred to agitators and the role of Libya in supporting or sponsoring their activities; the prime minister referred to "veritable insurrectionist commandos, well organized and coordinated," and announced that "the young people have been enticed and misled into demonstrations which appear spontaneous, but behind which lies a plan for destabilisation and elements more or less inspired by certain influences whose declared objective is the overthrow of the regime"; and the Tunisian ambassador in Paris assured a French television audience that the price increases "had very little to do with the rioting," and blamed "uncontrolled elements" (Seddon 1989b: 115).

In Morocco in 1984, King Hassan blamed Islamic fundamentalists, Communists and Marxist-Leninists, and "the Zionist secret services," for instigating the protests; in 1991, after the mass demonstrations and riots of the previous December, he referred to those involved as "criminals and bandits." In Sudan in 1985, students referred to as "ideologists" (an official euphemism for the recently banned Muslim Brotherhood) were initially blamed for the riots, while later the secretary of the official Sudan Socialist Union publicly accused Libya, Ethiopia, and the Soviet Union of involvement in anti-government activities and in sponsoring "communist" agitators and promised that Communists, Ba'athists and Muslim brothers would all be hunted down (Seddon 1989b: 116). In Algeria in 1988, there were several official references to "unseen hands" behind the demonstrations (although those involved remained unspecified, leaving it to speculation as to whether the reference was to Islamists, Berbers, students, communists, foreigners, or opposition elements within the FLN).

A general sequence in the mobilization of security forces can be identified: first, the police are brought in to maintain law and order;

then, when it becomes clear that they are unable to contain the protest, the national guard or other "special" security forces are deployed – it is generally at this point that the level of violence increases significantly; finally, the army is brought in, with heavy equipment (armored cars, tanks, etc.). In Morocco in 1990, for example, the police initially acted with restraint; shooting was reported to have started only when the "special units" were brought in. Eventually, after two days of rioting, "the streets were strewn with stones, broken glass, and the occasional burned out car. Shops, banks, factories and state buildings had been put to the torch. A sullen populace moved silently while armed troops guarded key crossroads and public buildings. Light tanks were positioned everywhere" (Hiett 1990: 12).

In only relatively rare cases, as in Iran in 1979 and in Turkey in 1978–9, do clashes between protestors and security forces involve major exchanges of fire; usually, it is the security forces alone who use firearms. Turkey in 1978–9 was exceptional in that many of the different warring political factions had their paramilitary groups, who were armed, and there were numerous clashes between such armed groups and the security forces even under the rule of martial law, prior to the coup in September 1980. Even in Iran it was only towards the very end of the shah's regime that armed confrontation was the dominant form of resistance: the preceding months were dominated by the street demonstration and the political general strike. In a few other cases also the protests involved the use of firearms on both sides, but always on a small scale. In Algiers in 1988, really violent clashes began on the third day; by this time some of the protestors were armed and in some districts (notably in El Biar) there were was shooting. It may well be that it was the fear of a potential armed uprising that encouraged the Algerian state to react so brutally in its repression of the subsequent demonstrations.

In some cases, as in Algeria in 1988, the violence of the state's response is such as to create a new climate of anger and outrage, which in turn creates pressure on the government to respond by removing those held responsible from power and, sometimes, to initiate political reforms; in others, it is the failure of the security forces to crush the protest sharply and effectively that precipitates limited political changes, as in Tunisia after the unrest of 1984, when the minister of the interior was removed and later indicted for treason, for failing to deal "properly" with the demonstrations. In that case, the prime minister declared (as he took over the post as an interim measure) that "the first lesson to be drawn from the events of January was that it is necessary to reorganise the forces of order so that they can respond adequately to all situations" (Seddon 1984: 16).

In some cases, the deployment of the security forces alone proves sufficient to crush the social unrest, but even in these cases the political threat posed by the popular protest generally leads to the arrest and harassment of known political activists; in some cases, the declaration of a state of emergency (Morocco in 1965, Sudan in 1985) or the imposition of martial law (as in Turkey in 1979) is considered necessary as a temporary measure.

Immediate State Responses: Restitution

Often, however, despite the efforts of the state and the security forces, popular protest has not been contained immediately by repression alone. In many such cases – in Egypt in 1977, in Tunisia and Morocco in 1984, in Sudan in 1985, in Algeria in 1988, in Jordan in 1989 – governments felt obliged to revoke publicly the price increases that, despite official denials, so often appear to have been the trigger for protest. In some instances, tactical offers to withdraw the measures which had led to price increases were made relatively early on.

In Egypt in 1977, for example, well before the announcement by President Sadat that he would rescind the price increases, the minister of state for parliamentary affairs indicated that the government was prepared to reconsider on this issue. Measures to increase minimum wage levels or to increase real wages by a certain percentage have also commonly been adopted, in some cases after direct discussions with trade-union representatives – as in Morocco in 1978–9 and in Tunisia in 1984. In Morocco in 1990, the government attempted to preempt the general strike threatened for December by announcing plans to implement "substantial rises in wages and other benefits" for workers and by holding "peace talks" with the unions concerned; and in January 1991, King Hassan announced a 15 percent increase in the minimum wage, calling for "a social pact for peace."

But all too often government-sponsored wage increases affect only those in formal-sector employment within the protection of the law and the scope of the trade unions, and fail to meet the needs of the majority of the urban poor. Pay deals with the unions are not, therefore, likely to reduce discontent among the urban poor. This was recognized by the Sudan government when it tried in early

April 1985 to. forestall the development of an organized opposition movement by announcing that wages would generally be increased between 20 and 40 percent, with the largest increases to go to lower-paid workers, to offset the effects of the recent devaluation of the Sudanese currency and the removal of subsidies on certain commodities.

In most cases, however, efforts by government to effect a tactical retreat by revoking the price increases and effectively recognizing the "social costs" of the austerity measures have proved largely successful in bringing popular protest to a halt. Just as the the price increases symbolize for the urban poor a denial of the state's responsibility for their basic needs (as well as a real increase in the cost of living and therefore increased deprivation), so the withdrawal of the price increases symbolizes a recognition by the state of the "justice" of the protestors' case, even if the real effects of such a concession might be limited. In Jordan in 1989, for example, Crown Prince Hassan (who was temporarily in charge while King Hussein was in Washington), flew immediately to Ma'an to listen to the people's grievances; when the king returned he pledged himself to "address the problem at its roots as soon as possible." He then dismissed the prime minister, al Rifai, who had been identified by the protestors as the architect of the economic-reform program, and appointed new economic advisers critical of the al Rifai government's policies.

Often, however, the "withdrawal" of the austerity measures is only temporary – a dramatic and visible response to popular demands. In the majority of cases, government economic-reform programs have acquired a momentum (for reasons associated both with domestic and with external forces) which could be brought to a halt only with enormous difficulty and is often only temporarily slowed down or postponed. In Tunisia, during the period after President Bourghiba's promise that the price increases would be revoked, the government continued, albeit more circumspectly this time, to pursue the economic reforms which had given rise to the dramatic price rises that triggered the popular protest in January 1984. In Algeria also, even after the events of 1988 and recognition by the government of the need for political reforms, the economic liberalization program was pursued, even though in the immediate aftermath of the riots the new prime minister presented a plan aimed at combining liberalization and economic reform with a reduction in unemployment, increases in wages for the low paid, and improvements in the availability of consumer goods. (This immediate attempt to meet some of the concerns of the protestors did not prevent a fresh outbreak of industrial action, with workers striking to demand improved wages and the sacking of incompetent managers – the most serious of these incidents, involving hundreds of dock workers at Skikda in eastern Algeria, alone cost more than $40 million in lost production. Unlike the strikes which preceded the October riots, however, these remained uncoordinated and relatively small-scale). But within a year, Merbah had been dismissed from office and reports suggested that "social instability is growing in the Algiers kasbah and poorer suburbs as the economic conditions that sparked off last October's riots fail to visibly improve" (Bamford 1989: 10). In Jordan, despite the dismissal of al Rifai and some discussion of the "national economic program" with protection for vulnerable groups proposed by the opposition movements, the government remained generally bound by its economic program (including the austerity measures) if the $250 million IMF Stand-By loan was to be obtained to facilitate the desperately needed rescheduling of the foreign debt.

In most of the countries which have experienced major upsurges of popular protest, economic reforms have been pursued even in the face of growing social dissatisfaction, popular protest and political opposition, as the economic pressures (particularly those exerted by western states, commercial banks, and the international financial agencies) to implement far-reaching "adjustment" continue to grow. Morocco, Tunisia, Algeria, Jordan, and Turkey are all cases in point. Despite a history of popular protest, and the continuing threat this poses to the stability of the regime, governments have continued to pursue economic liberalization while at the same time attempting to maintain control over what is, throughout the region, an increasingly turbulent political landscape. In 1992, after a decade of compromise, Egypt appeared to have joined the others. It would seem that even the threat of popular protest, with its increasing potential for fueling radical opposition and contributing to the overthrow of the regime cannot prevent the onward march of "structural adjustment." In the face of overwhelming pressures for continuing liberalization and adjustment, governments attempt to combine repression and political reform to prevent social unrest and popular protest from bringing about their downfall. This is not to say that popular protest has had no effect other than to stimulate short-term reactions on the part of the state. It is rather to emphasize that accommodations to popular protest over austerity measures as part of structural adjustment and economic reform have been made generally in the political, rather than in the economic sphere.

Longer-Term Political Consequences

The political consequences of popular protest have been particularly marked in the Middle East and North Africa. They range from the overthrow of a regime (in Iran in 1979 and Sudan in 1985), through diverse political reforms initiated from above to provide a greater variety of channels for political expression (Tunisia after 1984, Algeria after 1987, and Jordan after 1989), to various forms of repression and "states of emergency" (Morocco after 1965, Egypt after 1981, Turkey in 1979–80, Sudan in 1985, and Algeria after 1991) and military coups (Turkey in 1980, Sudan in 1985).

The range of responses is clearly considerable and the factors determining them complex. Two initial observations, however, can be made: first, that, during the 1970s and 1980s, the most systematic state repression of popular protest occurred in those countries with the strongest democratic traditions and strongest organized opposition; and second that the moves towards political reform took place in states where previously the scope for political expression was strictly limited and controlled by the state. Although it is perhaps significant that political liberalization was generally initiated in the second half of the 1980s by regimes that felt themselves to be relatively secure, it is not possible to identify, as some (e.g. Deegan 1992) have suggested, a general progression towards democratization – although for a short while at the end of the 1980s this seemed a possibility – for there has subsequently been a significant increase in repression again in the early 1990s as the rise of Islamic movements threatens the limited political reforms embarked upon in some states and appears to pose a major challenge to many existing regimes. All of the states considered in fact exemplify different variations on a theme: state repression with strictly limited forms of democratic expression.

State Repression

In those states where long-term and systematic repression (serious restrictions on civil and human rights, persistent arrests of suspected "activists," use of heavy prison sentencing and torture, banning of political movements and opposition trade unions) was implemented in response to popular unrest – as in Morocco from 1965, Turkey from 1980, and arguably Iran from 1980 – there was very limited social unrest until repression eased. It could be argued that Syria and Iraq – both heavily repressive regimes, where popular protest has been extremely limited – have been able in the same way to crush any potential social unrest. A contributory factor in countries like Turkey and Morocco during the periods referred to may be the high level of external support provided by the IMF and World Bank and other lenders during the period of "strong government," which made possible a degree of expansion and "cushioning" in the economy which would otherwise have been impossible; in the case of Syria and Iraq it may well be the relatively limited extent of liberalization and economic reform.

For Egypt, a somewhat similar argument could apply. Here, despite a general commitment to economic reform since the 1970s, the government has also maintained relatively high levels of subsidies and public expenditure and has persistently failed to adopt economic and fiscal reforms as stringent as the IMF and World Bank would like. Egypt has, with great difficulty, been able to survive with a massive and mounting foreign debt, largely as a result of support from the United States and other western states, although pressure from external creditors to implement major reforms was growing to the point where it could not be ignored in the period just prior to the outbreak of the Gulf War (Seddon 1991). In the aftermath of the Gulf War, Egypt finally came to terms with the IMF and agreed to implement economic reforms with stringent austerity measures; at the same time, state repression, particularly against Islamic groups, intensified.

In the case of the Islamic Republic of Iran, the precise opposite might be suggested: the sense of national solidarity in the early years of "the revolution" resulting from the political isolation of the regime and the war with Iraq, combined with severe repression, served to inhibit popular unrest until towards the end of the decade, despite the rigors of a devastated war economy. But when President Rafsanjani initiated economic reforms at the end of a decade notorious for state repression of all opposition, the response was widespread and growing popular protest.

In Iran, the economic imperative for reforms was considerable. With subsidies costing the government an estimated $4 billion by 1990, it was judged essential to impose cuts in public expenditure: petrol rationing ended in February 1991, with subsidies partially lifted on certain foodstuffs in July; in August, bus fares in Tehran increased five-fold. The result was a wave of protests and demonstrations in Tehran and other cities against rising prices, lack of affordable housing, the cost of transport, and unemployment. But large demonstrations in Isfahan after the vice squads tried to detain women flouting the Islamic dress code indicated that social unrest was also connected to growing discontent with the repressive aspects of the regime. Generally, it was noted, "clashes between angry crowds and the Islamic authorities are becoming commonplace. Many white collar workers are working to rule, strikes are frequent and shortages of every kind are widespread. Worse for the government, people are losing their fear of its organs of repression, such as the Islamic Komitehs" (*Middle East International*, August 16, 1991).

During the first half of 1991, some 2,000 strikes were recorded. Many of these were settled within a few days by a government struggling to implement economic reform while also containing social unrest; indeed, it was suggested in early 1992, "strikes by workers trying to catch up with inflation have become so routine since early 1991 that the authorities hardly seem to notice them" (*Middle East Economic Digest*, February 21, 1992). But if strikes were becoming "routine" and apparently not threatening to the new government, the outbreak of riots and demonstrations that began in Shiraz in mid-April 1992 and were repeated in other cities, including Arak and Mashhad, in May were not. Amnesty International reported in June 1992 that the demonstrations in Mashhad were the latest in a series of protests sparked off by attempts on the part of the municipal authorities to clear up the shantytowns, and by more general discontent with the government's economic and social policies. As so often, the authorities (and the press) refused to recognize these demonstrations as evidence of popular protest, referring to the involvement of "insurgents," "foreigners and agents of arrogance," "counter-revolutionaries" and the "corrupt on earth" (Amnesty International 1992). Mass arrests followed the demonstrations; four people were subsequently hanged, several were given long prison sentences and many more were flogged.

There is at first sight some support here for the argument, popular among supporters of "structural adjustment," that strong (even repressive) government is necessary for the effective implementation of radical economic reform. It could also be argued, however, that the introduction of economic reforms itself not only tends to create the basis for social unrest and popular protest but also to undermine the political as well as the economic centrality of the state and thereby engender, unavoidably, a degree of political disintegration.

Certainly those regimes within the region which have attempted to combine economic reform with a degree of political liberalization, presumably in order to head off further popular protest and draw the teeth of a growing yet unofficial opposition, have generally failed to prevent increasing political divisions.

Political Reforms, Islamism, and Democratization

In several cases (e.g. Tunisia, Algeria, Jordan, Turkey), particularly towards the end of the 1980s, governments responded to the political threat represented by popular protest by implementing what were intended to be controlled political reforms. While such moves reduced the immediate pressure from below, however, they opened up new opportunities for the organization of political opposition to the existing regime. In particular they increased the room for maneuver for the various Islamist movements which had, throughout the 1970s and 1980s, taken strength from the social discontent that underlay the austerity protests but generally suffered from state repression. Both the growing strength of Islamic movements, and the "backlash" of state repression which has generally followed the relatively short period of political liberalization, make any notion of progressive political reform and democratization debatable to say the least.

In Jordan, where arguably political reforms have been pursued most systematically, the liberalization of politics included the Islamic movements; in Tunisia, it did not. Both states have subsequently faced a growing Islamic movement, and if the threat to social and political stability from such movements currently appears greater in Tunisia than in Jordan – and has led to an appreciably higher level of repression in Tunisia than in Jordan (where the Islamists are represented in government) in the last couple of years – it seems likely that both regimes face significant pressure for more far-reaching political change from this quarter in the coming years.

In the case of Algeria also, attempts were made to reduce the risk of social unrest by a program of political reforms; here, however, the reforms themselves undoubtedly accelerated a process of political disintegration, giving rise to even greater political instability and social unrest. In November 1989 it was reported

> Algeria is living through an extraordinary autumn of revelations, realignments of old political alliances, and an unprecedented void with the sudden fragmentation of the ruling National Liberation Front after 30 years in power. The street and the mosque are the rising political forces – their strength and anger visible on every street of Bab el Oued and Belcourt – the sea-level working-class areas where people live 20 to a room. (*Brittain 1989*)

During 1990, the crumbling of the ruling FLN was accompanied by the formal recognition of numerous new political movements and parties, and by massive demonstrations orchestrated by the new parties, including the Islamists. Towards the end of April 1990, some 50,000 members of the Islamic Salvation Front (FIS) marched through the streets of Algiers to indicate their strength; in May, hundreds of thousands marched in support of democracy and against the FIS, chanting "Algeria, Freedom and Democracy"; in June the FIS swept into control of several municipal councils in the local elections (Seddon 1990).

But if an unprecedented political transformation was taking place in Algeria, as the monolithic power of the FLN disintegrated, the pursuit of economic reforms continued. It provoked further unrest. In October 1990, nearly 7,000 workers in Jijel in northern Algeria demonstrated against the rising cost of living. The workers' protests came in the wake of riots by youths over high prices and unemployment. Protest was not confined to one area. The government responded to these new outbreaks of social unrest with a commitment to increase the minimum wage by two-thirds and to restore subsidies on basic foods.

With the rise of the FIS in particular the "politicization" of popular protest rapidly increased. At the start of 1991, as the Gulf crisis deepened, some 60,000 people, organized by the FIS, marched through Algiers calling for the resignation of Chadli Bendjedid and the establishment of an Islamic Republic in Algeria, as well as protesting against the attacks on Iraq. Throughout the year the FIS gained support among the mass of the Algerian population; by the end of the year, when the first round of the general elections was completed, it threatened to take power in the second round at the start of 1992. Undoubtedly, the Islamists had reaped the the benefits of growing support from the disenchanted urban poor who had previously taken to the streets in protest at the government's economic policies and their social effects; now they were voting for a movement that promised to transform not only economic and social life, but also to create an Islamic Republic in Algeria. The army coup which in 1992 banned the second round of elections and effectively initiated a new period of political repression, directed specifically against the Islamic movements, preempted this possibility, but left Algeria in an effective state of emergency.

Elsewhere in the region, popular protest has increasingly been channeled into support for popular political movements offering far-reaching change. There is relatively little support, however, for leftwing parties. The threat of Islamism, in much of the region, comes from the fact that it taps the sense of disillusionment with existing regimes and their policies and practice so widespread among the mass of the population, especially among the urban poor. As long as the governments of the region continue to pursue programs of economic reform which undermine the living standards of the urban poor, sharpen social inequalities, and contradict popular notions of social justice and the moral economy of welfare, popular protest in the form of demonstrations and "riots" remains likely.

In most Middle Eastern and North African states, the capacity of Islamic movements to capitalize on widespread social discontent is evident, and explains in large part their success during the late 1980s and early 1990s as political movements. In most states within the region the threat of the populist Islamists is now seen as the major political problem. One strategy to contain this threat is increased repression (as in Morocco, Tunisia, Algeria, Egypt, and, to some extent Jordan) of the Islamists; another is to attempt to restore the legitimacy of government by a more emphatic official commitment to "Islamic principles" (as in Sudan, and also to a certain extent in Morocco).

But where an explicitly "Islamic" regime attempts to introduce its own economic reforms, there too popular protest may break out. In the Islamic Republic of Iran, as we have seen, economic liberalization and austerity measures have produced a reaction broadly similar to that experienced elsewhere in the region. This suggests that popular protest against the effects of economic liberalization respects or adheres to no particular religious or political ideology. Indeed, in Iran, popular protest against economic liberalization looks set to continue, with a strong possibility that it will develop into a more effective and coordinated political opposition. In Sudan, however, where a combination of "Islamic rule" and severe repression prevails, the capacity for popular protest seems limited. In this case, though, it would seem to be the latter rather than the former which explains the apparent quiescence of the population.

Austerity protests are clearly "political," in the sense that they involve collective action in opposition to government policies, and are directed against both specific and more general targets; they are, however, not associated intrinsically with any particular political movement or political ideology. Popular protest is not merely a response to economic and social adversity; it is also a demand for social justice and for renewal of the social contract between state and civil society in which the role of the state is to ensure the economic and social welfare of "the public." Significantly, in the Middle East and North Africa, it is Islamism, with its emphasis on the notion of "community" (*'umma*) and the "moral economy," that provides the most suitable discourse, readily acceptable to the mass of the urban poor, at the present time.

It has been argued recently that the first few years of the 1990s have seen an increasing tendency towards the use of the language of "democratization" in the region (Deegan 1992). However, even in those cases where a program of more far-reaching political reforms has been initiated in response to the pressures manifested in popular protest, the state continues to maintain a high degree of control over the political process, and may even intervene to reverse its political liberalization. In Algeria, for example, in 1992, when the Islamic opposition legalized by the reforms threatened to gain political power, the army moved in to stop the elections and the state embarked on a program of severe repression of the Islamic Salvation Front; while in Tunisia, where the Islamists were never officially recognized despite a degree of political liberalization, the state has maintained a policy of severe repression of the Islamic movements since the mid-1980s and has intensified its repression during the 1990s. Elsewhere, as in Egypt, a similar intensification of conflict between the state and the Islamists has taken place during the last few years.

While there is, undoubtedly, increasing pressure from below for political reforms throughout the region, it is also the case that embattled regimes are evidently unprepared as yet to relinquish control without a struggle. On the other hand, the growing strength of the Islamic movements, which presents a direct threat to the existing regimes (and explains their continued repression of such populist politico-religious movements) also presents a threat to the secular political movements, of whatever political tendency, for whom generally political liberalization and democratization are the major objectives.

It seems probable, however, that only when secular democratic movements and political parties are able to develop a comparable coherent moral philosophy and appeal, as well as economic and social policies capable of securing at least the basic needs of the people whom they claim to represent, and only when they develop the organizational capacity to promote the active and continuing participation of those who have so often felt obliged over the last 25 years to take to the streets to express their grievances and demand justice, will they be able to challenge effectively either the repressive character of the Middle Eastern and North African state or the strength of Islamism as a populist political ideology and movement.

7

The Asian Debt Crisis: Structural Adjustment and Popular Protest in India

Mridula Udayagiri

At least seven demonstrators were killed by Nepalese police following clashes between left wing demonstrators and security personnel in Kathmandu on 6 April. The police opened fire on members of left wing groups, who were protesting against the government's market-oriented economic policies, on the second anniversary of demonstrations that removed the power of the monarchy and led to Nepal's first democratically elected government in three decades. The protesters claimed that 22 people died in the shooting. The government later imposed a night curfew on the city and the neighboring town of Patan.

(*Far Eastern Economic Review, 16 April, 1992: 14*)

While Latin America has been at the forefront of austerity protests that have accompanied Third World debt crisis, Asia has been characterized by democratic struggles and economic miracles. By the 1970s Newly Industrializing Countries such as South Korea, Taiwan, and Hong Kong were considered exemplars of industrialization for other Third World nations according to purveyors of international development, the World Bank and the IMF (Garnaut 1980; Robison, Higgott and Hewison 1987). However, the mid-eighties have seen an economic downturn which resulted in pressure from international sources to undertake major structural adjustments of Asian economies (*Far Eastern Economic Review*, 26 September, 1984). Thus it can be argued that far from being exempted from this Third World adversity, debt crisis in Asia came later in comparison with Africa and Latin America, and was more selective in its incidence.

The task of this chapter is to examine Asia's seeming immunity from the debt crisis, and to show how this crisis is somewhat delayed in comparison to Latin America and Africa. The debt problem has already manifested itself in some nations and austerity protests are gathering force in some of the heavily indebted nations such as India, the Philippines, and Nepal. This chapter will provide a brief discussion of the probable explanations for the variation in intensity and timing of Asia's pattern of austerity protest and in particular, analyze India's experience of the structural adjustment programs that were instituted in July 1991. Although austerity protests have been common in countries such as Bangladesh, Nepal, and the Philippines, India's new economic program marks Asia's introduction into the wave of large-scale international austerity protests. The arguments presented here will be based on consideration of only those nations in Asia which are loosely referred to as Third World, that is, nations categorized by international organizations as developing and so thereby excluding Japan. China as a centrally planned economy is also excluded from the analysis.

India is a significant case for comparative study of international austerity protests as a modern democracy is at stake: it is acknowledged that never before has such a large and diverse and desperately poor population been held together in a commonly accepted, basic framework of democratic rights for as long as four decades (Bardhan 1984). A great aspiration of the founders of the Indian republic was to relieve the crushing burden of poverty that India had inherited at the end of British rule and this has been the ongoing litany of various Five Year Plan documents, electioneering slogans, and political speeches. Although the state is committed to structural adjustment reforms, socialist and nationalist objectives are deeply embedded in the Indian polity not only on the basis of purely altruistic motives but because they constitute the single largest source of power and patronage for its own legitimacy. Indeed, the large-scale protest articulates questions of moral economy, which in turn may deflect hard economic choices before the government and blunt the effect of austerity reforms. Explanations of an apparent lack of a debt crisis in Asia need closer consideration in view of changes already under way in the world's largest democracy and of what those portend for the rest of Asia.

1 SCALE OF ASIA'S DEBT

Although many poor nations are located in Asia, they have escaped the scale of debt adversity of some Latin America and African nations. The geography of debt crisis reveals that the major debtor nations are located in Latin America although countries of Africa and Eastern Europe are also included in this crisis. In the 1970s, southern African nations showed a tremendous increase in debt compared to Latin America (Altvater and Hubner 1991: 9). It was estimated that at the end of 1985 low-income countries of this region had average debt ratios (i.e. total external debt to exports) of around 400 percent, ranging from less than 50 percent (Gabon, Botswana, and Lesotho) to more than 1,000 percent (Sudan, Mozambique, and Guinea-Bissau). The following section provides a brief overview of the impact of the debt crisis in Asia, mainly to establish that several nations in the region have experienced both debt and austerity programs.

Debt Crisis in Asia

The 1960s and 1970s did not show any major variation in economic growth in different regions in the Third World. In the 1980s however, the differences manifested themselves. They are reflected in the intensity of economic crises that affected Latin America and Africa even as economic growth in Asia remained somewhat steady in comparison to the other regions. Comparative data from Africa, Asia, and Latin America presented in table 7.1, are instructive as to the level economic growth in the three regions. Decline in growth rates was most dramatic in Latin America in the 1980–90 period. Although some of the aggregate values of growth rates are positive in table 7.1, the low values reflect negative growth rates in the 1980–4 period especially for countries in Africa and Latin America. The countries with negative growth rates include Benin, Burkina Faso, Morocco, Nigeria, Tunisia, Zambia, and Zimbabwe in Africa; and Argentina, Bolivia, Brazil, Mexico, and Venezuela in Latin America (IMF 1992b).

A superficial look at regional economic performance excludes Asia from the crippling burden of the international debt crisis. Aggregate figures, given in table 7.2, for the debt-service burdens of Africa, Asia, and Latin America, show that the debt crisis in Asia has not shown the same alarming proportions as that of Latin America and Africa. For Asia, the debt problem peaked from 1985 to 1987. But regional aggregate figures obscure national realities, and we may tend to assume an optimistic picture based on the NIC experience.

Comparing national figures for individual debt-service burden or debt-service ratio in table 7.3 yields a disaggregated picture of

Table 7.1   Annual GDP growth rate for selected countries in
Africa, Asia, and Latin America, 1960–1990

Country	1960–70	1970–81	1980–90
Asia			
India	3.4	3.6	5.3
Indonesia	3.8	7.8	5.5
Korea, South	8.6	9.5	9.7
Philippines	5.1	6.2	0.9
Sri Lanka	4.6	4.3	4.0
Taiwan	—	—	—
Thailand	8.4	7.2	7.6
Median	5.1	6.7	4.6
Latin America			
Argentina	4.3	1.9	−0.4
Brazil	5.4	8.4	2.7
Chile	4.5	2.1	3.2
Ecquador	—	8.6	2.0
Mexico	7.2	6.5	1.0
Peru	4.9	3.0	−0.3
Venezuela	6.0	4.5	1.0
Median	5.1	5.0	1.1
Africa			
Algeria	4.3	6.9	3.1
Côte d'Ivoire	8.0	6.2	0.5
Egypt	4.3	8.1[a]	5.0
Kenya	5.9	5.8	4.2
Morocco	4.4	5.2	4.0
Nigeria	3.1	4.5	1.4
Tunisia	4.7[b]	7.3	3.6
Median	4.4	6.2	3.6

[a] 1970–80 figures
[b] 1961–70 figures

Source: World Bank 1983b, 1992

the debt crisis in Asia. Walton and Ragin (1990) argue that debt
service as a percentage of export earnings is a better measure than
absolute debt. The measure of debt burden used in this table includes
workers remittances under exports, which is useful as many Asian
nations export labor in significantly large numbers, especially to the
Middle East.

Table 7.2 Regional debt indicators and debt-service payments, 1981–1991

	1981	1985	1986	1987	1988	1989	1990	1991
Debt % of GNP								
Africa	44.4	59.9	74.9	92.4	96.1	99.8	98.2	99.6
Asia	21.3	29.2	30.6	32.1	27.5	25.3	26.1	26.5
Latin America	37.3	60.9	62.9	64.0	53.9	47.4	40.7	37.3
Debt % of export								
Africa	146.2	224.0	303.1	325.3	320.1	308.2	263.1	260.3
Asia	121.3	172.9	182.6	169.1	143.6	133.0	128.2	124.4
Latin America	233.1	331.7	399.3	388.8	333.1	290.5	266.7	280.6
% Debt service to export								
Africa	18.7	26.4	30.0	24.9	28.4	27.3	24.0	25.6
Asia	11.6	16.1	15.8	15.5	12.1	10.5	10.0	9.3
Latin America	0.4	37.6	43.3	37.5	39.5	29.2	25.2	29.4

Source: United Nations 1992

Table 7.3   Debt indicators for selected countries in Africa, Asia and Latin America, total debt service to export of goods and services, 1980–1989

Country	1980	1985	1989
Africa			
Algeria	27.2	35.8	68.9
Côte D'Ivoire	28.3	44.7	40.9
Egypt	20.8	23.6	21.8
Kenya	22.3	41.9	33.3
Latin America			
Argentina	37.3	58.9	36.1
Brazil	63.1	38.6	31.3
Mexico	49.5	51.5	39.5
Peru	46.5	30.2	6.8
Asia			
Bangladesh	23.2	21.6	19.9
India	9.1	22.3	26.3
Indonesia	13.9	29.5	35.2
Korea, South	19.7	27.3	11.4
Nepal	2.9	7.2	17.2
Philippines	26.5	32.0	26.3
Sri Lanka	12.0	16.5	17.8
Taiwan	–	–	–
Thailand	18.7	31.9	15.5

Source: World Bank 1992

At the beginning of the eighties, the countries in the Latin American region had the heaviest debt burden, followed closely by African nations. A careful analysis of table 7.3 reveals first, that fiscal crises are creeping into nations once considered invulnerable to international economic shocks; and second, that the debt crisis is geographically more diffused. Several Asian nations such as India and Indonesia, and Algeria in Africa have seen a significant escalation of the debt burden compared to Latin American nations. Peru shows the lowest debt burden, falling from 30.2 percent in 1985 to 6.8 percent in 1989.

Studies show that the variations in the timing and intensity of economic crisis in Africa, Asia, and Latin America stem from Asia's dependence on "self-reliance" and import substitution industrialization (ISI) (Maddison 1985; Singh 1985; Hughes and Singh 1991).

The choices suggest that ideological motives underpin economic strategies. More generally, the delayed debt crisis in Asia is attributed to nationalist and socialist principles. Nationalist and socialist claims constitute Asia's moral economy and legitimize patriotically driven development strategies. The fundamental goal for newly independent Asian nations was to become politically autonomous, free-standing actors in the international economy and this imparted a powerful influence on development strategies. State involvement in the economy contributed to socialist goals in addition to providing the impetus to nationalist sentiments. The state had a legitimate role to play in promoting social objectives to temper the effects of colonial policies. Legitimacy for the interventionist state was also provided by a strident promotion of domestic investment, which could be made possible only by controls over foreign companies and investment. This dual trend, of national capitalism with socialist goals, was and is evident in countries with politically diverse systems such as Indonesia, India, Malaysia, and Thailand. Although the goals have been subverted over time through international and domestic pressures, the ideological construction of an autonomous nation has been a powerful force in directing development strategies.

The broad pattern of economic policy that dominated in Asian nations therefore derived from nationalist ideology and was an attempt to wrest autonomy from colonial relations. Anderson (1991) proposes that contemporary nationalism is a conscious *policy* and that as an *official* policy it always emanates from the state. Indeed, state intervention for economic growth turns on nationalist assumptions and in the case of Asia is legitimated on grounds of socialist objectives. Economic policies that stress self-reliance and self-sufficiency are as much cultural outcomes of nationalism as are poetry, prose, fiction, and music. Economic nationalism as a powerful ideology which emerged within the context of anti-colonial struggles provided a fertile ground for strategies such as import substitution industrialization in the first developmental decade. It restrained multinational investment and openness to the world economy, but it also demonstrated that nationalist economic strategies were limited by the structural constraints of an international economy.

Nowhere is this more sharply illustrated than in the experience of countries such as Brazil and Mexico which left them more vulnerable to international economic downturns. Similarly, import substitution industrialization seemed feasible in Asia as a strategy for growth that relied on tariffs, quotas and import licensing. Some nations moved into import substitution production of intermediate and capital goods, but the limitations of this strategy became apparent when it reached saturation point (Portes and Walton 1981). The failure of ISI was predictable as it relied on a narrow base of consumer goods production that was not sustained by sufficient domestic consumer demand. Waning arguments for the ISI strategy resulted in a push towards export-oriented production primarily advocated by international finance institutions in East Asian nations such as Malaysia, the Philippines, and Thailand. ISI could not be abandoned easily as elite patronage was vested in this strategy. Besides there was a ready availability of finance capital in the international markets which was selectively handed out to those countries which were well integrated into the world economy (Robison, Higgott, and Hewison 1987). There was no immediate urgency to meet the expenses of high-cost industries with increase in exports or foreign-debt payments and the 1970s proved to be economically stable for Asia on the whole. By the end of the decade however fiscal crisis overtook some nations as international recession was more intensely felt in some of these impoverished Asian nations.

The fiscal crisis brought political turmoil to the fore and led to conflicts over policy and development strategies. In particular, the fiscal crisis expressed the tensions of an international aid regime (Wood 1986). The strain was between the power of international financial institutions on one hand and domestic concern for nationalist and socialist obligations on the other. One way that multilateral aid agencies sought to alleviate the economic crisis in Asia in the early 1980s, particularly in countries like the Philippines, Thailand, and Malaysia, was to push for export-oriented industrialization (EOI) again. But structural constraints limited EOI solutions for the Asian economic crisis. The "look East" policy could work in the presence of certain geopolitical conditions such as in South Korea, Taiwan and Hong Kong, and Thailand but could not be expanded to other countries. In addition, there were protectionist pressures from advanced capitalist nations along with a decline in demand associated with the recession in the early eighties (Cho 1985; *Far Eastern Economic Review* September 26, 1985). Thus EOI provided only partial amelioration from burgeoning deficits.

In addition to the limitations of the ISI and EOI strategies, Asian nations had to weather global recession and falling commodity prices in the late seventies and the early eighties that affected traditional agricultural, mineral, and energy exports, and economic shocks such as the oil-price crash. A conjunction of factors was responsible for the differential impact of global recession in Asia.

Reliance on an ISI strategy based on oil exports in Indonesia staved off an intense debt crisis, although the oil-price collapse of the early seventies and early eighties led to an escalating debt burden and a restructuring of the economy. Robison (1987) argues that state control over the economy since 1949 has emphasized nationalist objectives, allowing power and patronage to accrue to local elites. In the aftermath of a failed communist coup and the fall of the Sukarno regime in 1964, there was a reversal in economic nationalism as a result of a fiscal crisis that led to increasing dependence on foreign investment. But, a reassertion of economic nationalist policies began in the mid-seventies and reached well into the eighties. However, the oil-price collapse in the beginning of the eighties created an adverse balance-of-payments situation that was met with fiscal intervention from international finance institutions such as the World Bank. The package of reforms suggested removal of fuel and food subsidies, and reduction in state investment in resource and industrial projects (World Bank 1981b; *Far Eastern Economic Review*, May 16, 1985). Although cutbacks in food subsidies were first imposed in the 1982–3 budget, they have been reinstated over subsequent years (Dick 1982). State-owned and managed industrialization and growth is now moving towards deregulation and privatization in what is called a "quiet revolution" (*New York Times*, October 11, 1989). Austerity has resulted in reduced social spending for health, education, and industrial projects (*New York Times*, January 7, 1987). Radical austerity programs have been instituted as conditionalities for debt, which grew from $27 billion to $51 billion in 1989 (*Economist*, November 17, 1990).

Indonesia's attachments to nationalist and socialist objectives are gradually unraveling. Tariffs have been lowered, financial services have been deregulated, and foreign firms allowed easier entry into Indonesia than into South Korea and Taiwan. The government has eased restrictions on foreign direct investment portending a dramatic increase in domestic private investment. Sweeping changes have been instituted with no threat to political stability which can be explained by the absolute state control that military rule has imposed over Indonesia.

While Indonesia's debt crisis emerged from an overreliance on oil exports, the Philippines' earlier introduction to the debt crisis no doubt stemmed from political factors such as crony capitalism, rampant corruption, and profligate election spending which saddled the nation with a deep fiscal crisis. By 1979 this was compounded by the falling prices of agricultural commodities which constituted the core of its exports (Bello 1982; Boyce 1990; Broad 1988). The Philippines obtained formal political independence in 1946, but its economic and political policies are still influenced by Americans.

Although ISI was advocated as a strategy of economic nationalism, Jayasuriya (1987: 83) finds that the Philippines had the least nationalistic stance among Asian nations owing to its clientele status with the United States. The first fiscal crisis was predictably brought about by the Marcos government's heavy spending in the 1969 election year. An emergency mission from IMF in January 1970 resulted in an economic package that included a drastic currency devaluation. Consequently, national consumption was also reduced, but austerity measures provoked mass protest by youth and students. The militancy forced the government to temper the intensity of austerity measures.

Discontent with austerity measures and rampant government corruption accumulated in the late seventies and early eighties. The austerity protests induced Benigno Aquino's return from political exile in mid-1983, initiated the democratic movement after his assassination, and helped the overthrow of the Marcos government. In the 1983–4 period public displeasure could no longer be contained; there were several protests in Manila against unpopular economic measures. Although these protests are not singularly defined as "austerity protests" as they mounted demands for democratic reforms, economic issues became precipitating factors for protests in 1983–4. One such protest that articulated both economic discontent and demands for democratic reform took place on October 5, 1983 in the financial district of Manila. A peaceful protest by 3,000 people, mostly office workers and students, against the Marcos government came several hours after the second devaluation of the peso in less than 6 months (*New York Times*, October 6, 1983). Protesters called for an end to the Marcos regime amidst the growing fiscal crisis that necessitated IMF intervention and austerity measures.

By the late eighties external debt had accumulated to alarming proportions. It was left to the Aquino government to confront the debt burden with the help of the IMF. The Philippines government committed to redress the debt crisis and secured a loan of $1.3 billion of which $1.1 billion was used to repay old loans, mostly a legacy of the corrupt Marcos government (Pineda-Offreneo 1991). The debt conditionalities that directly affected the public were increased taxes, the transfer of debt from private corporations to the national government, the removal of government subsidies for rice, increased charges for public utilities, and the limitation of government personnel expenditure.

Some economic policies have been particularly harsh, especially those affecting the lives of the poor. Opposition to austerity measures has been expressed in protests in urban areas to force the attention of the government. One of the most protracted protests emerged from teachers who have resisted the deteriorating standard of living, falling wages, and crowded school rooms. The Philippines Constitution (1987) guarantees that the state will accord the highest priority to education as a means to acquiring jobs and employment. In 1990 it was estimated that debt service accounted for 37 percent of the budget whereas education received only 14 percent. For teachers, this translates into low salaries and increasing teaching loads. In September 1990 teachers went on a strike for four weeks which resulted in the dismissal of 844 teachers and the suspension of 2,000 more. Punitive actions did not deter the teachers from protesting. Several more went on a hunger strike the same year. In the case of the Philippines, resistance to austerity measures may force the government to temper their intensity, but in the absence of a long-term solution for a self-sustained economy, political and financial instability remain a reality.

Although the impact of global economic shocks were not as widely and deeply felt as in African and Latin American nations, they did expose Asian economies to reform pressures from international finance institutions. The delayed and modified debt crisis in some countries can be explained by three economic factors. Oil exports, export-oriented development (in the Asian NICs such as South Korea, Taiwan and Singapore, and Thailand), and import substitution have worked either singly or in combination to protect Asia from the severity of the global debt problem. In conclusion, a disaggregated analysis of Asia reveals that several nations are already in the throes of a debt crisis. The intensity may not be on the same scale as that of other severely indebted African and Latin American nations, but the situation is serious enough to warrant loans to alleviate the debt crises by structural reforms. By the end of the eighties, at least two Asian nations, Indonesia and the Philippines, had to grapple with sizable debt burdens and austerity programs. Meanwhile, India quietly became the second-largest borrower from the IMF in 1991, having run up a $70 billion external debt in the late 1980s.

2 INDIA: DEBT, DEVELOPMENT, AND POLITICAL INSTABILITY

The process of liberalization began in the late eighties during the Rajiv Gandhi regime pursued through a liberalized export–import policy between 1985 and 1988 (*Economic and Political Weekly*, August 24, 1991). The new economic reforms introduced in mid-1991 to secure financial reprieve from a large debt burden represented a rupture with state-led development that had guided India to a semblance of self-sufficiency and political autonomy within the global order. National elections in 1991 in India, which brought the Congress party back into power after a two-year hiatus, introduced economic liberalization as an official, state ideology and transformed the political and moral economy as far as the tenets of distributive justice were concerned. Despite some vacillation towards privatization from 1947 to 1991, the public role of the state had expanded steadily, resulting in a controlled economy which made elimination of poverty its central task. The 1991 election was a triumph for liberalization and for the now-deceased Rajiv Gandhi's vision of taking India into the twenty-first century by means of a break with Nehruvian socialism. The Congress party's commitment to structural adjustment reforms provided for a speedy introduction of economic changes with the new government's fiscal budget in July 1991. The changes which were intended to transform the structure of the economy included devaluing the rupee, ending restrictions on import licenses, encouraging foreign investment and collaboration, and scaling back public-sector investment. The present Indian government's concern is less with poverty elimination than with freeing the Indian economy from state controls, to enable "freedom to open a firm, to choose the price at which you will sell the product, to select the destination of your sales" (Basu, *Economic and Political Weekly*, August 31, 1991) and bring in a new market regime.

An important implication stems from India's experience with market reforms: the post-reform period has been marked with an escalation in the scale and degree of political instability. Indeed, religious aggression in this period suggests a complexity to the politics of liberalization and austerity programs. There are two wrinkles to this protest, one that is characteristic of coalitional politics in India, and the other that is embedded in the cultural politics of Hindu militancy. First, the outcome of the 1991 elections necessitated political coalitions; the Congress party won a slim majority and needed the support of the Hindu party, Bharatiya Janata Party (BJP) to obtain a majority standing in the parliament. Thus, interreligious tensions have been shaped by the legitimacy needs of a government which could retain its ruling authority only with the support of the BJP, the largest opposition group. The fragile coalition enabled the minority government to implement its economic reforms while at the same time providing a tacit approval for the BJP's religious militancy. Police complicity in communal riots (*New York Times*, February 4, 1993) suggests that the state was able to mediate religious tensions to subvert the momentum against growing opposition to the economic reforms and place a temporary break against austerity protests.

Second, cultural politics intersect with economic liberalization in its promise for "modernization" and this gives Hindu religious militancy the impetus "to redefine Hinduism as an ideology for modernization by the middle class" (Thapar 1991: 139). If economic liberalization is to succeed, it must be as a "modern" version of Hinduism, i.e. it must have a text, prophet, and geographically identifiable location, which can provide the necessary cultural idiom for modernization. Economic ideologies and religious dogma have combined to foreground Hindu militancy in contemporary Indian politics in an exceptional manner that promises long-lasting consequences.

In the midst of the 1992–3 Hindu–Muslim riots that engulfed the subcontinental region, the most disruptive and wide-spread since the partition of India and Pakistan, the fate of the new economic reforms continued to be a prominent feature of public debate. The IMF and World Bank both expressed concern that the government would not be able to carry out its reforms as scheduled (*Times of India*, December 23, 1992) especially as the fiscal deficit could not be contained due to the substantial loss in revenue incurred from the violence. Viewed as a threat to political stability in the region, communal disturbances injected an element of uncertainty into the government's negotiations with the IMF for a loan of $7 billion under the Extended Fund Facility, which took place in December in the capital, New Delhi, days after the violence erupted in India. Although the government's commitment to secular principles had been severely compromised, its commitment to the structural reforms was absolute. Although the reforms dominated public discourse, communal riots diverted attention from the nationwide protest that had been gaining momentum by the end of 1992, "the movement is stifled as the focus of the debate has changed" said Malini Bhattacharya, member of Parliament for the Communist Party of India.[1]

India presents a fertile case for study of austerity protests for the reasons outlined above and provides insights into diverse responses to international debt crisis. The next section lays out the context for structural adjustment programs introduced in 1991 even as the drama of austerity protest in India unfolds on the international stage. The first part presents a brief review of the post-independence political economy in India and will illustrate the conditions before the institution of the new economic reforms. Second, an analysis of the protest will be given the implications of which will be drawn out in the concluding section.

3 POLITICS OF PROGRESS AND REDISTRIBUTIVE
JUSTICE: THE INDIAN ECONOMY 1947–1991

India's stable economic performance is often attributed to nationalist-oriented growth (see Hughes and Singh 1991).[2] Certainly, state intervention in the years following independence provided substantive economic wherewithal to weather the global recession of 1980–3. In the post-Nehru era, state intervention was overcome by patronage and inefficiency, and growth rates fell with a decline in public investment (Bardhan 1984). Political instability, together with dismal economic performance, has been largely prevalent since the late sixties. The escalation of public demonstrations in the early seventies, largely as a response to liberalization and austerity measures, reveals that austerity protests have recurred in Indian politics and were precursors to large-scale protests in the early nineties. This is not to make the claim that liberalization initiatives introduced in the late sixties and early seventies were of the same nature or on the same scale as the liberalization program introduced in 1991. Earlier versions of liberalization included certain elements of the post-1991 plans, and certainly heralded contemporary conditionalities of World Bank or IMF strictures for alleviating debt crises. But they did not represent prevailing neo-liberal orthodoxy. The following section will briefly discuss these events within the context of India's political economy in the post-independence period. Contrary to conventional wisdom about Asian economic stability, evidence indicates that India experienced a fiscal crisis in the seventies, although not of the same order as African and Latin American nations. In fact, the crisis is illustrative of India's struggle to achieve self-sufficiency and autonomy in a global economy.

Politics of Economic Planning 1947–1991

Although the record of commitment to democratic principles is suspect in the light of events in the last two decades, the founders of an independent India had cherished a vision of parliamentary democracy that was equitable and just. They envisioned a different path of development where they formulated an "approach to planning under a democratic pattern of socialism as a new model for Asian and African development" (Frankel 1978: 3). Jawaharlal Nehru, the architect of the new nation "pointed to his country as an area of agreement between the opposing ideologies of capitalism on the one hand and communism on the other" (Frankel 1978: 3). Indeed, democratic socialism was an integral part of economic strategy for India. The objective for development was to combine the two goals of growth and distribution of resources to redress the burden of inequity that colonialism left behind.

Pursuit of wealth and power permeates the Indian political economy. To achieve socialist objectives, state actors are concerned about national power, social justice, and collective goods (Rudolph and Rudolph 1987: xv). The Indian Constitution's resolutions for socio-economic development have provided the moral energy for successive governments in the post-independence period. Central to the government's legitimacy has been its stated commitment to socialist goals, and the political culture has demanded that obligations to the poor are met (Calman 1985). This is clearly laid out in Article 38 of the Indian Constitution which guarantees the state shall

> strive to promote the welfare of the poor by securing and protecting as effectively as it may a social order in which justice, social, economic, and political, shall inform the institutions of national life.

However, India's socialist manifesto has been punctuated with significant departures since its inception. Far from an absolute adherence, state implementation of socialist principles has been remarkably inconsistent. Nehru himself reflected this ambiguous commitment to a socialist path,[3] the ambiguity is inhered in the organization of Indian politics. The Congress party, a motley group unified under a nationalist agenda became the ruling party at independence in 1947. In the post-1947 period this motley group has exerted various ideological pulls, ranging from conservative to socialist approaches to planning and growth in India. Consequently, the Congress regime's plans to bring a socialist transformation of Indian society through a politics of consensus and compromise diluted much of the promise of "an Indian road to socialism" (Harriss 1989).

Inconsistency in meeting socialist obligations is evidenced in the various constitutional and extra-constitutional means that have been used to contest the Indian government's legitimacy. Paul Brass (1990: 17) shows the disjunction between rhetoric and reality, in the contradiction between the language of planning, equality, socialism, and social justice, and the practices of everyday politics. Despite constitutional guarantees, politics in India rest on patronage. Bardhan's (1984) analysis of the Indian state's role in dispensing patronage is relevant here. He argues that labor tensions and mismanagement in the public sector are due to the nature of the political regime.

Senior appointments in the public sector are sometimes made more on the basis of political patronage than of merit (leading often to low morale in the ranks of the technocracy in the enterprises). Headships of public sector units, particularly under the State Governments, are indiscriminately used as political sinecures. Efficient managers who fail to satisfy the Minister's political clients are often arbitrarily transferred. Expensive projects are hastily initiated on grounds of political expediency or regional favoritism, without proper design and preliminary spade-work, resulting in long delays and cost-escalation. (*Bardhan 1984: 69–70*)

Although the politics of patronage constrains socialist goals, the model for achieving distributive growth emerged from nationalist ideology, forged during anti-colonial struggles, and a "modernization imperative" (Nayar 1972). It emphasized industrialization to achieve autonomy from colonial forces that encumbered India's growth in the pre-independence era. Policies of growth and industrialization were undertaken by the Planning Commission and were laid out in the Five Year Plans, the blueprints for India's development. The central debate in the planning process has been over the roles of public and private sectors in economic development planning (Brass 1990: 249). The economy was expected to be "mixed" with complementary roles for both private and public investment (Ahluwahlia 1985: 147). As Brass notes, this strategy in the early phases of India's planning emphasized dependence on imports and foreign aid to encourage import substitution industrialization which would bring self-sufficiency in the long run.

Evaluating India's economic growth after Independence, Balasubramanyam (1984) finds that in comparison to a slow growth rate of 1 percent per year prior to independence, the economy registered an annual 3.5 percent growth rate between 1950 and 1980. But India's economic performance when contrasted with other factors reveals that growth has been far from encouraging. India is comparable to low-growth countries like Pakistan, Kenya, and Indonesia when contrasting economic growth against increase in population. India's standing in the world economy also shows that it is not a strong economy. As Surendra Patel (1985) points out, in 1980 share in world trade declined from 2 percent to 0.5 percent, and contribution to world output fell from 1.2 to 0.7 percent, thus revealing that India has been losing its standing in the world economy over the years. Economic planners in India have to grapple with the threat of a fiscal crisis even as they try to find the best media for public- and private-sector investment.

Frankel (1978) notes that the first attempt at liberalization was taken as a response to the food crisis that appeared in 1955 at the end of the First Five Year Plan (1951–6), and placed a considerable pressure on the planning objectives for the Second Five Year Plan. The First Five Year Plan emphasized the role of public investment, attacked private investment, and institutionalized controls over private investment with the Industries (Development and Regulation) Act of 1951 (see Harriss 1989). State-led development became an unrealistic goal even before the end of the Five Year Plan. Fiscal crisis set in by 1957–8 and deterioration of foreign-exchange reserves in March 1958 created an opportunity for international aid. Aid was secured in order to purchase food grains; the amount bought was twice the requirement originally envisioned. With import substitution industrialization as a priority, import licenses were granted freely to the private sector for import of capital goods, iron, and steel which made considerable inroads into India's foreign-exchange reserves. The food crisis strained foreign-exchange reserves even further, as the government was forced to respond to growing political instability. Agitations against food shortages appeared in Calcutta, a stronghold of the Communist Party of India (CPI) (Franda 1971). By August 1959, the Communist Party of India undertook massive food protests in Calcutta, calling for detection and forced sale of hoarded rice stocks. Violent demonstrations ceased only after the government announced food concessions, but not before food shops had been looted and at least 12,485 people arrested.

The food crisis directed attention to the failure of the formal planning process. Harriss (1989) marks the mid-sixties as a "crisis of planning", which he attributes to resource constraints and weaknesses in the formulation and implementation of the Five Year Plans. The Planning Commission came under the scrutiny of the World Bank, which had expressed concern since the fiscal crisis of 1958 that India's public-sector programs were too ambitious. The Indian government realized by the end of 1964 that economic progress in India was possible only with large inflows of foreign aid. World Bank assistance was sought at this juncture and recommendations for a package of economic reforms soon followed. The package was presented as a condition for substantial inflow of aid, estimated at $1.5 billion, during the period of the Fourth Five Year Plan (1969–74). It represented a fundamental departure from the Nehruvian socialist plan but it was pursued nonetheless as a means of addressing the fiscal crisis. The package contained what later became standard conditionalities of assistance from the World Bank and the IMF under structural adjustment programs. It included export-oriented industries, relaxation of import licensing, import liberalization to stimulate investment, and devaluation of the rupee.

Even before populist opposition to liberalization could emerge, World Bank conditionalities were met with resistance from government representatives. The finance minister, T. T. Krishnamachari refused to devalue the rupee on what was clearly nationalist grounds and argued that devaluation would, in the long run, slow import substitution programs. He proposed seeking bilateral aid from friendly countries instead and recommended stringent control of imports with an increase in tariffs. As a consequence of the political resistance to World Bank measures, the Indian government was unable to follow through on all the reforms and partially implemented the Bank's recommendations on agricultural policy which emphasized high-technology inputs.

By the mid-sixties the economic promises of independence were yet to come for the majority of the population. Industrial growth in the fifties and sixties were characterized by a substantial increase in indebtedness, expansion of multinational capital, and stagnating levels in employment and real wages (Bagchi 1975; Patnaik 1972). Economic grievances dominated opposition-party concerns with food shortages, spiraling prices, and income disparities providing much of the basis for protests (see Frankel 1978). There was a tremendous growth in appeals to strike and *bandhs* to protest the "anti-people's policies" of the government. Between April and August 1966 particularly acute food shortages provoked *bandhs*, and demonstrations demanding reductions in food prices and rationing (Rudolph and Rudolph 1987). According to Baldev Raj Nayar (1975), the ratio of riots to population rose steeply after 1967, industrial unrest increasing dramatically along with student unrest.[4] Strikes were led by government employees for higher salaries and dearness allowance (cost-of-living adjustment). Trade unions agitated for higher salaries as a result of rising prices. Student protests were common at this time, frustrations with unemployment and irrelevant curricula provoked destruction of government property such as buses, post offices, and railway equipment. Nowhere was this more apparent than in West Bengal, the center for left-front politics. Food crises provoked urban protest which converged with the aims of the revolutionary Naxalite movement (see chapter 2).[5] Deemed an agrarian revolutionary protest that had emerged in the countryside, the Naxalite movement was responsible for CPI winning state-level elections.

The "crisis of planning" of the mid-sixties had already led to a gradual erosion of socialist objectives. Harriss notes that a retreat from socialist growth which started during Nehru's tenure was completed in the brief regime of the succeeding prime minister, Lal Bahadur Shastri (Harriss 1989: 77). Frankel argues that liberal economic policies introduced during the mid-sixties under Prime Minister Lal Bahadur Shastri, produced income inequality leading to political instability (Frankel 1978: 38). The concentration of economic power in large business houses increased disparities between the opulent lifestyle of prosperous factory owners and their executives and the marginal existence of the masses of the urban poor and unemployed. In agriculture, the Green Revolution was implemented at enormous social cost, deepening regional and class inequalities (see Frankel 1971, for an excellent analysis). There was a growing tension between liberalization and nationalist protectionism during the planning process as a response to the instability of the late sixties. It opened up the debate of state responsibility for economic and social transformation in the midst of a growing financial crisis. The conundrum of India's economy was best represented in Indira Gandhi's initial policies as she took office in 1967. A nationalist with a socialist stance, she devalued the rupee in trying to meet the World Bank's conditionality for more aid and later nationalized all private banks in 1969.

In the early seventies, the government came under pressure from the IMF to undertake stabilization programs[6] as a condition to cover the massive balance of payments deficit incurred by various events. The Indo-Pakistan war over Bangladesh, natural disasters such as floods and droughts in 1971, 1972, and 1973, and the international oil crisis in 1973 were largely responsible for the deficit. Recommendations included fiscal discipline, and policies to freeze wages, increase imports, promote exports, and provide incentives for private investments. In addition to the IMF, the World Bank also pressed the government to "open the economy along western lines." Most of the anti-inflationary measures were implemented by presidential ordinances and legislative powers that increased the absolute authority of the state by July 1974. But it was the urban middle and lower classes who bore the brunt of these anti-inflation measures in the face of growing unemployment, soaring prices, and shortage of commodities. As John Wood sums up "as 1973 ended, the only question was where and how oppositional reaction would take place" (1975: 315).

Strikes, closures, and demonstrations soon followed. When the reactions set in, they were marked in certain regions. The state of Maharashtra recorded the maximum number of disputes and closures in the early seventies, and Bombay led in the number of strikes, closures, and demonstrations (Gandhi 1990b; chapter 3 in this volume). One of the earliest and sustained urban movements against austerity measures was launched by women in Bombay during 1972: "Prices affect everyone but more so women because we look after the family. Then we have to look for work or do more work to be able to buy enough."[7] Nandita Gandhi makes women's participation in austerity protests more visible, and describes the movement:

> What became popularly known as the Mahangai Pratikar Sahyukta Mahila Andolan or the Anti Price Rise Movement of Bombay (APRM) was one of the many struggles against inflation. In 1972, the two communist parties and the socialist party women leaders who had individually, and through their parties been taking up the issue of prices, routinely met to discuss the possibility of joint action. A large number of women answered their call to protest against inflation in general and for the availability food grains, sugar, cooking oil and kerosene in particular. The objective of the joint front was to pressurize the government to check the price rise and ensure an adequate quota of subsidized essential commodities through the public distribution system. Sporadically, but fitfully, over a period of three years, middle class and working class women – young, old, housebound mothers, mahila mandal (women's club) members, those working at home, on piece rate work or as domestic servants, those belonging to unions or having joined the demonstration because of friends, marched with rolling pins, plates and spoons. (*Gandhi 1990b: 52*)

Economic grievances provided a mobilizing impetus. By 1972 a continuous three-year drought and expenditures on wars with Pakistan led to a 25–30 percent increase in prices of food grains, oil and sugar, wage freezes and credit controls which touched working-class families in Bombay. The movement attracted 10,000 to 20,000 women and gathered wide press coverage. The movement was disrupted with the imposition of Indira Gandhi's authoritarian rule in 1975 and the arrests of its leaders.

The most vehement opposition to economic austerity was launched in 1974. It was directed at state authorities and centered on the tenure of the central government; resulted in political repression; and led to nationwide imposition of authoritarian rule. Two states, Gujarat on the western side and Bihar, towards the north and east, led intense populist agitations initially motivated primarily by economic grievances. Although the protests did not emerge simultaneously, the Bihar agitation followed the Gujarat resistance almost immediately, reason enough to consider them as emerging from a particular historical context. The Gujarat agitations called the *Nav Nirman* ("social reconstruction") are significant as they demonstrate

the "capacity of an indignant middle class to paralyze and overthrow elected governments" (Jones and Jones 1976: 1013). They were
of symbolic importance for the Bihar agitations in confronting the
ruling party at the center directly. The proximate causes were food
scarcities and escalating prices. Urban lower and middle classes,
mainly white-collar employees and professionals such as lawyers and
doctors, considered food shortages and rising prices artifacts of
"manipulative politics." Wood (1975: 328) views price increases and
unemployment as having possible consequences along with other
political factors. Comparison of the consumer price index for non-
manual employees showed that Gujarat and Bihar experienced the
highest price increases between 1972 and mid-1974.

Gujarat led the country in austerity protests in 1974. Engaged in
factional party politics, the state's chief minister removed government
control over the oil industry and sanctioned export of oil products
from the state. By the end of 1973, cooking-oil prices had not only
doubled, but there was a scarcity on the market. Known as a food-
deficit area, Gujarat also experienced a drastic cut in public grain
supplies. The cut by two-thirds in the food grains provided through
the public distribution system resulted in a 100 percent increase in
prices within a year. The central government cut grain supply from
105,000 tons per month in January 1973 to 75,000 tons in July, and
again to 35,000 tons by the end of the year. Reduction in food supply came even as news of a good harvest in rice, millet and ground-
nuts was announced. The responses were inevitable, and students
led the food protests.

In early 1974, students at an engineering college in Gujarat state
protested at the rising costs of meals, and set fire to college dining halls and to the rector's home. Repressive action by the police
provoked a sympathetic strike by other university students who
demanded reductions in dining-hall costs. The students demands,
linked to popular economic grievances, called for state action against
those responsible for sharp price rises in good grains and cooking oil.
Support for the food riots snowballed. Other young people attacked
municipal buses and looted food-grain shops in Ahmedabad, the
capital. Trade unions – which had a wide following among state
and city employees, banks and insurance companies, and college
and school teachers – supported the *bandh* on January 10, 1974 to
protest against police brutality and rising prices. Although the city
of Ahmedabad was completely shut down, looting of food and oil
shops, and arson of government milk supply booths were widespread.
Within two days, the rioting had spread to other urban centers in
Gujarat state. Protest forms included rallies of people carrying empty

oil tins and grain sacks, and beating metal eating plates (*thalis*); silent marches; relay fasts; and bus hijackings.

The riots in Gujarat were followed by a spate of rioting in Bihar state in March 1974. Again students were at the forefront of the protests agitating against rising prices; shortage in essential commodities; unemployment; and outdated curricula. Large-scale violence prevailed in Patna, capital of Bihar state, as the students attempted to force the dissolution of the legislative assembly. Two people were killed in police gunfire that day and more deaths followed in the urban centers of Deoghar, Monghyr and Ranchi. Jayaprakash Narayan, a popular political leader, joined the agitation at the students behest and led several protests "to paralyze" the state government. The Bihar agitations continued through 1974, culminating in a three-day non-violent *bandh* from October 3, considered longer than any *bandh* in Indian nationalist history. A month later in November, despite the state government canceling water, road and railway transportation, a massive demonstration was successfully organized in the state capital.

Besides regional, middle-class urban protests, a general strike by railway employees was organized. The strike, to be started on May 8, 1974, had the support of 1.7 million railway workers representing 200 unions. Demands included doubling wages, additional dearness allowance, payment of annual bonus, and supply of essential commodities at subsidized prices. In spite of political and ideological schisms among the unions, at least 50 percent of railway employees refused to work. The strike, which lasted 20 days, was successfully broken with the arrests of 20,000 railway workers sanctioned by the Indian government's invocation of the Defense of India Rule and Maintenance of Internal Security Act (MISA).

In June 1975, an increase in political instability, opposition to government policies, and a deteriorating law and order situation compelled Indira Gandhi to declare a nationwide state of emergency, institute central-government rule, and retain the legitimacy of her regime. Major reforms promoted economic nationalism, fulfill the goals of India's socialist manifesto, and bring political stability to ensure the longevity of the Congress regime. Essential commodities became readily available, prices stabilized, and inflation rates were brought under control through anti-inflationary government ordinances. Good weather conditions yielded successful agricultural harvests. The increase in food supply was matched by a massive procurement scheme by the government. While the economic measures met populist demands for decent living standards, they were incurred at the cost of political corruption and the violation of human rights (Nayar 1977).

Since protests and riots have punctuated post-independence Indian politics, progress towards self-sufficiency has been far from smooth. Socialist and nationalist goals are under constant duress as the Indian government grapples with the pressure of changing international structures whose interests are often inimical to the objectives of distributive growth. Austerity protests of the early seventies highlight the tensions between domestic concerns of maintaining political legitimacy and pressure from international financial institutions to confront fiscal burdens. India's political economy continues to demonstrate these tensions rendering the socialist vision impractical in the face of global recession.

The Janata party, which defeated Indira Gandhi in the 1977 elections, pursued a contradictory strategy of economic liberalization with the socialist goals of agricultural development, self-sufficiency; and income redistribution (Stiles 1991: 112) but the Indian government also accumulated a current-account surplus in the 1977–9 period (Hughes and Singh 1991: 91). The second oil crisis and the drought of 1979 persuaded the government to increase exports and relax import controls. When Indira Gandhi succeeded in unseating the Janata government by political machinations in 1979, she reclaimed a nation that had slid further into economic uncertainties. In preference to protectionist policies of the past, the Gandhi government opted to internationalize the economy, in part, continuing the momentum of liberalization created by the Janata government.

While the Indira Gandhi administration liberalized imports by April 1980, it also expanded state controls over the banking industry for two reasons. First, it anticipated increased foreign borrowing, and second, the government wanted to appease members of the ruling party who opposed liberalization (*Far Eastern Economic Review*, May 9, 1980; Stiles 1991). Liberalization programs resulted in a steep increase in the prices of crude oil and fertilizers. By the end of 1980, the Indian government was negotiating for an IMF loan. The debt incurred by India in 1981 for $5 billion under the Extended Fund Facility was small, and not all of it was utilized. Patel (*Economic and Political Weekly*, January 4–11, 1992) notes that the only reason for underutilization of funds was to evade IMF-prescribed fiscal discipline. This would have most certainly compromised the ruling party's legitimacy, secured after a bitter struggle only two years before in 1979. The 1981 IMF loan was extended to India with a "soft" agreement: there was no pressing need for the customary structural adjustment program as India's economic crisis was deemed reasonable compared to other Latin American nations. The Indian government undertook minor liberalization mainly in easing trade restrictions; realistic exchange rates for the rupee, healthy savings rates and sizable foreign-exchange reserves did not warrant an extensive austerity program according to the IMF.

In conclusion, India's emerging indebtedness in the first decades of nation building was insignificant relative to the debt burdens of some Latin American and African nations. But the fiscal crisis that emerged in the mid-sixties led to major dislocations in the economy. Several other factors also contributed to what, by comparison with the situation in the sixties and early seventies amounted to economic stability in the late seventies: a decline in food imports; and an increase in migrant remittances as a consequence of the employment boom in the Middle East. India was also able to expand its oil production as a consequence of which oil imports fell by 30 percent in the 1980–3 period.[8] This happy conjunction of economic factors for India's prosperity was short lived. By 1991 global crises had overwhelmed the economy.

4   THE 1991 STRUCTURAL ADJUSTMENT PROGRAM: THE POLITICS OF PROGRESS AND PROTEST

The workers' struggle against privatization of UP Cement Corporation (Dalla, Churk and Chunar) has achieved a historic and heroic victory recently. At the height of UPCCL workers "do or die" struggle launched in the state capital, Lucknow, the UP [Uttar Pradesh] government has withdrawn the decision to privatize cement units owned by the corporation by an ordinance on October 11, 1991. (*Economic and Political Weekly, October 26, 1991*)

The victory of the Congress Party in the national elections of June 1991, albeit as a minority ruling party, hastened the spread of liberalization undertaken on a smaller scale under the aegis of Rajiv Gandhi from 1985 to 1989. The economic reforms, proposed in the annual budget presented by the finance minister, Manmohan Singh, included a package of privatization, liberalization, and austerity measures, and came as preparation for an initial IMF loan of $1.75 billion to $2 billion to bail India out of a serious debt crunch (*India Today*, July 31, 1991). To establish the sincerity of their intent, the Indian government devalued the rupee twice; once on July 1 and again on July 3, which amounted to a reduction of almost 20 percent against the basket of hard currencies. The human resource development minister, Arjun Singh, stated, "all these economic changes had already been contemplated and were part of our election manifesto"

(*India Today*, July 31, 1991). They were clearly not schemes hatched overnight. Economic developments in the eighties culminated in their logical outcomes in the debt crisis.

Even as the economic reforms were announced to "clean up India's economic mess" (*India Today*, July 31, 1991) the success of a workers' struggle against privatization of a cement factory in the state of Uttar Pradesh was reported in the press (Mukul 1991). Although the workers had appealed to the state and central governments, it was an appeal to the judiciary that proved successful for the striking workers. Court judgments denounced the underhand way that privatization had been introduced in the cement factory. The strike against privatization elicited a nationwide support: protest demonstrations by the Confederation of Public Sector Trade Unions workers were held all over India; and the Center for Indian Trade Unions staged a *dharna* in front of the prime minister's residence before submitting a memorandum of demands. On September 17, 1991, the All India Trade Union Convention against the Economic Policies of the Government held at New Delhi called for a national industrial strike on November 29, and the cement workers' struggle provided the symbolic rhetoric for their resistance to privatization. The cement workers' struggles were long, hard, and intense, having lasted more than a year. Starvation and police gunfire had claimed several lives, and families joined the workers in their protests against privatization. The state government handed down an ordinance to open the cement factories in "public interest," enabling the workers to claim victory against market forces.

Public debate on India's economy blames bureaucracy, inefficient planning, and an overextended public sector for the economic crisis and absolute poverty that deeply entrenches India. Although this is seen as an endemic problem, India's debt burden has been accumulating over the past decade. Warning of an economic crisis was first given at a meeting in New Delhi in 1989 organized under the auspices of *Social Scientist* at which about 40 economists raised the first alarm. A report on the meeting shows that despite differences of opinion they unanimously agreed that "the economic policy and management of the government was misconceived and harmful to the development of the economy in keeping with the needs of the mass of the people" (BM 1989).

The meeting ended with a joint statement which acknowledged an impending economic crisis. The burgeoning external and internal debt problem could be addressed only with public investment, interventionism, and by imposing import restrictions. Government planners did not offer any opposition to these views; at another meeting organized by the Institute of Development Studies in Jaipur, there was wide-ranging criticism of the government's economic policy of encouraging liberalization in the face of an increasing foreign-debt burden. The plan to increase growth rate to 6 percent with a foreign-aid flow of about 2.6 percent of the GDP was considered detrimental to the economic and political sovereignty of the nation, leading the economy into a crunching debt trap. By 1989, external debt payments amounted to 30 percent of the foreign-exchange earnings, causing grave concern in a political milieu that encouraged foreign investment and the private sector. Public concern was caused by a familiar theme: unemployment, poverty, and re-distributive growth had to be tackled before neo-liberal policies exacerbated economic vulnerability.

While economists and concerned government planners feared the impact of a debt crisis, politicians proceeded with liberalization, which had received considerable support during the Rajiv Gandhi regime (Ghosh 1991). Despite tremendous growth in the deficit in the 1988–9 period, the government favored purchase of food grains, fertilizers, electrical machinery, and technical services in the world market (*Economic and Political Weekly*, April 15, 1989). A report by the Economic Advisory Council of the Indian government identified some of the causes for an increasing debt burden. These were a liberalized export–import policy between 1985–8; leveling off of workers' remittances from abroad; and stagnation of indigenous oil production (Nayak 1991). Some of the factors that contributed to economic stability in the late seventies had failed to do the same by the mid-eighties. The foreign-exchange crisis was further intensified with the Gulf War, when there was a sharp fall in expatriate remittances, and the government incurred expenses through evacuating workers stranded in Kuwait and Iraq. While agricultural surpluses and competitive domestic production capacities for electrical machinery and turnkey projects suggested progress towards self-sufficiency there was also a marked increase in imports. As Nayak (1991) angrily notes about the exclusion of the public sector:

> The imports have not only aggravated the payments problems but also led to an under utilization of the domestic capital goods industry ... most stark is the plight of BHEL [Bharat Heavy Electrical Limited] which is being denied orders for power plants so that its capacity utilization this year is likely to be less than 30 percent. (*Nayak 1991: 1996*)

Clearly, imports were geared for elite consumption as industrial growth In the Rajiv Gandhi regime accommodated automobiles, entertainment electronics, and telecommunication gadgetry.

Import statistics reveal that the sharpest increase in India's import bill was for "capital goods" which grew eight-fold in a 10-year period, from $658 million in 1980–1 to $3 billion in 1989–90 (Nayak 1991). Now, in the early nineties, India's debt crisis is of the same order as that of other indebted nations in Africa and Latin America. External liability is estimated at $70 billion making it the third highest indebted country after Brazil ($122 billion) and Mexico ($101 billion). Debt service as a percentage of exports of goods and services is around 26 percent, where a burden of 20 percent is considered a serious encumbrance.

The alarm raised by the economists at the New Delhi and Jaipur meetings about the looming debt crisis were well founded. The brief hiatus of two years from the Congress regime was no respite from neo-liberalism, which was gathering momentum in the country. The attempted privatization of the UP cement factory in 1990 bears out the commitment to liberalization. The short-lived Chandrashekhar regime (November 1990–March 1991) had already approached the IMF for assistance. The union budget was expected to contain fiscal adjustments backed by the IMF (Patel 1992) but the budget was never submitted to the parliament as political conditions forced the government to resign.

It is useful to consider in some detail the way in which IMF conditionality was introduced as "economic reforms", in order to be able to place in context the response and resistance to these reforms. The primary instrument of the economic reforms was the industrial-policy statement announced by the finance minister, Manmohan Singh, in July 1991. It is "totally subversive of the content and direction of the IPR [Industrial Policy Resolution] of 1956" (BM 1991). The industrial-policy statement supersedes the Industrial Policy Resolution,[9] a keystone of social legislation, which ensured a socialist pattern of society in India. Although the industrial-policy statement is tantamount to a new industrial-policy *resolution*, the minority ruling party refrained from introducing it as a resolution as it would need ratification in the parliament, which it would be hard pressed to obtain. Monitoring the process of IMF conditionalities in India, Ghosh (1992: 13) warns that "the terms of the IMF loan far exceed the normal stipulations of that body for an "upper tranche" loan.[11] These range from easing import restrictions on consumer goods aimed for elitist consumption, reform of the financial system to permit entry to foreign banks, and amendment of the public-sector system to sell up to 20 percent of the equity of profitable public enterprises.

An example of how the IMF conditionality reneges on the socialist covenant is exemplified in paragraph 32 of the IMF memorandum. This particular section calls for reform of the financial system, in obvious reference to the Committee on the Financial System, which advocates a reduction in priority-sector lending by commercial banks from 40 percent to 10 percent. Considered a retrograde step, this is designed to reduce credit to the agricultural sector, small-scale industries' artisans, and small transport firms which account for priority lending. It is considered especially deleterious to the unorganized sector that contributes 50 percent of the value added by manufacturing industry. The appeal to the public to reject structural adjustment programs is clear in this statement: "IMF conditionalities are likely to take us deeper into the morass of dependence on external support" (Ghosh 1992: 15). Press coverage of the government's plans remain favorable: "Liberalization heralded the illiberal hour. ... the press, mostly owned and controlled by tycoons dreaming profit-expanding dreams, must be under instruction to treat economic reforms as absolute commandments; dissenting opinions have all but disappeared from the papers" (AM 1992: 442). Press censorship raises several concerns: the most significant is its association with state repression during 1975–7.

Other commentators see the economic reforms as necessary to lift India from stagnation. India, epitomized as a Third World paradox (because it has both high levels of poverty and an expanding base of high-tech industry), provokes exhortations for progress. The *Economist* (May, 1991) declared:

> India is not merely capable of making great inroads into poverty over the coming decade; that should be the least of its ambitions. ... India is a tiger caged. This tiger set free, can be as healthy and vigorous as any in Asia. ... The challenge is political.

The implication here is that the necessary imperative is for a political will to liberalize the economy, i.e. a throwback to the prescriptives of developmentalism and modernization. Thus socialist concerns, forged in anti-colonial struggles, have become archaic in a post-Cold War global economy. It is the desertion of nationalist and socialist principles that contours the nature of contemporary populist protest in India.

5 ECONOMIC REFORMS AND PUBLIC PROTEST: LABOR MILITANCY AND COMMUNAL RIOTS

Large-scale protest, singularly exceptional in its form and character has accompanied liberalization since 1991. The protest has emerged from religious groups who seek to assert a new identity for India, and from labor unions who resist the government's liberalization program. Another movement gaining momentum is a nationwide coalition of farmers' organization voicing ecological concerns, and determined to keep multinational companies out of agricultural production. While resistance to liberalization was not unanticipated, the rise of Hindu religious fundamentalism at this juncture suggests that opportunities for mobilization were created by the politics of liberalization. This section will briefly review the context of communal riots, and give an overview of collective protest from labor unions and farmers organizations.

Urban riot has been a recurring feature of Indian politics since 1947, but the demolition of the mosque in Ayodhya, Uttar Pradesh, on December 6, 1992 that triggered communal riots created a crisis for India's secular order.[10] The destruction of the mosque was carried out under the auspices of the Bharatiya Janata Party, who claimed that 465 years ago, the mosque was built by the Moghul emperor, Babar, on the site of a temple dedicated to Lord Ram (the mythic hero in one of the Hindu epics, *Ramayana*). The demolition sparked large-scale violence from Muslims and Hindus across the nation in a week-long frenzy of rioting in December. Bombay, a city with a multi-lingual, culturally heterogeneous population, which is characterized by a tolerable level of communal harmony, was particularly affected by religiously motivated violence. The government's inaction towards preventing the demolition, and its weak responses to contain violence and mayhem in the major urban centers have important implications for the politics of economic liberalization. So far, the BJP has been the only party to endorse the government's IMF/World Bank-backed economic reforms. Since it was not likely to build coalitions with the left-front parties in parliament as they bitterly resisted liberalization, the minority Rao government formed an alliance with the BJP to secure the required majority in parliament. This alliance was fortuitous for the BJP's religious militancy as it could pursue its political projects for Hindu nationalism under the aegis of a secular state. The Rao government, in ensuring its own legitimacy and tenure, gave the BJP *carte blanche* to pursue its antagonistic concerns; to provoke communal riots; and perhaps to obfuscate the growing opposition to liberalization by labor unions which was gathering force and popular support by late 1992.

The largest protest demonstration against the Indian government's industrial policy took place on November 25, 1992, in the capital, New Delhi. Estimated to be the biggest gathering of workers in the post independence period, the rally was attended by 250,000 to 300,000 participants (*Mid Day*, November 25, 1992). The rally held up the capital's traffic, forcing detours all through the day, and caused major traffic problems during rush hours. The demonstration followed two nationwide strikes held on November 25, 1991, and June 16, 1992. Organized by a broad coalition of trade unions and confederations, it included workers from central and state governments, banks, insurance companies, railways, and private and public industrial units; and farm laborers from various parts of the country, who demanded a halt to liberalization and unrestricted entry of multinationals into the Indian economy. Their rallying call was *Bharat Choro* or Quit India (*Times Of India*, November 26, 1992), reverting to a protest strategy of Indian nationalists during anti-colonial struggles against the British. The disciplined and orderly demonstration was a powerful signal to the government that its economic reforms were going to be met with resistance. The Sponsoring Committee of Indian Trade Unions also denounced the rise in prices of essential commodities, retrenchment in public-sector industries, and a slow-down in industrial and agricultural growth. Although the protest march was covered by most national and regional daily newspapers, government-supported media blacked out news of the demonstration.

The demonstration on November 25, 1992 succeeded major strikes held on November 29, 1991 and June 16, 1992. The strikes were organized as *bandhs* by coalitions of left-front trade unions. Labor declared them a complete success (*Working Class*, December 1991) although some dissenting unions abstained from the strike. Major cities were affected by the strike. In Bombay, nearly all the textile mills were closed for the day, along with other industries and the Bombay port docks. Publicly owned banks and insurance companies were also closed as the employees joined the resistance against the government's economic policies. This strike was particularly successful in the public sector which bears the brunt of the economic reforms in privatization. The *Times of India* remarked in its editorial that "the fact that significant sectors of the economy like financial services, airlines, railways and much of the heavy industry were seriously affected, points to the discontent among a broad spectrum of workers" (November 30, 1991).

The second nationwide strike followed about six months later in June 1992 and was marked by violence with the death of one left-front union member. The strike was successful through the participation of 12 million workers from public-sector firms (*India West*, June 19, 1992). Banks, insurance companies, domestic airlines, and other industries were closed for the day, bringing the country to a complete halt. Reports disputed the prevalence of the strike with government officials downplaying the amount of worker participation. Although the strike was peaceful, news agencies reported the arrests of thousands of workers as a preventive measure in the southern states of Kerala and Tamil Nadu (*India West*, June 19, 1992). Once again, trade unions called for the rejection of IMF/World Bank economic measures which imperiled India's economic sovereignty.

The nationwide strikes have forced the government to slacken the pace in implementing the economic reforms.[11] One major concern of the trade unions is the extensive retrenchment in public-sector firms. Euphemistically called "exit policy", the retrenchment is expected to affect firms with less than 300 employees. The IMF estimates that around 450,000 workers are likely to lose their jobs through voluntary retirement schemes and retrenchments.[12] The World Bank has extended a $3.2 million loan towards a "retraining" scheme for unemployed workers.

Other strikes have emerged as responses to specific austerity measures and liberalization policies. For example, in July 1992, truck drivers struck in reaction to the $3.00 toll imposed on trucks entering about eight states and the national capital, New Delhi. The All India Motor Transport Congress organized the strike among truck drivers to demand an abolition of highway toll taxes. An end to highway tolls has already been in demand for about four years at the time of writing, the strike is significant as austerity measures are being resisted with greater fervor in the post-reform period. The strike was called off after a week, when the government agreed to meet the unions demands. Negotiations with truck drivers were imperative since a shortage of essential commodities such as gasoline, garden produce, poultry, and milk constituted a threat to political stability in urban areas.

Protest in the public airline industry has serious implications for government revenue and the process of privatization. The Indian Airline pilots strike does not yield to such simple explanation; the causes are certainly based in complex politics of liberalization in India. The pilots struck on December 10, 1992, four days after communal riots raged in the subcontinent. The timing was inconvenient for the public but this was a better time than any for the pilots to make their demands heard. Their proposals included a 200 percent increase in the meal allowance and a salary competitive with those of private airline companies (*India Today*, January 15, 1993). The pilots also refused to operate unsafe airfields. Discussions with labor leaders suggest that the government's refusal to negotiate with the pilots was a strategy to dismantle the publicly owned, domestic airline company to ease privatization. Yet another explanation is that private airline companies are manipulating the situation to lengthen the strike and garner the government's business. In addition to the strike, Indian Airlines has been losing pilots to private airlines with no attempt made to retain their services.

One of the more serious threats to political stability is posed by a reduction in subsidies for fertilizer use. In a nation that relies on the public allotment system to reach the goals of distributive growth, ensuring adequate food grains is central to its socialist vision. While the public distribution system is not the most efficient organization, it remains one of the few means to alleviate starvation and provide food in a country marked by regional inequalities. One of the first fiscal acts of the Narasimha Rao administration was to cut fertilizer subsidy, a conditionality imposed by the IMF. As the government faced resistance to this move from its party ranks, farmers' lobbies and opposition parties, it prescribed a hike of 30 percent for fertilizers and decreed that small and marginal farmers would be exempted from this hike (*Economic and Political Weekly*, August 24, 1991). A scale back in agricultural subsidies has already manifested itself with a sharp drop in use of fertilizers (*India Today*, February 15, 1993). Consequently, agricultural production is expected to fall, creating the specter of food shortages and concomitant political unrest.

Austerity measures in the agriculture sector constitute only one piece of the liberalization mosaic. Opposition to liberalization has also been voiced, based on ecological concerns. Multinational entry into biotechnology and seed production has provoked a militant reaction from certain farmers' groups since liberalizing India's somewhat closed economy is bound up with international trade treaties, specifically, GATT.[13] The protest against GATT adds a new wrinkle to the protest against liberalization and structural adjustment programs. As far as the farmers are concerned, the Dunkel draft is closely linked with liberalization programs. On December 28, 1992, a few hundred farmers held a demonstration outside the offices of Cargill Seeds India Ltd, on St Mark's Road, a busy commercial area of Bangalore, capital of Karnataka state. About 500 farmers stormed into the offices of Cargill Seeds, threw out papers, files, and seed samples and burnt them in a huge bonfire. The police claimed it was a spontaneous protest, to explain their inability to contain the militancy. However, according to Dr Nanjundaswamy, the president of the Karnataka Rajya Raitha Sangha (Karnataka State Farmers' Association),[14] the police had been informed that a demonstration would be held near the Cargill office. This protest is part of a well-organized movement against several GATT proposals which ease multinational entry into domestic seed production, eventually denying Indian farmers the right to produce and sell seeds.

The heart of this controversy lies in a series of proposals introduced by Arthur Dunkel, director-general of GATT, in the Uruguay round of talks launched in 1986, that includes patenting of genetic resources. The proposal threatens food production in India as genetic resources are likely to become the private property of patent holders, mostly multinational companies such as Cargill and Sons. The real threat is the loss of economic sovereignty in food production according to the Karnataka Rajya Raitha Sangha (KRRS) and the Gene Campaign, a group of concerned scientists who are involved in mobilizing public opinion against the Dunkel proposals.

While the economy is still in the process of transformation, the effects on the people, especially the urban population, have been real and immediate. The landmark budget of 1991−2 along with the quick devaluation of the rupee resulted in a marked increase in prices. The immediate impact of the devaluation was to register an increase of 1.2 percent in prices in three weeks. Soon after the fiscal budget for the year was announced, the increase was 2.3 percent in two weeks (*Economic and Political Weekly*, August 24, 1991). Most commodities showed a sharp increase in prices: they included cooking gas, sugar, cigarettes, TV sets, air travel, machinery, cement, and organic and inorganic chemicals. Realizing that the brunt of rise in prices would be borne by women from urban middle and working classes, the finance minister acknowledged "I must apologize to all housewives" (*India Today*, August 15, 1991: 11). As of March 1993, the rise in prices continues: the 1993−4 budget announced on February 27, raised costs of petroleum products, rail fares, and telecommunication services. The question of reducing the coverage of the public distribution system has been discussed. Taking middle classes off the food-subsidy system is viewed as a real possibility adding another wrinkle to the politics of food production and distribution in India (see *India Abroad*, February 12, 1993).

To summarize, the post-reform period has been characterized by large-scale protest. Labor militancy, ecological protests by farmers, and communal violence have emerged during this period. As Birtill (1992) remarks, the opposition to western-style market economics is both creative and broad-minded. Labor militancy and farmers' protests have emerged specifically against liberalization and privatization, and judging from the participation in demonstrations and rallies, enjoy wide support. Their populist support is premised on appeals to nationalist and socialist principles that evoke anti-colonial memories and resist "anti-worker" or "anti-people" policies. Communal violence was empowered by the politics of state legitimacy. The Rao government, intent on retaining its tenure, formed an alliance with the BJP; received ratification for economic reforms; and created the conditions for militant Hindu protest that seeks to promote a version of Hinduism which is intolerant, bellicose, male supremacist, "Aryan", social Darwinist; and casteist (Bidwai 1993). While labor and farmers' protests have been, by and large, peaceful, militant Hinduism aided by new political opportunities created under liberalization, has brought a version of violent and divisive collective action unprecedented in post-Independence politics.

6   LIMITS TO ECONOMIC REFORMS: POWER, PATRONAGE AND DOMESTIC POLITICS

> Finance Minister Manmohan Singh acknowledged for the first time that thinking within the Congress Party could affect the economic reform program. In an interview with the *Economic Times* on November 9, Singh was quoted as saying "Reforms can proceed only at a pace at which they will be accepted by the ruling party, by Parliament and public opinion. (*India Abroad*, November 13, 1992)

Several conclusions can be drawn from the Asian experience with international financial restructuring. First, invincible as it may seem in comparison to Africa and Latin America, Asia's economic growth has been far from stable. While economic nationalism and socialist principles have exerted powerful ideological influences on industrial and growth strategies, they have not been adequate in protecting Asian economies from international financial downturns. Even invincible Asian NICS have proved to be vulnerable to global economic restructuring. In disaggregating national experiences, we find that austerity protests and opposition to market reforms have been largely prevalent in Asia and occurred as early as 1972 in India. Despite repressive, authoritarian rule, South Korea, often exemplified as a stable NIC, experienced protests in late 1979 and early 1980 that culminated in popular democratic struggles.

Second, introduction of market reforms is not accomplished smoothly since this entails a retreat from nationalist and socialist principles that often provokes fierce populist opposition. The resistance has often compelled Asian governments to scale back these reforms, in effect, promoting a diluted version of privatization. The realization of a full-scale market economy is often incomplete, the result is most often a weaker version of an IMF/World Bank ideal type. Growth and industrialization often rest on contradictory canons. These are shaped by legitimacy needs to retain national sovereignty within the constraints imposed by international finance capital. The varied experiences of countries such as Indonesia and the Philippines demonstrate this, and in particular, India which institutionalized its own variant of socialism.

Not long before communal violence burst into a regional disaster, the IMF and the World Bank endorsed the economic reforms undertaken by the Indian government as part of its loan obligations. The world's second-largest borrower at $2.4 billion in 1991,[15] the government carried out sweeping economic reforms, moving farther away from Indian-style socialism of the previous four decades. The annual meetings of the IMF and World Bank held in Washington DC in 1992 lauded India's efforts in securing market-oriented reforms. The president of the IMF was even moved to remark that he looked forward to India becoming a "tiger" as a result of her macro-economic stability and high growth. From the IMF and World Bank standpoint, the reforms were being implemented as planned, with no major setbacks. But Indian politicians and financial institutions knew otherwise. The Reserve Bank of India's annual report noted that there is "still a hiatus between policy formulation and implementation at the ground level" (*India West*, September 11, 1992). The tension between domestic politics and international pressures articulates the politics of state benefaction, especially of a regulatory state (Bardhan 1984) that derives legitimacy from an extension of privilege and rights for populist support. The Congress party's role in creating a regulatory state is well documented in the literature on Indian politics (Kochanek 1968; Kothari 1967). The lag in economic reform and halfhearted attempts at liberalization can be explained by the reconciliation of class interests.

Although Harriss (1989: 90), in an optimistic speculation argues that the Indian state has the ability to resist liberalization due to a developed capital and intermediate goods industrial base, an accumulated foreign debt of $70 billion dollars opened the doors to large-scale liberalization in 1991. Economic reforms, instituted as part of debt negotiations and liberalization, promoted multinational investment; and threatened retrenchment mobilized protests and strikes from labor unions and farmers' organizations in the post-reform period. In the earlier phase of austerity protests in the seventies, steep increases in the price of food grains and cooking oil, staples for survival, precipitated popular protest especially from women of urban working-class families in Bombay. Later, in 1973–4, students and urban middle classes perceived increases in food prices as a result of manipulative politics, indulged in by corrupt politicians who were only interested in safeguarding their positions of power and patronage. The protests in Gujarat and Bihar led to the imposition of authoritarian rule in 1975, and induced Harriss (1989) to predict that any attempts at liberalization in the economy would reimpose authoritarian rule.

Finally, outcomes of the contemporary phase of liberalization have been distinctive. It has led to protests from labor and farmers, and also enabled Hindu militancy. Protest that stems from a moral economy, compared to religiously militant, divisive politics that economic liberalization may engender, is benign as it appeals to humane values. The ability of the BJP to organize was largely enhanced by the political opportunities it was confronted with in the 1991 elections when the Congress party obtained a minority vote and forged a coalition with the BJP. The BJP's electoral successes that brought them to the forefront of constitutional politics has largely stemmed from a conjunction of factors which include a gradual collapse of the Congress party; the reaction of upper-caste Hindus against affirmative-action policies; and India's ideological shift to the right in the eighties (Bidwai 1993). A combination of forces such as the reorganization of the global economy in the post-Cold War period and shifts in domestic political power and factional alliances, ushered in liberalization and created the necessary legitimate political space for communal politics; a crippling debt and an alliance with the minority ruling party paved the way for the BJP's communalism to become a constitutional practice.

While the BJP's capacity to organize was greatly improved by electoral outcomes in the post-1991 period, liberalization, and concomitantly, modernization have also provided a fertile ground for communal politics. Rudolph and Rudolph (1993) propose that liberalization and economic growth in the 1980s brought widespread social mobility which transformed class and caste hierarchies among the Hindus, and migratory labor to the Middle East has provided employment opportunities to Muslims elevating them from an economically backward status. While Nehruvian secularism is questioned for its protectionism of Muslims, the retreat from Nehruvian socialism through liberalization enables such communal politics to become legitimate in contemporary India. The BJP's attempt to assert a new Hindu national identity for India is an attempt to redefine Hinduism as an ideology for modernization. As Romila Thapar (1991) points out, the Hindu militants' interpretation stems from the understanding that capitalism (which brings modernization) thrives among Semitic religions such as Christianity and Islam, and in order for capitalism to succeed in India, Hinduism has to be molded into a Semitic form with a historically attested prophet, a sacred book, and a geographically identifiable location, thus stamping out diversity and the diffuse nature of Hinduism.

The Indian debt crisis delineates a significant development in the global economic structure in which an archetype Third World socialist state's obligations are superseded by market imperatives. The political context of this development has provided an opening for religious militancy that foregrounds communalism in dangerous, unprecedented ways. While austerity protests were an anticipated outcome, escalation of religious fervor was an unintended consequence and points to the different expressions of social disruption. The question remains whether popular austerity protests can force the articulation of humane concerns in emerging modes of capitalism.

NOTES

1 Television interview with India Vision, USA, January 12, 1993.
2 Although they do not use the precise term nationalist-oriented growth, Hughes and Singh (1991: 62) argue that "self-reliance" (i.e. nationalist) and import–substitution industrialization account for India's and China's stable economic performance in the seventies and eighties. This is in contrast to Brazil's and Mexico's industrial strategies based on multinational investment and foreign debt. Maddison (1985) makes a similar argument.
3 Nehru's plans for public investment were often compromised by his support for big businesses in India. See Hanson 1966; Weiner 1962.
4 Rudolph and Rudolph (1987) provide quantitative evidence for the increase in riots, student unrest, and industrial conflicts in the post-1965 period, and include a discussion of violent events from 1952. The scale of violence was extensive: in a ten-year period from 1964 to 1974, riots increased from 33,000 to 81,000; student "indiscipline" grew from 395 reported incidents to 11,540; and number of workdays lost in industries rose from 7.7 million to 40.3 million.
5 Various analyses of the Naxalite movement are available. These include Banerjee 1984 and Franda 1971.
6 Between 1974 and 1977 India entered into renegotiations of bilateral

official debt under the auspices of the Paris Club. The debt fell from $179 million in 1974 to $110 million in 1977. See Robert E. Wood 1986.

7 Ranjana Koli, aged 35, a fisherwoman from Bombay, cited in Gandhi 1990: 60.

8 See Hughes and Singh 1991: 91; and Singh 1985.

9 Frankel (1978) provides a detailed account of the Indian government's plan for industrialization as specified by the Industrial Policy Resolution of 1956.

10 A number of articles provide succinct and perceptive analyses of the communal riots from December 1992 to January 1993 within a historical perspective. These are Bidwai 1993; Rudolph and Rudolph 1993; and Sen (1993).

11 While communal riots have delayed the government's action in implementing the economic reforms following the incidents of December 6, 1992, large-scale protests from trade unions had already slowed the process down (*India Abroad*, November 13, 1992).

12 Interview with S. N. Rao, *Frontline*, January 15, 1993.

13 The debate over GATT has become particularly acrimonious. Seabrook (1992) outlines the political and economic implications of some GATT proposals that may be enforced as part of liberalization.

14 Personal interview, Bangalore, January 1, 1993.

15 Argentina was the largest borrower at $3.19 billion, and Brazil was the third at $2.22 billion (IMF 1992a).

8

Explaining Sri Lanka's Exceptionalism: Popular Responses to Welfarism and the "Open Economy"

Ronald J. Herring

Aside from the difference between despotic and libertarian governments, the greatest distinction between one government and another is the degree to which market replaces government or government replaces market. Both Adam Smith and Karl Marx knew this.

(Lindblom 1978: ix)

1   PROTEST AND QUIESCENCE IN A DEPENDENT WELFARE STATE

The politics of liberalization is the politics of moving the boundary between markets and politics as determinants of economic outcomes. In this sense, liberalization is an episode in the continuing political dialog over the public moral economy.[1] The "great transformation" to market society described by Karl Polanyi (1944/57) is inevitably incomplete; what we find in virtually all contemporary societies are periodic shifts of the boundary between market determinations and authoritative determinations as political forces for public intervention wax and wane.

A global shift towards markets over states began sometime in late 1970s, often as a result of powerful international actors' selection pressure for market-oriented development strategies. The insecurity and deprivation which followed so frequently produced mass protest that the term "IMF riot" appeared in the literature. Sri Lanka presents a dual anomaly in the politics of liberalization-driven protest. First, mass anger at deprivation caused by public food policy, organized through a powerful general strike in 1953, preceded by decades the emergence of food-related social upheavals connected to the worldwide spate of liberalization which began in the late 1970s, as discussed in chapter 1. Second, retrenchment of the welfare state after the elections of 1977 – which were in effect a referendum on the "closed economy" – produced unexpected, perhaps even anomalous, quiescence.

Mass protests in 1953 are not theoretically surprising; a budding – "premature" in comparative terms – welfare state ratcheted up public expectations of affordable food as an entitlement. Unaffordable food produced a general strike which brought down the government. Yet deep cuts in entitlements after 1977 produced no large-scale protests organized around food, even in this intensely politicized society accustomed to holding political elites responsible for social welfare. Indeed, breaking a strong precedent of Sri Lankan politics, the incumbents were re-elected.

Together, these anomalies suggest refinement of the perspective that associates liberalization with mass protest. Economic forces in a peripheral economy may well produce the familiar protests against the market as prime allocative mechanism of human welfare, as Polanyi suggested, with or without a shift to liberalization. In Ceylon, precisely because of the inability of a particularly dependent state to insulate mass publics from international market-driven shocks, such protests led to persistent, but ultimately ineffectual, attempts to protect society from international markets – the "closed economy." Second, Sri Lanka's liberalization in the 1970s suggests that the international carrots associated with compliance in a liberalization project may substantially attenuate the connection between neoliberal policy packages and popular deprivation.

Liberalization in Sri Lanka has hardly been orthodox; "state shrinking," fiscal orthodoxy, privatization, deregulation, and other elements of the standard liberalization package were either not achieved or remained relatively insignificant in comparison to deregulation of external relations and redirection of public spending from consumption to investment. After exploring liberalization conceptually, this chapter examines the origins of state interventionism and the causes and consequences of its reversal in Sri Lanka. The causal logic stresses the interplay between structural vulnerability and democracy of a particular form: clientelistic, closely competitive, and highly politicized.

The relative docility of Sri Lanka's public in the face of increasing income inequality and cuts in the social wage is explained in part by displacement, particularly via ethnic conflict, but more importantly reflects the uncharacteristic leniency of external actors, hence a Keynesian deficit-driven expansion in place of the IMF prescription of induced recession. Analysis focuses on the period 1977–83. After 1983, escalation of "ethnic conflict" into civil war submerged liberalization as the central focus of political forces and rendered analysis of economic consequences of liberalization *per se* moot. In the elections of 1988 and 1989, welfarism was reinstated into legitimation practices by the party which had championed liberalization. This double movement reflects a political dialectic of elite and mass responses that underscores the power of Polanyi's vision of economic change.

2 UNPACKAGING LIBERALIZATION

Liberalization is frequently presented as a coherent concept because liberalization as a policy package is embedded in the projects of powerful international actors, particularly the IMF and World Bank (Dell 1984; Girvan 1980; Krueger 1981). Moreover, political support for "freeing up" and "opening up" the economy tends to be associated with discrete episodes of social change. Finally, there is coherence in social philosophy which reverses the logic of at least a century of thinking about state–economy relations; liberalization theory squarely reverses welfare-state logic and sees public interventions not as solutions to, but as causes of, economic problems. Nevertheless, the political logic of moving the boundaries toward markets produces variations across time and political systems which suggest the usefulness of disaggregation in understanding variance in response to the neo-liberal package.

External Boundary Liberalization

The state deregulates transactions with the international system. Most importantly, restrictions – both quantitative and qualitative – on imports are relaxed in the direction of free trade. Controls on incoming and outgoing capital flows are relaxed. "Artificial" maintenance of target exchange rates is disallowed (almost always meaning devaluation). Political interests (immediate and short term, since the long-term consequences of liberalization are moot) can be sketched. Free trade threatens the interests of capital and labor in firms and industries which are not internationally competitive. Easing restrictions on foreign investment advantages entrepreneurs with viable joint-venture projects, but threatens their competitors in the domestic economy. Devaluation hurts consumers generally, proportionate to the import content of their consumption basket (thus typically urban more than rural).

Conflict between the interests of individuals as consumers and as producers is inherent; the small gains from price reduction of some imported goods (if not offset by devaluation) are no compensation if increased competition destroys livelihoods. Workers who retain their jobs, and owners who retain their businesses, are of course in a different position from those who lose out to greater competition. Unlike discrete internal policy shifts, the ramifications of external boundary liberalization are difficult for the average citizen to conceptualize clearly. The greater availability and variety of consumer goods creates powerful symbols of new possibilities and generalized prosperity at the same time that new economic differentiation reorganizes the objective and subjective class configuration.

Internal Deregulation

The economic logic stresses broad growth benefits from removing the strangling effect of "red tape" on entrepreneurs. The greatest potential gain to consumers is increased price competition from reduction of protected monopolies or oligopolies. The immediate losers are powerful actors: (a) capitalists who control coveted permits to produce in restricted-entry sectors; (b) rent-seeking operatives of the administrative apparatus and their political brokers, i.e. a significant part of the state. Less powerful losers include the working class, to the extent health and safety regulations are relaxed; and citizens generally, to the extent that regulation protects their interests. The immediate and politically salient effects are likely to be negative for the state and protected capital, positive for unprotected capital, negative for formal-sector workers, and mixed for consumers generally.

State Shrinkage

A decrease in the state's share of resources and employment, usefully disaggregated into two components.

1 *Privatization*: to the extent that public-sector firms are losing propositions, their collective drain on the treasury may constitute a

burden for all taxpayers and recipients of public services "squeezed out" by the necessity of subsidizing inefficiency. Of course, some losses of public-sector firms are advantages to specifiable groups, and are tolerated for reasons of a presumed collective good. Public-transportation firms may keep fares low to insulate commuters from external shocks of petroleum prices, for example, and to facilitate the movement of labor from areas with affordable housing into more developed areas for work. Infrastructural services such as electricity and goods transportation may be priced low to subsidize profits in sectors to which their services represent a major cost (for example, irrigated agriculture and mineral processing). The major losers from privatization are operatives of the state apparatus, and the governing class of professional politicians who use the public sector as a source of patronage and funds (compare Bardhan 1984).

2 *Fiscal retrenchment*: deregulation and privatization could reduce the size of the state itself; public wages, salaries, and benefits constitute a major expenditure in the developmental mixed economy. But fiscal retrenchment is sought as well through the logic of "crowding out"; private-sector investment is assumed to be crowded out by public dominance of credit and a large tax take. Fiscal retrenchment is hard on the state apparatus, as its power and opportunities vary with the size of the budget. Other losers vary with their political power to protect class-specific or selective expenditures in the shrinking process. Beyond the gross guns vs butter trade-off, there is a wide range of coalitions possible in selectively protecting expenditures. In the classic IMF-induced state shrinkage, social consumption expenditures shrink faster than public infrastructural investments, which are legitimated by the necessity of creating a favorable investment climate consonant with the foreign-capital-led growth model. Vulnerability of the very weakest sectors to fiscal retrenchment is, along with devaluation effects, the core of the "IMF-riot" phenomenon.

Disaggregation of the effects of a liberalization package has suggested more losers than winners, at least in the short term. In long-standing genuine democracies, this conclusion is reinforced by the logic of origins of state intervention. However imperfect the translation of numbers into political power and interests into policy, specific interventions are expressions of political dynamics which indicate, on balance, support by a sufficiently powerful coalition.[2] The evolution of interventionist practices was analyzed by Karl Polanyi as one in which "society" (in a very Durkheimian formulation) "protected itself" against the "perils inherent" in a market-dominated economic system (1944/57: 76, *et passim*). For Polanyi, important societal values – particularly security – were threatened by the market, producing countervailing "protections" guaranteed by the state.

Polanyi's "society" is of course too much a black-box formulation. Specific interventions have been driven by the political mobilization, or threatened mobilization, of specific groups and classes, often with privileged allies, in the face of selective market-induced insecurity. Though "societal values" may be a partial explanation for prohibition of child labor, prostitution, environmental degradation, and other manifestations of morally offensive market outcomes, much of the history of intervention is that of class-based mobilization and struggles. Perhaps the Keynesian revolution in policy and theory, which made the modern state politically responsible for economic performance, fits Polanyi's model best, as depressions unified the interests of capital, labor, and regime legitimacy, and in so doing generated a protective coalition around macro-economic intervention.

Whatever the source of specific state interventions in economic processes, intervention itself builds vested interests in the state apparatus for continuation or expansion of discretionary authority. In poor nations, the institutional embeddedness of the developmental consensus produces further presumptive obstacles to dismantling the state's role. In democratic systems, the interests of rent-seeking bureaucrats are merged with those of the political class, which uses discretionary authority to pay off supporters, buy off opposition, and service patron–client relations (Scott 1972; Bardhan 1984: chs 6, 9). To counteract these inertial pressures, liberalization policies must be generated from some powerful new constellation of political forces.

What is the origin of this new force? Political scientists (before 1989) typically answered: the Bank and Fund. For many economists, the obvious answer was that political intervention in markets is inevitably counterproductive, and thus produces widespread discontent as mass publics learn this fundamental law. There is political naivety in this view: the failure to understand the interests served by "failure." Low rates of GNP growth, large deficits and chronic current-account deficits are aggregate phenomena which affect individuals differentially and often indirectly. On the other hand, the patronage plums, subsidies, sinecures, protected markets, and transfer payments have immediate and positive impact on individuals – mostly powerful, sometimes humble – in their struggles with the insecurity of market society. What is seemingly economically irrational is frequently politically rational (Bates 1981).

The Sri Lankan case points to the critical role of temporality, ideology, and politics in the framing of answers to this question. If the critics of public intervention are correct, the immediate losses and dislocations of liberalization are overwhelmed by the effects of growth and an expanding-sum game in the long run. The political-ideological problem for champions of liberalization is to convince mass publics, or at least politically salient sectors thereof, of this logic. Chances of success in this project are closely linked to pre-vious experience with alternatives and the political framing of cau-sality. To the extent that this ideological project is successful, mass protests against particular losses will be blunted. Failing that con-version, politics continues to revolve around the short-term effects of liberalization in generating identifiable winners and losers, who have differential ability to mobilize and influence public policy. If the preceding logic is correct, liberalization projects will proceed unevenly along the dimensions identified, as responses to new in-securities produce changes in regime practices.

3 DEVELOPMENTAL INTERVENTIONISM IN SRI LANKA

The elections of 1977 in Sri Lanka provided for a profound altera-tion of public moral economy and positive theory concerning growth and welfare. The expansion of the functional scope of government in the economy had been fairly steady until 1977, though accelerated by the 1970–7 United Front government (Shastri 1986). The result was a heavily taxed, tightly regulated economy. The 1977 elections were largely a referendum on perceived failures of the "closed eco-nomy"; the champions of a liberalized "open economy" triumphed decisively (Warnapala 1979). The rhetoric of open and closed itself signals the predominance of external boundary liberalization in the victorious United National Party's economic strategy.

Yet the new government inherited the institutions and expecta-tions of a dependent welfare state. Despite internal and external critiques, and well-documented failures (e.g. Pieris 1982; Marga Institute 1981), the pre-1977 welfare state demonstrated concretely the possibility of significant development at very low levels of per capita income and extreme dependence. For the bottom of the income pyramid, public programs, despite failings, contributed to security and well being quite remarkable in comparison with other low-income nations (Isenman 1980; Dreze and Sen 1989: 227–30 *et passim*). Welfarism also slowed the premature urbanization which plagued many poor countries by making rural life comparatively less nasty, brutish, and short.

The new regime had strong legitimation interests in disaggregating the liberalization package. A tension was apparent from the beginning, as the logic of the new economic philosophy entailed not so much state-shrinking as a shift in priority from social consumption to public investment, and from social security to aggregate growth. The public's response to the United National Party's request for a mandate for liberalization, and their quiescence in the subsequent difficulties, must be viewed through the prism of historical experience with the alternative.

Ceylon/Sri Lanka has been one of the world's most vulnerable and dependent economies. Classically dualistic[3] in the separation of an export-oriented plantation enclave from a large peasant subsistence sector, the colony depended on the sale of plantation crops in international markets to earn foreign exchange for the purchase of food imports and other necessities. At independence in 1948, half the dietary staple (rice) was imported and 90 percent of foreign-exchange earnings came from three crops (tea, rubber, coconut). Uncharacteristically, given its structural position and national poverty, Ceylon developed an extensive set of social welfare policies. These policies were condemned in the official international development community as "premature welfarism," diverting resources from investment toward social consumption and thus retarding growth.

With the global paradigm shift of the early 1970s, Sri Lanka somewhat ironically became a positive rather than negative development model.[4] For example, by the criterion of the "Physical Quality of Life Index" (PQLI) (composed of equally weighted measures of literacy, infant mortality, and life expectancy), Sri Lanka in the mid-1970s ranked higher than much richer nations such as Venezuela or Chile, with a life expectancy near that of some European countries and far greater than subcontinental neighbors India, Pakistan, Nepal, Afghanistan, and Bangladesh and a composite score somewhat better than China (see table 8.1). For a rough comparison of these data, consider that Sri Lanka's PQLI of 82, with an annual GNP per capita of about $200, came closer to that of Sweden (97) or the United States (95), than to that of India (42) or Afghanistan (17).

The PQLI is not without problems as a measure,[5] but the magnitudes of differences suggest important variations in policy priorities, which can be empirically verified. Among low-income Asian nations, Sri Lanka's welfare-state configuration contributed to extraordinary results in terms of human development. The control for income is crucial, since quality of life indicators is highly and positively correlated with national wealth; about two-thirds of the variance in PQLI scores can be explained by GNP per head alone (Moon and Dixon 1985).

Part of liberalization logic is that social consumption expenditures, of which welfare spending constitutes an important part, compete with growth-inducing investment, but the reality is more complex. Comparative growth rates of the nations compared in table 8.1 do not suggest that social consumption expenditures depress aggregate growth rates. Sri Lanka did better than the South Asian mean for the period 1960–77, despite decidedly welfarist priorities in spending. In broader comparative perspective, Sri Lanka's growth performance was right at the mean for poor countries in the 1950s and 1960s, though there was a dip in relative performance in the 1970s (Goldsmith 1986) for reasons discussed below.

Comparatively superior performance on human welfare measures is correlated with budgetary priorities. Spending on the IMF's aggregate category "Social Security and Welfare" on the eve of liberalization in Sri Lanka constituted a much higher priority than in any other nation of the subcontinental region, as illustrated in table 8.2. Sri Lanka stood closer to the priorities of advanced industrial nations than to those of its neighbors; in 1977, the percentage of central-government expenditures of this sort actually exceeded those of the United Kingdom (24.7 percent). While Sri Lanka's percentage (25.8) was only half that of Sweden (47.8), it dwarfed that of India (2.3 percent). Of special importance, Sri Lanka's priorities privileged human welfare spending over military expenditures; Asia nations as a whole allocated 23.9 percent of central-government spending to the military, compared to 2.2 percent in Sri Lanka.[6]

The expansion of the public intervention in terms of regulation, production and welfare was conditioned by two legacies of colonial rule: democratic politics and an extensive public sector before independence. In the independent period, patronage politics in a competitive democracy, linked to severe deterioration in Sri Lanka's external exchange position accelerated these dynamics. The plantation economy was born in mercantilism (Bandarage 1983) and required extensive infrastructure; the colonial state owned and developed relatively advanced railways, electrical, postal, telegraphic, telephone, and water-supply services, as well as the monopoly on salt production. Quasi-public financial institutions serviced the commercial sector. Because of the colony's strategic importance, the colonial state established production units during World War II for

Table 8.1 Development and growth: Indicators for South Asian nations and China, late 1970s

Nation	1 1977 GNP/capita	2 Average real annual growth rates (GNP/c) 1960–77	3 Crude death rate	4 Infant mortality rate	5 Life expectancy at birth	6 Literacy	7 PQLI[a] score
	(US$)		(per 1,000)	(per 1,000)	(years)	(%)	
Afghanistan	190	0.2	23	205	40	12	17
Nepal	110	0.2	14	150	43	19	28
Bangladesh	90	−0.4	19	136	46	26	35
Pakistan	190	3.0	21	126	51	24	40
India	150	1.3	15	123	49	36	42
China	390	5.1	7	45	65	66	75
Sri Lanka	200	2.0	7	37	65	85	82

[a] Physical Quality of Life Index (unweighted arithmetic average of columns 4–6; see Morris 1979 for procedure)

Sources: columns 1, 2: World Bank 1979: appendix table I; columns 3–7; appendix C3 World Bank 1983b.

Table 8.2   Governmental priorities in spending (percentage of total central government expenditures), 1976

Nation	Defense	Social security and welfare 1976	1977	Education	Health
Nepal	7.2	0.7	0.6	12.2	6.7
Bangladesh	9.3	6.3	2.8	9.2	5.0
Pakistan	36.2	1.6	2.7	2.8	1.8
India	23.3	3.2	3.3	2.3	2.5
Sri Lanka	2.2	19.9	25.8	11.3	6.2
Asian mean	23.9	n/a	n/a	9.4	3.3
Industrialized nations	14.1	38.0	37.8	5.6	11.5

Source: IMF 1984: 46–7

plywood, quinine, drugs, leather, coir, paper, ceramics, acetic acid, glass, and steel (Karunatilake 1976).

Welfare policies likewise began under colonial rule – a network for subsidized rice and flour distribution and rationing in 1942, for example. Free education (through the university level), poor relief, and subsidized or free medical care were all introduced in the late colonial period.[7] Howard Wriggins goes so far as to argue that the structure of the colonial Donoughmore constitution created "every incentive to take advantage of government revenues and virtually no inducement to think except in the most parochial terms" (Wriggins 1960: 87). The colonial state also took an extraordinarily active role in planning and subsidizing "colonization schemes" from 1935 onwards to remove the landless and land-poor from the deteriorating peasant sector in the wet zone to free farms in new irrigated tracts in the dry zone.[8]

Distribution of these boons, coupled with penetration of government programs and politicians into village society, produced politics of patronage rather than class (Perera 1985). Mick Moore correctly argues that welfarism became the dominant "meta-agenda" of politics (1985: 203).

Emerging patron–client politics of an intensely competitive form, in conjunction with Ceylon's specific mode of insertion into the world economic system, had implications for state intervention. Structural dependency proved to be a double-edged sword. Export concentration in primary commodities may, under specific (often transitory) conditions, improve national capacity to meet domestic needs, as apologists for colonialism argue from the logic of comparative advantage. With buoyant export prices, Ceylon's plantation economy provided a dependable and readily taxed revenue stream and generated the foreign exchange necessary to import food and other necessities (World Bank 1953: 146), similar to the potential later presented to oil exporters. The welfare system in Ceylon was built on precisely this base.

But dependency also means vulnerability. Political pressures produce responses to deterioration in exchange position through attempts to insulate mass publics from immiserization and to modulate external shocks. Public institutions create clienteles; in a political democracy, distribution and expansion of spoils (i.e. jobs, contracts, services, and subsidies) become objects of partisan competition for votes and means of servicing electoral machines. While remaining a colony, Ceylon received universal franchise very early (1931); though politicians could not control levers of real state power, they could compete in patronage and promises.

A wealthy plantation economy supported such predictably popular programs as subsidized food and free farms, but as the terms of trade turned against Ceylon after independence, the economy's capacity to bear the costs eroded. When the government in 1953 attempted to reduce rice subsidies because of increasing costs during the Korean War, a well-established leftist opposition called for the "Great *Hartal*" (general strike) which paralyzed the nation (Wanasinghe 1980; Wriggins 1960: 75–6; Ponnambalam 1981: 25). The prime minister resigned; the finance minister (and later president of Sri Lanka during the liberalizing period) lost his seat in the following elections. A well-organized and strategically placed working class, in concert with a mass public politicized around the issue of welfarism, clearly established constraints on development strategy; "rice politics" became fundamental in determining electoral outcomes and policy (Ponnambalam 1981). Strong feedback loops connected welfare policy, budgetary priorities, and structural dependency in a logic recognized by political elites.

Few nations have experienced so drastic and long-term a deterioration in terms of trade as did Ceylon from the mid-1950s to 1976. From 1950 to 1975, the export price index rose from 17 to 29 while the import price index rose from 8 to 49. The terms of trade index thus fell from 208 to 58 (Central Bank of Ceylon 1984b: 6.8, 6.9; Herring 1987: table 3). Concretely, though the volume of exports increased by more than 35 percent over that 25-year period, the purchasing power of exports *fell* by about 70 percent. Imports did not decline proportionately (falling only from index 62 to index 52); the structure of the economy limited import-cutting possibilities. Once luxury imports (whiskey, automobiles, etc.) had been restricted, further reductions in imports were difficult without harming either the economy (fuel, spares, intermediate and capital goods) or the basic needs of the population (food, medicine). The gap was met by borrowing, and debt servicing further reduced import capacity. Debt-service obligations rose from negligible levels in the 1950s to over 20 percent (excluding short-term credits) of all export earnings in 1975. Though the economy was exporting substantially more in 1975 than in 1950, those exports had a purchasing power little more than a quarter of the smaller volume of 1950. Moreover, as government revenues were heavily dependent on taxes on trade (60 percent of revenues in the early 1950s), deterioration in the terms of trade contributed significantly to burgeoning domestic budget deficits.

When foreign-exchange reserves of the early 1950s dwindled and the nation's vulnerability to exogenous shocks became apparent – most dramatically in the Great *Hartal* of 1953 – import-substituting industrialization predictably appeared. Indigenous entrepreneurs seemed more drawn to the plantation economy and import–export trade than to risky long-term industrial investment; the state took up the slack under both conservative and populist regimes. As current-account deficits became chronic, some nationalizations were justified by the necessity of "stemming the drain of foreign exchange and the evasion of controls" (Karunatilake 1976: 183). A similar concern for private-sector leakages of foreign exchange and extensive abuses of regulations (Wickramasinghe 1974) led to the establishment of state trading corporations, tighter regulations and export-oriented public-sector firms (petroleum products, for example). Fed by concern over shortages of imported consumer goods and the volatility of "rice politics" in a highly politicized society, governments expanded state control of distribution of necessities (both goods and services) at administered prices. Political elites found further nationalizations and controls attractive for narrowly partisan purposes as well in a political system evenly balanced between the major contenders, the United National Party (UNP) and Sri Lanka Freedom Party (SLFP) (which alternated in power until 1982). By 1975, roughly a quarter of GNP was in government or public-sector hands, a remarkable figure given the importance of peasant production in the economy as a whole.

The accumulation of these forces was inexorable, and reached crisis proportions in the early 1970s with food- and fuel-price shocks. Like many structurally similar poor nations in the mid-1970s, Sri

Lanka faced an economic crisis largely external in origin (Kappagoda and Paine 1981: 101–10): slow growth, austerity budgets, mounting internal and external debts, high unemployment. It was the world-wide economic dislocations of this period, most intensely felt in the periphery, that fed popular disillusionment with the "closed economy."

4   ELECTORAL RESPONSE TO THE "CLOSED ECONOMY"

Extreme scarcity and discretionary authority combine to produce conditions fostering corruption, victimization, and favoritism. The leftist United Front (UF) regime (1970–7) was widely perceived to be guilty of these and other abuses of power and eventually un-raveled internally (Shastri 1985: chs 6, 7). More importantly, the United Front's policies, which clearly produced hardship and faci-litated corruption, did not appear effective to the public: suffering was widespread, unemployment reached 25 percent, growth rates declined, and essential goods were scarce. Underemployment was severe and dissatisfaction with jobs "inappropriate" to level of edu-cation or expectations widespread and bitter (International Labour Office 1971: vol. 1, ch. 2).

Though the electorate judged economic performance under the "closed economy" in the early 1970s very harshly, it is not clear that alternative policies would have fared better in a small, dependent economy in the face of the extraordinarily adverse conditions – natural and economic – of the period. The economic crisis of the mid-decade was genuine, and severe, but the performance of the economy over a longer stretch of time was not noticeably worse than that of other poor nations.[9] Nevertheless, the UF government was identified with economic hardship. The extent to which deteriorating terms of trade and increasing budget deficits impinged on domestic politics is illustrated by the austerity budget of 1971. Political op-position prevented the government from increasing the price of flour and sugar, but the price of rice was increased 25 percent and medical subsidies reduced. N. M. Perera, one of Ceylon's leading Trotskyites, as minister of finance laconically noted:

> This has been a hard budget. It has not been a pleasant or easy task for me. Poignant memories of the past keep crowding around me. All my life I have fought to ease the burden of the poor and the humble. I am now the instrument not of easing, but of heaping additional burdens on them. (*in Halliday 1975: 210*)

Erosion of social welfare spending thus set in before the sweeping 1977 UNP electoral victory (140 of 168 seats), as the United Front government cut subsidies reluctantly, in response to the budgetary and foreign-exchange pressures (Shastri 1986). The left protected its political constituency more than the right arguably would have, but the room for maneuver was narrow. Though the government continually asked for the forbearance of the poor and unemployed and promised that the austerity measures were temporary responses to external conditions, an important section of the militant left rejected both the program and the analysis of the government.

The JVP (*Janatha Vimukhti Peramuna* or People's Liberation Front) was already mobilizing and organizing in the countryside for revolution, a process accelerated by the failure of the United Front government to produce radical structural change. The Insurgency of 1971 was not launched from a well-conceived strategic position, but nevertheless succeeded in wresting areas of the island from state control until the reinforced armed forces could regroup and, with heavy international technical assistance, crush the rural youths' rebellion.[10]

The Insurgency had a profound impact on Ceylonese politics. The demands of the JVP were centrally concerned with Sri Lanka's dependency; party lectures spoke of independence and self-reliance, rejection of World Bank advice and foreign loans, as well as foreign-trained and English-educated ruling elites. The central symbol of Sri Lanka's international dependence was attacked; the JVP promised to uproot the tea bushes and plant food. There was also a call to collectivize the land (Wijeweera 1975; Jupp 1978: 302–7). The revolt acted as a catalyst in generating a significant land reform which had not been mentioned in the coalition's election manifesto (Herring 1983: ch. 6), and in raising the priority of expanding employment. It also dislocated the economy, and added to pressures emanating from abroad.

The dramatic worldwide escalation of food prices in 1973–4 hit Sri Lanka's poor especially hard and added to budgetary and foreign-exchange crises. Long queues formed for bread and rice and the local press documented cases of corruption to obtain both. A common joke had to do with families turning down marriage proposals from cabinet ministers in favor of proposals from bread-shop owners. Prime minister Sirimavo Bandaranaike reacted to the "national disgrace" of being forced to wander the globe with a begging bowl; Sri Lanka was to be made self-sufficient in food through a war-footing mobilization of land and labor. Manioc (cassava) and yams were planted virtually everywhere by school children, Boy Scouts, government servants and Buddhist monks. Hillsides were denuded and planted (often with predictably catastrophic results). The minister of agriculture threatened to confiscate any land not growing food.[11]

Suffering and deprivation in the 1973–4 period were severe, particularly among the plantation proletariat – the Tamil tea laborers.[12] In 1973–4 the quantity of rice imports was cut by 12.5 percent, and yet the rice import bill *increased* by 166 percent. Likewise, the precipitous rise in costs of petroleum-based products dislocated the economy further and added to unemployment and distress. Factories dependent on foreign imports of machinery, fuel, and raw materials reduced production, or shut down (Balakrishnan 1977: 202, 210). Between 1973 and 1974, manufacturing value fell by 4.1 percent and capacity utilization fell to about 40 percent. The transportation system suffered, slowing commercial activity; and fertilizer, critical for the food war, became increasingly difficult to obtain.

The United Front regime, because of both positive ideology and economic exigencies, produced the culmination of state intervention. Critical consumer goods were rationed for lack of foreign exchange (which itself was rationed directly); movements of domestic food grains were controlled; new laws regulated land use and land ownership; state-sector employment expanded; and general austerity was proclaimed and managed by the state. These measures were, however, not ameliorative in popular perception, and provided clear evidence of inefficiency and corruption. The result was an electoral debacle for the parties of the Front. The irony is that for all the political costs of "closing" the economy, in fact it remained in a critical sense open to external shocks.

5   LIBERALIZATION

The core assumption of the United National Party government which won the 1977 elections was that the economy had been shackled by excessive regulation, an excess of consumption expenditure over investment, and "wasteful and complacent" public-sector enterprises. Market forces were to play a greater role in allocating resources and public enterprises were to compete with the private sector. The Central Bank termed the new ensemble of policies "a sweeping departure from a tightly controlled, inward-looking, welfare-oriented economic strategy to a more liberalized, outward-looking and growth-oriented one" (Central Bank of Ceylon 1978: 2).

Key elements of the new strategy included powerful investment incentives to foreign and domestic capital, a shift in the composition of public spending, and a liberalized international-trade policy, premised on export-led growth. Employment creation was a central objective, both through encouragement of domestic and foreign capital, and through ambitious public works such as the Accelerated Mahaweli Development Scheme for bringing new tracts of irrigated land under cultivation while substantially increasing hydroelectric capacity (Sri Lanka 1979, 1980c). Attracting foreign investment necessitated large infrastructural investments. These objectives implied neither *laissez-faire* doctrine nor state-shrinking, but were tailor-made for patronage politics if someone would foot the bill.

There is no doubt that the liberalization strategy from the beginning assumed increased and extraordinary dependence on external funds. Fiscal logic suggests that the very boldness itself was dependent on international support; if capital is granted tax incentives and yet the government increases infrastructural investment when budget deficits are already large and chronic, additional financial resources must be found externally. Likewise, relaxing import controls can be expected to put pressure on the balance of payments, chronically in deficit.

Despite its proclaimed economic philosophy, the Government did not dismantle the large public sector;[13] capital and current transfers to (public corporations, as well as revenue derived from the operation of government enterprises, rose steadily in the early years of liberalization (Herring 1987). Much of this expansion was driven by the strategy's reliance on attracting private foreign capital. Ironically, foreign aid, through project loans and grants, increased the size of the public sector, most significantly in the Accelerated Mahaveli (irrigation and power) Project. Employment in state industries fell from 73,224 in 1979 to 54,929 in 1986 (Central Bank of Sri Lanka 1986: table 30). Nevertheless, total expenditures on salaries and wages by the government increased both in absolute terms and as a share of GDP, reaching 9.9 percent in 1985 (Central Bank of Ceylon 1985: table 1.41).

Actual transfer of productive assets from the public sector to the private sector was minimal in the first five years of liberalization – a few textiles mills, some agricultural land – but the regime significantly reduced the public sphere in terms of exclusivity. Trading monopolies, both international and domestic, were broken, foreign banks were permitted (and invited) to establish branches; and bus transport was opened to the private sector. Regulation of economic activity declined, especially in the Export Promotion Zone, where a decidedly *laissez-faire* attitude prevailed; not only were long-established legal protections of labor in abeyance, but even data collection and monitoring were accorded very low priority.

Sri Lanka has traditionally been one of the most heavily taxed of poor nations. Government revenue as a percentage of GDP was 26.5 percent in 1978, compared to 11 percent in India and 12 percent in Pakistan; government *expenditure* was 40.9 percent of GDP. By 1985, government revenues were down to 23.4 percent of GDP, but spending exceeded the pre-liberalization level, constituting 42 percent of GDP (Central Bank of Ceylon, 1979a: table 2.1, 1985: tables 1.40, 1.41). The gap between the two figures underlines the IMF's pressure for "financial discipline," meaning large expenditure cuts.

Though the government cut some areas of public consumption, it expanded others; patronage remained a central political dynamic. In 1979 a National Housing Development Authority was established to construct 100,000 living units (later expanded to a target of 1,000,000) either directly or through "aided self-help" programs. An "Electoral Housing Program" undertook direct construction of 155 houses per electorate. IMF opinion was hostile to both the diversion of investment funds from capital formation, and to the interest subsidies to "aided" home-builders. Nevertheless, the plan was attractive to USAID, which contributed heavily, and is tailor-made for servicing regime patronage interests. Not only can significant boons be selectively allocated, but ruling politicians gain attractive opportunities for skimming operations. Likewise, the massive Mahaveli (river valley) development programs provided ample opportunities for patronage, ranging from lucrative contracts to subsidized irrigated land for farmers.

The public-investment program was ambitious, but was not meant to increase the public sector's share of final goods production. Rather, as the financial minister stated in July 1984, "public investment is to be viewed basically as a means of providing the infrastructure facilities necessary to support private entrepreneurship" (*Ceylon Daily News*, July 28, 1984). Public capital expenditures as a percentage of total public expenditure increased from 21 percent in 1971–2 to 43 percent in 1982 (Central Bank of Ceylon 1982: 250), though it was widely acknowledged in Sri Lanka that the rapid expansion of capital spending produced considerable waste and corruption. Gross domestic investment increased from an annual average share of GDP of 16 percent for the 1970–7 period, to an annual average of 27.7 percent for the 1978–83 period. Coupled with cuts in taxes to capital, the ambitious public-investment program inflated budget deficits. Budget deficits reached 26.1 percent of GDP in 1980 and 22.1 percent in 1982, contributing to mounting public debt.

International support was a necessary condition for these policies. While the share of public investment more than doubled as a percentage of GDP in the 1978–82 period, compared to 1970–7 averages, international assistance (grants, loans) almost quadrupled as a percentage of GDP (IMF 1984: 42, 24). Still, by 1984, interest on the public debt – domestic and foreign – was the largest single expense in the budget, exceeding capital transfers, salaries, and subsidies and grants (*Economic Review*, September 8, 1983: 116). Foreign financing typically covered around 50 percent of the annual deficits after 1977 (Central Bank of Ceylon 1983b: appendix table 18; table 1.41; Central Bank of Ceylon 1983b: appendix tables 67, 64). The significant grant element in foreign assistance enabled the government to escape a debilitating debt-service burden.

6 NUTRITIONAL SECURITY AND LIBERALIZATION

Given the vulnerability of the national economy and the volatility of "rice politics" in Sri Lanka (most dramatically in the Great *Hartal* of 1953, which prompted resignation of the government), regimes have sought to assure stable food supplies at affordable prices. As food imports were a major part of the balance of payments difficulties during the 1960s, strenuous efforts were made to increase the domestic production of rice, particularly under the UNP regime after 1965. The success of these efforts was dramatic, with paddy production tripling between 1952–3 and 1970–1, almost doubling the cereal self-sufficiency ratio. This achievement represented, in the words of Gavan and Chandrasekera, "what may have been the most spectacular record of any rice-growing country" (1979: 25). In the early 1970s, rice alone accounted for up to 20 percent of the total import bill; in 1983, rice imports were less than 2 percent of total import costs, and in 1984, less than 0.2 percent (Central Bank of Ceylon 1984a: appendix table 21).

Gains in paddy production came both from significant increases in area, largely through costly state-subsidized development of irrigated colonization schemes in the dry zone, and from increased yields obtained through propagation of high-yielding varieties, heavily subsidized fertilizer distribution, provision of rural credit with a large *de facto* grant element, and price supports to encourage production (Ponnambalam 1981: ch. 4; Moore 1985). Though these policies contributed significantly to reducing the food dependency of

the national economy, their costs contributed directly and heavily
to the fiscal crisis faced by the government in the following decade.
By one estimate, subsidies to rice producers and rice consumers in
the 1965–70 period were equal to 36 percent of public-sector capital
expenditure and in some years exceeded 50 percent (Gavan and
Chandrasekera 1979: 48).

Aggregate food production may not, however, have any positive
influence on food consumption by the most vulnerable sections of
the population. Increases in yields do lower the size threshold of
security for small landowning farmers, assuming costs of production
do not escalate beyond their financial reach. This yield–security
ratio is important in nations such as Sri Lanka in which a high
percentage of the poor own some land and the size distribution of
holdings is heavily loaded at the bottom end. The average size of
holding in what used to be called the "peasant sector" was 1.95
acres; more than three-quarters of all holdings were less than 3 acres,
covering little more than one-third of the area cultivated. More than
two-fifths of the holdings in this sector are less than one acre, averaging 0.37 acres each (Ministry of Plan Implementation 1982).
About 36 percent of the holdings are operated as tenancies by families owning no land at all or only home and garden sites; rental
demands deepen poverty on many small holdings.

Even in the peasant sector, only a fraction of the population can
be considered nutritionally secure, despite higher yields and greater
aggregate production. For the urban marginal population, nutrition
is even more dependent on public-welfare and food-pricing policy.
Though the empirical situation is by no means clear, it seems that
real incomes lagged behind food costs for the weaker sectors of the
economy after liberalization. This would not be surprising, since
there was rapid inflation after "opening up" the economy, trade union
power diminished, and an unemployed pool of labor remained to be
absorbed despite a fall in unemployment rates.[14]

One strand of the celebration of Sri Lanka as a "basic needs"
success story in the mid-70s, was the reduction of income inequality
for the decade 1963–73.[15] Data from the 1981–2 Consumer Finance
Survey indicated increased inequality between 1973 and 1981–2;
indeed, the Gini coefficient, which had fallen to 0.41 in 1973, and
was precisely the same in 1978 as in 1963 (0.49), increased to 0.52,
the highest level since the surveys began in 1953. Since property
income increased after 1977, tax concessions were granted to capital,
and indirect taxes were increased, income inequality after taxes and
before subsidies almost certainly increased (compare Lakshman
1980; Samarasinghe 1980). Moreover, the real value of the most

important consumer subsidies was significantly eroded by inflation. Likewise, management of public-sector enterprises historically had a purposive redistributive impact (Lakshman 1980: 122) which was contrary to liberalization logic.

Food policy has been central to both domestic politics narrowly conceived and to conflicts between Sri Lankan regimes and important international actors. The long-established policy of heavily subsidized food (at times gratis) for the population at large (over time limited somewhat by income criteria) was specifically targeted for criticism by the World Bank as early in 1953 (World Bank 1953: 128). A fundamental change in food policy was effected in June of 1978 when the general subsidy of food consumption was restricted to households earning less than Rs3000 per year. Approximately 7.72 million people – about half the population – claimed to be eligible. Further targeting accompanied a revision of the program from a ration provision to a food-stamp program limited to those with incomes less than Rs300 (then $12) per month (Oberst 1985).

The government undercut the subsidy by refusing to revise the purchasing power by indexing either the income criterion or the stamp values to counter inflation. Moreover, despite the dynamics of economic change, which accelerated after 1977, new additions to the rolls were forbidden. Between the inception of the program and July, 1981, the purchasing power of a typical family's food stamps had been cut in half (Sri Lanka 1981: table 3). Subsequent inflation cut the benefits in real terms even further. The bottom 20 percent of the income pyramid spend about three-quarters of their total income on food; in the poorest decile, food stamps account for 22 percent of food purchases (Edirisinghe 1985). An evaluation by the Food and Nutrition Policy Planning Division of the Ministry of Plan Implementation found that the effect of policy changes has been a deterioration of the nutritional status of pre-school children and an increase in the number of cases of serious malnutrition (Sri Lanka 1981: 30; see also Sahn 1983). That study concluded that the food-stamp system, although cheaper, put more families at risk nutritionally than the older ration system. An analysis of consumption data from the periodic Consumer Finance Surveys concluded that "there is no significant difference in the *average* nutritional situation between 1978/79 and 1981/82, but the calorie intake levels of the bottom 20 percent of the households have undergone serious deterioration" (Edirisinghe 1985: 49; see also Sanderatne 1985).

These dynamics produced a political-ecological niche for a program of redistributive populism focused on the food and the poor. It was just that strategy which was adopted by the UNP in the presidential election of December 1988 and the parliamentary elections of February 1989. President Premadasa's promises of poverty alleviation ran counter to the fiscal logic of the positive theory of liberalization, and to the chronic fiscal deficits. Nevertheless, these symbolic responses by political elites contributed to the absence of mass militance on the issue of food and poverty. Safety nets were in place, though gradually deteriorating, and the ruling party, in seeking a new mandate, acknowledged public responsibility for nutritional security.

7　EXTERNAL SUPPORT FOR LIBERALIZATION: FROM CARROTS TO STICKS

International resources to reduce the dislocation stress of readjustment were arguably a necessary condition for the domestic sustainability of liberalization. Following a sharp devaluation of the rupee in November of 1977, the IMF announced support for "the comprehensive program of economic reform ... in support of which the present stand-by arrangement [of SDR 93 million] has been approved" (*IMF Survey*, June 23, 1977). Banking on the IMF's seal of approval, the finance minister visited groups of investors and officials of aid-giving nations and agencies. In the first full year of the new policies, official loan commitments more than doubled the 1977 level, in marked contrast to the experience of other South Asian nations at the same time.

These official loans carried a grant element of 64.8 percent (World Bank 1980b: vol. I, 191). The net flow from all lenders increased from $48 million in 1977 to $175.9 million in 1979 (ibid.: I, 102). The finance minister was able to claim that "due to the confidence placed by the international community in our new economic policies, we have been able to obtain greater volume of foreign aid and foreign assistance *per capita* than perhaps any other third world country" (Sri Lanka 1980a: 2). As importantly, the minister noted that more than a third of the assistance was in the form of outright grants, the balance as long-term loans "at minimal interest." The minister acknowledged the direct connection to the new economic policy: "Without the courageous and imaginative steps we took ... nothing would have moved, nothing would have happened" (Sri Lanka 1980b: 2).

The effect of international factors in facilitating a higher level of imports and, indirectly, exports (since the import component of intermediate goods is over 75 percent) extends beyond the balance of payments. Domestic capabilities of the government in so dependent an economy are in large part a function of levels and terms of international trade. Taxes on international trade provided a larger share of revenue, reaching a high of 55 percent in 1979, far above the Asian mean. Sri Lanka became increasingly dependent on taxes on trade for revenue and on non-revenue sources for expenditure, recording the lowest ratio of revenue to expenditures in Asia for 1980–2 (IMF 1984: 24, 42). Without strong international support, current account deficits would have curtailed the level of trade and exacerbated the government's fiscal and political dilemmas.

Liberalization was initially lauded, both internally and externally, as a rare success story, primarily because of the relatively high growth rates after 1977. Nevertheless, there were caveats even for the short term.[16] But by any measure, the acceleration of economic activity was significant in comparison with the difficult period preceding liberalization. The politically salient question was whether higher growth rates represent self-sustaining processes or were simply the effect of a large influx of external resources into a very small economy, combined with initially favorable terms of trade and the short-term explosion of pent-up demand once the restrictions on imports were lifted. Fiscal liberality was facilitated by two mechanisms inconsistent with the typical neo-liberal orthodoxy: deficit spending driven by an expanded public sector and increased public control of investable resources, both enabled by external official largesse.[17]

Domestic political elites read international acclaim and material support as an open ticket. After a 1980 budget deficit amounting to more than 26 percent of GDP, accompanied by a rate of inflation of at least 30 percent, the consortium of donors, meeting in Paris in July, pressured the government to cut current-account and budget deficits and to raise more resources internally. The finance minister predictably responded that "external factors beyond our control" were responsible and that cuts in the investment program would dampen the enthusiasm the government had worked so hard to instill among investors (*Asian Wall Street Journal Weekly*, June 6, 1981, July 20, 1981). Familiar aid-budget disputes were repeated in meetings with the Aid Sri Lanka Consortium and IMF in the summers of 1982 and 1983; "belt-tightening" was urged, the government pleaded domestic constraints and blamed external factors, and compromises were made. In 1982 the government was particularly unwilling to cut expenditures because of the upcoming presidential elections (Samarasinghe 1983). There was reluctance to cut health, education, and welfare subsidies further, as the nation's remarkable records in

these areas "are our pride and we cannot afford to throw them away."
Resisting further devaluation, the minister said (*Far Eastern Economic
Review*, June 23, 1983): "We have only so much to export and any
further devaluation can only make imports more expensive," fueling
inflation.

External concessions made the liberalization strategy sustainable,
but did not erase vulnerability. The national economy was empirically more vulnerable to exogenous shocks under the liberalized
regime than under the "closed" economy (Jayatissa 1982). The IMF
noted that the sharp deterioration in terms of trade from 1980–3
increased the current-account deficit from 5.5 percent of GDP to
16 percent (IMF *Survey*, September 19, 1983). The net deficit in
national accounts for investment payments increased steadily from
Rs153 million in 1977 to Rs3,410 million in 1985. Reverse flows of
hard currency have increased with foreign investment and commercial borrowing (Herring 1987). While not high by contemporary
standards, the debt-service ratio eventually exceeded the historic
high experienced during the "oil shock" period of 1973–4, standing
at 26.2 percent in 1986 (Central Bank of Ceylon 1987: 228). By
1990, the debt-service ratio had declined to 13.8 percent; foreign
debt to GNP hovered near 74 percent. Over 70 percent of the external debt was on concessional terms.[18]

Given the historical experience of economic vulnerability, the net
effects of Sri Lanka's liberalization were not unambiguously destabilizing. Moreover, expansion of many sectors of the economy
and vigorous growth during part of the period separate the liberalization *project* of the UNP government politically from the imposition of unalloyed austerity by international forces beyond domestic
control characteristic of episodes of liberalization elsewhere. Indeed,
the UNP, albeit in a more populist mode, won the elections of
1988 and 1989.

8   THE QUIESCENCE PUZZLE

There have been persistent arguments that state-shrinking – particularly under IMF auspices – requires an authoritarian regime,
both because elected politicians are reluctant to impose severe hardships on their constituencies and because repression of the resulting
social conflicts is more easily accomplished when the state is not
constrained by the norms of liberal democracy (see, for example,
Sheahan 1980). Joan Nelson (1984: 1005) counts Sri Lanka as one
of the successful cases of stabilization politically; there were no

violent protests despite the fact that "subsidies and rations were successfully slashed."

One dominant reason for the exceptional quiescence of Sri Lanka's population through a liberalization episode is the departure of its policy from the "common set of neo-liberal reforms" addressed in chapter 1. The traditional IMF medicine of inducing a recession while cutting subsidies was offset by a Keynesian expansion, funded by internal deficits and external largesse, which produced higher levels of growth and employment than had been the norm for the preceding decade. To some extent, lower levels of income equality and nutritional security were counterbalanced in popular perceptions by increasing job opportunities and imported goods. Certainly a major determinant of the presence or absence of mass protests against liberalization is variable severity of austerity. In Sri Lanka, as in much of southeast Asia, liberalization was associated with growth, not contraction.

But as importantly, there are variations in the historical experience of *alternatives* to liberalization and the plausibility of claims that prosperity will follow temporary dislocation. Experience with the "closed economy," as well as the political-electoral process of assessing that path, differentiate Sri Lanka from many liberalizing countries. The severe hardships of the 1973–4 period discussed above rendered liberalization shocks mild by comparison.

Though there has been discussion of Sri Lanka as an "IMF success story," the reality is a dependent welfare state operating at somewhat lower levels of coverage. Domestic welfarism could not have been maintained without foreign support. In exchange for this extraordinary treatment, the international community was more insistent about some things than others. In political rhetoric (the "open economy"), and in practice, external boundary deregulation was dominant. Foreign investments were courted and are explicitly protected in the new (1978) constitution. Liberalization of imports and devaluation produced inflation, but widened consumer choice and improved industrial performance (as capacity utilization rose significantly).

Compared to the sweeping changes in state–economy relations at the international boundary, internal deregulation was less significant, with some exceptions. An expensive Export Processing Zone (EPZ) was created to attract foreign and domestic capital; labor protections were waived and state regulation was minimal. Outside the EPZ, deregulation mainly meant abolishing public-sector monopolies in such fields as trading and transportation and reducing the scope of licensing of industrial activity. For some of the public, the result was symbolically a reduction of the arrogance and inefficiency of the state.

State-shrinking did not happen. Privatization was urged on the government from abroad, but resisted in the early stages. Limited privatization was not much of a threat to the state apparatus because expansion characterized more sectors of state activity than contraction. Massive inflows of project assistance probably increased the net rental opportunities of the bureaucracy. Certainly public projects continued to be utilized for patronage functions and thus retained their political utility despite liberalization. For the first eight years of liberalization, the state expanded at roughly the same pace as the economy. After 1983, the civil war made extraordinary fiscal demands; the Ministry of Defence now claims about three times the percentage of expenditures it did in 1978.[19] Fiscal retrenchment did not extend to welfare expenditures as extensively as the IMF urged. Indeed, the political sensitivity of the safety nets was illustrated over time in the prominence of distributive populism in the successful UNP election campaigns of 1988 and 1989.

That the rhetoric of liberalization has outrun the reality is not surprising given its importance to symbolic politics in a Janus-faced state. To external audiences, the official rhetoric of liberalization signaled compliant behavior; to internal audiences, the promise was of genuinely new solutions to chronic economic difficulties while maintaining social safety nets. Given the extraordinary dependence on international aid and finance, Sri Lanka's experience suggests that international pressures for liberalization are not so monolithic or consistent as they are often portrayed (Girvan 1980; Dell 1984). Sri Lanka maintained a working relationship with the Fund despite budget deficits in excess of 10, even 20, percent of GDP. Domestic political pressures restricted wholesale destruction of the welfare state.

The interest of international actors is concentrated at the external boundary – opening new markets for international capital, insuring orderly adjustments of balance of payments, increasing world trade by reducing restrictions. The net effect of the heterodox reality is to improve the investment climate by improving public infrastructural investment and maintaining a cheap labor force by permitting maintenance of an internal welfare state, despite budget deficits. But why was Sri Lanka treated so much more generously and leniently than many other poor nations?

One of the leading proponents of liberalization at the World Bank identified a dilemma and a solution:

One of the apparent dilemmas of official development assistance has been the way to define its role when the private international capital market is providing a ready source of funds to credit-worthy borrowers. To extend public financial assistance to credit-worthy countries has seemed redundant because those countries are in any event growing rapidly and can obtain private funds. Yet it appears contradictory for aid to be allocated to countries where returns are low ... It would make eminent sense for the World Bank, and individual national donors, to concentrate much more assistance than now on facilitating the transition of developing countries from (i) policy stances in which direct controls pervade their trade and payments regimes and domestic economic activities to (ii) more liberal policies involving considerably greater participation in the international economy. (*Krueger 1981: 271*)

This logic may well be the most important insight into Sri Lanka's anomalous treatment internationally. The conjuncture of 1977 produced a regime openly committed, with democratic electoral support, to reversal of an especially long-standing interventionism in an economy small enough for relatively small flows to make an enormous difference in outcomes. Largesse sufficient to produce similar outcomes would be inconceivable in Brazil or India. Moreover, Sri Lanka was attractive as a genuine democracy with a pro-western foreign policy. Simultaneously, for all the bad press of IMF disasters, a plausible success story in the making had great appeal.

But if a debt-incurring Keynesian expansion goes far in explaining quiescence, there was nevertheless some pain in a very politicized society; other factors contribute to a full explanation. First, political process is important. Liberalization was not imposed top down on an unsuspecting public; the 1977 elections were a referendum on the move to an "open economy." Ineffectual "closing" of the economy over previous decades had produced a perception that new policies were unlikely to be as bad as previous strategies and stood some chance of success. International support for the government and the initial doubling of growth rates sustained this perception. Moreover, the experience of mass publics under Thatcher and Reagan suggests that even without international support, it is possible to sustain electoral support for a liberalizing trickle-down redirection of policy if costs are borne by a small and politically marginalized section of the population. Serious nutritional deprivation in Sri Lanka was probably limited to the bottom decile or two in the society − not a politically effective coalition.

History also matters. Unlike 1953, when a well-organized left opposition with strong roots in the trade unions was able to use collective muscle, the left and the unions had been disabled by the mid-period of liberalization. The same elections which ushered in the liberalizing UNP regime saw the elimination from parliamentary representation of the orthodox leftist parties for the first time. Trade unions had withered with decline of the left parties and the growing power of rival unions (JSS) linked to the governing party. Crushing the strike of public-sector employees in 1980 demonstrated the government's power and will. The populist SLFP, which had led the United Front government (under which the decline of labor and the left had begun), was likewise decimated in the 1977 elections. There was a stronger, more centralized state in place at the same time that the sources of organization and support for protest were weakened.

Mass protests at cuts in the social wage were also blunted in Sri Lanka, I believe, by the diversion of frustration into ethnic hostility. This argument has several strands. First, scapegoats are commonly victimized during periods of economic stress. Second, the impact of liberalization itself provided both symbolic materials and exacerbation of real cleavages to facilitate a scapegoating response.

The riots of 1983 in Colombo – the largest pogrom against Tamils in the nation's history and a turning point in the escalation of regional conflict to civil war – were, in Ganath Obeyesekere's account, driven by urban lumpen elements, characterized "by the hatreds and frustrations that slum dwelling breeds everywhere" (1984: 153). S. J. Tambiah (1986: 57) likewise attributes the increase in ethnic violence to "political manipulation" of marginalized populations "in protest of their lumpen proletariat condition."

The argument for liberalization's contribution to ethnic conflict was made by Newton Gunasinghe in a controversial three-part work (1984a,b,c). The regulated economy allowed many Sinhalese businessmen with connections to establish, via the permit-quota-license system mediated through patronage, niches that a market would not have provided. Tamil entrepreneurs largely lacked patronage and connections. Liberalization wiped out many of the inefficient small (Sinhalese) businessmen who had survived behind protective regulations. The anger in the business community was partly directed into anti-Tamil chauvinism. This ethnic antagonism was exacerbated by a member of the cabinet who utilized virulent anti-Tamil nationalism to cement and augment his political base.

Gunasinghe's argument is plausible, but is presented with only scattered evidence. He used the match industry as an example, but it is not clear how typical it was. The firms in the match industry represented three paths of response to liberalization. The strongest firm met international competition (from India and China) with investment for modernization, and survived. The second large firm had less deep pockets, and survived only by modernizing as a subsidiary of foreign capital. The smallest firm simply went under (Gunasinghe 1984b: 17). At the bottom of society, Gunasinghe argued that the urban poor experienced increased opportunity as well as increased insecurity. There was a great deal of internal class differentiation, and a movement from a "shared poverty" mentality to the "colour TV in the slum tenement" syndrome (Gunasinghe 1984c: 10). New material consumption possibilities fed new relative deprivation, and anger. Economic change "converted the urban poor into inflammatory material" (ibid). Since markets were seen as the source of both insecurity and mobility, Gunasinghe implied, the state became less the object of anger.

New definitions of national identity and threats to same, as well as a business class and politicians with something to gain, led to targeting and redirecting anger by this argument. It was widely believed that Tamils in Colombo were making a killing under liberalization because of their position in real estate and trade. Gunasinghe argues that Tamils were overrepresented in trade; resentment was fed by views similar to those represented in the Sinhala newspaper *Divayina* that "Tamil entrepreneurs [were] getting rich at the expense of the Sinhala" (Gunasinghe 1984c: 12). Pogroms allowed for the literal elimination of competition. In summary, Gunasinghe argued:

> As the economic role of the state appeared to them to be marginal, some other object of hostility had to be discovered to be held responsible for the current malaise. It is precisely here that the Sinhala chauvinist ideology, which first emerged from the ranks of the middle-level traders, found a fertile ground, engulfing numerous social strata among the Sinhala. (*ibid.*)

On the reverse side of the coin, liberalization badly hurt Tamil agriculture in the Jaffna area (Moore 1985: 109–10). Tamil insurgents in the north were convinced that the external flows were being pocketed by Sinhalese supporters of the regime; that virtually all of the carrots of developmental projects were accruing to the Sinhalese community; and that the extensive irrigation and settlement program funded from abroad was aggravating Sinhalese incursion on their historic turf, making decentralization a less attractive compromise solution to ethnic disputes.[20] Ethnic violence had flared just after the 1977 elections; any coalition of disaffected

Sinhalese and Tamils against liberalization became an impossibility as new cleavages dominated the political landscape. Moreover, the resurrection of the insurgent JVP in 1987 was likewise framed in terms of a nationalist (Sinhala) discourse after the Indo/Sri Lankan accords.

Moreover, diversion or displacement of frustration induced by economic distress and uncertainty is by no means automatically political or collective. There is something particularly painful in the perception that fortunes are being made all around and yet one's own welfare is declining. With clear evidence of economic boom, it is difficult to focus collective protests, and psychologically easy to blame an ethnic outgroup or oneself. If we believe politicians to be especially perceptive observers of popular moods, the anti-poverty themes of the UNP in 1988 and 1989 indicate that alternative sources of quiescence were wearing thin.

The puzzle, then, of why a democratic government (albeit somewhat less democratic) weathered a period of retrenchment and liberalization similar to that which has produced "IMF riots" in other countries has several interrelated answers. First, the Fund was extraordinarily tolerant of budget deficits in Sri Lanka. Second, this tolerance, and extraordinary financial concessions from abroad, fueled a Keynesian expansion rather than recession; aid projects allowed significant expansion of employment and politically targeted payoffs, as well as opportunities for rent-seeking bureaucrats. Third, the escalation of ethnic conflict created both scapegoats for mass frustration and at least some perception among the Sinhalese majority that "our government" is besieged by Tamil insurgents and deserves support. Political discourse and cleavage were literally remade. Fourth, mass protests of any kind confront repression, and thus significant risk for the individual; the government showed itself to be quite tough on threats to the economic miracle it claimed to be unfolding. And finally, firmly established and vigorous democratic processes permitted the reassertion by political elites in 1988−9, in a very Polanyi-like fashion, of promises that traditional safety nets for those ground to the bottom by market mechanisms would be re-established.

The political mechanism for liberalization sketched in the preceding sequence does not suggest mass political support for liberalization as utopia, as is now commonly claimed. The erosion of legitimacy of the developmentalist state followed mainly from its inability to deliver. The legitimacy of a patron−client political system and a welfare-state economy depends on state capacity which in turn is critically contingent on international trade and finance. The worldwide difficulties of the 1973–4 period were most severe in the most dependent societies, and served to delegitimize both interventionist development strategies and specific political forces (who cooperated by behaving badly) caught in that conjunctural crunch.

The demonstrable failure of state interventionism to meet popular expectations may then lead to support for a dramatic shift in political-economic philosophy. In the pragmatic discourses of ordinary politics, specific groups demand continued protection from unrestrained markets, despite the covering symbolic attachment to liberalization. The negotiation of these specific group demands – selective bulges in the politics–markets boundary – determines the vector-sum movement of the liberalization strategy. Liberalization is then premised not so much on people's low evaluation of public policies which offer protections from the jungle of market society in pure form, but rather on their high, but unmet, expectations.

What Blackhurst (1981) calls the "Twilight of Domestic Economic Policies" contains a political message. If traditional domestic economic-management tools are no longer effective because of international dynamics, the political coalition which accepted a Keynesian and social-welfare state becomes endangered in the rich nations for the same reasons that it does in the poor. Following two decades of quite extraordinary growth, the 1970s and 1980s presented common dilemmas. Compressed boom–bust cycles in commodity prices, unprecedented balance of trade and payments difficulties, financial instability, erratic growth rates, and the "debt crisis" have introduced common uncertainty in the management of both domestic economies and the international political economy. As traditional methods of assuring domestic economic performance sufficient to produce legitimacy have come under pressure, political elites search out new policies for "international competitiveness." Liberalization is one such strategy, though it coexists in a peculiarly uneasy partnership with strands of global neo-mercantilism.

NOTES

1 The concept of "moral economy" as a paradigm for peasant societies has aroused considerable controversy, often personalized in terms of the "Popkin–Scott debate." The error in the conventional moral-economy model is the assumption that peasant societies are in some way unique in the presence of "defensive reactions" to market capitalism. In fact, as Polanyi (1944/57) stresses, the legitimacy of market outcomes has been continually challenged by losers. In the "moral-economy" tradition, the *locus* of pre-market and anti-market economic norms is the "village

community." With increased integration of society generally, and particularly with the development of democracy, ethical questions concerning the legitimacy of market outcomes become part of a broader dialogue in which public authority is expected to intervene to prevent undesirable outcomes. Formulations such as an "excess profits tax" and "fair trade" in practice represent continuity with the just-price theories of medieval moral economy. The welfare state specifically appeals to a moral position defining limits to human misery regardless of market-driven distributions. Virtually all economic interventions are justified as in some way producing a more just or fair outcome than would unrestrained market dynamics.

2   There are two obvious caveats. First, numbers do not really count, even in relatively participatory democracies. Imperfections in the aggregation of interests always permit certain interests to gain selective benefits at the expense of some notional "general interest." Producer groups are notoriously able to win at the expense of consumers generally, as in the case of protectionism. At a more general level, what Lindblom (1978) calls the "privileged position of business," or the structural imperative of retaining "business confidence," works to limit democratic interventions in capitalist society. Second, there are not all that many functioning democracies in poor nations; models such as bureaucratic authoritarianism or some notion of the "parasitic state" explain the expansion of state authority contrary to the interest of mass publics. Nevertheless, the emergence and persistence of specific interventions reflects, in democratic systems, the operative distribution of political power, and may be presumed to have a political base at least under those economic conditions which produced them.

3   The conventional use of "dualism" to characterize the Ceylonese economy has been challenged by Bandarage (1983); see Herring 1985. Though Bandarage's work rightly stresses the complex interaction between plantation economy and village society historically, the notion of a dualistic economy need not, and should not, be taken to preclude certain interactive effects, but rather the disarticulation of sectors as stressed in dependency literature.

4   On Sri Lanka's exceptional position in comparative terms, World Bank 1980c: 90; Jayawardena 1974; Isenmen 1980; Morris and McAlpin 1980; Herring 1987.

5   The aggregate measure may obscure significant differences by class, sector, gender, and region; literacy may be overweighted; and problematic and non-comparable data are the norm. For a critical discussion, see Hicks and Streeten 1979; on Sri Lanka, Mattis 1978. On the inadequacy of traditional measures, and a defense of the PQLI, Morris 1979. On the persistence of severe poverty in Sri Lanka despite the impressive aggregate indicators, Marga Institute 1981; Isenman 1980; Lee 1976; Pieris 1982; Richards and Gooneratne 1980. For an empirical

analysis of the relationship between PQLI and income in 116 societies, along with a defense of the basic-needs measure, see Moon and Dixon 1985.

6 The escalation of civil conflicts to near civil-war proportions in the period after 1983 has altered this expenditure profile, but the basic point remains valid. By 1991, the figure had reached 5 percent of GDP, which the IMF found acceptable. Figures in table 7.2 introduce some distortion because of differences in political structure; Sri Lanka is highly centralized in a fiscal sense, as the central government accounts for more than 95 percent of total public spending, whereas in federal systems such as India the central government accounts for between 60 and 70 percent of total spending.

7 See Corea 1975: chs 5, 6; Wickremeratne 1973; Gavan and Chandrasekera 1979; 11–15; Gunatilleke 1978; Lakshman 1980: 17; Karunatilake 1975; and Herring 1981.

8 Farmer 1957; Herring 1983: ch. 5. The colonization schemes have contributed not only to improving the PQLI (via transfer of the landless and land-poor to new subsistence farms) but also to improving the cereal self-sufficiency ratio dramatically by opening up highly productive tracts, and to reduction of the potential for agrarian discontent, by making landed proprietors of large sections of the most marginal agrarian classes. An excellent review is Moore 1985. Because of the spatial spread of colonization schemes, land policy has added to tensions in the current social upheaval, as Sinhalese peasants populate areas traditionally considered to be Tamil turf.

9 Even the World Bank, long critical of Sri Lanka's heavy expenditures on education, health, and nutrition (about 10 percent of GNP over the previous two decades) commended the results in terms of "human development" and argued (1980c: 90) that (a) the "trade-off" between human development and growth "has not been so sharp as is sometimes suggested"; and that (b) growth rates deteriorated "for reasons generally independent of human development spending" (largely the weather and terms of trade).

10 On the Insurgency, see Obeysekara 1973; Halliday 1975; Jupp 1978: 193–5. The international participants in aiding the regime in its suppression of the revolt represent a remarkable aggregation: Great Britain, India, Pakistan, Australia, the United States, the USSR, Egypt, Yugoslavia, and (less directly) China. For a statement of the ideology and goals of the JVP, see the presentation of its leader, Rohana Wijeweera (1975).

11 Author's observations and local press reports in Sri Lanka during parts of 1973 and 1974. Colvin R. de Silva, Minister of Plantation Industries, threatened estate owners: "Grow food crops or lose your land" in a speech to the Kandyan Planters Association, reported in *Ceylon Daily News*, August 18, 1973. The prime minister, in a national broadcast on September 21, 1973, spoke of possible famine if the food war failed. She

lamented that Sri Lanka was in desperate straits because "we ate" the money previously borrowed abroad.

12 E. L. H. Lee (1976) documents deterioration of real wages in the estate sector as well as in urban areas. Gunatilleke (1978: 48–51) discusses the sources which led him to report widespread malnutrition in Sri Lanka in the mid-1970s. Nutrition data presented by Gavan and Chandrasekera (1979: table 7) indicate serious malnutrition effects, especially in the estate sector. The available nutrition data of a systematic sort relate to a period after the most severe stage of the food crisis. Paul Isenmen (1980: 244) presents data and analysis to link an increase in mortality, particularly on the estates, to the food crisis in 1974. See Marga Institute 1981; Sahn 1983. On Sri Lanka's international food situation, Agarian Research and Training Institute, 1976.

13 More than 60 percent of industrial production was by the public sector in the early 1980s (Central Bank of Ceylon 1982: 430). Setting the index of public sector industrial production for 1977 at 100, there have been swings between index 124.6 (1982) and 106.7 (1983), with the index standing at 115 for 1987 (Central Bank of Sri Lanka 1987: 55). Increases in public-sector industrial production clearly would have been greater except for disruptions of the civil war.

14 To be more precise than the preceding paragraph is possible but precarious. Data on inflation are unreliable; though the Colombo Consumer Price Index (CPI) is frequently used, it is easy to confirm with some on-the-street price comparisons that inflation is understated by the published numbers. The GDP deflator is a more accurate measure for some items, but obviously not for food produced domestically. Nevertheless, food prices by year's end, 1984, were more than triple prices in 1977. Given problematic data on inflation, real wages are of course difficult to analyze. By *official* calculations, the real minimum wage rate index for workers in agriculture improved significantly over that period (from 76.3 to 96.3), whereas the real wage index for workers in industry and commerce declined significantly (93.7 to 77.7) (Central Bank of Ceylon 1983: table 63). However, if we use David Sahn's (1986) calculations based on the Alternative Consumer Price Index, we find *declining* real wage rates in both agriculture and industry, though agriculture remained relatively better off. Sahn (1986: table 11) goes on to compute the real average daily wage rates in selected sectors, adjusted by the Alternative CPI. This series starts only in 1979, but shows declining average real wage rates in the paddy sector, coconut, tea, and construction industries (Herring 1987: table 10).

15 As measured by the Consumer Finance Surveys (Jayawardena 1974). The reality of that phenomenon has, however, been called into question, generating a serious empirical dispute (E. L. H. Lee 1976, 1977; Dahanayake 1979; Lakshman 1980). The disagreement hinges on the validity and reliability of the data in the Consumer Finance Surveys conducted by the Central Bank in 1953, 1963, 1973, and 1978–9 and 1981–2.

The numbers are problematic because of reporting biases at the upper end, particularly during the leftist United Front period (1970–7), and arguable evaluations of income in kind (higher rice prices artificially raise the "income" of subsistence farmers).

16 First, the new strategy was launched in an unusually auspicious economic juncture; the terms of trade, which had experienced a trend decline since 1950, showed a 35 percent improvement in 1976, and 31 percent in 1977; tea prices experienced an unprecedented rise of 80 percent, contributing to an unprecedented current account surplus of Rs1,259 million. Real gross national product grew at a rate of 8.2 percent in 1978, a very high rate by historical standards, then slowed to 6.2 percent in 1979, 5.5 percent in 1980, 3.9 in 1981, 5.0 percent in 1982, and 4.0 percent in 1983, 5.1 percent in 1984, 5.3 percent in 1985, 4.5 percent in 1986 and 1.5 percent in 1987. The rate of growth in real national *income* has fluctuated widely, however, because of subsequent deterioration in the terms of trade, and was −0.4 percent in 1985.

17 Public investment expanded at the expense of larger budget deficits and consequently higher public indebtedness (Sri Lanka 1984). This changing investment profile, and absolute level of investment, was sustainable only through increased levels of foreign financing, which reached almost four times the level of the 1970–7 period as a percentage of GDP. The foreign contribution to financing of the net cash budget deficit in 1976 was 32.5 percent; in 1980, 70.4 percent (Central Bank of Ceylon 1979b: table 10.1). The Public Investment Programme of the Ministry of Finance and Planning, 1980–4, projected a strategy in which net external inflows would be greater than domestic sources, constituting 54 percent of total public investment over the 5-year period (Sri Lanka 1980c).

18 Data from Economist Intelligence Unit 1992: 3, 22. The *Economist* continued to comment on the especially generous aid and conditions received by Sri Lanka in comparison to other nations.

19 Total expenditures remained close to pre-liberalization levels as a percentage of GDP, though slightly exceeding that level in 1985 (42 percent of GDP). Though subsequent budget deficits were large (10 percent of GDP in 1984, 19 percent in 1985), it would be wrong to attribute deficits primarily to military spending. The deficit reached 26 percent of GDP before the real beginnings of internal war in 1983. Rather, budget deficits are a reflection of ambitious development projects premised on increased availability of foreign funds on the expenditure side and severe responses of revenues to falling export prices on the income side.

20 This crude summary of sentiments is based on my own discussions with people in Sri Lanka and reading of newspaper accounts during the period under discussion. My discussion is also stimulated by a draft paper by Mick Moore, that cannot be cited, which disagrees with the text.

9

The Politics of Economic Reform in Central and Eastern Europe

1 INTRODUCTION

During the 1970s and 1980s, the Soviet Union and Eastern Europe as a whole, and virtually every individual state in the region, experienced a deepening economic crisis. Reforms were introduced in many states during this period, designed primarily to strengthen the economy and to revitalize state socialism as a viable alternative to capitalism. The particular strategies adopted, however, tended to deepen the crisis (and the problem of foreign debt in particular), while the combination of economic reform and continued political repression increasingly threatened the moral economy of state socialism, generating dissidence, social unrest, popular protest, and political opposition. This eventually culminated in a fundamental political crisis, giving rise to "the revolution" of 1989 in Eastern Europe and the subsequent disintegration of the Soviet Union.

Despite its economic, political, and ideological distinctiveness, the formal political autonomy of "the socialist bloc" in Europe (the Second World), with its commitment to state-controlled national socialist development, proved inadequate (as it did in the Third

World) to prevent ever closer integration into the international capitalist economy; and, as in the case of the Third World, this increasing integration, at a time of deepening global recession, both highlighted and exacerbated growing internal contradictions. In the Soviet Union, as in Eastern Europe, attempts to reform the economy while at the same time maintaining the central features of state socialism (i.e. *perestroika*) eventually proved impossible. By the end of the 1980s, profound changes, both political and economic, were taking place which brought about the collapse of state socialism and the redefinition of central and eastern Europe as part – even if a distinctive part – of "the developing world."

The crisis of state socialism in Central and Eastern Europe and the identification of the region as part of "the developing world" has been accompanied since the early 1980s (and even more dramatically since 1989) by increasing intervention on the part of the international financial institutions (e.g. the IMF and World Bank) and the major capitalist states in the "development" of the economies of Central and Eastern Europe. Their intervention is explicitly directed towards the capitalist development of Central and Eastern Europe through the provision of financial and technical assistance and by the promotion of further economic reforms, designed essentially to reduce the role of the state in the economy (and to restructure the basis for the provision of social welfare – Fitzgerald 1991), and to encourage the emergence of "the free market."

In less than a year after the collapse of state socialism in Eastern Europe, the substantial liberalization of the economies of many of these states was under way. Almost immediately, however, popular dissatisfaction began to surface in the form of strikes and demonstrations against the adverse effects of the austerity measures that constituted a crucial element of the new economic reforms. In Central and Eastern Europe, as elsewhere in "the developing world," economic liberalization has been accompanied by widespread popular protest.

While this wave of austerity protests has to be understood in terms of the region's distinctive political and economic history, and "the moral economy" of state socialism (which more than any other political system has emphasized the crucial role of the state in ensuring the welfare of its citizens), it is also, we would argue, an integral part of the global response to global adjustment. Furthermore, even before the dramatic events of 1989, Eastern Europe experienced deepening economic and social contradictions which strikingly resemble those of many other "semi-industrialized" developing countries (see Fitzgerald 1991). Consequently, we feel able to analyze popular responses to economic reform in Central and

Eastern Europe in broadly the same terms as we analyze them else-where in the developing world.

In this chapter, we focus on the period of economic liberaliza-tion (1989–92) and the forms of protest which have accompanied the process. It is important to recognize, however, that popular protest against the effects of economic reform began in the 1970s. In Poland they gave rise to a social movement which became a major political force – Solidarity.

2 POPULAR PROTEST AND THE RISE OF SOLIDARITY

The first major outbreaks of popular unrest in response to govern-ment economic reforms were those which occurred in Poland dur-ing the 1970s. In December 1970, the government of Wladyslaw Gomulka attempted to remedy Poland's worsening economic situation by raising prices and cutting wages. Street demonstrations and strikes broke out all along the Baltic coast in response. In Gdansk, workers occupied the Lenin shipyards and refused to leave; troops were brought in, killing 45 and injuring nearly 1,200. As the protests started to spread, Gomulka resigned.

The new government of Edward Gierek – who led the Polish United Workers" Party (PZPR) from 1971 to 1980 – launched a "great leap forward" (under the Five Year Plan for 1971–5), de-signed to ensure economic growth while maintaining and developing workers' rights and welfare. An essential part of the new economic strategy was to "open up" Poland to the world economy, taking substantial loans and importing technology with a view to boosting domestic production and increasing exports. Economic growth in-creased dramatically (by 1975, GNP was 50 percent greater than in 1970) as did wages, which rose by 40 percent. But while wages grew, so too did consumer demand, particularly for meat (annual per capita meat consumption rose from 53 kilos in 1970 to 70.3 kilos in 1975). With food prices strictly controlled, the government was obliged to increase subsidies (for meat they rose from 12.3 billion zloties in 1971 to 91.4 billion in 1979), without being able to guarantee increased supply. The economic pressures created by this level of subsidy were enormous.

In June 1976, the Polish government tried to raise food prices by 60 percent. Widespread strikes and demonstrations followed, with factory occupations providing the strategic core of the protest move-ment. The government, under the pressure of concerted protests and threats of a general strike, rescinded the unpopular price increases but proceeded to victimize the most active militants. However, a group of prominent intellectuals set up a Workers' Defence Committee (KOR), ostensibly as a semi-charitable organization providing financial and legal aid for victims of persecution as well as monitoring and exposing the worst cases of corruption and police brutality (Deutscher 1981: 62). The government was forced to back down, suffering a massive loss of authority and encouraging the dissidents to combine forces, which added a political dimension to the deepening economic crisis. The economy deteriorated rapidly after 1976 and the government became increasingly dependent on western creditors; between 1971 and 1980 the foreign debt grew from $1.2 billion to $24.7 billion. Central planning was increasingly compromised, living standards stopped rising and then fell back, spending on social services was reduced, social inequality grew, and the black market blossomed. Consequently, "the working class became increasingly angry, not only at the frustration of its quantitative demands, but especially at what it saw as the violation of its socialist social rights" (Macdonald 1983: 12).

During the last three years of the decade, economic and political tensions increased as the government struggled to maintain its commitment to growth and welfare in the face of a deepening economic crisis. In order to forestall social and political unrest, the government repeatedly granted wage increases and raised subsidies on foodstuffs, financing these with loans from the West. It attempted, in particular, to satisfy the industrial workers in the large factories with relatively high wages, cheap and well-stocked canteens, and other benefits: these plants were hailed as "the citadels of Polish socialism." Despite this, however, anger mounted at increasing inflation (it reached 103 percent by 1981), generally declining living standards and welfare provision, and the perceived betrayal by the state of the principles of socialist justice. The growth of corruption within the ranks of the party and state officialdom contributed to popular unrest. Between 1977 and 1979 the number of strikes reached around a thousand, with the majority settled in the workers' favor.

Attempts by the government during 1979 and 1980 to put up food prices produced widespread anger and outrage. The growing social unrest came to a head with the strike movement of August 1980, which started in the Gdansk shipyards – under the leadership of Lech Walesa, who had been fired from the shipyards in 1976 for his role in the strikes – and spread rapidly to become a national movement affecting all the major industrial centers and no less than 4,000 enterprises. The strikes began as an immediate response by workers to price rises; rapidly, however, they became more carefully orchestrated and gave rise to a set of strategic demands: striking workers should be compensated; there should be a flat-rate increase for all employees (aiding the low paid); the "commercial" and hard-currency shops should be closed; the privileges of the police and party cadres should be abolished; family subsidies should be equalized; there should be rationing rather than free-floating prices; and there should be a massive shift in public spending towards social welfare.

As one observer remarked,

> this social programme was classic in the socialist egalitarian assumptions underlying it. So too were the radical democratic freedoms called for in their "twenty-one demands": freedom of speech, the press and publication; availability of the mass media to representatives of all faiths; the release of all political prisoners; and measures to enable all sectors and social classes to take part in discussion of the reform programme. (*Macdonald 1983: 16*)

This program was very different from that espoused during the late 1970s by the majority of the Polish intelligentsia, who had developed a broad consensus that market reforms were needed, despite their economic and social effects – including unemployment and price increases.

At the outset the strike movement was essentially a workers' protest against government policy. Gdansk was the only industrial center where previously active opposition groups played a significant role in organizing the August strikes. They played no role, for example, in Szczecin or Silesia; and the two cities where opposition groups were by far the strongest – Warsaw and Cracow – were among the least affected by the August strikes. The role of the church was also limited initially. In Gdansk, Bishop Kaczmarek's first response to the appeal by the strike committees for a mass to be said in the Lenin shipyard was to refuse until they had gained permission from the provincial party secretary. The Bishop of Szczecin was equally conservative and in his only public speech during the crisis (broadcast on TV) urged the strikers to return to work.

But if the August strike movement was not orchestrated by opposition groups or the church, neither was it simply a "spontaneous" outburst; members of the PZPR were heavily involved from the outset. In Gdansk itself, about one-third of the Inter-Factory Strike Committee (MKS) delegates were PZPR members, while "a cursory glance at the forces initiating the big leaps in the strike movement beyond Gdansk shows a very strong presence of PZPR members – workers, technicians and foremen – amongst the leadership of the movement and, in many cases, amongst its initiators" (Macdonald 1983: 15). The experience of the workers' protests of 1970–1 and the earlier demands for independent trade unions, the right to strike, and freedom of information – which had achieved particular strength in Gdansk and in Szczecin – were undoubtedly significant. In 1980, the Gdansk workers used the interfactory strike committee as an organizational structure – something that had proved successful on the Baltic in 1971. Also, the Workers' Defense Committee (KOR) established in 1976 was still active and in close contact with factory activists, while the semi-clandestine newspaper *Robotnik* ('The Worker'), edited by a group loosely connected with KOR, played an important role in providing liaison between various local and regional strike committees and helping coordinate strike action.

The strike movement of 1980, although initiated as an immediate response by workers to massive price rises, drew on the previous experience of workers' protests and rapidly became an effective organization. It also began to involve intellectual activists from an early stage and soon transformed itself from a workers' protest to a politically oriented trade-union federation of strategic significance. Of the "twenty-one demands" presented by the workers in Gdansk in August 1980, the most momentous was that calling for the right to form autonomous trade unions, independent of state and party. Within three weeks the new federation – Solidarity – was allowed to deposit its statutes at the Warsaw District Court with a demand for formal registration. The Warsaw Court turned down the application, but two days before a general strike, threatened in support of Solidarity's recognition, the Supreme Court overturned this verdict and accepted Solidarity's registration. Within a year, Solidarity had around 7 million members, nearly a fifth of the Polish population, and had become a broad-based political movement.

In December 1981, however, with the support of the Kremlin, the Polish army took power and General Jaruzelski became Communist Party first secretary and prime minister. Thousands of Solidarity activists were arrested, including Walesa; strikes were put down by force, and Solidarity went underground. The struggle, however, continued and, despite the repression, Solidarity was eventually to acquire even more widespread support and, at the end of the decade, to form the government.

3   GROWING PRESSURE FOR REFORM: 1980–1989

In Poland, the struggle of the state against Solidarity during the 1980s took place against a backdrop of increasing economic difficulty. With a foreign debt of $21 billion in 1981 (whose servicing alone threatened to consume the total value of its annual exports), the Polish economy was on the edge of bankruptcy. Meanwhile, the very success of the new trade-union movement exacerbated the economic crisis, with the overall wage bill increasing by 20 percent in the aftermath of the strikes of summer 1980 and the volume of production declining with the introduction of a shorter working week in heavy industry and mining. Low productivity in agriculture remained a crippling handicap for the economy as a whole, with gross inefficiency in the state sector and the system of fixed food prices discouraging small-holders from selling their produce or expanding production. The government was only able to raise agricultural prices without incurring the wrath of the newly organized urban workers by providing costly state subsidies, which in turn increased the foreign debt. Structural change was increasingly required.

Time and time again over the next few years, massive price rises of sometimes several hundred percent were proposed; but since the population reacted violently, often with strikes, to these measures, they were generally only implemented in a directly or indirectly reduced form. Although by the end of 1986 the government had succeeded in reducing the proportion of the national budget spent on subsidies to 30 percent (from 50.5 percent in 1982) largely by cutting grants given to enterprises, in that year alone price subsidies for essential consumer goods increased by 46 percent. In addition, deficiency payments were made to groups earning less than 13,000 zloty in order to compensate them for the price increases. In April 1987, an attempt to raise the price of foodstuffs by 14 percent and coal by 100 percent was met with massive protest; even the new state-organized trade union (the OPZZ) threatened strike action. Prices eventually rose by 50 percent for coal, 25 percent for petrol and gas, 23 percent for electricity and just under 10 percent for food; at the same time, additional deficiency payments and wage increases were announced (Wachs 1991: 201).

In 1987, the Jaruzelski government released the last of the Solidarity activists from jail in a bid to gain greater support for government policies. New strikes broke out, however, under the familiar banners of Solidarity (still technically illegal) and in February 1988 a series of "roundtable talks" was initiated which brought Solidarity into discussions with the government. In 1989, Solidarity was made legal and elections held.

Poland was not alone, however, in embarking on a process of controlled economic reform which was to generate significant and unintended political changes; in the Soviet Union, in particular, the pressures for change were growing. The dramatic transformation of central and eastern Europe from 1989 onwards was provoked not only by the internal contradictions within each of the countries concerned but also by the effects of changes in Soviet policy towards its "allies" in the region as a result of its own program of *perestroika*. It is therefore appropriate to consider first the dynamics of change within the Soviet Union before turning to the developing contradictions in Eastern Europe which eventually gave rise to the "revolution" of 1989.

In the Soviet Union during the 1970s (as in Poland), the maintenance of fixed prices for food, despite low productivity in agriculture and a steady increase in effective demand, led to the state paying millions of roubles in subsidies while the population had to stand in queues complaining about the shortage of produce. In 1973, Roy Medvedev argued that democratization was the precondition for an acceleration of the economic, political, social, and cultural development of the Soviet Union. But he also spoke, pessimistically, of the "political passivity of our population below," suggesting that

> people have learnt to become so silent, and have acquired such a sense of guilt, that no individual dissenters – not even small groups of dissenters – can give rise to a mass movement capable of bringing about any real political change. The masses could move only as a result of serious political or economic crises. Yet the prospect of such crises seems neither probable nor desirable. (*Medvedev 1973: 33–4*)

Throughout the 1970s, however, the pressures for reform were growing as the contradictions within the Soviet political economy became more acute; without recognizing it at the time, the Soviet Union was sliding towards an economic and political crisis, which was to provoke both mass protest and profound transformation.

With the death of Brezhnev in 1982, these pressures rapidly increased. The selection of Andropov as party general secretary was testimony to the political crisis of Brezhnevism. In his very first declarations the new leader gave notice of his intention to introduce major changes not only in the economic but also in the political sphere. But resistance to any proposed reforms remained strong and not a single one of the reformist projects considered at the highest level became an official document. The struggle continued after Andropov's death in 1984.

From the outset, there were those who foresaw the dangers for ordinary working people of any economic reform which relied solely on promoting market forces and called for protection against the possibility of unacceptable social costs. For some – and these were not just "old guard" communists – economic reform could be seen as progressive only if it increased democratic control over the economy. In the early 1970s, Roy Medvedev had argued that

> our country's development cannot be accelerated unless a rational decentralization is effected, unless the right to decide many questions is transferred to authorities at a much lower level, unless the rights and responsibilities of all local organs are enlarged, unless self-management is extended, unless public opinion is enabled to participate in the taking of decisions, unless there is free discussion of all questions of social and political life – in short, unless society is made democratic. (*Medvedev 1974: 73*)

He articulated the views of those who emphasized the importance of "the moral economy" of socialism and the political prerequisites for socialist economic reform, as against those who saw economic reform essentially as a means of improving efficiency to restore economic growth.

Kagarlitsky has argued that "the characteristic features of the 1979–82 period were, on the one hand, a strengthening of reformist tendencies within the establishment and, on the other, the emergence of a new socialist opposition" (Kagarlitsky 1988: 69). The selection of Mikhail Gorbachev as general secretary in spring 1985 tilted the balance of power towards the reformers, and from summer 1986, *perestroika* (restructuring) became a central preoccupation in the Soviet Union. Initially, it was linked to the idea of *uskoreniye* (acceleration) of socio-economic development; and to *glasnost* (political openness). However, as the World Bank has observed,

> *uskoreniye* proved elusive. Real output stagnated, and the fiscal deficit rose from 2.5 percent of GDP to 8.5 percent. The program's failure spurred more serious efforts to reform the economy in 1987 and 1988. The material allocation system was scrapped. Prices were allowed to move in a freely negotiated range. The soft budget constraint was hardened. Cooperative enterprises were encouraged, and private family enterprises were legalized. Foreign trade was decentralized and, and a currency retention scheme was introduced along with a system of

differentiated exchange rates and limited foreign currency auctions. (*World Bank 1991b: 20*)

But the reforms were piecemeal and while the dismantling of the traditional planning system began, the official price system and state distribution agency were left largely intact.

While socialists and democratic reformists argued for economic transformation (emphasizing the need to restructure the entire system of production, recommending self-management of production and democratization of planning), the technocrats and emerging "free-marketeers" had a more limited program. After January 1987, when several departments moved to self-financing, prices began to rise ominously across a wide range of goods and services. Critics of this strategy argued that "under the guise of 'reform', workers are being forced to pay for the economic miscalculations of the bureaucracy, bad management, structural imbalances and the pre-crisis situation of the economy" (Kagarlitsky 1988: 81). In such an approach to *perestroika*, *glasnost* certainly played little part, and evidence from surveys at the time suggested that more than 70 percent of the population were opposed to such a strategy and such "reforms." Indeed, workers began during the latter part of 1987 to demand *glasnost* at the workplace: changes in the organization of labor, dismissal of incompetent and corrupt leaders, a shortening of working time, and an end to overtime. The press reported strikes and spontaneous protest meetings in many enterprises towards the end of 1987, calling for more extensive reforms.

In August 1987, the newly formed Federation of Socialist Social Clubs (FSOK) viewed the extension of market factors in managing the economy as "natural and inevitable," but stressed "the dangers of triumphant technocracy and the substitution of market fetishism for plan fetishism." The clubs agreed that the reform should be carried out without a drop in workers' living standards and should maintain social provision for cheap accomodation, free medical care, full employment, and other benefits. In other words, the "moral economy" of socialism should be respected even while a greater role for the market must be accepted.

Many intellectuals as well as workers were concerned to combine economic reform with a commitment to effective welfare provision. In January 1988, for example, the influential Soviet economist, V. Seliunin, argued that although structural shifts were required in the economy, *perestroika* would in its turn only be possible if it maintained the living standards of the masses and developed the industrial, political, and local democracy which gave workers the opportunity for real participation in decision-making – "it is necessary to turn from work for its own sake to people and their needs" (cited in Kagarlitsky 1988: 82). Others stressed the need to create an alternative to the bureaucratic "reform from above" – a "radical, reformist project," which would include "political democratization, the development of industrial and local self-management, the maintenance of social provision, a redistributive, anti-bureaucratic policy under democratic control from below, defence of the interests of the consumer, and a gradual reorientation of the economy, taking into account ecological and humanitarian factors, towards the satisfaction of human need" (Kagarlitsky 1988: 82–3). But the reforms undertaken by the Soviet government took a somewhat different path from that envisaged in this model of "socialist transformation." And even by 1989, when the transformation of the political order across central and eastern Europe brought to power new governments ready to embark on major economic-reform programs, the extent to which economic and political reform had been implemented in the Soviet Union remained strictly limited.

In Eastern Europe, as the economic crisis deepened towards the end of the 1970s, there was a growing consensus over the need for reform. In Hungary, while certain elements of economic reform had been introduced as early as 1968, under the so-called New Economic Model (one of the consequences of which, incidentally, was an increase in retail prices to a level which, as Nove remarks "upset many citizens, though without leading to riots, as was the case in Poland" – Nove 1983: 130), economic restructuring really began in the early 1980s. Hungary joined the IMF and the World Bank in June 1982, and a string of reforms followed which began to generate more characteristics of a market economy, even if the government failed to develop a coherent approach to economic reform (Swain 1989: 13–4). It was only in the summer of 1988, however, following a major reconstitution of the leadership of the ruling Hungarian Socialist Workers' Party, that a full commitment to economic reform was finally made. During 1988 and 1989, the economy and the nature of reforms required became the central focus of political debate; there was general agreement that a greater role for the market was essential.

In Yugoslavia at the beginning of the 1980s, the foreign-trade deficit was over $7 billion and that of the balance of payments, $3.7 billion. In 1981 its external debt passed the $20 billion mark. A commission was established in 1982 to examine the roots of the problem; by the summer of 1983, the commission had compiled 17 reports with conclusions which were to form the basis of the Long-Term Program for Economic Stabilization, to be put into operation from early 1984. By 1985 the leadership itself acknowledged that the country was facing an economic crisis, with a 5.5 percent decline in social product since 1979, a foreign debt of over $20 billion and rampant inflation (which reached 100 percent by 1985).

The Yugoslav government had entered into negotiations with the IMF for new loans and the restructuring of its existing debt every year since the beginning of the debt crisis in 1981. Although relatively successful in reducing the foreign-trade deficit, making possible a modest current-account surplus and holding the foreign debt at around $20 billion, the austerity and stabilization program failed to reduce inflation: retail prices and the cost of living soared during the first half of the decade. At the same time, productivity stagnated (showing a decline of 0.6 percent a year between 1981 and 1985, as compared with a 6 percent growth rate between 1973 and 1979). During 1985, Yugoslavia's creditors demanded that it continue to work with the IMF, but "on the basis of increased supervision of its economic performance" (Conert 1991: 224); the government was to account to the IMF quarterly, and the IMF was to undertake "consultations" twice yearly.

The party leadership of Slovenia, Croatia, and Serbia, although deeply divided on political issues, shared a commitment to the radical liberalization of the economy as a solution to the crisis. But the federal government, while committed to economic reforms, failed in its attempt to establish a commission for social welfare. The crisis affected ordinary working people with particular severity as unemployment increased (by March 1986 the number registered as seeking employment was around 1.1 million) and personal consumption slumped (down by 7.7 percent between 1979 and 1985). Increases in earnings were unable to keep pace with the galloping depreciation of the currency: from 1981–4 real income fell by an average of 6.2 percent a year; in 1985 it rose, but only by 2.8 percent. As one commentator has observed,

> the social costs of Yugoslavia's debt crisis and the stabilisation policies designed to overcome it are unmistakeable, though the extent to which their true scale and manifestations are revealed in statistical data is limited. There is much to suggest that real income actually fell by considerably more than is officially reported. When assessing the consequences, it is also necessary to remember that before the outbreak of the crisis real average income levels were barely above subsistence level ... Poorest of all are those who are forced to live

without, or on below-average incomes in economically backward regions. (*Conert 1991: 227*)

For, in addition to the wage differentials that exist within the republics there are also significant differences in wage levels as between republics: wages in Slovenia, for example, were in 1991 double those for Macedonia.

It has been suggested that "considering the extent to which living conditions have deteriorated ... and the extent to which the little developed and retrogressive state of the system of social benefits has contributed to that deterioration, social protest has been surprisingly limited" (Conert 1991: 227). On the other hand, the number of strikes recorded rose from 384 in 1984 to 699 in 1985 and 847 in 1986, and "the number of strikes taking place increased to such an extent in March 198/ as a result of the failure to freeze prices as well as wages that in Croatia one might even talk in terms of a wave of strikes" (Conert 1991: 227–8). In fact, the trade unions, deeply concerned about the social implications, particularly for the low-income workers and the underdeveloped south of the country, of the state of the economy (inflation passed 250 percent by the end of 1988), brought down the government at the end of 1988.

In Czechoslovakia, and in the Balkans, despite an appearance of immobility, the forces for change were growing. Even in Albania, following the death of Enver Hoxha in April 1985, a gradual process of "opening up" was initiated by Ramiz Alia, who had become head of state in 1982. Ever since his appointment, Alia had called for modernization and greater foreign contacts. But liberalization was slow until 1989, when the "revolution" in Eastern Europe was to sweep across the region to engulf even this most isolated and idiosyncratic of southern socialist states.

The German Democratic Republic remained, throughout the 1980s, one of the strongest economies in central and eastern Europe, and internal pressures for economic reform appeared limited. In 1989 per capita GNP in the GDR was $9,700 (compared with $7,900 in Czechoslovakia, $6,100 in Hungary and under $6,000 for all the others – Roskin 1991: 110). Yet it too, was deeply in debt, and increasingly dependent on the Federal Republic of Germany; by the end of 1988 the GDR's foreign debt amounted to $20.4 billion (or $1,250 per person). And when the "revolution" of 1989 swept through central and eastern Europe, the GDR experienced one of the most dramatic upheavals of all. Within a year it was part of a unified Germany.

4   THE "REVOLUTION" IN EASTERN EUROPE

The limited economic reforms introduced by the regimes in power during the 1970s and 1980s proved generally unpopular. They were seen by the "old-style communists" or "conservatives" as too rapid and threatening to the status quo, by the "free-marketeers" or "radicals" as insufficiently rapid and far-reaching, and by the democratic socialists as authoritarian "reforms from above" threatening the essentials of "the moral economy" of socialism. They were also largely ineffective in resolving the growing economic crisis and could even be said to have contributed to it.

The "revolution" of 1989, which transformed Eastern Europe, was the result of an upsurge of deep and growing dissatisfaction with the combination of economic stagnation, political repression, and ideological bankruptcy which was widely felt to have come to characterize state socialism during the preceding decades. The mass movements which, in different ways in different states, gave rise to the "revolution" were undoubtedly popular movements of protest; their concerns were explicitly political and their objective was to challenge and displace the existing governments and their state apparatus. Their shared perception was that of the failure of what one dissident called "actually existing socialism" (Bahro 1981) – political failure, ideological or moral failure, and economic failure – exemplified respectively by repression, corruption, and stagnation. The moral economy of the Eastern European crowd was a crucial inspiration for the new emerging dissident forces in civil society.

The catalyst, however, for the political transformation of Eastern Europe was the shift in Soviet policy towards the region which began in 1988. In March, during his visit to Yugoslavia, President Gorbachev foreswore "any interference in the internal affairs of other states under any pretext whatsoever," arguing that all nations had the right to "their own roads of social development." Later in the year, he told the United Nations General Assembly that freedom of choice for all nations to decide their own path was "a universal principle which allows no exceptions" (Roskin 1991: 130). In 1989, the final communiqué of the annual meeting of the Warsaw Pact stated: "there are no universal models of socialism." The growing pressures for reform in Eastern Europe were thereby encouraged and those seeking reform emboldened.

But if the Soviet leadership was evidently prepared to accept and even encourage reforms in Eastern Europe, it was significantly more cautious about change at home. There also, however, the contradictions of limited reform from above were growing. In the summer of 1989, the coal miners went on strike and effectively increased the momentum for change in the Soviet Union itself.

The strike began in a single mine in the Kuzbass city of Mezhdurechensk in western Siberia; within a week, 158 Kuzbass mines had closed and nearly 200,000 miners were on strike. The minister of the coal industry flew to the Kuzbass to begin negotiations, but by the time a tentative agreement had been reached, the strike had spread throughout the region. From the Kuzbass, action spread to Karaganda, Pechora, the Lvov region, Rostov, and the Donbass in the eastern Ukraine. There was a link between the Siberian strike and action in the Donbass – a delegation of Siberian miners had visited the mines of the region and urged them to join the strike. Beginning in Makeevka, the strike spread to Pavlograd and from there to Donetsk. Within 2 days all 21 coal mines in the city were on strike.

The July strike could not have come as a total surprise to the Soviet authorities. It had been preceded in March by two brief strikes in Donetsk when dissatisfaction had been expressed in a demand that the minister of the coal industry should resign. Gorbachev himself had been informed of the ferment and its background while visiting Donetsk in June. There were two brief strikes in the Pavlograd coal mines of western Donbass in the spring of 1989; and the Kuzbass strike of July was also preceded by a brief, unorganized strike in the spring. Although the strike movement was spontaneous and at the outset had no organizing body, the miners soon developed a complex structure of strike committees (see Friedgut and Siegelbaum 1990: 10–13). The strike committee membership was generally youngish (averaging about 35 years) and predominantly male, although women were also involved; one-quarter were Party members.

Views are divided as to the specific causes of the strikes. Some emphasize the fear of the miners regarding the adverse effects of economic reform on their economic and social welfare (Seppo 1989); others, rather the anxiety that *perestroika* was passing them by (Friedgut and Siegelbaum 1990: 13–18). Undoubtedly, the underlying determinants included poor working and living conditions fort despite the fact that the average coal miner earns about twice the average industrial worker, life is extremely hard and the physical environment appalling. In a survey carried out for the Soviet Sociological Association among Donetsk miners, specific grievances included lack of consumer goods (mentioned by 86 percent of respondents); low pay (79 percent), inadequate vacations (62 percent), poor pension provision (50 percent), high prices (41 percent), and poor housing (41 percent). For some, another major factor was resentment at corrupt and inadequate management (frictions with management were mentioned by 38 percent of respondents to the survey): "a total distrust of the local administrative and political stratum ... lay at the root of the strike, and influenced both the way the negotiations were conducted and the specific form of settlement" (Friedgut and Siegelbaum 1990: 17–18).

The effect of the miners' strike was considerable. Throughout late 1989 and into 1990, the strike committees remained a powerful force, able to exert influence not only locally but also nationally. In April 1990, for example, "Gorbachev's Presidential Council, fearful of igniting a new wave of strikes, postponed implementation of Polish-style shock therapy for the Soviet economy" (Friedgut and Siegelbaum 1990: 32).

But throughout the Soviet Union, during 1989, the pressures for more radical political change were growing. They were contained for a while by the Soviet leadership, but eventually proved irresistible: in November 1989, for example, President Gorbachev refused to consider parliamentary debate over the deletion from the Soviet Constitution of Article 6, giving the Communist Party a monopoly of power; but early in 1990 the Article was repealed to end more than 70 years of exclusive Communist Party domination of Soviet politics. In less than two years" time, the Soviet Union was to disintegrate and the Communist Party itself be effectively dissolved.

In Poland, where Solidarity had been legalized, the government proposed a power-sharing arrangement. But when elections took place in July 1989, Solidarity gained substantial support from some of the smaller parties and occupied the opposition benches as a major independent force. And in August, when President Jaruzelski, nominated a Solidarity activist, Tadeusz Mazowiecki, as prime minister, he was confirmed by the Sejm (the Communist Party dominated legislature) by an overwhelming majority to take command of Poland's first non-Communist government since 1947.

Poland was first, but Hungary was not far behind. In 1988, the elderly Janos Kadar was replaced as party chief by Karoly Grosz. Kadar was blamed for Hungary's deteriorating economic situation, but Grosz managed little better. By the end of 1988, Hungary had the highest per capita foreign debt of all the Eastern European economies ($1,800). The pressures for major political reform increased. In February 1989, amidst growing public discontent with the Grosz government, Hungary's parliament legalized non-Communist political parties. Groups that had previously existed as informal associations or "forums" now reconstituted themselves as parties. At the same time, the more liberal Communist Party members of the government began to call for meetings with opposition groups and for further economic liberalization.

In March, 75,000 marched in Budapest to demand free elections and the withdrawal of Soviet forces from Hungary; the authorities did not stop them, and Gorbachev pledged not to interfere in Eastern Europe. In May, the Communist government decided to stop enforcing an agreement to prevent Eastern European visitors to Hungary from fleeing to the West across Hungary's borders, and thousands of East German "tourists" fled into Austria, encouraging further pressures for change within the German Democratic Republic. In October 1989, the ruling Hungarian Socialist Workers' party renounced its leading role to become the Socialist party; and free elections were called for early 1990.

By September 1989, over 13,000 East German "refugees" had crossed the Hungarian–Austrian border; Czechoslovakia also opened its borders to enable those wishing to do so to leave the GDR and more than 17,000 persons fled through Czechoslovakia to the FRG. In September, massive demonstrations started in the GDR, centered in Leipzig. In October, President Gorbachev visited the GDR to urge reform. During October and November, major demonstrations took place in the cities of the GDR calling for political reform and the resignation of Erich Honecker. The city of Leipzig experienced the first pro-democracy demonstration after borders were opened with the West; between 200,000 and 300,000 people thronged its squares and thoroughfares. In spite of the reforms announced by Honecker's replacement, Egon Krenz, and the promises of more to come, demonstrators called for free elections and an end to the Communist Party's monopoly of power. In November, the Berlin Wall was dismantled; and in December, Chancellor Kohl of West Germany addressed the Hungarian parliament to give thanks for "the unforgettable days" from May to November that led from the Hungarian border opening to the removal of the Berlin Wall and the beginning of German reunification.

In Czechoslovakia, a rally of 3,000 held in August 1989 in favor of political reforms was broken up by the police; a larger demonstration in October, involving some 10,000 people, received the same response. Despite advice from President Gorbachev to undertake reforms in order to prevent social unrest, the Prague regime under Milos Jakes continued to repress any such demonstrations of protest; a student rally was dispersed brutally in early November, and the numbers of supporters of such opposition groups as Civic

Forum and (in Slovakia) Public Against Violence mushroomed. On November 19, 1989, some 20,000 protestors marched in Prague, and the next day an estimated 250,000 gathered to demand the resignation of the government. Jakes quit and was replaced by a relative liberal, Karel Urbanek. Alexander Dubček, hero of the 1968 "Prague Spring," returned to Prague to the cheers of a crowd of 300,000; a day later, half a million people rallied in Prague and workers staged a two-hour general strike that brought Czechoslovakia to a standstill. At the end of November, parliament voted to end the political monopoly of the Communist party; and in December, a coalition government of 16 Communists and 5 non-Communists was formed. This proved unacceptable to the Czechoslovakian people, who staged mass rallies in protest; by the end of the year, Dubček was elected speaker of parliament and the playwrite Vaclav Havel president of Czechoslovakia. State socialism in Czechoslovakia had collapsed, in what Havel called "the velvet revolution."

Elsewhere also, the pressures for change could not be contained. But while in the "northern" countries of Eastern Europe (Poland, Hungary, the GDR, and Czechoslovakia) the Communists were to lose power almost entirely by the end of 1989, further south in the Balkans, despite widespread social unrest and popular protest, they managed to retain a degree of control for the time being.

In Bulgaria, President Gorbachev's advice was taken seriously by the political leadership; under Todor Zhivkov, the Bulgarian Communist Party had maintained a strict control over the economy and political life for 35 years; but in November 1989, the day after the Berlin Wall was opened, Zhivkov was replaced as Party chief by the relatively liberal reformist Petar Mladenov. Mladenov nominated a reformist cabinet, permitted political opposition, changed the Communist Party's name to the Socialist Party, and led it to a narrow victory in elections which were held in 1990. Popular unrest, which had begun to grow during 1989, was contained and sufficient support retained for the reconstituted Communist Party to stay in power.

The same dexterity was not shown by the Romanian regime, although there too the Communists were to retain power. Widespread social unrest and overt opposition to the government of Nicolae Ceauşescu began when demonstrations in Timisoara (initially organized to protest the repression of Hungarians in Romania) were brutally crushed by the security police, the Securitate, who opened fire, killing hundreds. Protests spread and social unrest became pervasive. Towards the end of December, after Ceauşescu had been shouted down by protestors at his own rally, the regular army joined in the struggle against the government and its supporters in the security apparatus. Fighting continued for some days and hundreds were killed; but the former dictator and his wife were captured, given a quick military trial and executed by firing squad on Christmas Day. Relatively liberal Communists, some of whom had been under house arrest for criticizing Ceauşescu, then formed a Council of National Salvation and pledged democracy; the council named Ion Iliescu president. Critics of the "new" regime demanded the resignation of all former Communists from the government, but Iliescu held firm and was confirmed in power at the elections held in spring 1990.

The overthrow of Ceauşescu left Albania as the only state-socialist regime in Europe not to experience massive popular unrest and political upheaval. That was to change in 1990.

5 THE LAUNCHING OF LIBERALIZATION

The economic problems facing the new governments of central and eastern Europe were enormous. In 1989, Poland's debt was around $40.4 billion (up over $10 billion on 1985 and equivalent to 470 percent of exports); that of the GDR about $21 billion (compared with $14–15 billion in the mid-1980s); while Hungary owed just over $20 billion (up $7 on 1985). Bulgaria and Czechoslovakia had smaller, but also rapidly increasing debt burdens – rising from around $4 billion in 1985 to $10 billion, and from $5 billion to $8 billion, respectively. Total debt in convertible currency for Eastern Europe as a whole was $116.8 billion at the end of the decade, with debts to banks equaling $56.1 billion (48 percent of the total). Furthermore, output growth had fallen from around 4 percent a year in 1986 to 0.2 percent in 1989; and while the GDR and Czechoslovakia managed growth of 2 percent in 1989, Bulgaria declined by 0.4 percent, and Poland by 3 percent.

During the summer of 1989, the United States doubled an earlier offer of $50 million in food aid to Poland, while the European Community approved a figure of $325 million; Poland's needs, however, were estimated at between $1 billion and $1.2 billion. There was now overwhelming pressure, particularly from external agencies, to liberalize the economy. So, the country in deepest economic difficulties took the lead in introducing far-reaching reform measures. In December 1989 an agreement was concluded with the IMF which provided a substantial but conditional loan (£350 million) and the Mazowiecki government committed itself to a rapid and radical reform (a "big bang") program to start in 1990. The stated objective was: to transform the economy, through rigorous stabilization, liberalization, and restructuring, into an economy based on private institutions, with market determination of prices and a convertible currency. Food and other subsidies were to be reduced by 50 percent and it was anticipated that real wages would decline by 20 percent (Deacon 1992: 26).

Retail prices had already been increased in October 1989, and in the following quarter, food consumption had fallen by 10–15 percent as household real income dropped by an average of 30–40 percent. One of the most striking effects of the new policy measures was a rapid increase in unemployment, which rose from virtually zero prior to January 1990 to over 6 percent of the labor force by December 1990, increasing at the rate of about 100,000 per month (Sachs 1991). According to the Economic Commission for Europe, open unemployment had reached 1 million by the end of the year. Industrial output dropped by about 25 percent in 1990 and real GDP by some 12 percent. Real wages fell sharply by about 25 percent immediately after the January 1990 reforms and then continued on a downward trend. Meanwhile, the total foreign debt had reached nearly $50 billion.

Foreign advocates of "the big bang" approach to economic reform remained boldly optimistic. They hoped that "cuts in military spending and investment in heavy industry, combined with new external financing from abroad, can reduce the need for large cuts in current consumption" (Sachs and Lipton 1990: 87). Popular tolerance for the austerity measures adopted was taken for granted.

In April 1991, the Paris Club agreed to an unprecedented debt-forgiveness package, canceling up to 50 percent of the $33 billion owed to western governments; the deal was conditional on Poland's agreement to a three-year adjustment program with the IMF (also signed in April) and on successful implementation of the agreed program. But a plan to cancel or at least renegotiate Poland's debt to western commercial banks failed to materialize. The economy remained in deep recession: GDP and output both fell significantly during 1991 (by an estimated 8–12 percent and 12–18 percent respectively). Inflation remained high, at around 80 percent, against an initial IMF target for 1991 of 36 percent.

In Hungary, in December 1989, the IMF concluded an agreement with the government which provided for a substantial loan (£460 million) in return for a program of tough economic reforms, including cuts in the budget and in particular in subsidies on food and other goods, increases in rents and mortgages, and progressive privatization. The first free elections since World War II, held in 1990, brought to power a coalition government led by the right-of-center Hungarian Democratic Forum, which began a radical restructuring of the economy. During 1990, Hungary implemented what the World Bank called "a determined stabilisation compatible with a shift toward a private market economy" (World Bank 1991b: 8). But social unrest began to grow. At the end of October, taxi drivers went on strike, provoked by an overnight increase by 65 percent in petrol prices; the strike paralyzed Hungary as drivers blocked all the major cities and roads between cities.

The government, facing growing discontent over its handling of the economy, now abandoned caution and announced a radical program of reforms. The new six-month program, to be put to parliament in December 1990, was expected to push inflation to above 35 percent, to bankrupt one in three companies, and more than double unemployment to 200,000. "The economic programme will demand a single but huge sacrifice and throw open opportunities for breakthroughs," argued the top economic adviser to the prime minister, Gyorgy Matolcsy. The program would slash state subsidies (mainly on food, domestic fuel and electricity, and transport) by 50 billion forints. Wages and imports would be liberalized, as well as prices; and a 10 percent cut in personal tax was planned. To limit the negative impact of the reform program on welfare, a set of social-policy measures were proposed: the higher prices resulting from cuts in subsidies were to be offset by increased pensions and family allowances, at least for lower-income groups; larger budget allocations would be required for unemployment compensation, employment services and retraining programs provided under the Employment Policy Fund created in 1988 to counter the effects of higher unemployment. At the same time, all social welfare programs would be thoroughly reviewed and reformed; there would be an end to cheap housing, and both health-care and social-security programs would be revised to reduce costs and improve "targeting."

The impact of the economic-reform program was striking. The private economy boomed and foreign-investment inflows exceeded expectations. On the other hand, by the end of 1991, the government was reported to be deeply unpopular. Unemployment had reached an estimated 8 percent and real incomes had fallen during the year by around 2–3 percent. Unemployment rose from 80,000 to 400,000 in 1991. The reasons for the accelerating unemployment included a collapse in internal demand and in real wages, the closure of big state enterprises, the sacking of thousands of state employees, and a massive decline in trade with the former Soviet Union.

Yugoslavia, together with Poland and Hungary, was among the first states to initiate far-reaching economic reforms. A comprehensive set of what have been described as "soundly conceived economic adjustment reforms" (Killick and Stevens 1991: 16), were approved in 1988 by the federal parliament, and by 1990, Yugoslavia had embarked on a drastic stabilization program involving important elements of structural reforms. According to some observers, "on the whole stabilization measures brought about quick and encouraging results" (Killick and Stevens 1991: 16). But opposition began to grow to the undifferentiated application of reform measures at republican and provincial levels, and by mid-1990, the reforms had encouraged the centrifugal forces of nationalism: "the hardships and uncertainties that resulted inevitably from the liberalisation of imports and prices hardened opposing stances" (Killick and Stevens 1991: 17) both to reform itself and to the imposition of the reforms by the federal government.

The arguments in favor of "shock therapy" have always recognized the threat of social unrest in response to the costs of adjustment as a real risk but one to be avoided by pushing through the reform measures as rapidly as possible, "before opposition is able to build up." The supporters of the more gradualist approach, however, argue that a carefully phased strategy, with judicious intervention to reduce some of the most severe social costs, has economic advantages as well.

In Romania, where rationing had been expanded and strictly enforced after October 1989, the Ceauşescu government claimed that the transition to a market economy would take place gradually: a first stage, of 1–3 years, intended to lay the foundations; a second, of at least 5 years, to modernize the national economy. This gradualist approach of the old regime contrasts with the "shock therapy" approach of the new Polish government. The government of Iliescu, however, moved somewhat less cautiously; early in 1990, commerce in agricultural products was fully liberalized. The domestic supply of foodstuffs, however, remained inadequate; and during 1990, industrial production fell by nearly 20 percent and investment by 35 percent, while inflation rose by nearly 30 percent, nominal wages increased by only 8 percent and national income fell by 10 percent. At the end of October 1990, the Romanian prime minister, faced with a transport strike, ordered the use of army vehicles in emergency.

In late 1990, Romania embarked on a round of negotiations with the IMF. Agreement was initially hampered by concern over the removal of food subsidies. But prices, including food prices, were liberalized in early November 1990, with a second round of cuts in subsidies planned for January 1991. The European Community agreed that Romania now met the preconditions for EC aid (consolidation of democracy and moves towards a market economy). The scrapping of controls sent prices rocketing on all but a handful of essential items, such as bread and rents, which remained protected. Panic-buying left many shops empty. On November 5, it was reported that the price increases which had sparked demonstrations in the capital, represented only the beginning of the government's strategy to create a market economy. But, as Deacon reports, widespread strikes and street protests forced the government to postpone the planned second round of increases (together with measures to introduce unemployment benefit, reform the tax structure, and embark on large-scale privatization), and to adopt a somewhat more "moderate" strategy which limited price increases to between 100 percent and 200 percent (Deacon 1992: 27).

Some commentators have argued that

> [the] gradualist approach risks facilitating the resistance of the former party nomenklatura to the transition, while failing to accelerate sufficiently the production of badly-needed consumer goods. The appearance, or worsening, of open unemployment, declining production, the budget and balance of payments deficits, inflation, growing social inequalities and shortages may very well tempt the government to revert to some of the instruments of the old regime. (*Killick and Stevens 1991: 15*)

In the Soviet Union, President Gorbachev announced in April 1990 that the package of draft laws designed to introduce market principles into the Soviet economy would include controls on price increases. He stated that price reform would not occur for 6 to 9 months and even then some prices would be held stable. "Some people say that those at the top are planning to raise prices all in one go, to perform a 'shock therapy'. This is not the case," he said, during a visit to the industrial center of Sverdlovsk in the Urals. He conceded that the effect of the reforms would be a decline in employment and in production – but expected that many displaced from heavy industry would find new jobs in an expanding private sector (*Financial Times*, April 26, 1990). In fact, in 1990, net material product declined by some 4 percent and inflation reached 12 percent, while foreign debt totaled about 60 billion; in the words of the World Bank, "the traditional centrally planned system had largely collapsed, but a functioning market system had not yet replaced it" (World Bank 1991: 20).

In Czechoslovakia, in April 1989, the leadership had promised *perestroika*, a limited opening to the West, and even more limited democratization under the Communist Party. But over the next few months, political opposition generated massive demonstrations demanding free elections. In November, hundreds of thousands of Czechs took to the streets calling for the Communist Party leadership to resign. Early in December 1989, Czechoslovakia swore in a reformist government in which the communists were in the minority. Asked if he would start to institute "a heavy dose of monetarism" as he had indicated he might, the new prime minister responded to the press: "I would like to, but the question is, is the Czechoslovak public ready for it? And are my colleagues in the government ready for it?" In the same month, the new finance minister argued in an article in the *Financial Times* (December 1979), for "an evolutionary approach" in which the importance of pragmatic flexibility rather than moralistic or ideological fundamentalism was stressed and argued for "a new social contract" and a policy of "credible gradualism."

But Czechoslovakia applied to join the IMF and the World Bank in December 1989 and strains began to develop almost immediately over the pace of reform. According to one report, "some in the government want to capitalize on the strength of popular support by starting to impose painful austerity measures now. Others want tough measures deferred until after the [June] elections, hoping these will produce a government with a strong mandate for reform" (*The Guardian*, March 22, 1990). These divisions also reflected differences between Czechs and Slovaks within the government. In March 1990, however, the government proposed a program including severe austerity measures aimed at "curing inflation". The reforms, originally to be adopted in April, but eventually introduced only in 1991 after parliament's approval in the autumn, included the elimination of central planning and creation of an office of privatization, internal convertibility of the koruna, and price liberalization accompanied by the abolition of subsidies in stages. The deputy prime minister stated that, although price rises were among the most politically sensitive reforms, the sooner they were introduced the better, while the government enjoyed a popular mandate.

On January 1, 1991, the government initiated a substantial liberalization of both retail and wholesale prices; even before the effects of these measures had been seen, some experienced commentators were suggesting that "there is a risk that resistance to reform may grow as a result of the increased economic and social costs caused by the combined effects of economic reform and a deteriorating international environment" (Killick and Stevens 1991: 7). However, they also argued that "attempts to alleviate the social costs of adjustment often tend to preserve existing structures of employment and production, and thus slow down structural change" (Killick and Stevens 1991: 28).

In the first four months of 1991 Czech industrial output was down by 12 percent (around 9 percent of this resulting from the collapse of trade with the Soviet Union and COMECON). But, despite this, the finance minister in charge of the country's strategy for transformation to a "free market" economy ruled out any backtracking in the country's "shock therapy" privatization program. Any compromise between a centrally planned and a free-market economy was the impractical ambition of "intellectuals wanting to create the Brave New World of Aldous Huxley," he told the press. The currency was devalued for a second time in 1991 and made convertible for current-account transactions, and most international trade was liberalized.

The strains of economic reform, however, increased social tensions, including those between nationalities. In March 1991, separatists staged a mass demonstration in the Slovak capital, Bratislava, and demanded independence from Prague. The rally was in support of the campaign for the formation of a separate Slovak state which was launched with a declaration of sovereignty the previous week by a number of disparate nationalist groups. One of the concerns of the Slovak separatists was the tough program of economic reforms being undertaken by the federal government, and one of the promises offered was Slovak sovereignty and a softer program of economic reform. While Czechs generally appeared to accept the need to make sacrifices in the transition to a market economy, there were greater fears in Slovakia, already hit by higher unemployment and stranded with an outmoded heavy industry geared to the needs of the Soviet Union. The fears of the Slovaks about the possible consequences of economic reforms were acknowledged by government officials, who reassured Slovaks that special help would be forthcoming; but they insisted that a two-track reform would be disastrous for both republics. Since then, Czechoslovakia has divided into two separate republics.

In the Soviet Union also, growing tensions over economic (and political) reform had the effect of breathing new life into the forces seeking national independence. In early September 1990, the prime minister of the Russian Federation, Ivan Silayev, announced a sweeping program of privatization, abolishing most of the central-government ministries and switching to a market system over the next 18 months. The program was far more radical than that proposed by Soviet prime minister Nikolai Ryzhkov, and would amount to an almost complete reversal of 65 years of Soviet economics. These different approaches to economic reform, combined with growing pressure for political reform, were to accelerate the economic and political disintegration of the Soviet Union.

The removal from power of the Soviet president in the aftermath of the attempted coup of August 1991 and his formal dismissal in December, together with the dissolution of the Communist Party of the Soviet Union, heralded the disintegration of the Soviet political economy into a rapidly growing number of independent states, based on former republics of the USSR. While the coup was undoubtedly inspired by fears of further reforms, the political leadership of many of the new states espoused more radical economic reforms. In the Russian Federation, for example, although President Yeltsin and his colleagues in the Moscow mayor's office had declared that their plans for market reform and privatization would be accompanied by measures to defend the people's social rights and welfare, the appointment of Yegor Gaidar as deputy prime minister responsible for the reforms suggested a more radical liberalization was envisaged.

In Bulgaria, where the ex-communists were able to retain control, a significantly different approach to reform was adopted initially. As Deacon records, "in a series of social agreements between the government and the two trades union movements, a 70 percent compensation policy was [adopted] whereby all price rises would be compensated at that level in wages. A well structured unemployment benefit system was also agreed" (Deacon 1992: 27). Deacon recognizes that "such a policy was always likely to be costly and lead perhaps to a relative uncompetitiveness of the economy" (Deacon 1992: 27). In fact there was a widespread downturn in the economy during 1990, with the economic-reform program itself contributing to the problems. In March 1990, the Foreign Trade Bank revealed that it was practically insolvent, in August it was announced that output was down 10 percent on 1989, and rationing was introduced for many household essentials.

All the parties contending the June 1990 elections for the national assembly committed themselves to the creation of a market economy. But the Bulgarian Socialist Party (formerly the Communist Party) retained the mandate (with 47 percent of the vote) to pursue its relatively cautious program for economic reform. The Union of Democratic Forces, which won 37 percent of the vote, favored a "big bang" approach and declined to join the coalition government proposed by the BSP. The economic crisis continued, and the prime minister, Andrei Lukanov, was jeered by the political opposition and demonstrators at the beginning of November 1990 when he announced price increases of between 30 and 60 percent before the end of the year; electricity, and many food and consumer goods were already rationed or unavailable throughout the country. (Eventually, the cost of living rose by at least 100 percent during 1990 – Svindland 1992: 78). By the end of the month there was growing pressure on the prime minister to resign. He survived a no-confidence vote in parliament and won approval for an austerity budget. But demonstrations calling for resignation continued; and eventually the Podkerpa trade union called a strike, which brought the government down. In December a coalition government with strong UDF representation was formed under a new, non-party prime minister and with a commitment to radical reform.

During 1990, the Bulgarian foreign debt had reached $11 billion (136 percent of GNP). The government sought first a delay and then a halt to all payments related to the debt; it managed to obtain a massive loan through the IMF (£1,540 million), agreement on which involved the, removal of price controls on food and other basic goods and services. Prices were liberalized on February 1, 1991. In the same month, the Bulgarian government unified exchange rates, moved to a floating currency, and liberalized most foreign trade; it also liberalized most retail and producer prices, and adopted tight control on wages in the public sector. The price explosion (up to 1,200 percent for some goods) stunned the population. As one observer commented, "after months of rationing and queuing for the barest essentials as the old planned economy ground to a halt, Bulgarians have been confronted with the cruelty of a rudimentary market, with goods suddenly available but priced beyond the reach of most" (*The Guardian*, February 15, 1991). The cost of public transport increased by 12 times over the previous month; basic foodstuffs remained controlled, but at levels up to 7 times higher than in January. The government estimated that the measures would entail a drop in living standards of some 30 percent. Wages were planned to rise by 70 percent in March but there was a delay of six weeks between price liberalization and pay rises – which in any case failed to match the rise in prices. Responses among the population at large included horror and despair, "but little anger," according to this report.

In the GDR, the first steps to reform the economy through the institution of "a market-oriented planned economy" came at the end of November 1989, as the Communist party struggled to retain control. But the mass resignation of the Politburo at the beginning of December and subsequent decision to hold free elections in May 1990 in response to increasing popular opposition threw the party and the government into crisis. Meanwhile, calls for reunification with the FRG were growing, as were demands for a "socially oriented market economy." At the beginning of March, the prime minister warned that "the economic situation is worsening alarmingly; the strikes, slowdowns and other disturbances are leading to serious breakdowns in production" (*Financial Times*, February 1, 1990). Only hours later, 100,000 people demonstrated in Leipzig in favor of reunification. In the elections, brought forward from May to March in response to public pressure, the success of the center-right Christian Democratic Union and its political allies, and the defeat of the Social Democrats and the former Communist party (renamed the Democratic Socialist party), ensured that progress towards economic and political unification would accelerate. On July 2, 1990, monetary union took place as the first stage in economic reunification.

Food prices rose at once; to be followed immediately by popular protest. The higher prices for basic foods and the planned removal of subsidies for housing and transport triggered off a series of warning strikes in the metal-working industry; about 28,000 workers staged lightning strikes at 26 factories around East Berlin. By the end of the year, the social costs of economic unification were all too evident. Unemployment had soared, to reach nearly 760,000 by January 1991, with 1.8 million on short-time working. Independent forecasts predicted that combined unemployment and short-time working would rise even further in the coming year, to 3 million, unless wage demands were moderated. But a study by the economic research institute IFO in Munich concluded that rises in earnings in the former GDR had effectively been wiped out by the higher cost of living (*The Guardian*, January 1, 1991).

In March 1991, Chancellor Kohl committed 17 billion Deutschmarks

as tens of thousands of east Germans continued their protest against rising unemployment by staging lightning strikes, occupying plants and blocking streets. Dr Kohl made it clear that the new aid measures, on top of Dm 85 billion already earmarked by the federal government, were designed to head off an even greater wave of protest around July 1st, when hundreds of thousands of east Germans face the sack. (*The Guardian, March 1, 1991*)

The citizens of Leipzig marked the first anniversary of democratic elections on March 18, with a huge demonstration (involving an estimated 100,000 men and women) against unemployment and the state of the economy. Local trade unions organized the rally, which was treble the size of one held the previous week. One union official thought that social unrest could be kept within certain limits but warned that it would grow as unemployment increased. Towards the end of March there were massive demonstrations in Berlin, Leipzig, Dresden, Magdeburg, Jena, Chemnitz, and other cities; the crowds in Leipzig's Augustplatz chanted "Kohl must go" and roared "Pig" whenever the Chancellor's name was mentioned.

A prominent East German Social Democrat, who took part in the demonstration, defended Chancellor Kohl but admitted that the government had wasted a year in forming a proper economic policy. An opinion poll published at the end of March found two-thirds of East Germans felt their expectations of unification had not been met, while one in two blamed the West German government for their economic plight, rather than "40 years of communist misrule."

Two leading forecasting institutes estimated that overall industrial output in East Germany, which had fallen by 50 percent in the second half of 1990, would be 20 percent lower in 1991, largely because of the collapse in trade with the Soviet Union. This would push the jobless and those on short-time working to at least 3 million in 1991, while the employed labor force would fall from 8.73 million (in 1990) to 6.5 million. By late spring, there were growing fears that half the labor force (around 4 million) could be out of work by the summer – a higher proportion than in the world slump of the 1920s. (Before unification, 96 percent of the adult population was employed.) The murder, on Easter Monday, of the head of the Treuhand agency responsible for privatizing East German companies was a dramatic indication of the anger aroused by a program which had axed some of the biggest names in East German industry over previous months. The Treuhand had become the embodiment of East Germany's misery as it closed down more than 330 enterprises and eliminated more than 80,000 jobs. The same week, the government announced figures indicating the unemployment in East Germany had surged past the 9 percent mark.

In Albania, in January 1990, Ramiz Alia referred to the collapse of communism as a tragedy, but announced plans for economic and political reform which included multi-candidate elections to the People's Assembly, decentralization of light industry and transport, more private housing and even productivity linked wage increases. Economic stagnation during the 1980s had been disastrous for

Albania; but the strategy of borrowing from abroad to revitalize the economy, adopted by many of the other central and eastern European states during the 1970s and 1980s was precluded by the constitution which banned foreign debt. In February 1990, the introduction of "a new economic mechanism" permitted foreign investment for the first time in a decade. But the cautious pace of economic and political reform proved increasingly unacceptable to many Albanians; in March 1990, several hundred young men took part in a demonstration in Kavaje, 30 miles south of the capital, Tirana, which was broken up by the police with batons and rubber bullets; in May, about 2,000 workers at one of the biggest textile factories in the city of Berat went on strike to protest against low wages; and in July there were demonstrations in Tirana itself, calling for change. The official Albanian news agency ATA reported that demonstrators, numbering between 300 and 400 hundred people, "including vagabonds, and former prisoners as well as some deceived adolescents," had clashed with the security forces, throwing stones and bricks and breaking windows; foreign diplomats referred to large demonstrations and reported at least 30 people injured in police shooting. Significant numbers of dissidents subsequently forced their way into the western embassies, seeking refuge and emigration to the West.

In December, as thousands of students demonstrated for several days in the capital and clashed with baton-wielding riot police, the ruling Communist Party held a special conference to prepare for economic reforms and to fight the first contested elections ever. The election manifesto adopted by the party envisaged its total re-organization land significant changes to the political system (including the recognition of opposition political parties), as well as new legislation, economic reforms, and a greater opening up to the outside world. In the meanwhile, students, academics, and workers staged a rally to demand the prosecution of the riot police responsible for the injuries to demonstrators during the previous clashes; reports from Tirana suggested that the protest was on an unprecedented scale. There were also demonstrations and clashes with the police elsewhere in the country; in Elbasan, Albania's major industrial city, tanks moved in to quell protests.

During early January 1991, miners near Tirana went on strike over wages and working conditions; the strike spread rapidly to other parts of the country, with several thousand workers taking part. Transport and other industrial workers now also threatened action, demanding wage increases of up to 200 percent. Under increasing pressure from such popular protest, the government agreed immediate pay rises of between 30 and 50 percent for the miners, promising other workers wage increases shortly. The new Democratic party, established in December, staged well-attended rallies over Christmas, and its plea that elections be postponed in order to give it some time to organize was eventually agreed by the Communist Party leadership. In exchange for the concession, Ramiz Alia gained opposition support for an end to strikes and wage rises until May 1991.

The Communist Party proposed the gradual introduction of "market mechanisms" into a still largely state controlled economy, but the "democratic" opposition was already firmly committed to radical economic reforms. Its election manifesto called for "the creation of a shareowning democracy, the end of centralized communist control, and the distribution of land to the peasants working it." As one commentator observed, "the opposition proposals on the economy are in line with the marketisation policies being carried out by post-communist governments in eastern Europe; Mr Alia's recall the policies of Mr Gorbachev and pre-1989 Eastern Europe" (*The Guardian*, February 19, 1991). But the Albanian economy was on the brink of collapse. Increasingly, the government was obliged to concede the need for economic reform and to look to liberalization for a solution. It applied for membership of the IMF and the World Bank.

Elections were held at the end of March 1991; eleven parties and organizations contested the elections but the major struggle was between the Communist Party, now renamed the Party of Labor, and the Democratic Party. In the event, the Communists gained the majority (165 seats against 68), with overwhelming support (around two-thirds of the vote) from the rural areas. The towns strongly supported the opposition; in Tirana, the Democrats took 18 out of 19 seats (and Ramiz Alia lost his, with only 36 percent of the vote), while in the industrial towns of Durres, Shkoder, Elbasan, Korca, Kavaje, and Vlora, they captured all of the seats. The Communists offered the Democrats a role in a coalition government, but this was turned down. In several towns, notably in Shkoder, there were demonstrations in protest against the results of the elections, while on the streets of Tirana, "people wept openly, rubbing their stomachs to indicate their belief that more hunger was in store" (*The Guardian*, March 2, 1991).

Despite the publication in April of a new draft constitution abandoning many of the central tenets of the previous Marxist orthodoxy, popular protest in the urban areas continued to grow. In early May, a hunger strike at a pit outside Tirana (demanding improved wages and working conditions and the identification of those responsible for the deaths of anti-communist protestors in Shkoder) gave rise to calls for a general strike; in mid-May, a general strike, called by Albania's newly independent trade unions, brought many factories and public transport to a halt in several major towns. Four days later, tens of thousands of workers marched through the streets of Tirana, demanding pay rises of up to 100 percent. According to state radio, almost a tenth of the population took part in the strikes, which spread to all regions: "all forms of transport, mining, the oil sector, and other enterprises have been paralyzed," it was reported. President Alia appealed for an end to the stoppages, declaring that "economic and political life are almost at a standstill," and calling for dialog and an end to violence. A week later, a rally by thousands of strike supporters in Shkoder in support of the miners' strike was followed by a mass protest, involving tens of thousands, which clashed with security forces in the streets of Tirana. With the general strike about to start its fourth week and massive popular unrest in virtually every town throughout the country, the government felt obliged to resign.

In June 1991, following nearly six months of social unrest, only two months after the communists won their first contested elections, to end nearly half a century of Communist Party rule, a new coalition government was sworn in. The Democrats took control of most of the economic portfolios. Painting a grim picture of economic breakdown and mounting social unrest, the new prime minister, Ylli Bufi, appealed for foreign aid to help restore law and order, put the country back to work, and introduce the basic elements of a market economy; he promised to devalue the lek, free prices (apart from those on basic foods), and close down unproductive plants and factories.

In several parts of the country, however, including the northern town of Shkoder, where thousands had been made jobless, the food situation had become critical and was still deteriorating. In Shkoder, looting of shops and food stores, the sacking of the Communist party headquarters and an increase in crime were the immediate consequences of the deteriorating situation; but the food shortages affected not only Shkoder. In July 1991, shocked by evidence of spreading hunger, the EC proposed a multi-million pound emergency food- and medical-aid program for Albania. A visit to the country by European Commission vice-president, Frans Andriesson, revealed that the economy was near to collapse, with industrial output down by 50 percent and widespread food shortages as a result of drought and the collapse of state-controlled agriculture following hasty reforms in April which effectively dismembered the agricultural cooperatives. Official figures showed corn production down by two-thirds on 1990, milk output halved, acreage planted to cotton down by 80 percent and that to tobacco reduced by about a half.

The government was caught between the commitment to reforms and the growing economic and social costs of its reform policies. But in November, it withdrew subsidies from large enterprises and introduced price liberalization; prices rose four-fold in five weeks and unemployment soared. As food production fell, only $1 million of food aid arriving every day, mainly from Italy, prevented mass starvation. By December, food riots were becoming increasingly common and widespread, affecting small towns and larger urban centers (including the capital, Tirana) alike.

At the end of 1991, as economic and political situation became ever more desperate, the Democratic Party pulled out of the coalition government. The president, Ramiz Alia, at once appointed the former minister of food to head a caretaker government until the elections due in the spring of 1992. The last of the socialist regimes of central and eastern Europe to embark upon economic reforms entered 1992 in the most desperate state of all.

6   THE COSTS OF ECONOMIC REFORM 1989–1991

As the pace of economic reform began to accelerate through 1990 and 1991, and the measures associated with the reforms to become more rigorous, the social costs became increasingly visible and popular protest more widespread and more threatening. In some cases, conflict over the pace and character of economic reform contributed to ethnic and national divisions, and to the disintegration of existing states (e.g. the Soviet Union, Yugoslavia, and Czechoslovakia); in others, popular protest against the social costs of government economic policies began to give way to, or take the form of, ethnic and racial violence directed particularly against "foreigners" and other minority groups (e.g. Hungary, Romania, Poland, and East Germany). In many parts of central and eastern Europe, the prospect for a peaceful and successful restructuring of the economy had begun, by early 1992, to look extremely uncertain.

The Social Costs

To some extent, the social costs were foreseen. In its *World Development Report, 1990*, the World Bank emphasized the "revolutionary" changes and the potential for economic development in the long term but cautioned that, "[i]n the short and medium run, however, adjustment will probably involve significant costs. Average regional incomes failed to grow in 1989, and Poland's GDP is estimated to have fallen by 1 percent, with a sharper decrease likely in 1990" (World Bank 1990: 9). Already by the end of 1990, some commentators had warned that "the process of adjustment that would emerge from the unfettered market process would likely involve too little job creation, too much job destruction and too high a level of unemployment" (Blanchard et al. 1991).

In 1991, the World Bank predicted that Poland, Czechoslovakia, and Hungary would not regain their 1989 income levels until 1996. The prospects for Bulgaria, Romania, and Yugoslavia were even worse, with 1989 levels predicted unattainable until the next century. GNP was recorded as having fallen in all of these countries during 1990, with industrial production down by an average of 17.5 percent and agriculture experiencing the worst year for a decade. In central and eastern Europe as a whole, unemployment had risen to an estimated 2.5 million by the last quarter of 1990. The outlook for 1991 was grim, with a further decline of perhaps 5 percent in GDP in Poland and a slump of anything from 6 to 10 percent in Czecholovakia (World Bank 1991b; and sources cited by Killick and Stevens 1991: 681).

Looking back at the social costs of economic reform over the previous two years, UNICEF reported that unemployment in Hungary increased ten-fold between late 1989 and May 1991; in Poland, unemployment at the end of 1990 was 1.4 million (8 percent of the labor force) and was expected to be 2 million by the end of 1991. Czechoslovakia expected half-a-million unemployed by the end of 1992. For those who had work, incomes had fallen steeply. Average real incomes in Poland fell by around 25 percent in 1990. In Bulgaria, the fall was nearer 50 percent. In Czechoslovakia, the number of officially poor was expected to quadruple in 1991; in Poland and in the former Soviet Union, some 40 percent were estimated to live below the official poverty line (UNICEF 1992).

Within the former Soviet Union the experience of economic reform was particularly grim. According to one source,

national income fell by between 2 per cent and 7 per cent in 1990, the country's trade deficit trebled, even though the volume of trade actually declined, and an inflation rate of over 30 per cent has threatened to drift upwards to levels usually characterised as hyperinflation, leaving those on fixed incomes in dire circumstances ... Meanwhile, open unemployment has become an increasingly serious phenomenon, in circumstances in which the means of social protection are scarcely effective. (*Standing 1991: 1*)

By 1991, some estimates suggested that 80 million people, or more than a quarter of the entire population, had fallen into a state of bare subsistence, living on less than the official poverty level of 80 roubles per month. A radical redirection of social and labor policy had taken place, which coincided with a more "flexible" wage determination process, the abandonment of guaranteed employment and the recognition of unemployment as a "regrettable reality." According to Standing (1991: 1), "unemployment has already become a particularly severe prospect for women workers and for ethnic minorities in the various parts of the country."

After the break-up of the Soviet Union, the ending of subsidies and associated price rises were announced for Russia late in 1991, with none of the protective measures referred to earlier actually implemented. In January 1992, prices for all commodities rose by an average 3.5 times and the price of basic consumer goods increased by up to 7 times the cost a year before. Some wage earners received rises to "compensate," but were lucky to get a three-fold increase, as a result, the wage needed to sustain a basic standard of living increased to 550 roubles a month, compared with a minimum pension of 342 roubles a month. In March 1992, it was reported that "official Russian government figures reveal that the majority of the population now exists below the poverty line, and the impact is felt far up the social scale" (Livingstone 1992: 99). On the other hand,

the poorest among the population – particularly women – are, of course, the hardest hit. Women now comprise 90 percent of Moscow's unemployed. The average Russian woman spends at least two hours a day in the food lines, in addition to a full-time job and domestic work, with wages falling relative to men's, and an even higher risk of unemployment than men. (*Livingstone 1992: 99*)

Under such conditions, he remarks, the slogan seen on demonstrations that "Price liberalization is a crime against the Russian people" finds a genuine echo. Critics of government policy argued that "hyperinflation has the effect of definitively depressing the savings of intermediate strata and widening the gulf between those who already have power and property and those who live on wages, even if the latter increase in line with inflation. Students, retired people and the unemployed will run into many millions unless the present ruinous course is abandoned" (Kagarlitsky 1992: 89).

According to official figures for Eastern Europe, there were 2.1 million Poles (11 percent of the population) out of work by the end of 1991, along with 523,000 Czechoslovaks (6.6 percent), 500,000 Bulgarians (10 percent), 400,000 Hungarians (8.3 percent) and 300,000 Romanians (4.4 percent). Unemployment particularly affected young people, and women. In Poland, people aged 19–24 comprised 34.2 percent of jobless, while women constituted 58 percent of the total without work (although their share in the labor force was 46 percent); according to Malgorzata Tarasiewicz, formerly head of Solidarity's Women Division, women's employment was likely to be further undermined with continued restructuring (quoted in Baker 1991: 12). In all countries but Hungary, women outnumbered men among the newly unemployed (Moghadam 1992: 9). Where women previously experienced the highest rates of labor force participation in the world, they now faced unemployment in addition to loss of benefits from public social-welfare systems. As Fitzgerald remarks, "the economic reform process might well improve women's situation in terms of housing and queues but has already markedly increased the vulnerability of widows and single mothers who do not command commercial labour power" (Fitzgerald 1991: 25). In the GDR, where before unification and economic restructuring more than 90 percent of women had a secure job, female employees were the first to be made redundant, while childcare was the first benefit to be cut, making it ever more difficult to stay on (Mussall 1991). According to Moghadam, "experts expect one-fifth of the active population in Poland and Bulgaria to be jobless by the end of 1992, with figures of 13–14 per cent for Hungary and 12 per cent for Romania and Czechoslovakia" (Moghadam 1992: 17). In the former GDR, unemployment rose in January 1992 to a record level of 1.34 million (16.5 percent of the labor force); more than 300,000 extra people registered as unemployed in January, with women disproportionately affected. In Bulgaria, recent estimates suggest that unemployment "is nudging towards 25 per cent" (*The Guardian*, January 20, 1992). The World Bank estimated in 1991 that unemployment through the region would rise to nearly 11 percent by 1993; it expected that women would account for around 60 percent of the total jobless (World Bank 1991b).

As unemployment has risen throughout the region, the protection afforded by state welfare provision has been systematically undermined. As Fitzgerald points out, entitlement to welfare under state socialism, although legally the prerogative of all citizens, was in practice highly dependent on facilities supplied at the workplace (Fitzgerald 1991); as unemployment increased, so the basis of much welfare provision began to crumble. Young people and women were generally the hardest hit by unemployment, their "entitlement" to welfare being the most precarious. According to UNICEF, cutting subsidies changed relative prices and many families were now spending 50 to 60 percent of income on food alone. The consumption of bread, milk, and other basic foods declined in Bulgaria, Hungary, Poland, Yugoslavia, and the CIS. In Albania – the worst case – approximately 20 percent of all children were now malnourished, and infant mortality was more than double its 1989 level of 15 per 1,000 births.

"Social income" had also declined: minimum wages, unemployment benefits, child allowances, old-age pensions, and disability pay were theoretically maintained, but in practice they had been eroded by inflation. Companies had abandoned welfare services formerly provided to employees' families. Czechoslovakia cut spending on health by 20 percent in 1990 and on education by 10 percent in each of the previous two years. In Romania, there was an estimated inflation rate of 30 percent in 1990, compared to an increase in nominal wages of only 8 percent. Romanian pensions were also not fully adjusted to take account of the price rises; as of June 1991, prices had risen by 145 percent over the previous nine months. In part, the inadequacy of social safety nets was a result of miscalculations about the weight they would have to bear. Poland, for example, planned on a rise in unemployment to 400,000 with incomes falling by 5 to 10 percent, rather than 2 million and 25 percent.

UNICEF argued that reasonable indexing of benefits, sensitive monitoring of changes in child well-being, careful targeting of available resources, free school meals, food stamps to ensure minimum nutritional standards, and the maintenance of basic health and education services – all of these could have protected the most vulnerable, and especially the children. Such measures had, generally, not been adopted.

In Bulgaria, for example, one commentator observed, of the measures adopted in spring 1991, that

> the government has fulfilled its commitment to a consistent and rapid price liberalisation, but it has not carried out its promise of providing compensation to vulnerable sections of the population for the resulting increases in prices. Nor has it followed Polish-style wage indexation. It has followed IMF policy advice and limited wage indexation to 70 per cent of increases. (*Svindland 1992: 90*)

In October, on the eve of a general election, the government emphasized its commitment to a gradual transition to a market economy, with adequate social provisions (*The Guardian*, October 12, 1991). But in the event, the opposition UDF narrowly beat the Bulgarian Socialist Party to form a non-communist government, and openly proposed to speed up the pace of reforms. Deacon pointed out that "the intervention of the IMF in discussions with the newly elected UDF government of October 1991 has ... helped to ensure that the social agreements will be undermined. Responding to the close scrutiny of the IMF of the state budget, UDF politicians are now suggesting ways round these social protection measures" (Deacon 1992: 27). By the third quarter of 1991 inflation was reported to be running at an annual rate of 400 percent (Svindland 1992: 78); and at the beginning of 1992, the UDF leader, Zhelyu Zhelev won the country's first presidential election after declaring that "economic times will get worse before they get better and that there is no alternative to privatisation and a market economy" (*The Guardian*, January 20, 1992).

UNICEF argued that just as developing countries in the Third World began in the late 1980s to adopt special social policies to cope with the social costs of adjustment, so too the former "communist" countries of central and eastern Europe should take special steps to cope with the transition to "market economies." UNICEF insisted that these transitions be undertaken "with a human face."

More generally accustomed to focusing attention on the needs of developing countries in Africa, Asia, and Latin America, UNICEF now emphasized the social costs of the abrupt and dramatic changes in central and eastern Europe. In its report on *The State of the World's Children 1992* (UNICEF 1992), it observed that – as in the developing countries of "the Third World" – "adjustment" has involved spending cuts and the withdrawal of subsidies on food and other essentials. In both cases, the capacity of families to meet their needs by their own efforts has been undermined by rising unemployment, falling incomes, and rising prices; at the same time, cuts in social services have weakened the "safety nets" just when they have become particularly crucial. In a recent commentary on the UNICEF report it is argued that "the worst human consequences could have been avoided. Unfortunately, there are signs that the baby of minimum welfare measures is being thrown out with the bath water of state control" (UNDPI 1991–2: 18). At the start of 1992 it seemed clear that, in many cases governments remain committed to policies effectively undermining welfare. In January 1992 in Poland, for example, the government proposed a reduction in nominal unemployment benefits, as part of efforts to reduce public spending; while in Albania, in mid-February 1992, the rate of unemployment benefit stood at 750 lek (about $18) per month while a family's bread ration alone cost 600 lek.

But UNICEF's concerns about the social costs of economic reform and emphasis on the need for alternative strategies to the wholesale liberalization and privatization of economies and societies in which the state has hitherto played a central role played, are increasingly echoed by other agencies and "experts." The Economic and Social Committee of the European Parliament has adopted a broadly similar position, in which it emphasizes the importance of combining social and economic policy, and stresses that any negotiations with respect to possible association on the part of Poland, Hungary, and Czechoslovakia should pay particular regard to the eventual aim of overcoming the economic and social imbalances of the two halves of Europe and the Charter of the Fundamental Social Rights of Workers (cited in Deacon 1992: 32–3). Furthermore, as Moghadam (1992: 20) points out, Blanchard and associates (Blanchard et al. 1991) argue that governments must play an active role to minimize the social costs of adjustment; while Standing (1991) for the International Labour Office makes a case for "social adjustments," directly echoing the concerns of UNICEF regarding the unacceptable costs of economic reform in central and eastern Europe, as of structural adjustment in developing countries.

The arguments regarding the advantages and disadvantages of "shock therapy" versus "gradual reform" – which began to surface in discussions of the lessons of adjustment in the developing world towards the end of the 1980s, have begun to sharpen in the last two years with respect to Central and Eastern Europe. The initial enthusiasm for the "shock therapy" initiated by Poland, has begun to be qualified by the experience so far. Voices for "adjustment with a human face" in central and eastern Europe (as in the rest of the developing world) have become louder and more insistent (Blanchard et al. 1991; Standing 1991; Standing and Tokman 1992; UNICEF 1992).

It is important to recognize also that such arguments are not simply taking place among foreign agencies and expatriate analysts; from within central and eastern Europe, similar arguments have been developed by commentators and political activists alike. Critics of the economic-reform programs within the new "developing countries" have been equally, if not more, concerned at the social costs incurred and, significantly, with the politics of adjustment, notably the issue of how and by whom the reform process is to be controlled and made accountable – with the democratization of the reform process. Furthermore, while there is increasing concern both within Central and Eastern Europe, and outside, at the seriousness of the social costs being borne (particularly by the socially disadvantaged) and at the plight of the victims of economic reform, those who are experiencing the costs of reform have – as we have seen in previous sections – not remained silent or inactive.

Indeed, from the very start of the reform process, it has been clear that popular responses are not confined to grumbling or to individual survival strategies. Whether manifested in the most obvious forms – demonstrations, strikes, and other public forms of protest – or in less obvious ways – refusal to support parties or governments, creation of alternative social movements, or whatever – those who are the subjects of economic reforms have also intervened in the process and have often affected the outcome. And if it would appear that, in some cases (in East Germany for example) the level of popular protest directed at government economic policy has taken new directions as the horrific social costs of economic reform have mounted, elsewhere it remains a potent threat, serving as a brake on "shock therapy" or encouraging the maintenance of a degree of protection against rising prices and unemployment.

The Political Repercussions

Increasingly, however, it would appear that popular discontent at the dramatic deterioration in living conditions is feeding a great upsurge across central and eastern Europe of nationalism and ethnic violence, racism and xenophobia, which is itself contributing to the political transformation of the entire region.

If the social costs were, to some extent, foreseen, it is evident that the scale and significance of popular protest and the far-reaching political repercussions of economic reform were not foreseen, at least by the international agencies (despite their experience of "the politics of adjustment" in Africa, Asia, and Latin America through the 1980s). The general movement during 1990 and 1991 by governments across central and eastern Europe towards more "radical" economic reforms, however, clearly aroused widespread and growing popular protest and opposition (as we have shown in section 5). Only in a minority of cases, notably that of Bulgaria, did the mass of the population remain largely quiescent.

As Moghadam has pointed out, restructuring in Eastern Europe and the Soviet Union encompasses more than stabilization, adjustment and privatization. "The scope of restructuring even exceeds the entire economy, as it entails political, juridical, and ideological changes" (Moghadam 1992: 16). The economic reforms are part of a massive social and political transformation which affects the moral economy as much as it does the political economy. Here, as elsewhere in the developing world, the transition to a market economy implies a transition from one moral order to another; and here, just as in the Third World, the transition has given rise to anger and outrage in response to the costs of change as well as to excitement and optimism regarding the possible benefits of an emerging new order. And here, just as in many parts of the developing world (notably in South Asia, the Middle East, and Africa), the collapse of the old economic, political and moral order has given new force to movements for radical change, many of which draw on historical and cultural divisions and antagonisms for their strength, emphasizing the "return to traditional values" as the path to security and a new moral order.

As the social costs of economic reform and economic crisis increase across central and eastern Europe, the prospect of political unrest also looms. Even pro-reformers, like Jacques Attali (former President of the European Bank for Development), argue that the volatile political situation of central and eastern Europe is closely bound up with the economic plight of the region. But while their response is to encourage further liberalization and pin their hope on a relationship of hope with Western Europe, based on openness of market opportunity and equality under the law, our analysis suggests that if government economic reform cannot be made compatible with adequate welfare provision to constitute the basis for a broadly acceptable, new moral economy (combining economic development with social justice) within the existing framework of the state, then the rule of law will all too easily be disregarded on a massive scale and popular protest against the costs of economic liberalization all too easily be engulfed in the monstrous growth of ethnic violence and nationalism and break apart that framework from top to bottom. As Attali warned, "throughout the vast landmass of Europe, in the vast geographical zone once covered by the Soviet Union and its satellites, the clear potential exists for five, 10 or even 20 Yugoslavia-style civil wars" (*The Guardian*, September 8, 1992).

In some cases, like that of Yugoslavia, ethnic and national divisions and open political conflict have already torn apart the old state structures and economies, with appalling and continuing human cost; in others, like the Soviet Union, an initially less traumatic but nonetheless potentially destructive and violent process of disintegration has added new problems of nationalism and interethnic conflict to the difficulties of economic and social reform. In Poland, at the beginning of 1992, a report on internal security compiled by the ministry of the interior warned of the danger of social unrest, arguing that "there is a substantial threat to the fundamental interest of the Polish state ... due mostly to the disintegration of the state apparatus and economic breakdown" (cited in *The Guardian*, February 1, 1992). The report refers particularly to the susceptibility of the younger generation to extremist politics, fed by the deep recession and the threat of unemployment as the economy is restructured. In east Germany, and elsewhere (e.g. Hungary, Romania), the specter of an upsurge in reactionary ("neo-Nazi") violence is looming large.

Governments are, not surprisingly, becoming increasingly concerned at the terrifying potential for dissent, dissidence, and opposition to evolve into a violent holocaust of xenophobia, nationalism, and ethnic conflict. Most, nevertheless, appeared set at the start of 1992 to press ahead with radical economic-reform programs including severe austerity measures, despite the possible political repercussions. Whether such a commitment can be maintained remains to be seen.

Part III

Conclusion

10

Debt Crisis and Democratic Transition

From the less-developed nations of Africa and Latin America to the former socialist states of Eastern Europe, developing societies around the world have experienced two fundamental transformations in the last decade.

The first is a global trend toward neo-liberal economic reorganization – the shift from centrally-planned to market-oriented economies in Eastern Europe and the more general adoption of liberalization policies throughout the Third World. Although the introduction of market mechanisms in Eastern Europe has received singular attention, essentially similar liberalization reforms or "structural adjustment" programs were introduced somewhat earlier to developing countries in response to the debt crisis. In all instances, the result is a world economy more closely integrated and more intrusive in the domestic policy affairs of developing countries.

Second, and clearly related, is a global trend toward the democratization of authoritarian and one-party regimes in the wake of popular protest movements. In the early 1990s, for example, strikes, riots, and demonstrations forced 19 one-party states in Africa to institutionalize a democratic opposition. Continental powers such as Brazil and Nigeria moved from military rule to democratic reform in the 1980s, while Mexico and Algeria witnessed transformative struggles over the opening of their one-party systems to political competition. From Korea to Madagascar, movements of mass protest demanded an end to authoritarian rule. Even mini-states such as Nepal and Haiti held democratic elections.

We propose that these trends are causally interrelated. Of course, we recognize that historical changes of such vast comparative scope are highly complex and replete with processes of multiple and reciprocal causation ranging from deep structural shifts to adventitious political events. Yet we also find a regular and coherent pattern in the evidence of the preceding chapters. Stated in a few propositions, the debt crisis that began in the late 1970s was the result of profit-seeking in a globally restructured economy. First World bankers and Second and Third World borrowers equally indulged the fantasy that public-sector expansion and subsidized consumption would generate development. Profligate lending persisted even after the collapse of 1982. Structural adjustment, the international institutional response to this crisis, endeavored to restabilize the global financial and inter-state system. Yet stabilization in its quintessentially neo-liberal form rests on a contradiction. Its methods are regressive and, so, its social effects destabilizing. Austerity creates hardship and opportunity which generate protest. Economic reversals for poor and middle-income groups betray the commitment to social development that once sustained Third World states in times of unequal growth. Hardship is experienced as injustice. Neo-liberal reforms, moreover, foster the opportunity for popular participation in the processes of building a consensus and sharing the burden of change. International agencies want democratic reform and those who are asked to sacrifice for their own good demand a voice in public policy. Democratization results, always in locally conditioned ways. Yet the pressure is for bourgeois rather than egalitarian democracy, a result that may be both preferable to recent alternatives and disappointing to future promises.

In this conclusion, we offer an explanation for the sequence of events leading from crisis and austerity to democratization. Specifically, we propose a theoretical analysis focused upon the *mechanisms* that connect hard times and democratic reforms. It is convenient to distinguish two general categories or "levels" at which these mechanisms operate: first, the state in relation to international structural forces; and, second, the actions of popular movements. In practice, of course, these levels and mechanisms work in unison. The explanation for democratization merges action and structure.

From the standpoint of the state and global political economy, four mechanisms promote democratization. First, debt and austerity produce a *partial state breakdown*.[1] The degree of sacrifice required by structural adjustment goes beyond the effective limits of patronage and coercion practiced by authoritarian governments. On one hand, the state loses the financial capacity to ingratiate supporters and bureaucratic retainers through subsidies and favors. The "bureau-cratic-authoritarian" state, after all, was based on publicly supported technocratic elites in government, the military, and state-owned firms (O'Donnell 1978). On the other hand, austerity policies in the form of reduced income and consumption require cooperation from the large majority of non-elite, non-patronized sectors if they are to work. Wage restraint and price control, for example, are easily undermined by a public unconvinced of the state's commitment to equality and fairness.

Second, *neo-liberal ideology* propagated by the IMF, banks, lender governments, and economic experts favors weak, non-interventionist states in the Third World. Liberal democratic governments are best because they dilute state power to a level acceptable to diverse coalitions, just as they give greater power to the free play of markets. Austerity, moreover, comes with international pressures against corruption and clientism which restrain market principles of allocation. Rent-seeking officials are swept aside along with ambitious state planning (e.g. for publicly owned corporations or land reform). Market forces play a larger role in domestic policy, particularly those emanating from the international economy.

Third, the *end of the Cold War* eliminates the geopolitical rationale of authoritarianism. Prior to the 1980s, multilateral agencies, including the IMF, and liberal reformers were hamstrung by advanced country support for authoritarian states who traded on their anti-communism. Although these alliances were discomforting to liberals on the home front, geopolitical expediency required their tacit acceptance. Similarly, as long as the Soviet Union remained strong it backed leftist authoritarian states. The collapse of communism has had a dual effect on democratization. The West no longer needs embarrassing autocrats and the East cannot afford them. Indeed, both sides want liberal trading partners.

Finally, the opening of former socialist countries to western investors and the coincident privatization of state-owned enterprise in many Third World countries have created a *global competition for capital*. Investors prefer stable democratic countries safe from the prospects of expropriation or sudden changes of governments and their guaranties. The competition begins at home in the developed countries where labor unions and depressed communities organize to oppose deindustrialization, job export, and capital flight. Before the United States government can win congressional approval for a free-trade agreement with Mexico, for example, it must prove that Mexican labor enjoys the freedoms of collective bargaining and health and safety protections – that US capital will not profit from degraded labor abroad. The Mexican government, in turn, has taken a series of actions to promote, or at least publicize, reforms in the electoral system, human rights enforcement, labor freedoms, and pollution abatement. Democratization at home is a key selling point in the efforts of a great many debtor countries to attract needed foreign trade and investment. And if official reforms are sometimes intended only as window dressing, local dissidents have seized the opportunity to press substantive gains. For a variety of reasons, democratization has become good politics around the world.

These global forces are simultaneously prominent factors within the domestic political field. As Cardoso and Faletto (1979: xvi) argue in support of their "historical-structural" method for analyzing dependent development in Latin America, "external and internal forces [form] a complex whole whose structural links are not based on mere external forms of exploitation and coercion, but are rooted in coincidences of interest between local dominant classes and international ones, and, on the other side are challenged by local groups and classes ... [resulting in] the *internalization of external interests*." In this instance, changing international considerations reach directly into the occupational worlds, consumption habits, and local communities of the less developed countries. During these years, democratization has been as much a popular movement as a structural tendency.

At the level of grassroots political action. a parallel set of conditions facilitates democratization. First, the *collapse of clientism* as a mechanism of political integration changes long-established rules of the political game (Nelson 1979). As state spending shrinks programs that once purchased political loyalty with employment and public services are eliminated. Governments and political brokers strive to maintain these programs, sometimes with alternative loan funding from international sources. As the preceding chapters show, moreover, economic liberalization can produce paradoxical welfare-state expansion (e.g. chapter 8). And patron–client models of political control can be recreated with other kinds of resources in a market economy. Yet we believe that the broader trend is toward the decline of clientism and, conversely, the growing autonomy of urban low-income groups. As we argued in chapter 2. Eric Hobsbawm's (1967) portrait of a politically docile, immigrant urban population does not reflect a world of austerity and global restructuring.

Quite the reverse, as waves of IMF riots show. Recent research on Third World cities suggests that the old forms of domination are failing (Eckstein 1988, 1990; Gay 1990; Selby, Murphy, and Lorenzen 1990; Stokes 1991).

The patron–client model, second, represented more than a calculated exchange of services. It was also a social contract – a complex set of reciprocal rights and obligations governed by those normative expectations that we have come to call the moral economy. In the case of democratization, moreover, something new is added to the backward-looking moral economy of protest. Urban political movements have begun to press a new set of expectations in which *popular sovereignty is a condition of austerity*. If everyone is expected to sacrifice in the interests of economic reform, then everyone should have a voice in deciding how sacrifice is meted out and what reforms are adopted. Although less than decisive, popular movements have the resources of protest, publicity, and resistance to enforce these expectations.

This autonomous political initiative grows out of the institutions of *civil society* which have served the urban poor in all their efforts to adapt and persevere. Labor unions, neighborhood associations, religious groups (e.g. Latin American, Christian base communities and Muslim brotherhoods in Africa), regional associations, women's organizations, cultural and folkloric groups (e.g. Brazil's politicized Samba schools and East African dance groups), all these are the sinews of social organization that mobilize people to deal with the new challenges of neo-liberal reform. Just as the moral economy is transformed to define a new social contract, so traditional associations assume new political roles. A church-based group of "family mothers" in Latin America concerned about disappeared relatives, for example, may lead the struggle for human rights while an African trade union becomes the nucleus of a new political party.

Finally, in combination, social protest, a sense of justice, and organizational bases in civil society help to initiate *new social movements* for achieving human rights, class and gender equality, and democratic rule. In many instances, movements for multiparty democracy follow directly in the wake of structural adjustment programs and food riots as an effort to channel protest mobilization into longer term remedial directions. In other cases such as Eastern Europe, South Africa, and parts of Asia (Korea, Philippines), the new democratic movements capitalize on a longer history of resistance to authoritarian rule which the spread of neo-liberal reforms has energized. Depending upon the prevailing political system, movements for democratic reform may agitate for the overthrow of dictatorship (e.g. Zaire), real competition in corrupt one-party systems (e.g. Kenya, Mexico), or more effective and responsive representation in functioning democracies (e.g. Venezuela, India). The striking facts about contemporary democratic movements are their prevalence around the world irrespective of existing political conditions and the scope of their efforts to create effective democracy within formal institutional trappings.

The democratic transformation must be scrutinized soberly for what it is and what it is not. We observe a cross-national movement impelled by the foregoing forces, yet with differentially successful results. If efficacious reforms are achieved in one country, in another only superficial changes that paper over new styles of oppression are likely. Beyond this variation, moreover, neo-liberalism promotes a decidedly bourgeois form of democracy more concerned with free trade than individual freedoms, more attentive to property than human rights, and downright skeptical about the social progress promised by earlier developmental states in contrast to the economic progress now promised by the market. Democratization is no panacea. It does not necessarily solve the old problems of underdevelopment and it surely brings some new ones in train. In a few countries where structural adjustment has recently revitalized economic growth rates (e.g. Venezuela), inequality and immiseration have increased apace. The fitful social movement for democratization in authoritarian countries by means of multiparty systems, free elections, and human rights is not the same as functioning egalitarian democracy. Yet history suggests that democracy is reached through democratic struggle.

NOTES

1 This formulation of state-level forces conducive to democratization derives from a discussion following John Walton's presentation of a talk on "Civil society and the urban poor" to the Sociology Department at Northwestern University, November 1992. These four points emerged in an exchange between Bernard Beck and Charles Ragin, who later set them down on paper.

Bibliography

Abdel Karim, A., el Hassan, A., and Seddon, D. 1985: From popular protest to military take-over: an analytical chronology of recent events in Sudan. *Review of African Political Economy*, no. 33, 82–9.

Abrahamian, E. 1968: The crowd in Iranian politics, 1905–53. *Past and Present*, no. 41, 184–210.

Afshar, H. (ed.) 1985: *Iran: A Revolution in Turmoil*. London.

Agarian Research and Training Institute 1976: *Sri Lanka and the International Food Crisis*. Colombo: ARTI.

Ahluwahlia, I. J. 1985: *Industrial Growth in India: stagnation since the mid sixties*. Delhi: Oxford University Press.

Al-Azm, S. J. 1981: Orientalism and orientalism in reverse. *Khamsin: Journal Revolutionary Socialists of the Middle East*, no. 8, 5–26.

Al-Azmeh, A. 1976: What is the Islamic City? *Review of Middle East Studies*, no. 2, 1–12.

Alexander, M. 1990: ERP hits women hardest. *Msamankow*, no. 2 (August), 9.

Allen, C. H. 1992: Restructuring an authoritarian state: democratic renewal in Benin. *Review of African Political Economy*, no. 54, 43–58.

Altvater, E. and K. Hubner. 1991: The causes and course of international debt. In E. Altvater, K. Hubner, J. Lorentzen, and R. Rojas (eds), *The Poverty of Nations: a guide to the debt crisis – from Argentine to Zaire*, trans. Terry Bond. London: Zed Books, 3–15.

Alvarez, S. E. 1989: Women's movements and gender politics in the Brazilian transition. In J. S. Jaquette (ed.), *The Women's Movement in Latin America*, Boston: Unwin Hyman, 18–71.

A. M. 1992: Calcutta Diary. *Economic and Political Weekly*, February 29.

Amnesty International 1989: *Amnesty International Trade Union Bulletin*, no. 42. London. Amnesty International.

Amnesty International. 1991: *Women in the Front Line*. London: Amnesty International.

Amnesty International 1992: Mass arrests in Mashhad. *Urgent Action (UA 188/92)*, June 5. London: Amnesty International.

Anderson, B. 1991: *Imagined Communities: reflections on the origin and spread of nationalism*. London: Verso.

Andreas, C. 1989: People's kitchens and radical organizing in Lima. *Monthly Review*, 41 (6), 12–22.

Anker, R. and Hein, C. 1985: Why Third World urban employers usually prefer men. *International Labour Review*, 124, no. 1 (January–February), 73–90.

Armstrong, P., Glyn, A., and Harrison, J. 1984: *Capitalism since World War II: the making and breakup of the great boom*. London: Fontana Books.

Arnold, David 1979: Looting, grain riots and government policy in South India 1918. *Past and Present*, no. 84, 111–45.

Ashraf, A. and Banuazizi, A. 1985: The state, classes and modes of mobilization in the Iranian Revolution. *State, Culture and Society*, 1, 3, 3–40.

Association of Salvadorean Women (ASW) 1982: Participation of Latin American women in social and political organizations: reflections of Salvadorean women. *Monthly Review*, June, 11–23.

Bagchi, A. K. 1975: Some characteristics of industrial growth in India. *Economic and Political Weekly*, Annual Number, February.

Bahro, R. 1981: *The Alternative in Eastern Europe*. Verso: London.

Baker, S. 1991: Second sex takes second place in E. Europe. *Guardian* (New York), July 3.

Balakrishnan, N. 1977: Industrial policy and development since independence. In K. M. de Silva (ed.), *Sri Lanka: A Survey*, Honolulu: University of Hawaii Press.

Balasubramanyam, V. N. 1984: *The Economy of India*. London: Weidenfeld and Nicolson.

Bamford, D. 1989: Algeria: an unseemly struggle. *Middle East International*, September 22, 10–11.

Bandarage, Asoka 1983: *Colonialism in Sri Lanka: the political economy of the Kandyan Highlands, 1833–1886*. Berlin: Mouton.

Bandarage, Asoka 1988: Women and capitalist development in Sri Lanka, 1977–87. *Bulletin of Concerned Asian Scholars*, 20, no. 2, 57–81.

Banerjee, S. 1984: *India's Simmering Revolution: the Naxalite uprising*. Totowa, NJ: Zed Books.

Banton, Michael 1957: *West African City: a study of tribal life in Freetown*. London: Oxford University Press.

Bardhan, Pranab 1984: *The Political Economy of Development in India*. Oxford: Basil Blackwell.

Barnes, Sandra T. 1986: *Patrons and Power: creating a political community in metropolitan Lagos*. Manchester: Manchester University Press.

Bashir el Bakri, Z., Zahir, F., Badri, B., Khalid, T. A., and al Sanusi, M. 1990: Women in Sudan in the twentieth century. In S. Wieringa (ed.), *Women's Movements and Organizations in Historical Perspective*, The Hague: Institute of Social Studies.

Basu, K. 1991: Budget in the time of change: reflections on restructuring. *Economic and Political Weekly*, August 31.

Bates, Robert H. 1981: *Markets and States in Tropical Africa*. Berkeley: University of California Press.

Baylies, C. and Szeftel M. 1992: The fall and rise of multi-party politics in Zambia. *Review of African Political Economy*, no. 54, 75–91.

Beenstock, M. 1989: *The World Economy in Transition*, 2nd edn. London: George Allen & Unwin.

Beinart, William and Bundy, Colin 1987: *Hidden Struggles in Rural South Africa: politics and popular movements in the Transkei and Eastern Cape 189–1930*. London and Berkeley: James Currey and University of California Press.

Bello, W. 1982: *Development Debacle: the World Bank in the Philippines*. San Francisco: Institute for Food And Development Policy.

Beloff, Max 1938: *Public Order and Popular Disturbances, 1660–1714*. New York: Barnes and Noble.

Beneria, L. forthcoming: The Mexican debt crisis: restructuring the economy and the household. Prepared for inclusion in L. Beneria and S. Feldman (eds), *Economic Crises, Persistent Poverty and Women's Work*, Boulder, CO: Westview Press.

Berg, E. and Batchelder, A. 1984: Structural adjustment lending: a critical analysis. Unpublished paper, Elliott Berg Associates, Alexandra, Virgina.

Bernal Richard L. 1984: The IMF and class struggle in Jamaica, 1977–1980. *Latin American Perspectives*, 11 (Summer), 53–82.

Beulink, A-M. 1989: Women and the debt crisis. *Development – Journal of SID*, 1, 88–97.

Bidwai, P. 1993: Bringing down the temple: democracy at risk in India. *The Nation*, January 25.

Biersteker, Thomas J. 1989: Reducing the role of the state in the economy: a conceptual exploration of IMF and World Bank prescriptions. Unpublished manuscript, Los Angeles: School of International Relations, University of Southern California.

Birtill, P. 1992: A note on foreign investment in India's "new" economy. *Race And Class*, 34, 1, 17–22.

Blackurst, Richard 1981: The twilight of domestic economic policies. *The World Economy*, 4.

Blaikie, P. M., Cameron, J., and Seddon, D. 1979: *The Struggle for Basic Needs in Nepal*. Paris: OECD Development Centre.

Blanchard, O., Dornbusch, R., Krugman, P., Layard, R., and Summers, L. 1991: *Reform in Eastern Europe*. MIT Press: Cambridge.

Block, Fred 1977: *The Origins of International Economic Disorder: a study of*

United States international monetary policy from World War II to the present. Berkeley: University of California Press.

B. M. 1989: Liberalization road to economic ruination. *Economic and Political Weekly*, August 19.

B. M. 1991: Towards neo-colonial dependency. *Economic And Political Weekly*, August 3–10.

Bohstedt, John 1983: *Riots and Community Politics in England and Wales, 1790–1810.* Cambridge, MA: Harvard University Press.

Bohstedt, R. 1988: Gender, household and community politics: women in English riots. *Past and Present*, no. 120, 88–122.

Bolles, A. L. 1983: Kitchens hit by priorities: employed working-class Jamaican women confront the IMF. In J. Nash & M. P. Fernandez-Kelly (eds), *Women, Men and the International Division of Labour*, New York: SUNY (Albany) Press, 138–59.

Booth, Alan 1977: Food riots in the north-west of England 1790–1801. *Past and Present*, no. 77, 84–107.

Booth, M. 1987: Prison, gender, praxis: women's prison memoirs in Egypt and elsewhere. *Middle East Report (MERIP)*, November–December, 35–41.

Bornshier, Volker 1980: Multinational corporations and economic growth. *Journal of Development Economics* 7:2 (June).

Bornshier, Volker, Chase-Dunn, C., and Rubinson, R. 1978: Cross national evidence of the effects of foreign investment and aid on economic growth and inequality: a survey of findings and reanalysis. *American Journal of Sociology*, 84, 651–83.

Boyce, J. 1990: *The Political Economy of External Indebtedness: A Case Study of the Philippines.* Manila: Philippine Institute for Development Studies.

Bradshaw, York 1987: Urbanization and underdevelopment: a global study of modernization, urban bias, and economic dependency. *American Sociological Review*, 52 (April), 224–39.

Brandt, W. et al. 1980: *North–South: a programme for survival. The Report of the Independence Commission on International Development issues under the Chairmanship of Willy Brandt.* London: Pan Books Ltd.

Brandt, W. and Manley, M. 1985: *Global challenge. From Crisis to Cooperation: breaking the North–South stalemate. Report of the Socialist International Committee on Economic Policy.* London: Pan Books Ltd.

Brass, P. 1990: *The Politics of India since Independence.* The New Cambridge History of India, vol. IV. 1. Cambridge: Cambridge University Press.

Bratton, M. and van de Walle, N. 1991: Protest and political reform in Africa. Unpublished manuscript.

Bratton, M. and van de Walle, N. 1992: Towards governance in Africa. In G. Hyden and M. Bratton (eds), *Governance and Politics in Africa*, Lynne Reinner, Boulder, 27–55.

Bratton, M., Bjornlund, Eric and Gibson, Clark 1992: Observing multiparty elections in Africa: lessons from Zambia. *African Affairs*, 91, no. 364, 405–32.

Brett, E. A. 1983: *International Money and Capitalist Crisis: the anatomy of global disintegration*. London: Heinemann.

Broad, Robin 1988: *Unequal Alliance, 1979–1986: the World Bank, the International Monetary Fund, and the Philippines*. Quezon City: Ateneo de Manila University Press, and Berkeley: University of California Press.

Brumberg, D. 1991: Islamic fundamentalism, democracy and the Gulf War. In J. Piscatori (ed.), *Islamic Fundamentalisms and the Gulf Crisis*, Chicago: American Academy of Arts and Sciences, 186–208.

Burke, E. 1986a: Understanding Arab protest movements. *The Maghreb Review*, 11, no. 1, 19–25.

Burke, E. 1986b: Understanding Arab social movements. *Arab Studies Quarterly*, 8, 333–45.

Burke, E. 1988: Islam and social movements: methodological reflections. In E. Burke, E. and I. Lapidus (eds), *Islam, Politics and Social Movements*, California: University of California Press.

Burke, E. 1989a: Nationalism and Collective action in the Middle East: an overview. Unpublished paper, University of California.

Burke, E. 1989b: Towards a history of urban collective action in the Middle East continuities and change 1750–1980. In Kenneth Brown, et al. (eds), *Urban Crisis and Social Movements in the Middle East*, Paris: Edition L'Harmattan.

Burke, E. and Lapidus, I. (eds) 1988: *Islam, Politics and Social Movements*. California: University of California Press.

Caldeira, T. P. de R. 1990: Women, daily life and politics. In E. Jelin (ed.), *Women and Social Change in Latin America*, London and New Jersey: Zed Press and UNRISD.

Calhoun, Craig 1982: *The Question of Class Struggle: social foundations of popular radicalism during the Industrial Revolution*. Chicago: University of Chicago Press.

Calman, L. 1985: *Protest in Democratic India: authority's response to challenge*. Boulder: Westview Press.

Campbell, B. 1978: Ivory Coast. In J. Dunn (ed.), *West African States*, Cambridge: Cambridge University Press, 66–116.

Caporaso, James A. 1982: The state's role in Third World economic growth. *Annals*, AAPSS, 459 (January), 103–11.

Cardoso, Fernando H. and Faletto, Enzo 1977: *Dependency and Development in Latin America*. Berkeley: University of California Press (original Spanish edition, 1969).

Carr, Barry 1986: The Mexican Left, the political movements, and the politics of austerity, 1982–1985. In Barry Carr and Ricardo Anzaldua (eds), *The Mexican Left, the Popular Movements, and the Politics of Austerity*. San Diego, CA: Center for U.S.–Mexican Studies, University of California, Monograph Series 18, 1–18.

Carroll, B. A. 1989: "Women take action!" Women's direct action and social change. *Women's Studies International Forum*, 12 (1), 3–24.

Castells, M. 1977: *The Urban Question*. London: Edward Arnold.

Castells, M. 1978: *City, Class and Power*. London: Macmillan.

Castells, M. 1983: *The City and the Grassroots*. London: Edward Arnold.

Celasun, M. L. 1983: *Sources of Industrial Growth and Structural Change: The Case of Turkey*. World Bank Staff Working Papers, no. 641, Washington, DC: World Bank.

Central Bank of Ceylon 1978: *Annual Report*. Colombo.

Central Bank of Ceylon 1979a: *Annual Report*. Colombo.

Central Bank of Ceylon 1979b: *Review of the Economy*. Colombo.

Central Bank of Ceylon 1982: *Review of the Economy*. Colombo.

Central Bank of Ceylon 1983a: *Annual Report*. Colombo.

Central Bank of Ceylon 1983b: *Review of the Economy*. Colombo.

Central Bank of Ceylon 1984a: *Annual Report*. Colombo.

Central Bank of Ceylon 1984b: *Economic and Social Statistics of Sri Lanka*. Colombo.

Central Bank of Ceylon 1984: *Economic Performance in the First Half of 1983*. Colombo.

Central Bank of Ceylon 1985: *Annual Report*. Colombo.

Central Bank of Ceylon 1987: *Annual Report*. Colombo.

Central Bank of Sri Lanka 1986: *Review of the Economy*. Colombo.

Central Bank of Sri Lanka 1987: *Annual Report*. Colombo.

Chafer, T. 1992: French African Policy: towards change. *African Affairs*, 91, no. 362, 37–52.

Chalker, L. 1991: Good government and the aid programme', text of an unpublished lecture at the Overseas Development Institute/Chatham House, June.

Chipman, J. 1989: *French Power in Africa*. Oxford: Basil Blackwell.

Cho, S. K. 1985: The dilemmas of export-led industrialization: South Korea and the world economy. *Berkeley Journal of Sociology*, 30, 65–94.

Clark, J. and Allison, C. 1989: *Zambia: Debt and Poverty*. Oxford: Oxfam.

Clark, Peter 1976: Popular protest and disturbance in Kent, 1558–1640. *The Economic History Review*, 29, no. 3, 365–81.

Clement, J-F. 1985: Strategies repressives et techniques du maintien de l'ordre: les revoltes urbaines de janvier 1984 au Maroc. Unpublished paper, September.

Clement, J-F. 1986: Les revoltes urbaines de janvier 1984 au Maroc. *Reseau Scientifique et Documentaire Etats Villes: rapports sociaux et mouvements urbains dans le monde arabe*, Bulletin, no. 5 (November), 3–46.

Cline, William 1983: Economic stabilization in the developing countries: theory and stylized facts. In John Williamson (ed.), *IMF Conditionality*, Washington, DC: Institute of International Economics, 175–208.

Cline, William R. and Weintraub, Sidney 1981: *Economic Stabilization in Developing Countries*. Washington, DC: The Brookings Institution.

Cohen, R. 1982: Resistance and hidden forms of consciousness among African workers. In H. Johnson and H. Bernstein (eds), *Third World Lives of Struggle*, London: Heinemann Educational Books and The Open University, 244–57.

Cohen, R. 1991: *Contested Domains: debates in international labour studies*. London: Zed Books.

Coker, C. 1991: What future for southern Africa? *The World Today*, July, 116–20.

Colclough, C. and Manor, J. (eds) 1991: *States or Markets? Neo-Liberalism and the Development Policy Debate*. Oxford: Clarendon Press.

Collier, David 1976: *Squatters and oligarchs: authoritarian rule and policy changes in Peru*. Baltimore: Johns Hopkins University Press.

Commonwealth Secretariat. 1990: *Engendering Adjustment for the 1990s*. London: Commonwealth Secretariat.

Conert, H. 1991: Yugoslavia: the "socialist market economy" and the debt crisis. In E. Altvater, K. Hubner, J. Lorentzen, and P. Rojas (eds), *The Poverty of Nations: a guide to the debt crisis from Argentina to Zaire*, London: Zed Press, 219–28.

Cordera Campos, Rolando, and Gonzáles Tiburcio, Enrique. 1991: Crisis and transition in the Mexican Economy. In Mercedes Gonzáles de la Rocha and Augustín Escobar Latapí *Social Responses to Mexico's Economic Crisis of the 1980s*. San Diego: Center for U.S.–Latin American Studies, University of California, 19–56.

Corea, Gamini 1975: *The Instability of an Export Economy*. Colombo: Marga Institute.

Cornelius, Wayne 1975: *Politics and the Migrant Poor in Mexico City*. Stanford: Stanford University Press.

Cornia, G. 1987a: Adjustment at the household level: potentials and limitations of survival strategies. In G. Cornia, R. Jolly, and F. Stewart (eds), *Adjustment with a Human Face*, Oxford: Clarendon Press, 90–104.

Cornia, G. 1987b: Adjustment policies, 1980–1985: effects on child welfare. In G. Cornia, R. Jolly, and F. Stewart (eds), *Adjustment with a Human Face*, Oxford: Clarendon Press, 48–72.

Cornia, G., Jolly, R., and Stewart, F. (eds) 1987: *Adjustment with a Human Face*. Oxford: Clarendon Press.

Covington, Sarah 1990: Urban popular movements in Mexico: grassroots action for change. Working paper, U.S.–Mexico Studies Series, Graduate School and University Center of the City University of New York.

Crook, R. C. 1989: 'Patrimonialism, administrative effectiveness and economic development in Côte d'Ivoire', *African Affairs*, 88, no. 351, 205–28.

Crook, R. C. 1991: State, society and political institutions in Côte d'Ivoire and Ghana. In J. Manor (ed.), *Rethinking Third World Politics*, London: Longman.

Dahanayake, P. A. S. 1979: Growth and Welfare: some reflections on the effects of recent development policy reforms in Sri Lanka. CBC *Staff Studies*, 9.

Daines, V. and Seddon, D. 1991: Survival struggles, protest and resistance: women's responses to "austerity" and "structural adjustment". *Gender Analysis in Development Sub-Series*, no. 4, Norwich: School of Development Studies, 42.

Daines, V. and Seddon D. 1993: Confronting austerity: women's responses to economic reform. In M. Turshen and B. Holcomb (eds), *Women's Lives and Public Policy: the International experience*, Westport, CN: Greenwood Press, 3–32.

Daines, V. and Seddon, D. 1994: *Confronting Austerity: women's responses to economic reform*. London: Zed Press.

Darnton, Robert 1992: Reading a riot. *New York Review of Books*, October 22, 44–6.

Davies, R. and Saunders, D. 1987: Stabilization policies and the effect on child health in Zimbabwe. *Review of African Political Economy*, no. 38, 3–23.

Davis, Diane 1990: Social movements in Mexico's crisis. *Journal of International Affairs*, 43, 343–67.

de Groot, J. 1989: The formation and reformation of popular political movements in Iran. In K. Brown, B. Hourcade, M. Jolé, C. Liauzu, P. Slugett, and S. Zubaida (eds), *Urban Crises and Social Movements in the Middle East*, Paris: L'Harmattan Villes et Enterprises, 214–34.

de Janvry, Alain 1981: *The Agrarian Question and Reformism in Latin America*. Baltimore: Johns Hopkins University Press.

Deacon, B. 1992: *The impact of supranational and global agencies on central European national social policy*. Faculty of Health, Leeds Polytechnic, March. Paper presented at conferences on 'New World Order', Arundel Sussex, UK, May 1992, and on 'Social responses to political and economic transformation', Central European University, Prague, May 1992, and at the 'First European Conference of Sociology', Vienna, Austria, August 1992.

Deegan, H. 1992: Democratization in the Middle East – possibilities and pit-falls. Unpublished paper, Staffordshire Polytechnic.

Delamaide, D. 1984: *Debt Shock*. London: Weidenfeld and Nicolson.

Dell, Sidney 1984: Stabilization: the political economy of overkill. In Charles K. Wilber (ed.), *The Political Economy of Development and Underdevelopment*, New York: Random House.

Deutscher, T. 1981: Poland – hopes and fears. *New Left Review*, no. 125 (January–February), 61–74.

Diaz-Alejandro, Carlos F. 1981: Southern cone stabalization plans. In William R. Cline and Sidney Weintraub (eds), *Economic Stabalization in Developing Countries*. Washington, DC: The Brookings Institution, 119–47.

Dick, H. 1982: Survey of recent developments. *Bulletin of Indonesian Economic Studies* xviii(1).

Dietz, Henry. A. 1976: Bureaucratic demand-making and clientistic participation in Lima, Peru. In James Malloy (ed.), *Authoritarianism and Corporatism in Latin America*, Pittsburg: University of Pittsburg Press, 413–58.

Dreze, Jean and Sen, Amartya 1989: *Hunger and Public Action*. Oxford: The Clarendon Press.

Dunn, J. 1986: The politics of representation and good government in post-colonial Africa. In P. Chabal (ed.), *Political Domination in Africa*, Cambridge: Cambridge University Press.

Eckstein, Susan 1988: *Power and Popular Protest: Latin American social movements*. Berkeley: University of California Press.

Eckstein, Susan (ed.) 1989: *Power and Popular Protest: Latin American social movements*. California: University of California Press.

Eckstein, Susan 1990: Poor people versus the state and capital: anatomy of a successful community mobilization for housing in Mexico City. *International Journal of Urban and Regional Research*, 14, 274–96.

Economist Country Profile – Brazil No. 2 1987: London: The Economist Intelligence Unit.

Economist Intelligence Unit 1990: various reports.

Economist Intelligence Unit 1991: various reports.

Economist Intelligence Unit 1992: *Sri Lanka Country Report*. London: The Economist Intelligence Unit.

Edirisinghe, Neville 1985: Preliminary report on the food stamp scheme in Sri Lanka: distribution of benefits and impact on nutrition. Washington, DC: International Food Policy Research Institute.

Edwards, Sebastian 1989: The debt crisis and economic adjustment in Latin American. *Latin American Research Review*, 24, 172–86.

El Nacional 1989: El Dia que Bajaron los Cerros: El Saqueo de Carcacas. Caracas.

El Naggar, S. 1987: *Adjustment Policies and Development Strategies in the Arab World*. IMF: Washington, DC: IMF.

Ellner, Steve 1989: Venezuela, no exception. *Report on the Americas*, 23 (May), 8–100.

Elson, D. 1983: Dominance and dependency. In D. Elson, L. Morris, V. Pillay, John Toye, and Ben Turok (eds), *Third World Studies*, Block 4, Milton Keynes: Open University.

Elson, D. 1989: The impact of structural adjustment on women. In B. Onimode (ed.), *The IMF, The World Bank and the African Debt*, London: Zed Press, 56–74.

Elson, D. 1991a: Male bias in macro-economics: the case of structural adjustment. In D. Elson (ed.), *Male Bias in the Development Process*, Manchester: Manchester University Press.

Elson, D. 1991b: Structural adjustment with gender awareness? MS.

Epstein, A. L. 1958: *Politics in an African Community*. Manchester: Manchester University Press.

Epstein, Edward C. 1989: Austerity and trade unions in Latin America. In William Canak (ed.), *Lost Promises: debt, austerity, and development in Latin America*, Boulder, CO: Westview Press, 169–89.

Escobar Latapí, Augustín and Roberts, Bryan 1991: Urban stratification, the middle classes, and economic change in Mexico. In Mercedes Gonzáles de la Rocha and Augustín Escobar (eds), *Social Responses to Mexico's Economic Crisis of the 1980s*, San Diego: Center for U.S.–Mexican Studies, University of California, 91–113.

Espinal Rosario 1988: Torn between authoritarianism and crisis-prone democracy: the Dominican labor movement, Working Paper no. 116, Kellogg Institute for International Studies, Notre Dame University.

Fadda Cori, Giulietta 1986: Crisis urbana en el area metropolitana de Caracas. *Revista Mexicana de Sociologia*, V. 48, no. 4, 87–108.

Farmer, B. H. 1957: *Pioneer Peasant Colonization in Ceylon*. Oxford: Oxford University Press.

Feijoo, M. del C. and Gogna, M. 1990: Women in the transition to democracy. In E. Jelin (ed.), *Women and Social Change in Latin America*, London and New Jersey: Zed Books and UNRISD, 79–114.

Fieldhouse, D. K. 1986: *Black Africa, 1945–80: economic decolonization and arrested development*. London: Allen & Unwin.

Fitzgerald, E. V. K. 1991: *Economic Reform and Citizen Entitlements in Eastern Europe: some social implications of structural adjustment in semi-industrialized economies*, UNRISD Discussion Papers, no. 27, Geneva: UNRISD.

Fox Genovese, E. 1982: Placing women's history in history. *New Left Review*, no. 133 (May–June), 5–29.

Foxley, Alejandro 1981: Stabilization policies and their effects on employment and income distribution: a Latin American perspective. In William R. Cline and Sidney Weintraub (eds), *Economic Stabilization in Developing Countries*. Washington, DC: The Brookings Institution, 191–225.

Franda, M. 1971: *Radical Politics in West Bengal*. Cambridge, MA: MIT Press.

Frank, A. G. 1980: *Crisis in the World economy*. London: Heinemann.

Frank, A. G. 1981: *Crisis in the Third World*. London: Heinemann.

Frankel, F. R. 1971: *India's Green Revolution, Economic Gains and Political Costs*. Princeton: Princeton University Press.

Frankel, F. R. 1978: *India's Political Economy, 1947–1977: The Gradual Revolution*. Princeton: Princeton University Press.

Frenkel, Roberto and O'Donnell, Guillermo 1979: The "stabilization programs" of the International Monetary Fund and Their Internal Impact. In Richard R. Fagen (ed.), *Capitalism and the State in U.S.–Latin American Relations*, Stanford: Stanford University Press, 171–216.

Frieden, Jeffrey A. 1991: *Debt, Development, and Democracy: modern political economy and Latin America, 1965–1985*. Princeton: Princeton University Press.

Friedgut, T. and Siegelbaum, L. 1990: Perestroika from below: the Soviet miners' strike and its aftermath. *New Left Review*, no. 181, 5–32.

Friedman, John and Salguero, Mauricio 1988: The Barrio economy and collective self-empowerment in Latin America: a framework and agenda for research. *Comparative Urban and Community Research*, vol. 1. New Brunswick, NJ: Transaction Books, 3–37.

Fröbel, F. 1982: The current development of the world economy reproduction of labor and accumulation of capital on a world scale. *Review*, 5, no. 4, 507–55.

Gandhi, N. 1990a: "Mass mobilisation in the Indian Women's Movement – a case study of the anti price rise movement in Bombay, 1972–75", in S. Wieringa (ed.), *Women's Movements and Organizations in Historical Perspective*. The Hague: Institute of Social Studies.

Gandhi, N. 1990b: The anti price rise movement. In Ilina Sen (ed.), *A Space Within the Struggle: women's participation in people's movements*, New Delhi: Kali for Women, 108–16.

Garnaut, R. (ed.) 1980: *ASEAN in a Changing Pacific and World-Economy*. Canberra: Australian National University Press.

Gavan, James D. and Chandrasekera, Indrani Sri 1979: The impact of public foodgrain distribution on food consumption and welfare in Sri Lanka. International Food Policy Research Institute Research Report 13, Washington, DC.

Gay, Robert 1990: Neighborhood associations and political change in Rio de Janeiro. *Latin American Research Review*, 25, 102–18.

Gentleman, Judith 1987: *Mexican Politics in Transition*. Boulder, CO: Westview Press.

Ghai, D. and Hewitt de Alcantara, C. 1990: The crisis of the 1980s in Africa, Latin America and the Caribbean: economic impact, social change and political implications. *Discussion Paper*, no. 7, Geneva: UNRISD.

Ghosh, A. 1991: IMF borrowings: some myths exposed. *Economic and Political Weekly*, July 20.

Ghosh, A. 1992: Management of economy and IMF conditionalities. *Economic and Political Weekly*, January 4–11.

Gilbert, Alan and Gugler, Josef 1982: *Cities, Poverty, and Development: urbanization in the Third World*. Oxford: Oxford University Press.

Gill, S. and Law, D. 1988: *The Global Political Economy: perspectives, problems and policies*. London and New York: Harvester Wheatsheaf.

Girvan, Norman 1980: Swallowing the IMF medicine in the seventies. *Development Dialogue*, 2, 113–55.

Girvan, Norman, Bernal, Richard and Hughes, Wesley 1980: The IMF and the Third World: the case of Jamaica, 1974–80. *Development Dialogue*, 2, 113–55.

Glewwe, Paul and Hall, Gillete 1992: Pobreza y desigualdad durante un ajuste heterodoxo: el caso del Perú, 1985 a 1990. Documento de Trabajo de EMNV, no. 86S, Washington, DC: Banco Mundial.

Goldrich, Daniel, Pratt, Raymond B., and Schuller, Charles R. 1967: The political integration of lower-class urban settlements in Chile and Peru. *Studies in Comparative International Development*, 3, 3–22.

Goldsmith, Arthur A. 1986: Democracy, political stability, and economic growth in developing countries. *Comparative Political Studies*, 18, no. 4 (January), 517–31.

Gonzáles de la Rocha, Mercedes and Escobar Latapí, Augustín (eds) 1991: *Social Responses to Mexico's Economic Crisis of the 1980s*. San Diego: Center for U.S.–Mexican Studies, University of California.

Green, R. H. 1989: 'The broken pot: the social fabric, economic disaster and adjustment in Africa': B. Onimode (ed.), *The IMF, the World Bank and the African Debt*, vol. 2: *the social and political impact*, London: Zed Books, 31–55.

Green, R. H. 1991: Reduction of absolute poverty: a priority structural adjustment. University of Sussex, *IDS Discussion Paper*, no. 287.

Gunatilleke, Godfrey 1978: Participatory democracy and dependence: the case of Sri Lanka. *Marga Quarterly Journal*, 5, no. 3.

Guzel, M. S. 1989: La greve des 15 et 16 juin 1970 a Istanbul. In K. Brown, B. Hourcade, M. Jolé, C. Liauzu, P. Slugett, and S. Zubaida (eds), *Urban Crises and Social Movements in the Middle East*, Paris: L'Harmattan Villes et Entreprises, 163–78.

Halliday, Fred 1975: The Ceylon Insurrection. In Robin Blackburn (ed.), *Explosion in a Subcontinent*, Harmondsworth: Penguin.

Halliday, F. 1988: The Iranian Revolution: uneven development and religious populism. In F. Halliday & H. Alavi (eds), *State and Ideology in the Middle East and Pakistan*, Macmillan: London, 31–63.

Hanson, A. H. 1966: *The Process of Planning*. Oxford: Oxford University Press.

Harper, E. 1968: Social consequences of an unsuccessful low caste movement. In J. Silverberg (ed.), *Social Mobility and the Caste System in India: an interdisciplinary symposium*, The Hague: Mouton.

Harris, N. 1986: *The End of the Third World: newly industrialising countries and the decline of an ideology*. London: I. B. Tauris and Co. Ltd.

Harriss, J. 1989: Indian industrialization and the state. In Hamza Alavi and John Harriss (eds), *Sociology of "Developing Societies": South Asia*. New York: Monthly Review Press, 70–90.

Herring, Ronald J. 1981: The Janus-faced state in a dependent society: determinants of shifts in Sri Lanka's development strategy. Unpublished paper, American Political Science Association, New York.

Herring, Ronald J. 1983: *Land to the Tiller: the political economy of agrarian reform in South Asia* New Haven: Yale University Press. (In Asia, Delhi: Oxford University Press, 1983.)

Herring, Ronald J. 1985: Review of Asoka Bandarage, *Colonialism in Sri Lanka. Contemporary Sociology*, 14, 567–80.

Herring, Ronald J. 1987: Food policy in a dependent welfare state. In W. L. Hollist and F. L. Tullis (eds) *Pursuing Food Security, IPE Yearbook*, Vol. III, Boulder: Lynn Rienner, 158–80.

Hicks, Alexander 1985: Welfare expansion revisited. Draft MS, Northwestern University.

Hicks, Norman and Streeten, Paul 1979: Indicators of development: the search for a basic needs yardstick. *World Development* 7:6 (June).

Hobsbawm, E. J. 1959: *Primitive Rebels: studies in archaic forms of social movement in the 19th and 20th centuries*. New York: Norton.

Hobsbawm, E. J. 1964a: The machine breakers. In *Labouring Men: Studies in the History of Labour*, London: Weidenfeld and Nicolson, 5–21.

Hobsbawm, E. J. 1964b: Economic fluctuations and some social movements since 1800. In *Labouring Men: Studies in the History of Labour*, London: Weidenfeld and Nicolson, 126–57.

Hobsbawm, E. J. 1967: Peasants and rural migrants in politics. In Claudio

Veliz (ed.), *The Politics of Conformity in Latin America*, New York: Oxford University Press, 43–65.

Honeywell, Martin 1983: *The Poverty Brokers: the IMF and Latin America*. London: Latin American Bureau.

Hoogvelt, A. 1987: The crime of conditionality: open letter to the managing director of the International Monetary Fund (IMF). *Review of African Political Economy*, no. 38, 80–50.

Hughes, A. and Singh, A. 1991: The world economic slowdown and the Asian and Latin American economies: a comparative analysis of economic structure, policy, and performance. In Tariq Banuri (ed.), *Economic Liberalization: no panacea: the experiences of Latin America and Asia*. Oxford: Clarendon Press, 57–97.

Iliffe, John 1987: *The African Poor: A History*. Cambridge: Cambridge University Press.

International Labour Office 1971: *Matching Employment Opportunities and Expectations: a programme of action for Ceylon*, vol. 1, *Report*, vol. 2, *Technical Papers*. Geneva: ILO.

International Monetary Fund 1980: *Government Finance Statistics Yearbook IV*. Washington, DC.

International Monetary Fund 1984: *Government Financial Statistics Yearbook*, vol. XIII. Washington, DC.

International Monetary Fund 1990: *International Financial Statistics Yearbook*, Washington, DC.

International Monetary Fund 1992a: *Annual Report*. Washington, DC.

International Monetary Fund 1992b: *International Financial Statistics Yearbook*, Washington, DC.

Isenmen, Paul 1980: Basic needs: the case of Sri Lanka. *World Development* 8, no. 3, 237–58.

Jaquette, J. S. (ed.) 1989: *The Women's Movement in Latin America: feminism and the transition to democracy*. Boston: Unwin Hyman.

Jayasuriya, S. K. 1987: The politics of economic policy in the Philippines during the Marcos era. In R. Robison, K. Hewison, and R. Higgott (eds), *South East Asia in the 1980s: the politics of economic crisis*, London: Allen and Unwin, 80–113.

Jayatissa, R. A. 1982: Balance of payments adjustments to exogenous shocks during 1970–1981. Central Bank of Ceylon *Staff Studies* 12, no. 1, 41–92.

Jayawardena, Lal 1974: Sri Lanka. In Hollis Chenery, Motele S. Ahluwalia, C. L. G. Bell, John H. Duloy and Richard Jolly (eds), *Redistribution with Growth*, London: Oxford University Press.

Jelin, E. (ed.) 1990: *Women and Social Change in Latin America*. London: Zed Press and UNRISD.

Jiggins, J. 1989: How poor women earn income in sub-Saharan Africa and what works against them. *World Development*, 17 (7), 953–63.

Jones, D. E. and Jones, R. W. 1976: Urban upheaval in India: the 1974 Nav Nirman riots in Gujarat. *Asian Survey*, xvi, no. 11, 1012–33.

Joseph, R. 1976: The Gaullist legacy: patterns of French neo-colonialism. *Review of African Political Economy*, no. 6, 4–14.

Jupp, J. 1978: *Sri Lanka: Third World democracy*. London: Cass.

Kagarlitsky, B. 1988: Perestroika: the dialect of change. *New Left Review*, no. 169, 63–83.

Kagarlitsky, B. 1992: Russia on the brink of new battles. *New Left Review*, no. 192, 85–97.

Kalpagam, U. 1985: Coping with urban poverty in Indian. *Bulletin of Concerned Asian Scholars*, 17, no. 1, 2–18.

Kamen, Henry 1971: *The Iron Century: social change in Europe 1550–1660*. London: Weidenfeld and Nicolson.

Kappagoda, Nihal and Paine, Suzanne 1981: *The Balance of Payments Adjustment Process: the experience of Sri Lanka*. Colombo: Marga.

Karunatilake, H. N. S. 1975: The impact of welfare services in Sri Lanka on the economy. Central Bank of Ceylon *Staff Studies* 5:1 (April), 201–32.

Karunatilake, H. N. S. 1976: The public sector in the national economy. Central Bank of Ceylon *Staff Studies* 6:2 (September), 179–98.

Kaufman, Robert R. 1986: Democratic and authoritarian responses to the debt issue: Argentina, Brazil, Mexico. In Miles Kahler (ed.), *The Politics of International Debt*, Ithaca: Cornell University Press, 187–217.

Kearney, Robert N. 1979: The political impact of strikes and disorder in Ceylon. In Robin Cohen, Peter C. W. Gutkind, and Phyllis Brazier (eds), *Peasants and Proletarians: the struggles of Third World workers*. New York: Monthly Review Press, 248–64.

Khuri, Fuad I. 1975: *From Village to Suburb: order and change in Greater Beirut*. Chicago: University of Chicago Press.

Kibble, S. 1992: Zambia: problems for the MMD. *Review of African Political Economy*, no. 53, 104–8.

Killick, Tony 1990: *A Reaction Too Far: economic theory and the role of the state in developing countries*. London: Overseas Development Institute.

Killick, Tony and Stevens, C. 1991: Economic adjustment in Eastern Europe: lessons from the Third World. Paper presented at a conference on 'Reforming Eastern European Economies', University of Surrey, February, 1991. Later published as Eastern Europe: lessons on economic adjustment from the Third World. *International Affairs*, 67, no. 4 (October) 679–96.

Kochanck, S. A. 1968: *The Congress Party of India: the dynamics of one party democracy*. Princeton: Princeton University Press.

Korner, P., Maass, Gero, Siebold, Thomas and Teizlaff, Rainer 1986: *The IMF and the Debt Crisis*, London: Zed Books.

Kothari, R. 1967: India: The Congress System on trial. *Asian Survey*, 7, no. 2, 83–96.

Krueger, Anne O. 1981: Loans to assist the transition to outward-looking policies. *The World Economy*, 4, no. 3.

Kunz, F. A. 1991: Liberalisation in Africa: some preliminary reflections. *African Affairs*, 90, no. 359, 223–38.

Lakshman, W. D. 1980: Income and wealth distribution in Sri Lanka: an examination of evidence pertaining to the post-1960 experience. IDCJ Working Paper No. 16, Tokyo: International Development Center of Japan.

Lancaster, C. 1991: Democracy in Africa. *Foreign Policy*, no. 85, 18–26.

Latin America Weekly Report, May 11, 1984, January 16, 1992, January 30, 1992, June 4, 1992, September 17, 1992.

Lawrence, P. and Seddon, D. (eds) 1990: What price economic reform? *Review of African Political Economy*, no. 47, 3–7.

Leeds, Anthony and Leeds, Elizabeth 1976: Accounting for behavioral differences: three political systems and the responses of squatters in Brazil, Peru, and Chile. In John Walton (ed.), *The City in Comparative Perspective: cross-national research and new directions in theory*. Beverly Hills, CA: Sage-Halsted, 193–248.

Lemarchand, R. 1992: African transitions to democracy: an interim (and mostly pessimistic) assessment', unpublished paper.

Leslie, J. M., Lycette M., and Buvinic, M. 1986: *Weathering Crises: the crucial role of women in health*. Washington: Center for Research on Women.

Levine, Donald H. and Mainwaring, Scott 1989: Religion and popular protest in Latin America: contrasting experiences. In Susan Eckstein (ed.), *Power and Popular Protest: Latin American social movements*, Berkeley: University of California Press, 203–40.

Leys, Colin 1975: *Underdevelopment in Kenya: the political economy of neo-colonialism*. Berkeley: University of California Press.

Lindblom, Charles 1978: *Politics and Markets*. New York: Basic Books.

Lipton, Michael 1977: *Why the Poor Stay Poor: a study of urban bias in world development*. Cambridge, MA: Harvard University Press and Temple Smith.

Livingstone, K. 1992: Can democracy survive in Russia? *New Left Review*, no. 192, 98–104.

Lowe, S. 1986: *Urban Social Movements: the city after castells*. London: Macmillan.

Loxley, J. 1984: Saving the world economy. *Monthly Review*, September, 22–34.

Loxley, J. 1990: Structural adjustment programmes in Africa: Ghana and Tanzania. *Review of African Political Economy*, no. 47, 8–27.

Lubeck, Paul 1985: Islamic protest under semi-industrial capitalism: 'Yan Tatsine explained". *Africa*, 55, 369–89.

Lubeck, Paul 1985: *Islam and Urban Labor in Northern Nigeria: the making of a Muslim working class*. Cambridge: Cambridge University Press.

Lubeck, Paul 1990: Restructuring Nigeria's urban-industrial sector within the West African region: the interplay of crisis, linkages and popular re-sistance. Paper presented at the XII World Congress of Sociology, Madrid, Spain, July 9–13, 1990.

Lustig, Nora 1990: Economic crisis, adjustment and living standards in Mexico, 1982–85. *World Development*, 18, 1325–42.

Macdonald, O. 1983: The Polish vortex: solidarity and Socialism. *New Left Review*, no. 139 (May–June), 5–48.

MacEwan, Arthur 1985: The current crisis in Latin America and the international economy. *Monthly Review*, 36 (March), 1–18.

McFarlane, Anthony 1982: Riot and rebellion in colonial Spanish America. *Latin American Research Review*, 17, 212–21.

MacGaffey, J. 1988: Economic disengagement and class formation in Zaire. In D. Rothchild and N. Chazan (eds), *The Precarious Balance: state and society in Africa*, Boulder, CO: Westview Press, 171–88.

Maddison, A. 1985: *Two Crises: Latin America and Asia, 1929–1938 and 1973–1983.* Paris: OECD Development Center.

Maher, V. 1981: *Women and Property in Morocco: their changing relation to the process of social stratification in the Middle Atlas.* Cambridge: Cambridge University Press.

Mahfoudh, D. 1988: La syndicalisation des femmes en Tunisie. *Special issue of Peuples mediterraneens (Les femmes et la modernite)*, 44–5 (July-December), 29–47.

Mandel, E. 1980: *The Second Slump: a Marxist analysis of recession in the seventies.* London: Verso Books.

Mangin, William 1967: Squatter settlements. *Scientific American*, 217, 21–9.

Manor, James (ed.) 1984: *Sri Lanka in Change and Crisis.* London: Croom Helm.

Marga Institute 1981: An analytical description of poverty in Sri Lanka. Colombo.

Margulies, R. and Yildizoglu, E. 1988: Austerity packages and beyond: Turkey since 1980. *Capital and Class*, no. 36 (winter).

Mason, T. 1981: The workers' opposition in Nazi Germany. *History Workshop*, 11 (Spring), 120–37.

Massiah, J. 1988: Women's lives and livelihoods: a view from the Commonwealth Caribbean. *World Development*, 17 (7), 965–77.

Mattis, Ann R. 1978: An experience in need-oriented development. *Marga Quarterly Journal*, Colombo 5, no. 3, 1–29.

Mbilinyi, M. 1985: The changing position of women in the African labour force. In T. M. Sham and O. Aluko (eds), *Africa Projected: from recession to renaissance by the year 2000?* London: Macmillan.

Meade, Teresa 1989: "Living worse and costing more": resistance and riot in Rio de Janeiro, 1890–1917. *Journal of Latin American Studies*, 21, 241–66.

Medvedev, R. 1973: Problems of democratization and detente. *New Left Review*, no. 83, 27–40.

Medvedev, R. 1974: What lies ahead for us? *New Left Review*, no. 87–8, 61–74.

Mills, G. 1992: Zambia and the winds of change. *The World Today*, 48, 16–18.

Ministry of Plan Implementation 1982: *Census of Agriculture. Preliminary Report.* Colombo: Government of Sri Lanka.

Moffitt, Michael 1983: *The World's Money: international banking from Bretton Woods to the brink of insolvency.* New York: Simon and Schuster.

Moghadam, V. (ed.) 1992: *Privatization and democratization in Central and Eastern Europe and the Soviet Union: the gender dimension.* Helsinki: WIDER.

Molyneux, M. 1990: The "woman question" in the age of perestroika. *New Left Review*, no. 183, (September–October), 23–49.

Moon, Bruce and Dixon, William 1985: Politics, the state and basic human needs: a cross-national study. *American Journal of Political Science*, 29, no. 4, 661–94.

Moore, Mick 1985: *The State and Peasant Politics in Sri Lanka*. Cambridge: Cambridge University Press.

Morris, Morris David 1979: *Measuring the Condition of the World's Poor: the physical quality of life index*. New York: Pergamon.

Morris, Morris David, and McAlpin, Michelle B. 1980: Measuring welfare in South Asia. Paper distributed for the SSRC/ICSSR Conference on South Asian Political Economy, New Delhi (December 12–16).

Mosley, P., Harrigan, J., and Toye, J. 1991: *Aid and Power: the World Bank and policy-based lending*, vol. 1. London and New York: Routledge.

Mukul 1991: Workers' struggles halts privatisation moves. *Economic and Political Weekly*, October 26.

Mussall, B. 1991: Women are hurt the most. *Der Spiegel* (Hamburg); reprinted in *World Press Review*, June, 22.

Naipaul, V. S. 1991: *India: a million mutinies now*. New York: Viking.

Nash, J. 1990: Latin American Women in the World capitalist crisis. *Gender and Society*, 4, no. 3 (September) 338–53.

Nayar, Baldev, Raj 1975: *Violence and Crime in India: a quantitative study*. New Delhi: Macmillan India.

Nayak, P. B. 1991: On the crisis and the remedies. *Economic and Political Weekly*. August 24.

Nayar, K. 1972: *The Modernisation Imperative and Indian Planning*. Delhi: Vikas Publishers.

Nayar, K. 1977: *The Judgment: inside story of emergency in India*. New Delhi: Vikas Publishers.

Nelson, J. M. 1979: *Access to Power: politics and the urban poor in developing nations*. Princeton, NJ: Princeton University Press.

Nelson, J. M. 1984: The political economy of stabilization. *World Development*, 12, 10.

Nelson, J. M. 1989: *Fragile Coalitions: the politics of economic adjustment*. New Brunswick: Transaction Books.

Nelson, J. M. and Eglington, S. J. 1992: *Encouraging Democracy: what role for conditioned Aid?* Policy Essay no. 4, Washington, DC: Overseas Development Council.

Nove, A. 1983: *The Economics of Feasible Socialism*. London: George Allen & Unwin.

Oberst, Robert 1985: The food stamp scheme in Sri Lanka. Unpublished paper for Wisconsin Conference on South Asia, Madison.

Obeyesekere, Gananath 1984: The origins and institutionalization of political violence. In James Manor (ed.), *Sri Lanka in Change and Crisis*, London: Croom Helm.

Obeysekara, Jayasumana 1973: Revolutionary movements in Ceylon. In

Kathleen Gough and Hari P. Sharma *Imperialism and Revolution in South Asia*, New York: Monthly Review Press.

O'Donnell, Guillermo 1978: Reflections on the patterns of change in the bureaucratic-authoritarian state. *Latin American Research Review*, 13, 3–38.

Ofreneo, R. 1987: *Deregulation and the Agrarian Crisis*. Quezon City: University of the Philippines Institute of Industrial Relations.

O'Hanlon, R. 1988: Recovering the subject: subaltern studies and histories of resistance in colonial south Asia. *Modern Asian Studies*, 22 (1), 189–224.

Omvedt, G. 1986: *Women in Popular Movements: India and Thailand during the Decade of Women*, UNRISD Participation Programme. Geneva: UNRISD.

Paige, Jeffery 1975: *Agrarian Revolution: social movements and export agriculture in the underdeveloped world*. Berkeley: University of California Press.

Parfitt, T. W. and Riley, S. P. 1989: *The African Debt Crisis*. London: Routledge.

Patnaik, P. 1972: Industrial development in India since Independence. *Social Scientist*, 54–5.

Pastor, Manuel 1987: The effects of IMF programs in the Third World: debate and evidence from Latin America. *World Development*, 15(2), 249–62.

Patel, I. G. 1992: New economic policies: a historical perspective. *Economic and Political Weekly*, September 28.

Patel, S. J. 1985: India's regression in the World Economy. *Economic and Political Weekly*, September 28.

Paul J. 1984: States of emergency: the riots in Tunisia and Morocco. *MERIP Reports*, no. 127, 3–6.

Peacock, J. J. 1965: *Bread or Blood: a study of the agrarian riots in East Anglia in 1816*. London: Victor Gollancz.

Pearson, L. B. 1969: *Partners in Development, Report of the Commission on International Development*. London: Pall Mall Press.

Perera, J. 1985: *New Dimension of Social Stratification in Sri Lanka*. Colombo: Lake House.

Perlman, J. E. 1976: *The Myth of Marginality: urban poverty and politics in Rio de Janeiro*. Berkeley and London: University of California Press.

Petras, James and Brill, Howard 1986: The IMF, austerity and the state in Latin America. *Third World Quarterly*, 8 (April), 425–48.

Pieris, G. H. 1982: *Basic Needs and the Provision of Government Services in Sri Lanka*. Geneva: ILO.

Pineda-Ofreneo, R. 1991: *The Philippines: debt and poverty*. Oxford: Oxfam.

Pinstrup-Andersen, P. 1989: The impact of macro-economic adjustment food and nutrition. In S. Commander (ed.), *Structural Adjustment and Agriculture*, London: James Currey & ODI, 90–104..

Piscatori J. 1991: Religion and realpolitik: Islamic responses to the Gulf War. In J. Piscatori (ed.), *Islamic Fundamentalisms and the Gulf Crisis*, Chicago: American Academy of Arts and Sciences, 1–27.

Pittin, R. 1984: Gender and class in a Nigerian industrial setting. *Review of African Political Economy*, December, 71–81.

Piven, F. F. and Cloward, R. A. 1977: *Regulating the Poor: the functions of public welfare*. New York: Vintage Books.

Polanya, K. 1944/57: *The Great Transformation: the political and economic origins of our times*. Boston: Beacon Press.

Ponnambalam, Satchi 1981: *Dependent Capitalism in Crisis: the Sri Lankan economy* London: Zed Books.

Portes, Alejandro 1972: Rationality in the slum: an essay on interpretive sociology. *Comparative Studies in Society and History*, 14, 268–86.

Portes, Alejandro 1989: Latin American urbanization during the years of the crisis. *Latin American Research Review*, 24, 7–44.

Portes, Alejandro and Walton, John 1976: *Urban Latin America: the political condition from above and below*. Austin: University of Texas Press.

Portes, Alejandro and Walton, John 1981: *Labor, Class, and the International System*. New York: Academic Press.

PRELAC [Programa Regional del Empleo Para America Latina y El Caribe], 1987: *Newsletter*, no. 15 (December).

Pryer, J. 1987: Production and reproduction of malnutrition in an urban slum in Khulna, Bangladesh. In J. H. Momsen and J. Townsend (eds), *Geography of Gender in the Third World*, New York & London: State University of New York Press & Hutchinson, 131–49.

Raczynsky, D. 1989: Social policy, poverty and vulnerable groups: children in Chile. In G. Cornia, R. Jolly, and F. Stewart (eds), *Adjustment with a Human Face*, vol. 2, Oxford: Clarendon Press, 57–92.

Radford, J. 1989: Policing male violence – policing women. In J. Hanmer and M. Maynard (eds), *Women, Violence and Social Control*, London: Macmillan, 30–45.

Ragin, Charles C. 1987: *The Comparative Method: moving beyond qualitative and quantitative strategies*. Berkeley: University of California Press.

Ragin, C. and Walton, J. 1987: The international origins of polity instability. Draft MS, Northwestern University.

Reddock, R. 1990: Caribbean sub-project overview. In S. Wieringa (ed.), *Women's Movements and Organizations in Historical Perspective*, The Hague: Institute of Social Studies, 47–73.

Reddy, William M. 1987: *Money and Liberty in Modern Europe: a critique of historical understanding*. Cambridge: Cambridge University Press.

Richards, A. and Waterbury, J. 1990: *A Political Economy of the Middle East: state, class and economic development*. Boulder, CO: Westview Press.

Richards, Peter and Gooneratne, Wilbert 1980: *Basic Needs, Poverty and Government Policies in Sri Lanka*. Geneva: ILO.

Riley, S. P. 1984: The current political situation in Sierra Leone. In P. K. Mitchell (ed.), *Sierra Leone Studies at Birmingham: proceedings of a symposium*, Birmingham: University of Birmingham.

Riley, S. P. 1992a: Africa's new wind of change. *The World Today*, 48, 116–19.

Riley, S. P. 1992b: Domestic pressure or political adjustment? Democratic politics and political choice in Africa. *Third World Quarterly*, 13, no. 3, 539–52.

Roberts, Bryan 1989: Urbanization, migration, and development. *Sociological Forum*, 4, 665–91.

Robison, R. 1987: After the gold rush: the politics of economic restructuring in Indonesia in the 1980s. In R. Robison, K. Hewison, and R. Higgott (eds), *South East Asia in the 1980s: the politics of economic crisis*, London: Allen and Unwin.

Robison, R., Higgott, R., and Hewison, K. 1987: Crisis in economic strategy in the 1980s: the factors at work. In R. Robison, K. Hewison and R. Higgott (eds), *South East Asia in the 1980s: the politics of economic crisis*, London: Allen and Unwin, 16–51.

Rogers, John D. 1987: The 1866 grain riots in Sri Lanka. *Comparative Studies in Society and History*, 29, 495–513.

Rose, R. B. 1959: 18th century price-riots, the French Revolution and the Jacobin maximum. *Review of Social History*, IV, 432–45.

Rose, R. B. 1961: Eighteenth century price riots and public policy in England. *International Review of Social History*, VI, 277–92.

Roskin, M. G. 1991: *The Rebirth of East Europe*. Englewood Cliffs, NJ: Prentice Hall.

Rowbotham, S. 1980: The Women's Movement and organizing for Socialism. In S. Rowbotham, L. Segal, and H. Wainright, *Beyond the Fragments*, London: Merlin.

Rowbotham, S. forthcoming: *Women in Movement: feminism and social action*.

Roxborough, Ian 1989: Organized labor: a major victim of the debt crisis. In Barbara Stallings and Robert Kaufman (eds), *Debt and Democracy in Latin America*, Boulder, CO: Westview Press, 91–108.

Rudé, George 1964: *The Crowd in History: a study of popular disturbances in France and England, 1730–1848*, revd edn. New York: John Wiley, 1981.

Rudolph, L. I. and Rudolph, S. H. 1987: *In Pursuit of Lakshmi: the political economy of the Indian state*. Chicago: University of Chicago Press.

Rudolph, S. H. and Rudolph, L. I. 1993: Modern hate. *The New Republic*, March 22.

Rule, James B. 1988: *Theories of Civil Violence*. Berkeley: University of California Press.

Sachs, J. D. 1988: Recent studies of the Latin American debt crisis. *Latin American Research Review*, 23, 170–9.

Sachs, J. D. 1991: Lionel Robbins Memorial Lecture. London School of Economics, London.

Sachs, J. D. and Lipton, D. 1990: Creating a market economy in Eastern Europe: the case of Poland. *Brooking Papers on Economic Activity*, 1, 75–147.

Safa, H. I. 1979: Class consciousness among working-class women in Latin America: a case study in Puerto Rico. In R. Cohen, P. C. W. Gutkind and P. Brazier (eds), *Peasants and Proletarians: the struggles of Third World workers*, London: Hutchinson, 441–59.

Sahn, David E. 1983: An analysis of the nutritional status of pre-school children in Sri Lanka, 1980–81. Washington, DC: International Food Policy Research Institutes.

Sahn, David E. 1986: Malnutrition and food consumption in Sri Lanka: an analysis of changes during the past decade. Washington, DC: IFPRI.

Said, E. 1978: *Orientalism*. New York: Pantheon, and London: Routledge and Kegan Paul.

Said, E. 1985: Orientalism reconsidered. *Race and Class*, 27, 2, 1–15.

Samarasinghe, S. W. R. de A. 1980: Current economic policy: a comment. Unpublished paper for the Conference on Post-War Economic Development of Sri Lanka, Peradeniya, December 16–20.

Samarasinghe, S. W. R. de A. 1983: Sri Lanka in 1982. *Asian Survey*, XXIII, 2, 158–64.

Sanderatne, Nimal 1985: The effects of policies on real income and employment. In *Sri Lanka: The Social Impact of Economic Policies During the Last Decade*. Colombo: UNICEF.

Scarpaci, J. 1993: Empowerment struggles of poor urban women in the Chilean dictatorship. In M. Turshen and B. Holcomb (eds), *Women Lives and Public Policy: the international experience*, London and Westport, CT: Greenwood Press, 33–50.

Scott, James C. 1972: Patron–client politics and political change in Southeast Asia. *American Political Science Review*, LXVI, 91–113.

Scott, James C. 1976: *The Moral Economy of the Peasant: rebellion and subsistence in Southeast Asia*. New Haven: Yale University Press.

Scott, James C. 1985: *Weapons of the Weak: everyday forms of peasant resistance*. New Haven and London: Yale University Press.

Seabrook, J. 1992: The reconquest of India: the victory of International-Monetary Fundamentalism. *Race and Class*, 34, no. 1, 1–22.

Seddon, D. 1981: *Moroccan Peasants*. London: Wm Dawson.

Seddon, D. 1984: Winter of discontent: economic crisis in Tunisia and Morocco. *MERIP Reports*, no. 127.

Seddon, D. 1988: Popular protest and political opposition in Tunisia, Morocco, and Sudan. In Kenneth Brown, et al. (eds), *Urban Crises and Social Movements in the Middle East*. Paris: L'Harmattan Villes et Entreprises, 179–97.

Seddon, D. 1989a: The politics of "Adjustment" in Morocco. In B. Campbell and J. Loxley (eds), *Structural Adjustment in Africa*, London: Macmillan, 234–65.

Seddon, D. 1989b: Riot and rebellion in North Africa: political responses to economic crisis in Tunisia, Morocco and Sudan. In B. Berberoglu (ed.), *Power and Stability in the Middle East*, London: Zed Press, 114–35.

Seddon, D. 1989c: Zaio transformed: two decades of change in northeast Morocco. In R. Lawless (ed.), *The Middle Eastern Village: changing economic and social relations*, London: Croom Helm, 22–54.

Seddon, D. 1990: Elections in Algeria. *Review of African Political Economy*, no. 49, 70–3.

Seddon, D. 1991: Politics and the Gulf Crisis: government and popular responses in the Maghreb. *School of Development Studies Discussion Paper,* no. 219, University of East Anglia, Norwich, pp. 50.

Segal L. 1990: *Slow Motion: changing masculinities, changing men.* London: Virago.

Sen, A. 1993: Threats to secular India. *New York Review,* April 8.

Selby, Henry A., Murphy, Arthur D., and Lorenzen, Stephen A. 1990: *The Mexican Urban Household: organizing for self-defense.* Austin: University of Texas Press.

Sen, Amartya 1993: Threats to secular India: *New York Review* April 8.

Senghass, Dieter 1985: *The European Experience.* Leamington Spa and Dover: Berg.

Seppo, D. 1989: Miners' strike opens new act in perestroika. *International Viewpoint,* no. 170, 10–17.

Serrano, C. 1987: Crisis economica y mujeres de sectores populares urbanos en Santiago de Chile. Paper presented at the meeting of Development Alternatives with Women for a New Era (DAWN), La Paz, December.

Sharp, Buchanan 1980: *In Contempt of All Authority: rural artisans and riot in the West of England, 1586–1660.* Berkeley: University of California Press.

Shastri, Amita 1985: Politics of constitutional development in South Asia in the seventies: a case study of Sri Lanka. Unpublished Ph.D. Thesis, Jawaharlal Nehru University, New Delhi.

Shastri Amita 1986: Limits to the nationalist revolution in Sri Lanka: the united front regime, 1970–77. Unpublished paper, Association for Asian Studies annual meetings, Chicago.

Sheahan, John 1980: Market oriented economic policies and political repression in Latin America. *Economic Development and Cultural Change,* 28, 267–91.

Sheahan, John 1989: Economic adjustment programs and the prospect for renewed growth in Latin America. *Latin American Research Review,* 24, 159–71.

Sheahan, John 1991: *Conflict and Change in Mexican Economic Strategy: implications for Mexico and Latin America.* San Diego: Center for U.S.–Mexican Studies, University of California.

Shorter, Edward and Tilly, Charles 1974: *Strikes in France, 1830–1968.* Cambridge: Cambridge University Press.

Shoshan, B. 1980: Grain riots and the "moral economy": Cairo, 1350–1517. *Journal of Interdisciplinary History,* X, 3, 459–78.

SIC, Centro Gumilla 1989: El 27 de Febrero. 12, no. 513 (April). Caracas.

Siltanen, J. and Stanworth, M. 1984: The politics of private woman and public man. In J. Siltanen and M. Stanworth (eds), *Women and the Public Sphere: a critique of sociology and politics,* London: Hutchinson, 185–208.

Singer, P. 1982: Neighbourhood movements in Sao Paulo. In H. I. Safa (ed.), *Towards a Political Economy of Urbanization in the Third World Countries*, New Delhi: Oxford University Press.

Singh, A. 1985: *The World Economy and the Comparative Economic Performance of Large Semi-Industrial Countries*. Bangkok International Labor Organization, Asian Regional Team for Employment Promotion (mimeo).

Smith, P. H. 1991: Crisis and Democracy in Latin America. *World Politics*, 43, no. 4, 608–34.

Snyder, David and Tilly, Charles 1972: Hardship and collective violence in France, 1830–1960. *American Sociological Review*, 37, no. 5, 520–32.

Sri Lanka 1979: The new tax policy. Speech of the Minister of Finance and Planning in Parliament, April 4, 1979, Colombo.

Sri Lanka Minister of Finance and Planning 1980a: Budget speech, 1981. Colombo.

Sri Lanka 1980b: *Performance*. Colombo: Ministry of Plan Implementation.

Sri Lanka 1980c: *Public Investment Programme, 1980–84*. Colombo: Ministry of Finance and Planning.

Sri Lanka 1981: Evaluation report of the food stamp scheme. Colombo: Ministry of Plan Implementation.

Sri Lanka 1984: *Public Investment, 1984–1988*. Colombo: Ministry of Finance and Planning.

Standing, G. 1989: Global feminization through flexible labor. *World Development*, 17, no. 7, 1077–95.

Standing, G. (ed.) 1991: *The new Soviet labour market: in search of flexibility*. Geneva: ILO.

Standing, G. and Tokman, V. 1992: Towards social adjustment: labour market issues in structural adjustment. Geneva: ILO.

Staniland, M. 1987: Francophone Africa: the enduring French connection. *The Annals*, no. 489, 51–62.

Stevenson, J. 1974: Food riots in England, 1792–1818. In R. Quinault and J. Stevenson (eds), *Popular Protest and Public Order: six studies in British history, 1790–1920*. London: George Allen & Unwin, 33–74.

Stiles, K. W. 1991: *Negotiating Debt: the IMF lending process*. Boulder, CO: Westview Press.

Stokes, Susan 1991: Politics and Latin America's urban poor: reflections from a Lima shanty town. *Latin American Research Review*, 26, 75–101.

Sutton, Mary 1984: Structuralism: The Latin American record and the new critique. In Tony Killick (ed.), *The IMF and Stabilization: the developing country experience*. London: Heinemann, 19–67.

Swain, N. 1989: Hungary's socialist project in crisis. *New Left Review*, no. 176, 3–29.

Szeftel M. 1983: Corruption and the spoils system in Zambia. In M. Clarke (ed.), *Corruption: causes, consequences and controls*, London: Frances Pinter, 163–89.

Tambiah, S. J. 1986: *Sri Lanka: ethnic fratricide and the dismantling of democracy*. Chicago: University of Chicago Press.

Tello, Carlos 1991: Combatting poverty in Mexico. In Mercedes Gonzáles de la Rocha and Augustín Escobar Latapi (eds), *Social Responses to Mexico's Economic Crisis of the 1980s*. San Diego: Center for U.S.-Mexican Studies, University of California, 57–65.

Thapar, R. 1991: A historical perspective on the story of Rama. In Sarvepalli Gopal (ed.), *Anatomy of a Confrontation: the Babri-Masjid-Rama-Janmabhumi issue*, New Delhi: Viking/Penguin, 141–63.

Thompson, E. P. 1971: The Moral economy of the English crowd in the eighteenth century. *Past and Present*, 50, 76–136.

Tilly, Charles 1975: Food supply and public order in modern Europe. In Charles Tilly (ed.), *The Formation of Nation States in Western Europe*, Princeton: Princeton University Press, 380–455.

Tilly, Charles 1986: *The Contentious French*. Cambridge, MA: Harvard University Press.

Tilly, Louise A. 1971: The food riot as a form of political conflict in France. *The Journal of Interdisciplinary History*, II no. 1, 23–57.

Tilly, Louise A. 1983: Food entitlement, famine, and conflict. *The Journal of Interdisciplinary History*, XIV no. 2, 333–49.

Tilly, Louise A. 1992: The decline and disappearance of the classical food riot in France. New School for Social Research, Working Paper no. 147.

Tripp, A. M. 1989a: Excerpt from "The informal economy: labor and the state in Tanzania". Paper presented to the Midwest Political Science Association Annual Meeting, Chicago, Illinois, April 1989, *Participation and Needs Newsletter*, no. 4, Helsinki: WIDER.

Tripp, A. M. 1989b: Women and the changing urban household economy in Tanzanian. *The Journal of Modern African Studies*, 27, 4, 601–23.

UNCTAD Bulletin 1989a: New York: United Nations, July/August.

UNCTAD Trade and Development Report 1989b: United Nations Commission on Trade and Development. New York: United Nations, 1989.

UNDPI 1991–2: Eastern Europe: UNICEF alarmed over transition. *Development Forum*, Vol. 19, No. 6; Vol. 20, No. 1 (November 1991-February 1992), United Nations Department of Public Information (UNDPI): New York.

UNICEF 1989a: *Annual Report*. New York: United Nations.

UNICEF 1989b: *The State of the World's Children, 1989*. Washington, DC.

UNICEF 1992: *The State of the World's Children 1992*. UNICEF: Geneva.

United Nations. 1990: *World Economic Survey, Current Trends and Policies in the World Economy*. New York: United Nations.

United Nations. 1992: *World Economic Survey, Current Trends and Policies in the World Economy*. New York: United Nations.

Van Hear, N. 1988: Recession, retrenchment and military rule: Nigerian Labour in the 1980s. In R. Southall (ed.), *Trade Unions and the New Industrialization in the Third World*, London: Zed Books.

Vargas, V. 1990: The women's social movement in Peru: rebellion into action. Paper presented to the Social Movements Seminar, Institute of Social Studies, The Hague.

Velez-Ibanez, C. 1983: *Rituals of Marginality*. Berkeley and Los Angeles: University of California Press.

Villavicencio, M., Olea, C., and Vargas, V. 1990: Roots of the Peruvian women's movement. In S. Wieringa (ed.), *Women's Movements and Organizations in Historical Perspective*, The Hague: Institute of Social Studies, 149–64.

Wachs, F. 1991: Poland: out of the crisis with violence and reform. In E. Altvater, K. Hubner, J. Lorentzen, and R. Rojas (eds), *The Poverty of Nations: a guide to the debt crisis from Argentina to Zaire*, London and New Jersey: Zed Press.

Walter, John and Wrightson, Keith 1976: Dearth and the social order of early modern England. *Past and Present*, 71, 22–42.

Walton, John 1987: Urban protest and the global political economy. In M. P. Smith and J. R. Feagin (eds), *The Capitalist City*, London: Blackwell.

Walton, John 1989a: Debt, protest, and the state in Latin America. In Susan Eckstein (ed.), *Power and Popular Protest: Latin American social movements*. Berkeley: University of California Press, 299–328.

Walton, John 1989b: Labor and popular protest: Latin American responses to structural adjustment. Paper prepared for the International Conference on 'Impact of Foreign Debt on Latin American Unions', Center for Labor Research and Studies, Florida International University, Miami, Florida, December 5–8.

Walton, John 1991: Review essay. *International Journal of Urban and Regional Research*, 629–33.

Walton, John and Ragin, C. 1989: Austerity and dissent: social bases of popular struggle in Latin America. In W. L. Canak (ed.), *Lost Promises: debt, austerity and development in Latin America*, Boulder, CO: Westview Press, 172–93.

Walton, John and Ragin, C. 1990: Global and national sources of political protest: Third World responses to the debt crisis. *American Sociological Review*, 55 (December), 876–90.

Wanasinghe, Sydney 1980: The hartal of August 1953. *Young Socialist*, 2 (June).

Warnapala, W. A. Wiswa 1979: Sri Lanka 1978: reversal of policies and strategies. *Asian Survey*, XIX, no. 2, 178–90.

Warren, Bill 1980: *Imperialism: pioneer of capitalism*. London: Verso, New Left Books.

Weiner, M. 1962: *The Politics of Scarcity: public pressure and political response in India*. Chicago: Chicago University Press.

Wells, Roger 1977: The revolt of the South-west, 1800–1801: a study of English popular protest. *Social History* 6 (October) 713–44.

West, G. and Blumberg, R. L. 1990: Reconstructing social protest from a feminist perspective. In G. West & R. L. Blumberg (eds), *Women and Social Protest*, Oxford: Oxford University Press, 3–35.

White, C. 1986: Profiles – Women in the Caribbean project. In J. Massiah (ed.), *Women in the Caribbean*, Special Issue of *Social and Economic Studies*, 35 (2), 59–81.

Wickramasinghe, Wimal 1974: The faking of foreign trade declarations. Central Bank of Ceylon, *Staff Studies* 4, no. 1, 45–56.

Wickremeratne, L. A. 1973: The emergence of welfare policy, 1931–1948. In K. M. de Silva (ed.), *History of Ceylon*, Colombo: University of Ceylon.

Wickremeratne, L. A. 1977: Planning and economic development. In K. M. de Silva (ed.), *Sri Lanka: a survey*, Honolulu: University of Hawaii Press.

Widner, J. A. 1991: The 1990 elections in Côte d'Ivoire', *Issue*, 20, no. 1, 47–62.

Wieringa, S. (ed.) 1990: *Women's Movements and Organizations in Historical Perspective*. The Hague: Institute of Social Studies.

Wijeweera, Rohan (Rohana) 1975: Speech to the Ceylon Criminal Justice Commission. In Robin Blackburn (ed.), *Explosion in a Subcontinent*, Harmondsworth: Penguin.

Williams, Dale Edward 1984: Morals, markets, and the English crowd in 1766. *Past and Present*, 104 (August), 56–73.

Williamson, John 1983: *IMF Conditionality*. Washington, DC: Institute of International Economics.

Wiseman, J. A. 1992: Early post-redemocratization elections in Africa. Unpublished MS.

Women Working Worldwide 1991: *Common Interests: women organising in global electronics*. London: Women Working Worldwide.

Wong, R. Bin 1982: Food riots in the Qing dynasty. *Journal of Asian Studies*, 41, no. 4, 767–88.

Wood, Robert E. 1986: *From Marshall Plan to Debt Crisis: foreign aid and development choices in the world economy*. Berkeley: University of California Press.

World Bank 1953: *The Economic Development of Ceylon*. Baltimore: The Johns Hopkins University Press.

World Bank 1975: *The Assault of World Poverty*. Baltimore: The Johns Hopkins University Press.

World Bank 1979: *World Development Report, 1979*. New York and Oxford: Oxford University Press.

World Bank 1980a: *Annual Report*. Washington, DC: World Bank.

World Bank 1980b: *World Debt Tables*. Washington, DC: World Bank.

World Bank 1980c: *World Development Report, 1980*. New York and Oxford: Oxford University Press.

World Bank 1981a: *Accelerated Development in Sub-Saharan Africa* (the Berg Report), Washington, DC: World Bank.

World Bank 1981b: *Annual Report*. Washington, DC: World Bank.

World Bank 1983a: *Annual Report*. Washington, DC: World Bank.

World Bank 1983b: *World Development Report, 1983*. New York and Oxford: Oxford University Press.

World Bank 1985: *World Development Report, 1985*. Washington, DC: World Bank.

World Bank 1987: *World Development Report, 1987*. Washington, DC: World Bank.

World Bank 1988a: *Annual Report*. Washington, DC: World Bank.

World Bank 1988b: *World Development Report, 1988*. Washington, DC: World Bank.

World Bank 1989: *World Debt Tables, 1988–89: External Debt of Developing Countries*. Washington DC: World Bank.

World Bank 1990: *World Development Report, 1990*. New York and Oxford: Oxford University Press.

World Bank 1991a: Managing Development: the governance dimension. Unpublished paper, Washington, DC.

World Bank 1991b: *The Transformation of Economies in Eastern and Central Europe: issues, progress and prospects*. Washington, DC: Socialist Economies Reform Unit, The World Bank.

World Bank 1991c: *World Debt Tables, 1991–92*, 2 vols. Washington, DC: World Bank.

World Bank. 1992a: *Annual Report*. Washington DC: World Bank.

World Bank 1992b: *World Debt Tables, 1992–1993: External Debt of Developing Countries*, vol. 2, *Country Tables*. Washington DC: World Bank.

World Bank 1992c: *World Development Report, 1992*. Washington, DC: World Bank.

World Bank and UNDP 1989: *Africa's Adjustment and Growth in the 1980s*. Washington, DC:

World Economic Survey, 1990: New York: United Nations.

Wriggins, W. Howard 1960: *Ceylon: dilemmas of a new nation*. Princeton: Princeton University Press.

Wright, Thomas 1973: Origins of the politics of inflation in Chile, 1888–1918. *Hispanic American Historical Review*, 53, 239–59.

Young, A. 1990: *Femininity in Dissent*. London and New York: Routledge.

Zghal, A. 1989: "The Bread Riot" and the crisis of the one party system (in Tunisia). Paper presented to the Conference on 'Social Movements, Social Transformation and Democracy in Africa', organized by the Council for the Development of Economic and Social Research in Africa (CODESRIA), Algiers, July.

Zuckerman, Edward 1986: A study in red: Zambia succumbs to its debts. *Harpers*, April, 48–55.

Index

Gentleman, J. 124
Genya 168
Germany 8, 15, 155, 300, 304, 315; East
  see GDR; Nazi 61
Ghai, D. 59, 71, 72, 73
Ghana 13, 101, 107, 144, 165; *see also*
  PAMSCAD; Rawlings
Ghosh, A. 240, 241, 242
Gibson, C. 147, 151
Gierek, Edward 290
Gilbert, A. 45
Gill, S. 7
Girvan, N. 106, 114, 255, 278
glasnost 297
Glewwe, P. 104, 105
Glyn, A. 5, 10
GNP (gross national product) 265, 285n.,
  290; fall in 148, 321; low rates of growth
  258; per capita 104, 115, 260, 261, 300;
  ratio of debt to 15, 16, 276, 314
Gogna, M. 80, 83, 84, 85, 95
Goldrich, D. 45
Goldsmith, A. A. 261
Golub, Stephen 99
Gomulka, Wladyslaw 290
Gonzáles Tiburcio, E. 99, 124
Gooneratne, W. 284n.
Gorbachev, Mikhail S. 296, 301–5 *passim*,
  310, 318
government spending 103, 106, 124;
  profligate 41; *see also* cutbacks
Great Depression 6
Green, R. H. 59, 140, 142
Green Revolution 233
Greenham women 89
Grosz, Karoly 303
growth 14, 49, 229, 250, 285; appropriate
  economic policies for 17; creating market
  conditions conducive to 138; distributive
  growth 230, 237, 246; domestic investment 12; doubling 279; export 8, 12; far
  from stable 248; high 21, 249; highest
  average rates 98; import 138; improving
  efficiency to restore 296; industrial 232,
  241; longitudinal shifts 102; nationalist-
  oriented 228; negative 123, 217; obstacles to 18; output 306; performance
  101, 261; plan to ensure 290; plan to
  increase 240; redistributive 240; retarding 260; slower 7; steady 217; sustained,
  basis for 64; uneven 99; very considerable 11; vigorous 276
Guatemala 43, 112, 129
Gugler, J. 45
Guinea-Bissau 217
Gujarat 39, 234–5, 236, 250
Gulf crisis 212; War (1990–1) 174, 186,

209, 240
Gunasinghe, Newton 280–1
Gunatilleke, G. 285n., 286n.
Guzel, M. S. 87

Haiti 43, 44, 99, 111, 130, 334; violence
  108
Hall, G. 104, 105
Halliday, Fred 198, 266, 285n.
Hanson, A. H. 251n.
harassment 75, 77, 89, 91, 205; sexual 76
hardship 86, 99, 102, 133, 150, 309; absence of direct relation between protest
  and 31; experienced as injustice 334;
  exploitation of 132; imperfect association
  between protest and 44; indicators of
  115; measures which fueled 149; policies
  which clearly produced 266; political
  action and 108; protests with no effect on
  ameliorating 129; severe 38, 52, 277;
  stabilization as 42
Harper, E. 61
Harrigan, J. 10, 14, 16, 17, 19
Harris, N. 4, 11
Harrison, J. 5, 10
Harriss, J. 229, 231, 232–3, 249, 250
hartals 37–8, 264, 265, 271
Hassan, Crown Prince of Jordan 193, 206
Hassan, King of Morocco 87, 173, 203,
  205
Havel, Vaclav 305
health 70, 160, 308; general decline in
  124; reduced social spending for 223;
  services 47; subsidies 275
hegemony 146, 148, 158
Hein, C. 76
Hewison, K. 215, 222
Hewitt de Alcantara, C. 59, 71, 72, 73
Hicks, N. 284n.
Hiett, P. 204
Higgott, R. 215, 222
Hindu militancy 226–7, 243, 248, 250,
  251
hoarding 34, 111, 127
Hobsbawm, Eric J. 25, 26, 31, 36, 37, 38,
  45, 46, 336
homelessness 124
Honduras 77
Honecker, Erich 304
Honeywell, M. 41, 115
Hong Kong 77, 215, 222
Hoogvelt, A. 143
Houphouët-Boigny, Felix 17, 135, 152–3,
  154, 156–7, 158
Hoxha, Enver 300
Hubner, K. 217
Hughes, A. 220, 228, 237, 251n., 252n.

Sudan 43, 44, 107, 140, 173, 200–1, 203, 205–6, 217; "Arab socialism" 181; political consequences of popular protest 208; price increases revoked 205; "resource gap" 183; state role in private capital accumulation 182; women's involvement 88, 92–3; *see also* al-Numeiry; Khartoum
Suez 197
Sukarno, Achmad 223
supply 29, 30
survival strategies 57–96
Sutton, M. 42, 103
Svindland, E. 314, 324, 325
Swain, N. 298
Sweden 260, 261
Syria 171, 174, 175, 180, 208–9;; "Arab socialism" 181; "resource gap" 183
Szeftel, M. 148, 150, 151, 152, 166

Taiwan 215, 222, 223, 225
Tambiah, S. J. 280
Tamil Nadu 245
Tamils 280, 281, 282
Tanzania 63, 66, 68, 85, 136, 167
Tarasiewicz, Malgorzata 323
tariffs 101, 106, 223, 232; *see also* GATT
taxes 126, 270, 272, 275
technical assistance 267, 289
Telefunken 119
Tello, C. 123, 124
terms of trade 15, 275, 287n.; declining 11; deteriorating 14, 123, 148, 264, 276; international, secular changes in 183
Thailand 77, 221, 222, 225
Thapar, Romila 227, 251
Thatcher, Margaret, Baroness 279
Third World 38, 42, 48, 98, 104, 216, 288–9, 334; cities 337; classical price riots 106; debt crisis 215; economic stagnation 101; effects of neo-liberalism 24; end of 10–13; exports 41; industrialized oil exporters 40; liberalization policies throughout 333; net capital drain to industrial countries 100; peasant rebellions 32; privatization of state-owned enterprise in many countries 335; purpose of stabilization programs is to discipline economies 41; restructuring accompanied by economic crisis 20–1; socialist state's obligations 251; struggle and resistance among subaltern groups 61; unprecedented rise in lending of private bank capital to governments 14; *see also* developing countries
Thompson, E. P. 23, 27, 28, 29, 31–2, 34, 36, 48, 52, 167, 178

Tilly, Charles 23, 25, 26, 27, 28, 30, 31, 34, 36, 37, 132
Tilly, Louise 23, 25, 26, 27, 28, 31, 32, 34, 35
Timisoara 305
Togo 136, 144, 145, 167, 168
Tokman, V. 326
torture 89, 208
Toye, J. 10, 14, 16, 17, 19
trade: balance of 8–9, 183, 283; deficits 14, 187, 298; export 8; free 255; illegal gold 161; international, taxes on 275; *see also* terms of trade
trade unions 45, 119, 120, 122, 151, 168, 172, 201, 205, 235, 252n., 313, 314, 316, 337; banning of 208; broad coalition of 244; left opposition with strong roots in 279–80; left-front 244, 245; male-dominated 77; members sentenced by summary courts 191; newly independent 319; opposition to liberalization 244; organization of popular protest shifted to labor 35; popular movements in tandem with 46; significant growth in opposition 188; strong and significant 115; strong tradition 109; well-organized 141; women's role in 75–9, 85, 88, 95, 97; *see also* Solidarity
transfer payments 8, 258, 269
transitions 4, 35, 130, 133, 309
Transjordan 196
Traore, Moussa 136, 169
Treuhand agency 316
Tripp, A. M. 63, 66, 68
Trotskyites 266
Tshisekedi, Etienne 163, 164
Tunisia 42, 77, 140, 173, 174, 194, 195, 203–8 *passim*, 211; army given *carte blanche* during strike 191; communities actively organized 45; negative growth rates 217; price increases revoked 205; protest severity and overurbanization 44; "resource gap" 183; severe repression of Islamist movements 213, 214; state role in private capital accumulation 182; women's involvement in Al-Mabrouka 87–8
Turkey 13, 17, 43, 44, 107, 173, 174, 184, 189, 190, 204, 207, 209, 211; crisis 186–7; first Five Year Plan 180; largest strike wave in history 187; martial law 86–7, 205; miners' strike 197; political consequences of popular protest 208; "resource gap" 183; state role in private capital accumulation 182; *see also* Ataturk
turnkey projects 240